A CEASELESS WATCH

Titles in the series

Progressives in Navy Blue: Maritime Strategy, American Empire, and the Transformation of U.S. Naval Identity, 1873–1898

Learning War: The Evolution of Fighting Doctrine in the U.S. Navy, 1898–1945

Victory without Peace: The United States Navy in European Waters, 1919–1924

Admiral John S. McCain and the Triumph of Naval Air Power

Churchill's Phoney War: A Study in Folly and Frustration

COSSAC: Lt. Gen. Sir Frederick Morgan and the Genesis of Operation OVERLORD

The Emergence of American Amphibious Warfare, 1898–1945

U-Boat Commander Oskar Kusch: Anatomy of a Nazi-Era Betrayal and Judicial Murder

Warship Builders: An Industrial History of U.S. Naval Shipbuilding, 1922–1945

Mahan, Corbett, and the Foundations of Naval Strategic Thought

The Fall and Rise of French Sea Power: France's Quest for an Independent Naval Policy, 1940–1963

Studies in Naval History and Sea Power
Christopher M. Bell and James C. Bradford, editors

Studies in Naval History and Sea Power advances our understanding of sea power and its role in global security by publishing significant new scholarship on navies and naval affairs. The series presents specialists in naval history, as well as students of sea power, with works that cover the role of the world's naval powers, from the ancient world to the navies and coast guards of today. The works in Studies in Naval History and Sea Power examine all aspects of navies and conflict at sea, including naval operations, strategy, and tactics, as well as the intersections of sea power and diplomacy, navies and technology, sea services and civilian societies, and the financing and administration of seagoing military forces.

The Pacific and Far East

A CEASELESS WATCH

Australia's Third-Party Naval Defense, 1919–1942

Angus Britts

NAVAL INSTITUTE PRESS
ANNAPOLIS, MARYLAND

Naval Institute Press
291 Wood Road
Annapolis, MD 21402

© 2021 by Angus Britts
All rights reserved. No part of this book may be reproduced or utilized in any form or by any means, electronic or mechanical, including photocopying and recording, or by any information storage and retrieval system, without permission in writing from the publisher.

Library of Congress Cataloging-in-Publication Data
Names: Britts, Angus, author.
Title: A ceaseless watch : Australia's third-party naval defense, 1919–1942 / Angus Britts.
Other titles: Australia's third-party naval defense, 1919–1942
Description: Annapolis, Maryland : Naval Institute Press, [2021] | Series: Studies in naval history and sea power | Includes bibliographical references and index.
Identifiers: LCCN 2020050483 (print) | LCCN 2020050484 (ebook) | ISBN 9781682475331 (hardback) | ISBN 9781682475515 (ebook) | ISBN 9781682475515 (pdf)
Subjects: LCSH: Sea-power—Australia—History—20th century. | National security—Australia. | Australia—History, Naval—20th century. | Australia—Foreign relations—1900–1945. | Australia—Foreign relations—Great Britain | Great Britain—Foreign relations—Australia. | Australia—Foreign relations—United States. | United States—Foreign relations—Australia. | Australia—Military policy.
Classification: LCC VA713 .B75 2021 (print) | LCC VA713 (ebook) | DDC 359/.03099409041—dc23
LC record available at https://lccn.loc.gov/2020050483
LC ebook record available at https://lccn.loc.gov/2020050484

♾ Print editions meet the requirements of ANSI/NISO z39.48-1992 (Permanence of Paper).
Printed in the United States of America.

29 28 27 26 25 24 23 22 21   9 8 7 6 5 4 3 2 1
First printing

Maps drawn by Chris Robinson.

Contents

List of Maps and Tables	ix
Acknowledgments	x
List of Abbreviations	xi
Introduction	1
1. The Day That Never Dawned	3
2. Foundations: *1788–1918*	17
3. Paris, Washington, and Singapore: *1919–1923*	51
4. Not a Cloud in the Sky: *1924–1929*	84
5. The Onset of the Two-Ocean Dilemma: *1930–1935*	113
6. Something Less Than Fools: *January 1936–August 1939*	143
7. Conduits: *September 1939–December 1941*	175
8. The Far East: *December 1941–April 1942*	210
9. The Pacific: *December 1941–December 1942*	242
10. Threats and Interests: *January 1919–January 1943*	277
Notes	293
Bibliography	329
Index	343

Maps and Tables

MAPS

The Pacific and Far East	iv
Sinking of the HMS *Prince of Wales* and HMS *Repulse*, December 10, 1941	215
Battle of the Coral Sea, May 4–8, 1942	241
Battle of Midway, June 3–7, 1942	261
The Solomons Campaign, August–November 1942	265

TABLES

2.1 Participant Combatant Naval Strengths in the Pacific, 1914	41
5.1 Tonnage Rates for Cruisers, Destroyers, and Submarines	114
5.2 Australian Defense Expenditure (from Consolidated Revenue), 1926–1936	128
6.1 Heavy Ship Strength Available to Meet the German Fleet and Nine Modernized Japanese Heavy Ships	160

Acknowledgments

The author wishes to acknowledge the excellent support provided by Glenn Griffith and his colleagues at Naval Institute Press in the compilation and production of this work. A special acknowledgment is also made regarding the assistance provided by associate professor Neville Meaney, whose provision of his private papers and research material to the author has been a truly invaluable contribution to the writing of *A Ceaseless Watch*.

Angus Britts
December 10, 2020

Abbreviations

AA	antiaircraft
ABDA	American, British, Dutch, Australian
ANZAC	Australian and New Zealand Army Corps
AWC	Advisory War Council (Australia)
CIC	commander in chief
CID	Committee of Imperial Defence (Britain)
CINCPAC	commander in chief Pacific Fleet (USA)
COD	Council of Defence (Australia)
COS	chiefs of staff
FAA	Fleet Air Arm (Britain)
HMAS	Her Majesty's Australian Ship
HMNZS	Her Majesty's New Zealand Ship
HMS	Her Majesty's Ship
IGHQ	Imperial General Headquarters (Japan)
IJN	Imperial Japanese Navy
JAAF	Japanese Army Air Force
JNAF	Japanese Naval Air Force
PBY	Catalina long-range flying boat (USA)
RAAF	Royal Australian Air Force
RAF	Royal Air Force
RAN	Royal Australian Navy
RN	Royal Navy
SBD	Douglas Dauntless dive-bomber
TBD	Douglas Devastator torpedo-bomber
TBF	Grumman Avenger torpedo-bomber
UAP	United Australia Party
USAAC	United States Army Air Corps
USMC	United States Marine Corps
USN	United States Navy
USS	United States Ship

Introduction

Remember that day and night a ceaseless watch goes on all over the world, and keeps Australia just as safe and secure from all the Powers of the world as if every sailor and every British battleship belonged to you.

—Prime Minister George Reid, Empire Day 1905

When Prime Minister George Reid delivered the inaugural Empire Day address at Tamworth in northern New South Wales on May 24, 1905, Australia belonged to the mightiest maritime empire in history, her security protected by the most powerful fleet on earth. For the vast majority of those who celebrated Reid's stirring words, it was scarcely imaginable that at the moment of their nation's gravest peril, Australia's survival would hinge instead upon the intervention of a fleet from the other New World across the Pacific.

A Ceaseless Watch traces the events and circumstances over two decades that led to this very crisis during an eight-month period in 1942, a crisis centered upon the threat of an attack against Australia by the armed forces of imperial Japan. The central thread of the interwar narrative became the interplay of interests—national, international, and imperial—that both shaped and depleted the prevailing Anglo-Australian defense relationship in the course of the 1920s and 1930s. With the coming of war in Europe in September 1939, the maintenance of Australia's vital interests would become hostage to the realms of Allied grand strategy, within which Britain's vital interests lay elsewhere. And in the wake of the Royal Navy's abject failure to confront effectively Japanese naval air power in the Far East, Australia came to rely upon the presence of a still-battered U.S. Pacific Fleet to turn back the unfolding menace to the continent's Pacific coastline. It would take no less than four carrier engagements and five surface battles over eight months, a frequency of fleet and squadron-scale combat unequaled in modern warfare, for Japan's offensive momentum in the Southwest Pacific to be halted and Australia's protection be thereby secured.

Since the mid-1970s especially, Australia's postwar historians have grappled with this subject in great detail. It remains to this day a discourse that is public and at times controversial. Three aspects in particular, namely the conduct of Anglo-Australian relations, the importance of Prime Minister John Curtin's public appeal for American assistance on December 27, 1941, and the exact nature of Japan's military intentions toward Australia, have drawn the most heated debate among historians, prime ministers, and other prominent community figures. It is a conversation with an inexorable connection to broader questions of national mythology and national identity that are in play today. Beyond Australia, however, consideration of the topic within foreign publishing circles has been relatively limited. Published in the United States through the auspices of the Naval Institute Press, the following account thus seeks in some small part to redress this existing imbalance, and in doing so to highlight the peculiar dilemmas faced by nations whose external security was, or is, entirely dependent upon the intervention of a great-power protector.

1

The Day That Never Dawned

Several hours before sunrise on Tuesday, May 12, 1942, the first of almost two hundred airplane engines coughed and spluttered, then roared into life. Approximately 250 miles to the northeast of its designated strike zone, the Imperial Japanese Navy's elite First Air Fleet was preparing to unleash another of its massed aerial onslaughts against an unsuspecting opponent. For this operation, code-named QP, the carriers *Zuikaku*, *Shokaku*, and *Soryu* were accompanied by four heavy cruisers and a pair of destroyers, with the warships being supported by four fast fleet tankers. Otherwise known within the Japanese navy as the Kido Butai (Mobile Force), the fleet steamed under the command of Vice Admiral Ozawa Jisaburō, an expert in naval air tactics. Between them Ozawa's carriers fielded some 192 first-line combat aircraft, including 54 Navy Type 0 (Allied reporting name "Zeke") fighters, 68 Navy Type 99 ("Val") dive-bombers, and 70 Navy Type 97 ("Kate") attack bombers. The Japanese carrier formation had been assigned the task of neutralizing an important strategic target, and if the mission succeeded, the commander of Japan's Combined Fleet, Admiral Yamamoto Isoroku, foresaw no further impediment to the pursuit of his ultimate objective, namely the final destruction of the weakened U.S. Pacific Fleet.

Following the signing of the Tripartite Pact on September 27, 1940, Yamamoto had informed then-premier Konoe that in the event of war with the United States he would "run wild considerably for the first six months" but lacked any confidence in the outcome thereafter.[1] The admiral recognized that Japan's sole chance of prevailing against the Americans in the short term rested with the suppression of American naval power in the Pacific for as long as possible. By defeating the Pacific Fleet the Japanese would buy valuable time to strengthen their own defenses before a brand-new American armada emerged from the shipyards to stage the inevitable counterattack. But before Yamamoto could bring the enemy to battle via a setpiece showdown in the Central Pacific, his flank needed to be secured against any threat of an Allied naval counterthrust. In the course of planning conferences during late March 1942, he and the Japanese naval staff had seriously considered the merits of the proposed Operation MO, an aero-amphibious expedition to simultaneously occupy Tulagi in the Solomon Islands and Port Moresby in Papua. The prior successful employment of carrier air strikes against Pearl Harbor and other localities, however, eventually persuaded Yamamoto and his colleagues that their aim was best achieved through the execution of a similar attack. By crippling its facilities and sinking the Allied warships there assembled, the chosen target stood to be made unusable as a springboard for major enemy operations throughout the following months. And being deprived of the effective use of this crucial base would likely compel Yamamoto's opposite number, Adm. Chester Nimitz, to further concentrate the Pacific Fleet in Hawaiian waters.

That was precisely what Yamamoto wanted. With the bulk of the Pacific Fleet located in one place, he would bring the entire weight of the Combined Fleet to bear and would crush the enemy in one fell swoop. In order to ensure that the reduced First Air Fleet carried out the QP mission unhindered, a series of diversionary operations undertaken against Midway Island and the Aleutians were designed to fix Nimitz' attention upon a direct threat to America's main Pacific defense perimeter short of the continental United States itself. With the Japanese at the gates it was highly unlikely that authority would be granted for Nimitz, even if he were so minded, to redeploy any of the Pacific Fleet's precious carriers from the general vicinity of the Hawaiian island chain. And in concert with the damage inflicted by Ozawa's fliers, Yamamoto believed that such a daring long-range sortie into the enemy's rear area would undoubtedly deliver another stunning blow to Allied morale. Following the capture of the supposedly impregnable British base at Singapore on February 15, 1942, and the subsequent one-sided campaign that had resulted in the fall of the Netherlands East Indies the following month, the relentless Japanese southern advance was already being viewed as potentially unstoppable by many within the shaken Allied nations. A further Pearl Harbor–style episode should again hammer home to Japan's opponents the realization that none of their vital centers were immune from attack by a carrier spearhead that emerged and then vanished with virtual impunity.

With Ozawa having relieved Vice Admiral Nagumo Chūichi as its commander for the duration of the present mission, the First Air Fleet departed Palau in utmost secrecy on April 29, 1942. Total radio silence was in effect and any mention of QP in all other fleet transmissions was forbidden. Benefiting from bad weather that generated prolonged heavy overcast, Ozawa's ships reached the designated air strike launch point undetected throughout the entire passage. Meanwhile Yamamoto's diversions had swung into action. On May 7 a nuisance air attack was launched from the decks of the light carrier *Hōshō* against Dutch Harbor in the Aleutians. Though inflicting little damage, the raid aroused the Americans to the imminent prospect of further Japanese operations nearer to Hawaii. These were confirmed to be underway on May 8, when a PBY reconnaissance plane flying from Midway spotted a group of fifteen transports some three hundred miles to the west of the island; these ships were a key aspect in the overall Japanese deception. Supplied with further reports detailing the presence of a heavy escort, including multiple aircraft carriers, Nimitz ordered the Pacific Fleet's carriers to intercept the enemy force. Given the critical strategic importance of retaining Midway and equipped with seemingly irrefutable observation evidence of his opponent's intentions, the American commander could not have logically determined otherwise. At dawn on May 11, Midway was attacked by aircraft flying from the light carriers *Zuihō*, *Shōhō*, and *Ryūjō*, triggering a daylong series of skirmishes between the opposing carrier forces.

The central plank in Yamamoto's ruse was the ability of his commander on site, Rear Admiral Hara Tadaichi, to lead the Americans on a wild-goose chase, a task Hara accomplished with considerable skill. With only minimal damage inflicted upon both sides, by nightfall on May 11 the Pacific Fleet's carriers were well to the north of Midway and unable to interfere with Ozawa's forthcoming retirement. At 0430 hours on the morning of May 12, the first wave of attacking aircraft began departing the decks of the First Air Fleet's carriers: thirty-four Vals, thirty Kates, and twenty-seven escorting Zekes. They were to be followed shortly afterwards by Ozawa's second wave, thirty-four Vals and forty

Kates accompanied by a similar number of Zekes. For the protection of the Japanese carriers, nine Zekes from the mission reserves pool were available to form a localized combat air patrol. On the basis of recent undetected overflights by submarine-launched reconnaissance planes, the strike zone was expected to contain numerous Allied warships, auxiliaries, and merchant vessels. Encouragingly, Japanese naval intelligence adjudged the target's likely land-based fighter and antiaircraft defenses to be minimal. It had been correctly anticipated by Yamamoto's planning staff that, following recent changes to the enemy's command structure, virtually all available fighter aircraft in the vicinity had been redeployed elsewhere. Nevertheless, three airfields in the area were included among the initial targets for the first wave flying under the command of the highly experienced dive-bomber "ace" Lieutenant Egusa Takashige.

Following an evening of high winds and scudding showers, the skies above Sydney Harbour were largely clear of heavy clouds as the predawn darkness faded on the eastern horizon. At Dover Heights in Sydney's eastern suburbs the squall had left its imprint upon the Royal Australian Air Force's experimental radar site, with antenna damage forcing a shutdown of the detection equipment so that repairs could be made. Just after 0630 hours local time, lookouts stationed in the West Head defense area on the shores of Broken Bay, sixteen miles to the north of the city, observed two small groups of aircraft to their north flying westward in loose formation. Accustomed as they were to the routine conduct of RAAF training activities in the vicinity, the army personnel believed the distant planes to be Australian, most likely returning to Richmond after completing a night familiarization exercise. Twenty minutes later their colleagues located at North Head on the outer northern side of the entrance to Sydney Harbour sighted a large body of inbound aircraft flying at ten thousand feet some fifteen miles to the east of the headland peninsula. Simultaneously, observers based further south at Cape Banks reported the presence of twenty to thirty unidentified aircraft approaching Botany Bay. An emergency signal was immediately flashed to all armed services area commands, and within moments the teletype machine in Australian prime minister John Curtin's Canberra office chattered out a chilling message from RAAF Laverton: URGENT & CONFIDENTIAL: AIR RAID SYDNEY. REPEAT: AIR RAID SYDNEY.

At 0700 hours the first blows fell upon the targeted airfields as well as the flying-boat anchorage within the harbor itself. Located thirty-seven miles to the west of the city, Richmond came under attack from the supposed "friendlies" spotted earlier, namely nine Kate attack planes. With six Zekes flying top cover, the Japanese bombardiers were untroubled in releasing their payloads, with devastating effect. A stick of bombs incinerated two flights of armed and fueled Hudson bombers drawn up wingtip to wingtip on the tarmac below; other aircraft were destroyed or damaged by numerous direct hits upon hangars, maintenance shops, and dispersal areas. The carnage was replicated shortly thereafter at Bankstown, fourteen miles to the southwest of Sydney. Fifteen U.S. Army Air Corps fighters and twelve bombers, the latter including six B-17 Fortresses, were left ablaze as the aerodrome was thoroughly bombed and strafed by six Vals and an equal number of Zekes. Situated on the northwestern shoreline of Botany Bay, Mascot came under attack from a similar formation. The Zekes promptly shot down two American P-39 fighters that had just become airborne and shot up another four taxiing on the runway while the dive-bombers made short work of the two dozen training aircraft arrayed in neat rows nearby. In the skies over Sydney Harbour the aerial blitz commenced with a gaggle of Zekes raking the flying-boat anchorage in Rose Bay with cannon and machine-gun fire. Flying at wave-top height the Japanese fighters picked off the moored flying boats one by one, sinking five of their number and leaving three others in flames; an RAAF Catalina was likewise dispatched as it attempted an emergency takeoff.

Given that the Japanese flyers had once again achieved almost total surprise, only a handful of the antiaircraft defenses ashore and afloat had as yet gone into action as Lieutenant Egusa and his fellow dive-bomber crews arrived overhead. With the harbor lying virtually helpless beneath them, the first of the Vals proceeded to target the cruisers HMAS *Canberra* and USS *Chicago*, both vessels being moored to the east of the Royal Australian Navy depot at Garden Island. Plummeting down with deadly accuracy, the dive-bombers bracketed each ship with a fusillade of high-explosive and armor-piercing ordnance. Three direct hits and a number of straddles, a deliberate tactic utilizing bombs with time-delayed fuses to buckle the target's hull plates below the waterline, left *Canberra* burning and settling by the head. A hundred yards away *Chicago* suffered numerous impacts and straddles; she rapidly developed a serious list to port and capsized soon afterwards. Over on the northern shore in Athol Bay USS *Vincennes* had available steam to clear her mooring, but as the ship began making way toward the harbor entrance she was singled out for attack. Losing one of their number to AA fire from *Vincennes* as they commenced their dives, the plunging Vals scored several hits on the American cruiser; a near-miss adjacent to the steering compartment jammed her rudder and caused the vessel to begin circling slowly to port. Unable to maneuver freely, *Vincennes*' captain opted to save his ship by beaching her in the shallows at Taylor's Bay.

Anchored at the entrance to Shell Cove, the New Zealand light cruiser HMNZS *Leander* had been likewise able to get under way and was making fifteen knots down the western channel when she was set upon by dive-bombers. An armor-piercing bomb slammed into her forward superstructure, killing virtually all the personnel stationed on the bridge and causing the ship to veer sharply to starboard. Sustaining further hits that set her afire amidships, *Leander*'s progress was eventually halted when she ran aground in Rose Bay. By now the waters to the east of the Harbour Bridge were a scene of utter mayhem as a large, disorganized flotilla of smaller naval and civilian vessels sought to rescue the crews of the four stricken Allied cruisers. Manning a collection of craft ranging in size from tugs and harbor ferries to tiny dinghies, the rescuers continued attending to their task in spite of incessant strafing from the Japanese fighters. Stiffening light antiaircraft fire from ashore and afloat came to the aid of the little ships by shooting down two of the attacking Zekes, the second of which disintegrated in a fireball after spectacularly cartwheeling into the north eastern stone pylon of the Harbour Bridge.

While the Vals sought out the enemy cruisers, twenty-one Kates were hitting shipping and waterfront facilities on both sides of Sydney's famous landmark. Armed with bombs in preference to torpedoes, the multirole airplanes likewise unloaded on their targets with deadly accuracy. At Garden Island the armed merchant cruiser *Manoora* was disabled and several harbor patrol boats were sunk. Across Woolloomooloo Bay the attack planes struck a pair of freighters berthed at the Finger Wharf complex, while in nearby Circular Quay two other freighters and several commuter ferries came under attack. To the west of the bridge, the Kates concentrated their efforts against the extensive commercial wharfage located within the bays and coves of the southern shoreline and the principal RAN dockyard facility on nearby Cockatoo Island. Berthed at the latter, the old light cruiser *Adelaide* capsized and the corvette *Toowoomba* was left ablaze on the slips. Three freighters and three large transports were singled out in the southern dockland precinct, of which four were sunk or crippled at their berths. Throughout Walsh Bay, Glebe Point, and White Bay, the bombing sparked fires that rapidly spread to the warehouses on the wharves, while portions of the wooden wharves themselves began to collapse in the ensuing blazes. With the last of the Kates engaged in their bomb runs, the first Allied fighters arrived on the scene. Having escaped destruction at Richmond, two RAAF Wirraways succeeded in downing one of the Japanese attack bombers before being picked off in quick succession by the vastly superior enemy Zekes.

Elsewhere the Japanese staged several nuisance raids that were timed to coincide with the initial strikes against Sydney. Launched from the screening heavy cruisers, six Navy Type 0 ("Jake") reconnaissance seaplanes staged individual attacks against towns and hamlets located along a seventy-mile stretch of coastline to the north of the city. In each instance the aircraft "buzzed" the local civilian population, swooping low over houses and randomly dropping small bombs. Aside from the sinking of a prawn trawler anchored at Gosford, no material damage was inflicted; the primary rationale behind these sorties was their psychological impact. During recent operations in command of the Second Expeditionary Fleet in the Bay of Bengal, Vice Admiral Ozawa had employed similar tactics against settlements on the Indian coastline, resulting in a wave of fear and panic among the inhabitants, who believed that the raids would be followed by an amphibious invasion.[2]

Such fears were already in evidence among the members of Prime Minister Curtin's bipartisan Advisory War Council summoned to an emergency meeting at Parliament House in Canberra. From the reports received thus far, it appeared that catastrophic damage had been inflicted upon shipping in Sydney Harbour, with at least a dozen warships and merchantmen sunk or crippled and blazes burning out of control at various points along the commercial waterfront. As the meeting progressed, the atmosphere quickly degenerated when the question of Sydney's antiaircraft and fighter defenses came under discussion. Already furious that the attacks had unfolded with little prior warning, Curtin was visibly seething when informed by the RAAF that only two fighter planes had been able to intercept the Japanese formations. Accusations flew among the politicians as to who bore responsibility for Sydney's shambolic protection against aerial attack, but these recriminations faded as the conversation turned to what the enemy might do next. In spite of contrary advice provided by the military advisers present, a number of the AWC's members were convinced that an invasion alert should be issued for the southeastern Australian seaboard. With tempers again becoming frayed, this time between the politicians and the military, the receipt of a fresh teletype message informed the suddenly silenced room that a fresh swarm of hostile aircraft was rapidly approaching the harbor city.

Under the overall command of Lieutenant Tomonaga Joichi, Vice Admiral Ozawa's second wave entered the fray at 0805 hours, fifteen minutes after the last of Egusa's aircraft had departed the scene. Before them lay a dirty brown pall which now hung over the harbor and its surroundings, sustained by the multiple pillars of smoke that betrayed the extent of the destruction and chaos that the initial strike had inflicted. Leading the force of forty Kates, Tomonaga's orders were for thirty of his attack planes to concentrate their level bombing against the various shipyards and ancillary industries to the west of the Harbour Bridge, with the remaining aircraft to strike the oil terminal at Gore Cove. While the Kates bombarded their assigned shore targets, the Vals that accompanied them were instructed to hit enemy warships and the naval depot at Garden Island. Droning their way over Inner South Head, Tomonaga's airplanes flew through a heavy barrage of AA fire from the shore batteries, which came under fire themselves from a dozen strafing Zekes. At this point the Japanese encountered a nasty surprise in the form of a single RAAF Hudson inbound from an antisubmarine patrol. Using a nearby cloud bank as cover for an ambush, the Australian pilot chose the right moment to make a lengthy diving pass through his unsuspecting opponents, potting a Kate and a Zeke in the process. Thereafter pursued by four Japanese fighters, the Hudson's dorsal gunner accounted for another Zeke before the chase was finally broken off; the heavily damaged bomber performed a successful crash landing upon its return to Richmond.

Striking in six three-plane flights, eighteen Vals subjected the facilities on Garden Island to a hail of bombs, inflicting serious damage upon the various maintenance and storage premises assembled there. RAN headquarters sustained several hits, while scaffolding and machinery on the construction site for a large graving dock were set on fire. Unable to clear her berth, the previously damaged *Manoora* was likewise left burning, and when shortly thereafter the flames from the ship reached an adjacent shed crammed with paint supplies and solvents, a sequence of violent explosions showered sheets of flaming liquid debris upon nearby machine shops and supply stores. On the harbor itself both *Vincennes* and *Leander* commanded the majority of attention from the rest of the dive-bombers. Diving through intense light AA fire, two of the Vals were shot down, and the American cruiser suffered no additional harm when struck by a pair of bombs, both of which failed to explode. At the northern end of Rose Bay the similarly beached *Leander* was less fortunate: a well-aimed bomb pierced the ship's 6-inch rear magazine, causing a thunderous detonation that tore off the cruiser's stern and shattered windows for a mile in every direction. Within less than fifteen minutes, much of the waterway to the east of the Harbour Bridge became obscured under a dense plume of black and gray smoke as the dive-bombers commenced the return flight to their carriers.

With Tomonaga acting as the lead bombardier, twelve of the Kates set their sights upon Cockatoo Island. The naval base below them contained a large shipyard and slipway complex, two dry docks, a floating dock, and a range of machine shops, ancillary industries, and warehouses.[3] Facing no impediment from enemy fighters and with only sparse flak, the Japanese aircrews were again able to inflict telling blows. As the smoke from the bombing began to clear in places, it became evident that almost the entire facility had been impacted, with numerous secondary explosions further fueling fires that were raging unchecked across the island. Both dry docks had been severely damaged by the impact of armor-piercing bombs, with the collapse of several large cranes and gantries, while the floating dock was holed and eventually foundered. In the near vicinity, the attack planes likewise struck shipyards and slipways at Goat Island, Balmain, and Woolwich, including the historic Mort's Dock complex at Balmain, which was badly damaged. Approximately one hundred yards to the west of Cockatoo Island lay tiny Spectacle Island, which housed the RAN's armaments and ammunition bunkers. Here a stick of bombs touched off an appalling blast, instantly releasing a powerful shock wave that smashed into nearby suburbs from Birchgrove to Woolwich.

Overshadowed by a seething mushroom cloud, the blast front filled the air with exploding shells and flying shrapnel as it demolished many industrial sites and hundreds of business and residential premises that lay in its path.

Located at the entrance to Gore Cove on the harbor's northern shoreline, the discharge wharf for the adjacent oil refinery was the designated aiming point for five of the Kates assigned the task of neutralizing the installation. Hits to the pumping apparatus resulted, as the attackers had hoped, in the discharge of thousands of gallons of fuel oil into the surrounding waters of Balls Head Bay. The other four participants then exacerbated the situation by dropping a mixture of incendiaries and high explosives that ignited the spreading slick, which in due course engulfed a pair of oil barges anchored nearby. The resulting inferno proceeded to slowly wend its way toward the harbor proper, its progress only partially checked for the moment by the deployment of floating booms by rescue personnel, once again under heavy strafing from the ever-present Zekes. Banking sharply away from the conflagration below them, the remaining bomber crews retired eastwards, and by 0850 hours the skies over Sydney were at last devoid of Japanese aircraft.

Upon the recovery of his planes from the returning second wave, Vice Admiral Ozawa ordered retirement and the First Air Fleet steamed away at speed to the northeast. Although sighted by an American PBY to the north of the Santa Cruz Islands several days later, the Japanese ships completed their journey without further incident, receiving a rapturous welcome upon their eventual return to Kure on May 30, 1942. The punishment inflicted by the Japanese strikes rendered Sydney Harbour effectively incapable of supporting further Allied naval operations during the forthcoming window for Admiral Yamamoto's great showdown with the U.S. Pacific Fleet. With this objective having been achieved and at a trifling cost—just nine aircraft shot down—Ozawa's mission had orchestrated a comprehensive strategic success.

In Canberra the anxieties present among Prime Minister Curtin and his colleagues grew with each new report received from the various armed services headquarters in the Sydney area. They had been cheered to some extent by an earlier phone conversation between the prime minister and General MacArthur, in which MacArthur promised to redeploy three fighter squadrons together with American antiaircraft and searchlight batteries to Sydney as soon as possible. At the same instant MacArthur reiterated the advice given by Curtin's military advisers, cautioning him against drawing premature conclusions as to possible Japanese intentions in the aftermath of the strikes. By noon a search off the coastline by Catalinas flying from RAAF Rathmines had failed to find any trace of an invasion fleet nor any sign of Ozawa's carriers. The discussion, meanwhile, focused upon the present situation in Sydney, with particular attention being paid to the question of martial law. In spite of the heavy damage inflicted in a number of harborside suburbs, there had been no reports thus far of a general breakdown in public order, and in due course the prime minister determined that the circumstances did not yet warrant such a declaration. Nevertheless additional troops were to be dispatched by rail from their bases in the outer Sydney suburbs of Ingleburn and Holsworthy to assist the civilian authorities in maintaining order, as well as contributing to the rescue and fire-fighting efforts already under way.

The scale of destruction and damage rendered by the Japanese strikes massively surpassed the severe effects of the air attack against Darwin three months earlier. Beyond the confines of Sydney Harbour the scenes at the three military airfields that suffered the first bombs were emblematic of the general devastation inflicted. The raid on Richmond had resulted in the deaths of seventy RAAF personnel, with twenty-three aircraft destroyed and numerous buildings, including the main hangar, left in ruins. While the casualties at Bankstown amounted to no more than a dozen wounded, the base facilities were largely gutted; piles of charred metal and fabric marked the destruction of twenty-seven USAAC machines, including more than half of a pursuit squadron newly arrived from the United States. Several days earlier, six of that squadron's P-39 fighters had been transferred to Mascot to act as a rapid-response interceptor flight in the event of a surprise attack. Four of these airplanes now lay wrecked on that base's runway, the other two having crashed into Botany Bay when downed by the Japanese fighters. Although the hangars and other installations suffered only limited damage, the flight line at Mascot contained the remains of twenty-four burnt-out trainers; fifteen ground staff had been killed and many others wounded as they attempted to push the stationary aircraft out of harm's way. And within Sydney Harbour itself, Rose Bay sported the wrecks of eight flying boats and three small seaplanes, all of which had been targeted during the opening moments of the enemy onslaught.

Few of the warships and merchant vessels that were present in the harbor that morning had managed to avoid serious mishap. Of the five Allied cruisers attacked, only *Vincennes* escaped with a beaching and heavy damage. Of the remainder, *Canberra* was sunk outright, while *Chicago*, *Adelaide*, and *Leander* had all been rendered virtually unsalvageable. Other losses included the gutted *Manoora* and the similarly stricken *Toowoomba*, three harbor patrol boats, and at least half a dozen other small naval ancillaries. A transport and two freighters were likewise sent to the bottom and a further four burnt out, while the toll among the civilian craft that had participated in rescue activities stood at more than thirty vessels of all types sunk. The casualties sustained among the naval and civilian crews amounted to 750 dead and missing and in excess of 600 wounded. While the Japanese aviators had concentrated the majority of their efforts against legitimate military targets, two civilian commuter ferries foundered after being struck by bombs while approaching Circular Quay, resulting in fifty-five deaths and another ninety injuries. It was indeed fortunate for the RAN that the heavy cruiser *Australia* and the light cruiser *Hobart*, due back on port that morning after completing an exercise off the south coast, had delayed their scheduled return due to the effects of rough weather.

Equally grievous was the devastation that fell upon the chosen ground targets that populated the foreshores of the harbor and its resident islands. The Cockatoo Island dockyard was reduced to a bombed-out landscape of twisted metal, burnt-out structures, and destroyed plant and equipment that required many months to fully repair. A similar level of destruction and damage was likewise evident at Garden Island, while the nearby commercial Finger Wharf had collapsed in three places. Within the western docklands precinct, raging fires were responsible for the collapse of wharfage and the razing of numerous storage buildings. As for the commercial shipyards and slipways within the general vicinity, the majority of those attacked sustained substantial damage to their wharves and workshop facilities. The bombing of the oil installation at Gore Cove had resulted in the effective crippling of the vital pumping apparatus and a resulting impact upon adjoining shipyards, repair shops, and other factories; a number of these were eventually engulfed by the floating inferno of discharged fuel oil. And through the detonation of the ammunition magazines on Spectacle Island, reducing the island itself to a crater-strewn expanse of rock, more than twenty waterside factories and as many as five hundred residential and commercial premises throughout six suburbs were demolished or otherwise heavily damaged. Casualties ashore also proved to be heavy, amounting to approximately 220 military and 260 civilian dead and missing and more than 900 wounded. Even with the infusion of fresh troops and emergency personnel, the various rescue and recovery operations were continually compromised by unchecked blazes as well as by the toxic cloud of pungent smoke that billowed from the oil fires in Balls Head Bay.

With the coming of nightfall on May 12, the orange glow above Sydney Harbour was clearly visible to onlookers on board the Australian cruisers *Australia* and *Hobart* while the returning ships were still a considerable distance offshore. As of yet the fire services had been unable to bring several of the largest blazes under control, and these efforts would persist for many hours to come. Thanks however to the rapid intervention of the local civilian and military authorities, a major exodus from the city had been prevented by the prompt establishment of checkpoints on the major arterial roads and the commandeering of the railways for priority military traffic. Although there were some instances of looting, public order was generally secured by the presence of regular troops and militia patrolling the streets. Nevertheless an atmosphere of dumbfounded fear and apprehension prevailed among much of the city's population. Many residents were convinced that the morning's raids would be followed by an invasion, and the following hours of darkness proved to be a testing time for taut nerves, particularly within Sydney's coastal suburbs. If any remaining belief in the inviolability of Australia's southeastern seaboard had survived the bombing of Darwin, the first bombs to fall upon the Richmond aerodrome bludgeoned home the stark reality that virtually all the nation's vital centers lay under the thrall of Japanese naval air power.

Throughout the course of the day a series of official communiqués emanating from Canberra informed the Australian people of the raids against Sydney, but only with limited details supplied. No details had been officially released regarding the situation on the Central Coast to Sydney's north, where Ozawa's nuisance attacks had triggered spontaneous local evacuations in a variety of coastal and hinterland areas. Appreciating the pressing need to stabilize civilian morale across the continent, Prime Minister Curtin planned to address the nation on the radio at 1930 hours that evening. Just moments before his broadcast commenced, the prime minister was handed a translated copy of an intercepted announcement that had been made on Japan's NHK radio network a few minutes earlier:

> IMPERIAL GENERAL HEADQUARTERS TODAY ANNOUNCES THE ACHIEVEMENT OF A GREAT VICTORY IN THE SOUTH SEAS. THIS MORNING, NAVY PLANES BOMBED ENEMY SHIPPING AND PORT FACILITIES IN SYDNEY HARBOUR. SIX ENEMY CRUISERS HAVE BEEN SUNK, ALONG WITH OTHER NAVAL CRAFT, AND AT LEAST TEN MERCHANT VESSELS. APPROXIMATELY FIFTY ENEMY AIRCRAFT HAVE ALSO BEEN DESTROYED. ATTACKS MOUNTED AGAINST THE VITAL PORT FACILITIES WERE CARRIED OUT WITH COMPLETE SUCCESS, AND THESE TARGETS HAVE BEEN NEUTRALIZED. THE JAPANESE GOVERNMENT TAKES THIS OPPORTUNITY TO ADVISE THE AUSTRALIAN GOVERNMENT THAT UNLESS AUSTRALIA FORTHWITH ACCEPTS THE AUTHORITY OF THE NEW ORDER OF THE GREATER SOUTH-EAST ASIA CO-PROSPERITY SPHERE, FURTHER ATTACKS AGAINST AUSTRALIAN CITIES WILL TAKE PLACE.

2

Foundations

1788–1918

In fact, the sharp end of the Pacific conflict eventually found its way to Sydney Harbour on the night of May 31, 1942. Three weeks earlier on May 7–8, the Imperial Japanese Navy had received its first check of the war when Operation MO was turned back in the Coral Sea. As the American defenders on Midway Island prepared for an expected onslaught from Japan's Combined Fleet, Sydney's first experience of naval attack arrived in the form of three enemy midget submarines. Preceded by an unchallenged overflight of the harbor by a reconnaissance seaplane, two of the midgets successfully penetrated the boom-gate defenses and launched their attacks. The converted harbor ferry *Kuttabul* was sunk with the loss of nineteen RAN sailors on board; all three of the attackers were lost.[1] This daring sortie marked the summit of the Japanese menace to Australian shores, a menace that was substantially extinguished just five days later with the sinking of the *Hiryu*, the fourth of Vice Admiral Nagumo's large carriers to be sent to the bottom at Midway. For five previous months Australia confronted what remains to the present day the most serious security crisis in the nation's history. Yet the key factors dating from 1919 that were to shape the eventual onset of Australia's darkest hours were themselves symptomatic of a fundamental strategic dilemma that had prevailed since the foundation of white settlement in 1788.

"This Great South Land": January 1788–December 1850

When the British government determined to claim what was then described as "Terra Australis Nullius" as a keystone for imperial expansion into the Pacific, the subsequent rationale for colonization was initially a means to relieve chronic overcrowding in British prisons by means of overseas transportation. The military consequences of establishing a prison colony on the other side of the world were indeed apparent from the earliest days of the British presence on the eastern seaboard in January 1788, with the sighting of two unknown sailing ships off the coast preceding the movement of the First Fleet from Botany Bay to Port Jackson.[2] These were the French frigates *Boussole* and *Astrolabe* under the command of Jean François Galaup Comte de la Perouse, which were conducting an exploration of the South Pacific. Granted permission to anchor in Botany Bay by Governor Arthur Phillip, the French set up camp just inside the northern side of the bay's northern entrance, on the site of the modern Sydney suburb of La Perouse. During their stay the visitors erected an improvised stockade but evidently remained on friendly terms with the British until la Perouse's departure in early March 1788.[3] The French ships subsequently disappeared, yet they left behind them the first instance of a foreign naval scare in Australia's colonial history, a periodic bout of nervousness inevitably exacerbated by the sparseness of available defenses.

The separate voyages of exploration undertaken by la Perouse and Antoine de Bruny d'Entrecasteaux were part of a wider French scheme to chart the largely unknown coastlines of New Holland (Australia), New Guinea, and Van Diemans Land (Tasmania). In October 1800 the crack French navigator Thomas Baudin, who had previously visited the South Pacific in 1786 and 1789 in the service of the Austrian emperor Joseph II, departed France to continue this process under the following instructions from the French government:

> The aim of the Government . . . has been to have examined in detail the south-west, west, north-west and north coasts of New Holland, some of which are still entirely unknown, whilst others are known only imperfectly. By combining the work which will be done on these various parts with that of the English navigators on the east coast . . . we shall know the entire coastline of this great south land, which, situated not far from the countries of Asia . . . have seemed until recently to be condemned to a sort of oblivion.[4]

On April 8, 1802, Baudin's flagship *Le Géographe* crossed paths with *Investigator*, a British survey vessel commanded by Lieutenant Matthew Flinders. An accomplished navigator and cartographer, Flinders was likewise in the process of charting the Australian coastline, and the meeting between both men at the subsequently named Encounter Bay (on the South Australian coastline) proved cordial. Though wary of each other's motives, they nevertheless exchanged valuable navigational information and went their separate ways the following day. When the French visited Port Jackson in June of the same year, some of Baudin's subordinates took the opportunity to make observations of a different kind. In 1810 Napoleon authorized planning for the future seizure of the British colony on the basis of these officers' reports concerning the state of Sydney Harbour's defenses, but the subsequent reversal of French fortunes in the Napoleonic Wars ensured that no material preparations for such an expedition were undertaken.[5]

It was unsurprising that a veil of distrust existed between Baudin and Flinders given that both men separately believed that a state of war between Britain and France was in force at the time of their meeting; neither was aware that peace in the form of the Treaty of Amiens had been concluded in late March 1802. This situation illustrated one of the major difficulties for European exploration and settlement in the Pacific prior to the Industrial Revolution, namely the enormous vacuum in communications with the southern hemisphere. In the absence of the telegraph, the submarine cable, and regular shipping schedules, instructions and news from home could be many months old before they arrived. As such it was often impossible to know with certainty whether a sighted vessel was engaged in exploration or privateering. So from the earliest days, the new colony was exposed to its most serious practical threat. Entirely dependent upon the sea routes between Britain and Australia for its continuing sustenance, New South Wales could ill afford any attempt by a hostile power to target the settlement's slowly developing trade and commerce with the outside world.

Throughout the period from 1788 to 1815, France's periodic allies Holland and Spain were likewise regarded as potential menaces. In April 1799 the Spanish ship *Nostra Senora de Bethlehem* arrived at Sydney following her seizure by American whalers under letters of marque, to be followed in December of the same year by the similarly seized *El Plumier*, much to the alarm of then-governor John Hunter, who believed that the

Spanish might stage a revenge attack against the settlement.⁶ With the British gaining the ascendency in the Indian Ocean by 1811 the menace posed by these nations largely diminished, but the end of the Napoleonic Wars did not bring about a total abandonment of French interest. French survey expeditions visited the Western Australian coastline in 1818 and 1826, whereupon the British government ordered Governor Darling in New South Wales to establish a colony in Western Australia. Darling dispatched two small forces, the second of which reached the mouth of the Swan River in March 1827. On May 2, 1829, Captain Charles Fremantle proclaimed British possession of the west coast, which became known as the Swan River Colony, together with the remainder of the continent that did not already fall within the declared territory of New South Wales.⁷

Aside from the potential hostile interventions of western European imperial powers, the early colonial administrations in New South Wales had concerns about the motives of other visitors, namely those from Russia and the United States. In June 1807 the Russian supply ship *Neva* called at Port Jackson during her voyage to settlements near Alaska. She was followed in 1814 by *Suvorov*, and in 1820 no less than four Russian warships arrived at Sydney at varying stages during that year. Further warship visits to both Sydney and Hobart (Tasmania) took place from 1825 until 1835.⁸ The first American ship to enter Sydney Harbour was the civilian brig *Philadelphia*, in November 1792. Fears over American intentions were raised in 1813 when news of the outbreak of the 1812 war between the United States and Britain eventually reached New South Wales, but no incidents took place in Australian waters during the course of the three-year conflict. In December 1839 the peaceful visit of the two American sloops *Vincennes* and *Peacock* thrust the parlous state of Port Jackson's defenses into the limelight. Equipped with charts of their destination, the American ships determined to proceed up-harbor to Sydney Cove on the evening of November 30 without waiting for the services of a pilot. A subsequent account from Capt. Charles Wilkes, USN, detailed that at "half-past ten p.m. we quietly dropped anchor off the Cove in the midst of the shipping without anyone having the least idea of our arrival."⁹ The visit ended on an encouraging note, however, when Wilkes organized a gala ball at Fort Macquarie that attracted some one thousand guests. His gesture succeeded in creating a great deal of goodwill from the colonists toward the U.S. Navy.¹⁰

This incident highlighted the almost complete neglect of the colony's security by the British authorities since the arrival of the First Fleet some fifty-one years before. In 1819 Commissioner J. T. Bigge had been dispatched from England to report on conditions in New South Wales and make recommendations for civic and military improvements where necessary. Among Bigge's subsequent findings was a recommendation that Sydney's artillery defense be substantially upgraded, including the establishment of a battery at South Head.[11] In response, the Colonial Office repeatedly refused further requests from New South Wales' military governors that funding be allocated for the upgrading of existing fortifications and the construction of new sites. The standard argument employed by the British government was that these measures did not merit financing due to budgetary constraints and were unnecessary because of the Royal Navy's dominance of the sea lanes. Even the provision of an expert engineering officer (singular) was delayed until 1835. In 1847 the colonists were further angered by the withdrawal of British garrison units to New Zealand for deployment in the First Maori War. A letter to the *Times* from an unidentified correspondent in June 1845 succinctly identified the central issue that would cloud the Anglo-Australian security relationship for a century to come: "England has never shown any favour to her Australian colonies in time of peace, and if she neglects also to protect them in time of war, the colonists will soon discover that such an alliance is only detrimental to them, without producing any counterbalancing advantages."[12]

In spite of continuing obfuscation from London regarding the security situation (Bigge's proposed battery at South Head was finally constructed in 1859), by 1850 the existing Australian colonies had otherwise made considerable progress toward self-sufficiency. Reaching its peak during the 1830s, convict transportation had thereafter declined, increasingly superseded by an influx of free settlers under a government-subsidized assisted immigration scheme. Economic prosperity was on the rise, thanks in no small part to the development of a lucrative export trade in high-quality wool, alongside other profitable entrepreneurial activity.[13] Prior to the granting of royal assent for the Australian Colonies Government Act on August 5, 1850, three colonies—New South Wales, Western Australia (the Swan River Colony), and South Australia (1834)—had been formed. Three more were to follow; Victoria (1851), Tasmania (1856), and Queensland (1859), each of these being split off from the existing territory of New South Wales. Under this legislation the colonies were granted the right to govern their own domestic affairs, though British governance continued in external matters such as foreign relations and defense. The establishment of civil legislatures and the exercise of liberal Enlightenment principles in public administration provided the Australian colonists with a range of rights and freedoms that were still to be implemented within England itself.[14] Yet Australia remained an isolated periphery of the British Empire and was poised to enter a half-century in which the fear of foreign military incursion would eventually pave the way for the creation of a federated Dominion nation-state.

The Australian Colonies and Imperial Defense: January 1851–December 1900

During the course of 1851 the discovery of gold in both New South Wales and Victoria significantly transformed the position of the Australian colonies. With the exception of Western Australia, convict transportation had largely ceased and assisted migration was superseded for the next decade by a massive influx of unassisted immigrants.[15] The wealth derived from the goldfields resulted in the expansion of Sydney and Melbourne into thriving metropolises while ensuring that the path to economic self-sufficiency became further entrenched. In 1850 the white settler population in Australia stood at approximately 400,000 people; this number increased to more than 600,000 by December 1851 and reached one million in 1860.[16] The consequences of this newfound prosperity for the colonies did not, however, relax the trepidation of the colonists when it came to the matter of their defense against external threats. On the contrary, the wealth of gold bullion stored in Australia's coastal port cities stimulated even greater concern that hostile nations or privateers would be emboldened to ransack these largely undefended localities. The result was the outbreak of the largest naval scare seen in Australia since 1788 when on March 28, 1854, Britain declared war on Russia, and an Anglo-Franco-Turkish alliance proceeded to confront the Russians on the Crimean peninsula.

Following the receipt of this news in May 1854, a number of the city's most influential citizens held a large public meeting in Sydney to discuss maintaining the security of the colony on Britain's behalf, while at the same time deploring the vulnerability of the Australian colonies as a whole. One speaker saw things differently. John Dunmore Lang, a clergyman and prominent republican activist, subjected himself to public ridicule when he suggested that the bellicose attachment of the colonies to Britain in this instance could very well bring upon them the specter of foreign military aggression that they so feared. He also reminded the audience that in time of war it was unlikely that Britain possessed the wherewithal to defend all the empire's far-flung possessions.[17] As had been the case in earlier scares, the Crimean War ended in 1856 without incident in Australian waters, yet the brief panic it had engendered caused the incoming governor, Sir William Denison, to advise the Colonial Office of a means to prevent future reactions of this sort. Denison suggested that London employ greater emphasis upon "the community of interest between the Mother Country and the Colony which renders the defence of the latter as a matter of importance to the former."[18]

In making this suggestion Denison expanded upon the problem that had been raised in the *Times* in 1845. Whereas the powerful strength of the cultural bonds between the British and their Australian colonists was unquestioned, this did not mean that both parties necessarily shared mutual interests when it came to the formulation of foreign policy and military strategy. The major difficulty lay in reconciling Britain's policies toward her fellow European imperial powers with the differing regional circumstances faced by the Australians.[19] To be addressed in greater detail shortly, the British sought to negotiate agreements with foreign powers in order to achieve British aims in the power play of European diplomacy, yet the Australian colonies viewed some of these agreements, rightly or wrongly, as directly injurious to their own vital strategic interests.

As it happened the Crimean War did finally provide some tangible benefits for the long-suffering colonies. At long last London acknowledged, albeit reluctantly, that Australia's defenses did require a substantial upgrade, and financing was approved for the construction of new coastal fortifications and the upgrading of existing facilities. This included the overdue completion of Fort Denison on Pinchgut Island in Sydney Harbour, which had been initiated seventeen years beforehand as a consequence of Captain Wilkes' visit.[20] The most significant addition to colonial defenses came with the welcome establishment of the Royal

Navy's Australian Squadron on March 26, 1859. Under the command of Commodore William Loring, the squadron took up residence in Sydney and soon found itself engaged in the second Maori War in 1860.[21] Joining the British ships in the conflict was Her Majesty's Colonial (HMC) sloop *Victoria*, the first Australian colonial warship to serve with the Royal Navy in an overseas war. Lasting until 1864, the war produced the Australian Squadron's first major casualty when its flagship, the screw corvette *Orpheus*, was wrecked off Manukau on February 7, 1863, with the loss of 187 lives, including the squadron commander, Commodore William Burnett.[22]

The shelling of Fort Sumter in Charleston Harbor on April 12, 1861, marked the opening of the American Civil War and along with it a fresh bout of nerves for the Australian colonies. While British sympathies lay with the Confederacy, Russia tacitly supported the Union cause, and the tsar's Pacific Squadron represented a tangible threat to both Australian maritime trade and the continent's eastern coastline. In the first half of 1863, the flagship of the Russian squadron, the corvette *Bogatyr*, paid courtesy visits to Melbourne and Sydney. Though the exact nature of Russian intentions toward the Australian colonies in this instance remains a matter of conjecture, there was evidence that the visitors were deliberately gathering important field intelligence during their respective stays. In Sydney several Russian officers took detailed notes of the existing fortifications, with one such account detailing the ease with which the city could be attacked due to the paucity of effective defensive works.[23] While this latest threat from Russia again failed to materialize, the arrival of the Confederate warship *Shenandoah* at Melbourne on January 25, 1865, brought with it the prospect of a serious diplomatic incident. After sustaining damage in the course of its raiding operations against Union whaling fleets, *Shenandoah* received a rousing greeting from the city's citizens and remained at Williamstown until February 19, while undergoing repairs. The United States consul petitioned the Victorian governor to have the crew arrested as pirates; the request was politely refused and *Shenandoah* left Australian waters unscathed with forty-five additional recruits.[24]

Britain's participation in the tangled diplomacy of the Civil War held direct implications for Australia and British imperial naval strategy as a whole. On November 8, 1861, the U.S. warship *San Jacinto* had intercepted the British steamer *Trent*, with the result that two Confederate emissaries were forcibly removed from the latter.[25] Though the British did not respond with direct military force, the incident provoked discussion within both Whitehall and the Admiralty as to the best means to safeguard imperial trade and commerce. The provision of overseas-based squadrons, improved colonial fortifications and local naval defenses, and the establishment of a mobile "flying squadron" to deal with emergencies were all included in the conversation. The latter means was especially appealing to the then–British prime minister William Gladstone thanks to its lesser expense, and in 1868 it was put into practice.[26] In November 1869 a flying squadron of four frigates and two corvettes visited Sydney, Melbourne, and Hobart before proceeding to New Zealand. As Andrew Lambert noted in his essay on the subject, deterrence through mobile naval power was the most feasible option for guaranteeing the security of a global maritime empire.[27] Yet the introduction of the flying squadron concept did not set in stone the total abolition of the permanent overseas squadrons, and the debate over these varying strategic approaches was to continue well into the twentieth century.

In April 1865, the same month in which the Confederacy surrendered, the British parliament passed the Colonial Naval Defense Act. This legislation provided the colonies with the legal basis to raise their own naval forces for local defense and likewise allowed for such forces to be placed under the control of the British Admiralty in times of emergency. With the exception of Western Australia, the Australian colonies proceeded to develop their own small fleets over the next three decades, with the majority of the craft being constructed in British shipyards.[28] The policy of colonial self-sufficiency at sea was replicated on land, with the final withdrawal of British garrison troops from Australia during 1870, a decision that generated considerable concern among the various colonial legislatures. An editorial in the *Sydney Morning Herald* on August 25, 1870, suggested that the situation the colonies found themselves in was akin to the operation of an insurance policy: "It may be found that the principle of insurance has a wider range. The master mariner takes care of his ship, the householder watches against fire, but both accept the protection of a wider guarantee; and the time may come when it will be seen that, while no people should depend absolutely upon any but themselves, those changes which reduce distance and hasten intelligence, while they increase the danger of attack, require it to be counterbalanced by a wide and strong combination—the tutelary power of the whole Empire."[29]

Off Rottnest Island (Western Australia) on April 19, 1876, another diplomatic incident with the United States was fortunately averted after the hastily requisitioned government ship *Georgette* fired warning shots at the American whaling vessel *Catalpa*, which was carrying escaping Fenian convicts. The action ceased when the latter raised the American flag.[30] Two years before in 1874, the completion of a submarine cable link to the continent had finally eliminated the long-standing communications vacuum with the northern hemisphere. Now apprised of world events on a concurrent basis, the Australians were exposed to a new age of modernization, and along with it the emergence of a new and important participant in European affairs. Alongside another series of "Eastern Crises" involving potential hostilities between Britain and Russia, the defeat of France in the 1870 Franco-Prussian War heralded the rise of a unified German imperial republic. At the same instant, debate continued within British naval and military circles as to the competing demands of imperial and continental defense requirements, while opinions within the Royal Navy remained divided as to whether Britain's global requirements were best served by permanent overseas squadrons or by the flying squadron approach. The former option was ultimately retained for the remainder of the nineteenth century, and the 1879 Carnarvon Commission concluded that the colonies should be responsible for bearing at least part of the cost of hosting the Royal Navy's overseas deployments.[31] And in December 1884 the cause of colonial Australian naval defense was considerably advanced by the appointment of Rear Admiral George Tryon as commander of the Australia station. Though equipped with instructions from the Admiralty to pursue a united Australasian squadron under Admiralty control, in the course of his two-year tenure Tryon came to appreciate and support the need for an effective localized naval defense of Australia as a whole.[32]

At the April 1887 Colonial Conference in London, the question of future imperial naval defense formed the basis for a negotiated agreement between Whitehall and the colonies, albeit reluctantly from the latter's perspective. Operating under British command, an Australian Auxiliary Squadron would be established as a supplement to the Royal Navy's existing Australian Squadron. This auxiliary force could not be deployed beyond Australian waters without colonial consent, and the colonies would bear 5 percent of construction costs, together with an annual sum of £91,000 for maintenance expenses.[33] Beyond Australian coastal waters, the Royal Navy was to protect the all-important trade routes to the continent, without which Australia could be cut off and effectively isolated from the outside world. Two years later the primacy of the Royal Navy itself within British strategic thinking became enshrined in legislation with the passage of the 1889 Naval Defense Act, which provided for a fleet that would be larger and more powerful than the combined strength of the next two largest foreign navies in service.

The agreement reached in London took place during a period in which the inherent contradictions of Denison's proposed community of interest were becoming more apparent. Colonies such as New South Wales were prepared to dispatch volunteer units to the Sudan (1885) and the second of the Anglo-Boer Wars (1899), and though there were some who opposed these measures, opinions such as those held by William Bede Dalley, the premier of New South Wales, were in the majority. "We do not stop to question; we only know that British blood—that Australian blood—has been shed in the defence of England's rights, and we respond accordingly," Dalley stated in February 1885 in the course of justifying his government's decision to send troops to the Sudan.[34] Yet when the colony of Queensland proclaimed its annexation of New Guinea on April 13, 1883, in order to forestall German claims to the island, Whitehall was far from impressed. Despite the claim from Queensland's premier that "the establishment of a Foreign Power in the neighbourhood of Australia would be injurious to British, and more particularly to Australian interests," the initiative was rapidly quashed by the Colonial Office.[35] More odious still for the Australian colonies, all of which had supported Queensland's stance, was that the British and the Germans subsequently negotiated an agreement in April 1886 to divide New Guinea and other Pacific islands. The British likewise refused to heed Australian calls in 1886 to prevent the French from occupying the New Hebrides, and they were firmly opposed to any concept of an independent Australian "Monroe Doctrine" in the South Pacific.

These events were a sobering portent that when it came to the strategic interests of the Australian colonies, Britain's participation in the diplomatic machinations of the European great powers rendered any contrary

Australian ambitions as effectively null and void. This situation would persist throughout the 1890s, as a new phase emerged in the evolution of potential external threats that had afflicted the colonial Australian mindset for the past century. Australian fears over a mass influx of Chinese migrants, or, worse, the prospect of a Chinese invasion, had been stoked by various colonial politicians since the mid-1880s.[36] The fear of Chinese encroachment was primarily expressed in the context of domestic racial integration, although some of those who posed these warnings did point to the supposed danger posed by China's developing navy. It was Japan, however, that would come to assume an unchallenged hegemony over Australian anxieties for the next half-century, largely through the might of the Imperial Japanese Navy, a force that owed its genesis in the 1860s to direct material assistance from Britain.[37] Thanks to the ongoing training of the Japanese naval officer corps by the Royal Navy and the construction of major Japanese warships in British shipyards, Japan had given China a drubbing at sea in the course of the 1894–95 Sino-Japanese War. And in yet another instance of an evident split in Anglo-Australian interests, London and Tokyo concluded the 1894 Anglo-Japanese Commercial Treaty in the absence of any prior notice supplied to the colonial governments from Whitehall. With the exception of Queensland, the colonies reacted angrily; they refused to be party to the agreement and there were immediate calls in New South Wales for that colony's existing bar on Chinese immigration to be extended to the "warlike" Japanese.[38]

With the coming of the 1890s, the impetus for Australian federation grew apace, culminating in the royal assent for the Commonwealth of Australia Constitution Act on July 9, 1900, and its public proclamation in Australia on January 1, 1901. There exists little debate that of all the various forces that eventually propelled the Australian colonies into nationhood, the most crucial influence was the defense issue. In his celebrated "Tenterfield Speech" of October 1889, the renowned colonial statesman Henry Parkes stated that aside from collective defense there was no other genuine justification for federation to take place. In 1898 a jocular Rudyard Kipling remarked that if Australia wished to speed up the federation process, "you ought to make a syndicate to hire a few German cruisers to bombard Sydney Melbourne and Brisbane for twenty minutes... there'd be a federated Australia in twenty-four hours."[39] Yet federation did not alter the position that the new nation would find itself in from the outset.

Australia's external naval security essentially remained hostage to the ongoing British strategic debate between the imperial and continental schools and the associated division over naval dispositions within the imperial camp itself. It would be the outcomes of these wider questions that were to mold the development of Australia's seaborne defenses in the years prior to August 1914.

The Shadow of Tsushima: January 1901–July 1914

In short, the imperial school contended that Britain's might was sustained by the nation's status as a global maritime superpower, with the imperialist supporters, particularly those within the parliament, the press, and the Royal Navy, drawing sustenance from the ideas of the American naval theorist Adm. Alfred Mahan. For their part the backers of the continental school believed that the European continent represented the true source of power and were guided in their thinking by the so-called Heartland theory advanced by Halford Mackinder, the English geopolitical advocate.[40] With regard to the Royal Navy, the central question for both sides of the argument was the material disposition of the fleet. Whereas the imperial school held firm to a general policy of global deployment, the continentals emphasized the need to massively concentrate the nation's naval strength in the North Atlantic to ward off any threats to Britain itself. Likewise there still existed divergent views within the Admiralty as to the means by which a global defense posture could best be implemented. During the course of the four decades prior to 1900, reformers such as Captain John Colomb and Admiral Sir Alexander Milne had succeeded in promoting a number of necessary measures, including the establishment of a network of strategically placed coaling stations throughout the wider empire.[41] Yet as was the case in the broader debate, fleet disposition proved to be the sticking point, the choice being between maintaining overseas squadrons or detaching units from the fleet to deal with imperial circumstances as they arose, with trade defense remaining the key issue.

A possible solution was soon to materialize. In February 1902 the British and Japanese entered into the Anglo-Japanese Alliance. In spite of Australia's exclusion from the negotiations, members of the Australian government initially stated that the agreement was of the utmost benefit to the Commonwealth because the presence of the Imperial Japanese

Navy protected Australian commerce from the potential danger posed by Russia's Pacific Squadron based at Port Arthur.[42] Further afield, the Anglo-Japanese Alliance seemingly provided a solution to the imperial versus continental conundrum. With the Japanese possessing a modern fleet, the British could effectively subcontract their naval obligations to the east of Suez, allowing the Admiralty to reduce the size of its overseas squadrons or even disband them altogether. This course of action was especially appealing given the steady expansion of the German fleet during this period and permitted Whitehall the operational flexibility to exercise a de facto continental naval policy. Once again the British government had achieved a negotiated outcome in the Pacific that proved favorable to Britain's great-power interests.

Though the public reaction of the Australian government was one of cordial warmth when advised by cable of the signing of the alliance, the agreement fundamentally contradicted Australia's existent foreign and domestic interests. As will become apparent in due course, the ongoing acceptance of the alliance by Australia became at best lukewarm, an unsurprising sentiment given the nation's ongoing fears over Japanese intentions in the Pacific. From the domestic standpoint the contradiction proved to be even starker. On December 23, 1901, the Australian parliament had received royal assent for the establishment of the Immigration Restriction Act. Seeking to firmly establish Australia's future racial identity, the legislators were well aware that this initiative could strain relations with the Japanese.[43] Seven months earlier, on May 3, Japan's resident consul had written to the Australian government requesting that any racially based legislation not go forward, as "the friendship that exists between the Empires of Great Britain and Japan leads me to suppose that your Government would not willingly take steps calculated to wound the feelings of the people whom it is my privilege to represent."[44] The Commonwealth attorney general Alfred Deakin made no apologies for his nation's attitude when he spoke in the House of Representatives on September 12, 1901: "I contend that the Japanese require to be excluded because of their high abilities. I quite agree with the honourable member for Moreton that the Japanese are the most dangerous because they most nearly approach us, and would, therefore, be our most formidable competitors. It is not the bad qualities, but the good qualities of these alien races that make them dangerous to us. It is their inexhaustible energy, their power of applying themselves to new tasks, their endurance, and low standard of living that make them such competitors."⁴⁵

At the same moment Australia's leaders were settling the legal framework for a homogeneous society, the question of national defense likewise loomed large in their minds. Following federation, all existing colonial land units and naval craft were placed under Commonwealth control. The initial defense bill brought before the Australian parliament in 1901 largely confirmed the status quo of the colonial era, and in the naval camp this meant a continuation of the subsidy scheme with the British Admiralty. When it came to Australian naval policy itself, opinion was sharply divided. Those who desired a separate Australian navy were represented by Captain R. W. Creswell, the former commander of the Queensland colonial flotilla, who regarded complete Australian dependence upon the Royal Navy as both unfair to the British and the abrogation of Australia's legitimate naval defense responsibilities.⁴⁶ Creswell's position stood at odds with that of the commander of the Australian Squadron, Admiral Sir Lewis Beaumont, who broadly supported the retention of the subsidy scheme. One point of agreement between the two was that commerce raiding was the nation's major security concern; invasion hardly entered into their calculations.⁴⁷ At the 1902 Colonial Conference, Australian prime minister Edmund Barton opted for a compromise. With the Admiralty unwilling to accept any alternative to its policy of a single imperial fleet (under its command), Barton nevertheless negotiated a deal whereby Australia would pay a lesser subsidy than what the Admiralty had originally demanded, and the Admiralty would possess the right to deploy the Australian Squadron as it saw fit.⁴⁸ Back in Australia, debate over the naval agreement bill was conducted on national and imperial defense lines, but Barton at length secured enough support for its passage on August 23, 1903. For the moment at least, considerations of cost, Barton's principal argument against Creswell's proposals, sustained the subsidy scheme and the Australian Squadron remained on station.

From February 1904 until October 1906 a series of events were to exercise a considerable revisionary impact upon Australian defense thinking and thereafter facilitate the eventual creation of the Royal Australian Navy. On February 8, 1904, units of the Japanese Combined Fleet executed a surprise attack against the Russian Pacific Squadron based at Port Arthur, thereby initiating the Russo-Japanese War. In October of the same year Admiral Sir John Fisher took up the post of first sea lord at the British Admiralty. On May 27–28, 1905, Russia's Second Pacific Squadron was annihilated by the Combined Fleet in the Tsushima Straits. Two months later, in July, Britain and Japan agreed to extend the Anglo-Japanese Alliance. On February 10, 1906, Admiral Fisher's revolutionary brainchild, the first all big-gun battleship, HMS *Dreadnought*, was launched by King Edward VII. And in October 1906 the British and French successfully concluded negotiations that made the New Hebrides a joint protectorate, in the absence of prior consultation with the Australian government.[49] The Australians now found themselves confronted with three powerful regional neighbors—France, Germany, and Japan—whose strategic interests were scarcely in common with those of the new nation. Furthermore, the future external defense of the continent largely rested in the hands of a first sea lord whose primary ambition was to meet the naval threat from Germany by reconcentrating the bulk of the Royal Navy in the waters of the North Atlantic.[50]

Largely in response to the ominous display of Japanese naval might in the rout of the Russians at Tsushima, the Australians began to prosecute in a more unified fashion the case for a separate RAN. With his public standing restored following his appointment as director of naval forces in December 1904 by the then–Labor coalition government, Creswell found an ardent supporter in the new prime minister, Alfred Deakin, when the latter came to power in June 1905. Under instructions from the government, Creswell drew up a scheme for the composition of a future Australian navy, and likewise the means by which it could be employed in the defense of the country.[51] Deakin referred this assessment to the Committee of Imperial Defence (CID) in London, which responded in May 1906 by rejecting it outright. The British naval experts ridiculed Creswell's scheme, but Deakin was not to be deterred. On September 29, 1906, he politely defied the CID's adjudication and informed the House of Representatives that a three-year naval program would be commenced. But at the following Colonial Conference in April–May 1907 Deakin did not prevail. The British again rejected Australian naval aspirations and likewise the proposal from Deakin that a separate Department of Imperial Affairs—under joint British and Dominion administration—take over responsibility for Dominion affairs from the Colonial Office.[52] Still Deakin persevered, and on December 13, 1907, he announced the intended purchase of nine submarines and six torpedo boats. At the same moment, the prime minister emphasized the depth of Australian concern over foreign threats when he proposed the introduction of universal military service in peacetime.

Deakin had another card up his sleeve. Without informing Whitehall first, he issued a private invitation to the United States for a visit from the U.S. Navy's "Great White Fleet" on its forthcoming world cruise before a formal invitation was issued through the Colonial Office in January 1908. The offer was accepted and sixteen American warships arrived in Sydney Harbour in August to a wildly enthusiastic public welcome. Adm. Charles Sperry and his command were subsequently feted in both Sydney and Melbourne with glowing print coverage of the visit, at times verging on the embarrassing. The British were unimpressed. In response to the Australian initiative, Sir Edward Grey, the foreign secretary, reminded the Dominion government that "invitations to foreign governments should not be given except through us as circumstances are conceivable in which grave inconveniences might result."[53] Nevertheless the presence of the Great White Fleet provided Australians with a much-needed sense of reassurance that another friendly Anglo-Saxon power lay across the Pacific, a power that likewise had issues with Japanese expansionism. And during the course of the visit, Deakin did not shy away from publicly pronouncing his nation's desire to possess a blue-water naval capability of its own:

> But for the British Navy there would be no Australia. That does not mean that Australia should sit still under the protection of the British Navy—those who say we should sit still are not worthy of the name of Briton. We can add to the squadron in these seas from our own blood and intelligence something that will launch us on the beginning of a naval career and may in time create a force which shall rank among the defences of the Empire. We live in hope that from our own shores someday a fleet will go out not unworthy to be compared in quality, if not in numbers, with the magnificent fleet now in Australian waters.[54]

Though the visit of the American fleet was a triumph for public relations, those who observed it would perhaps have been more tempered in their enthusiasm if they had known at the time that planning existed for an assault by the U.S. Navy against both Sydney and Melbourne in the event of war between Britain and the United States. Since the mid-1890s the Naval War College had been actively considering precautionary plans, known as Plan RED, for the defense of America's eastern coastline if some form of conflict did arise, and from 1902 onward this likewise provided for the Pacific.[55] The Americans were mistrustful of the Anglo-Japanese Alliance and resolved that in the event of war with both the British and the Japanese, key ports in both New Zealand and Australia would have to be neutralized. Following an initial thrust against Auckland, elaborate schemes existed for Sydney and Melbourne to be attacked in turn, with supporting estimates of Australian force strength and the topography of both localities.[56] A sortie against Western Australia was also contemplated. However, any consideration as to the actual seriousness of such planning extending beyond an exercise for junior officers at the Naval War College would be necessarily balanced by its deficiencies. Most notably in this respect, the proposals lacked any consideration for the logistical support of a theoretical operation that spanned the breadth of the Pacific.[57]

Unbeknown to Deakin, events in the following year were to accelerate the arrival of the day he so desired. Since his appointment in October 1904 as first sea lord, "Jacky" Fisher had been busy applying a blowtorch to the fighting power of the Royal Navy. More than one hundred obsolete British warships had been scrapped or placed in reserve. The introduction of the *Dreadnought*-class battleships in 1906 was soon followed by the unveiling of another of Fisher's pet projects, the *Invincible*-class battle cruisers, thereafter escalating the naval arms race. The first sea lord regarded the new battle cruisers as ideal for service in the Pacific because they would easily outperform the likely types of enemy warships that would be deployed to interdict Australia's sea commerce.[58] When the Germans determined to follow suit, the first sea lord resolved to bury the naval challenge once and for all by outbuilding the kaiser. On the basis of largely circumstantial evidence, he persuaded the Asquith government that Germany was secretly building additional dreadnoughts to match the Royal Navy, and he obtained the necessary funding to build eight capital ships in a single year. In March 1909 this contrived scare went public, with the cry of "We want eight [dreadnoughts] and we won't wait" being taken up with vigor by the British press.⁵⁹ In Australia, too, the public pressure to aid the cause of the Empire by offering financing to construct a new British battleship was immense. Andrew Fisher, the Labor prime minister who had succeeded Deakin in November 1908, resisted calls for such a response, but his replacement by Deakin prior to an Imperial Conference called for August 1909 resulted in the dreadnought offer being renewed before the Australian delegation departed for London.⁶⁰

Before leaving office in June 1909, Prime Minister Fisher's government had set the scene for a potential showdown with the British by ordering in February, without first informing the Admiralty, three torpedo boat destroyers from British yards. What followed was a complete surprise for the Australian representatives at the Imperial Conference. Reversing its previous stance, the Admiralty now proposed that the Dominions be equipped with "distinct fleet units" (task forces), each equipped with a battle cruiser, three light cruisers, six destroyers, and three submarines.⁶¹ Furthermore, Admiral Fisher supported the concept of an Imperial Pacific Fleet made up of the Dominion units and the Royal Navy's East Indies and China Stations. Headed by Colonel J. F. G. Foxton, the Australian delegation accepted the proposal; the New Zealanders did so reluctantly (they still favored financial contributions), while the Canadians rejected the scheme, largely because of the shelter afforded them by the American Monroe Doctrine.⁶² Under a new Anglo-Australian naval agreement, the proposed gifted dreadnought would now become the battle cruiser flagship of the Australian fleet unit. A funding model for the new warships was agreed upon, with the subsidy of the existing Australian Squadron to remain in place until the vessels were ready for service. The Admiralty undertook to refurbish its East Indies and China Station squadrons to modern standards. And both parties consented to an arrangement whereby the Admiralty would assume control over the Australian fleet unit in wartime, but only with the prior consent of the Australian government.⁶³

Buoyed by the outcome of the conference, the Australians acted promptly to introduce legislation affirming the agreements struck and likewise formalized the introduction of compulsory peacetime military service. But subsequent efforts by Alfred Deakin to propose an extension of the Monroe Doctrine to the Pacific, which would include participation by Britain, Holland, France, China, and the United States, were quickly dismissed by the British.⁶⁴ In April 1910 Deakin suffered electoral defeat and was again succeeded by Andrew Fisher, whose government broadly supported the 1909 outcome, albeit opposing the continuation of the subsidy scheme. The new prime minister obtained the services of Admiral Sir Reginald Henderson, whose initial advisory brief was extended to a complete future plan for the RAN. Henderson recommended a twenty-two-year scheme of naval development, the details of which would be addressed by the federal Parliament following the conclusion of the 1911 Imperial Conference. Meanwhile the Australians had placed an order in March 1910 for the construction of the future battle cruiser HMAS *Australia*, and in November of the same year received *Yarra* and *Parramatta*, the first two of the three torpedo boat destroyers that had been ordered in February 1909.⁶⁵

Convened in May 1911, the latest Imperial Conference provided the Dominion representatives with the opportunity to discuss their contribution to the formulation of imperial foreign and defense policy. On May 26, Prime Minister Fisher and his colleagues were invited to a secret session of the CID, at which the British rationale for an extension of the Anglo-Japanese Alliance until 1921 was clearly articulated, as was the need for a single foreign and defense policy to ensure the feasibility of a unified imperial defense.⁶⁶ In open session at the conference, discussion turned to the mechanism that would best allow for Dominion consultation. Both Australia and Canada rejected the concept of an Imperial Parliament, the Australians doing so in the belief that such an instrument would be dominated from the outset by British representation. Fisher wanted a more direct form of consultation with Whitehall in times of crisis and successfully moved a motion for adopting a future means that did not impair Britain's freedom of action but nevertheless provided the Dominions with an effective voice for airing their concerns.⁶⁷ While no final determination was reached, the Australian leader was clearly delighted with the outcomes that had been achieved: "All the barriers of reserve have been broken down and mutual confidence has been established for all time. A community of interests of the highest immediate importance and vast possibilities has been created. I will go back equipped with knowledge that will qualify the federation I represent for co-operation with the mother country of a more effective kind than has ever been possible before. By the revelation of the British policy, Australia has been admitted into the very innermost confidences of the Imperial government."[68]

Unfortunately for Fisher, the euphoria would soon evaporate. In July 1911, with the prime minister still in transit to Australia, a crisis arose between France and Germany following the arrival of the German gunboat *Panther* in the Moroccan port of Agadir. This particular great-power play over a perceived French attempt to annex Morocco came to encompass the British through the possibility that the Germans may establish a naval base on Morocco's Atlantic coast, thereby posing a threat to Britain's maritime interests.[69] In the aftermath of the Agadir episode (which was resolved peacefully via negotiations between France and Germany), those in Whitehall concluded that the Admiralty had been caught flat-footed in its response to the crisis. A change of personnel loomed large and with it came the onset of profound Australian disillusionment. The good ship community of interests was about to collide with a similarly metaphoric sunken reef in the abrasive and unforgiving form of one Winston Spencer Churchill.

Churchill took office as first lord of the Admiralty in October 1911. As colonial secretary in 1907 he had repudiated Deakin's efforts to remove Dominion affairs from the authority of the Colonial Office, and, as subsequent events were to demonstrate, he had little sympathy for Australian strategic interests. After negotiations between Britain and Germany broke down in the wake of the Agadir crisis, Churchill advised the House of Commons in March 1912 that four extra dreadnoughts and a new fleet base at Gibraltar were required to safeguard British interests in the Atlantic and the Mediterranean.[70] The passing of a supplementary naval appropriations bill by the German Reichstag in May 1912 and the enactment of the so-called German Fleet Law provided Churchill with the ammunition he required to divert the proposed establishment of an Imperial Pacific Fleet. In July 1912 he obtained the consent of the visiting Canadian prime minister Robert Borden for Canada to contribute three dreadnoughts to a British Mediterranean force.[71] On July 12 the foreign secretary, Sir Edward Grey, informed the Commons that because of the developing international situation, Britain was compelled to concentrate her naval forces in European waters, regardless of the risks that could arise in the Far East. And in November of the same year Churchill reaffirmed the Admiralty's belief that Dominion naval participation would only be effective if placed under the overall control of the Admiralty.⁷² Under the spell of Churchill's naval stewardship, Whitehall had effectively repudiated the consensus reached with the Dominions at the 1909 Imperial Conference.

Shocked by this apparent British about-face, the Australian government made its feelings known in a letter dated December 3, 1912, from George Pearce, minister for defense, to Sir Henry Muirhead-Collins, the Australian representative in London, the contents of which were published by the *Sydney Morning Herald* on January 22, 1913:

> We had the Imperial naval conference in 1909 which drew up a scheme for the co-operation of the Imperial government and Dominions in matters of defence. The proposals were not rejected at the 1911 Conference, although they were extant; yet what happened? Australia is the only one of the parties to the 1909 Conference that has carried out its share of the scheme then arrived at. None of the other governments have stated that they will not carry out their share: they have merely ignored it, and in my mind this action on the part of these governments is the greatest blow yet dealt to Imperial co-operation.... It seems to me that it would have been better for the 1911 Conference to have frankly and clearly advised that the 1909 Conference resolutions should not be given effect to.⁷³

In spite of his dismay over the situation, Fisher kept his powder dry in the belief that further public criticism would be counterproductive. He held firm to this attitude even after Churchill had informed the House of Commons on March 26, 1913, that a flying squadron would be based in Gibraltar and that the force in question was capable of reaching any Far Eastern hot spot within a month if required. For the present, the Australian government occupied itself with considering the recommendations of Admiral Henderson's 1911 report, which Churchill in due course rejected, along with New Zealand's support for Australia's stance.⁷⁴ In the face of these machinations, the question of Admiralty control over Australia's future naval assets remained a live issue. For the Australians, a change of government following the federal election in May 1913 meant that the new Liberal prime minister, Joseph Cook, would take up the cudgels with Whitehall in a period where Anglo-Australian relations over the naval question were being sorely tested by suspicion and mistrust.

Unlike Fisher, Cook was something of a blue-water imperialist at heart, and at first he followed Fisher's lead by having little to say on the public record. In August 1913 he inquired of the Colonial Office as to what would occur with the Australian fleet unit. The Admiralty responded in October by blandly informing Cook that because of the present naval situation the 1909 agreement should be deferred and that the new dispositions did not compromise Australia's security. But on October 4, Sydney Harbour witnessed the material manifestation of the Australian unit when *Australia* and the cruisers *Melbourne* and *Sydney*, accompanied by HMS *Encounter* (on loan from the Admiralty), entered the roadstead to a rapturous welcome. With the formal handover in command of the Australian Station on October 21, Australia became the first of the Dominions to take complete responsibility for its own naval defense, and the RAN, which had been given official status by King George V on July 10, 1911, now possessed a formidable squadron in its own right.[75]

When Cook responded to the Admiralty's October 1913 reply on February 28, 1914, the frustration felt by his government was unmistakeable. Both he and his defense minister, Senator E. D. Millen (in a subsequent April 1914 memorandum), directly criticized Whitehall for reneging on the 1909 agreement and failing to consult Australia and New Zealand over Churchill's activities.[76] For his part Churchill suffered a major blow in the same month when the Canadian parliament voted down the appropriation bill for the three dreadnoughts. In March the first lord vigorously sought extra funding for more dreadnoughts from the Commons in a speech in which he unwaveringly defended his views on naval dispositions and the effectiveness of the Anglo-Japanese Alliance.[77] The response from Australia and New Zealand was highly critical of Churchill's stance, and the majority of Australian press and public opinion followed suit. Millen's April memorandum specifically repudiated Churchill's contentions, together with what the Australians perceived as the first lord's arbitrary means of policy making. When the Admiralty responded in May, it showed no signs of wavering from its existing position, whereupon the Colonial Office warned the Admiralty that the

Australians must be provided with a full and proper explanation. Acting on its own initiative, the Colonial Office attempted to mollify Australian anger by sending a conciliatory dispatch to the Commonwealth on July 28, 1914.[78] On the same day, Austria-Hungary declared war on Serbia, and within a matter of days the onset of mass mobilization across Europe initiated the outbreak of hostilities between the Entente and the Central Powers.

In spite of Churchill's high-handed approach to Australian defense concerns, he and the Australians did share one common view. In 1914 he told the House of Commons that if British sea power "were shattered on the sea, the only course of the five million of white men in the Pacific would be to seek the protection of the United States." In his response, Andrew Fisher, now the leader of the Federal Opposition, agreed: "In the event of an Asiatic attack on the Australian dominions, following the defeat of Great Britain by a naval power, the only course that would be open to us would be an appeal to the United States."[79]

A Dose of Realpolitik: August 1914–November 1918

In a 1912 essay, the contents of which flow into the following chapters, the Australian diplomat and theorist Frederic Eggleston posed the question of whether a nation could "depend for its defence upon a foreign policy conducted by statesmen responsible to another nation?"[80] Such a dependence came into practicable effect for Australia in wartime as of August 3, 1914, two days before the outbreak of hostilities between Britain and Germany. On that day the Australian government advised Whitehall of its consent to place the Royal Australian Navy under Admiralty control as well as providing an expeditionary force of 20,000 troops to be deployed "to any destination desired by the [British] Home Government."[81] Squadron-scale naval activity in the Pacific theater would be principally confined to the period from August to November 1914, with a subsequent latter-war campaign involving the commerce raiding activities of Germany's disguised merchant cruisers. As for existent Australian concerns over the ambitions of the nation that now provided the material bulk of the country's third-party naval defense, Japan's occupation of the various German-controlled island groups to the north of the equator was to occupy the wary attention of Australia's leaders for the balance of the Great War.

Table 2.1. Participant Combatant Naval Strengths in the Pacific, 1914

Japan	4 dreadnought battleships, 1 battle cruiser, 10 predreadnought battleships, 15 armored cruisers, 18 light cruisers, 51 destroyers, 13 submarines.
Great Britain	2 predreadnought battleships, 2 armored cruisers, 5 light cruisers, 8 destroyers, 2 submarines.
Australia	1 battle cruiser, 4 light cruisers, 3 destroyers, 2 submarines.
New Zealand	3 light cruisers.
France	2 armored cruisers, 3 destroyers.
Russia	2 light cruisers, 20 destroyers, 8 submarines.
Germany	2 armored cruisers, 3 light cruisers, 2 destroyers.
Austria	1 light cruiser.
Italy	1 light cruiser.

CPP, 1914 Session, vol. II, no. 33. "Navies relative strength in the Pacific. Return showing strength of Navies of the various powers now stationed in the Pacific," doc. 107, in Meaney, *Australia and the World*, 212–15.

Of greatest immediate concern for the Admiralty in the Pacific theater was the presence of Germany's East Asia Squadron commanded by Vice Admiral Maximilian von Spee. Based at the heavily fortified Chinese port city of Tsingtao, von Spee's force included the armored cruisers *Scharnhorst* and *Gneisenau*, two light cruisers, and a fleet train of colliers and supply vessels. On June 20, 1914, the German squadron departed Tsingtao on a training cruise, arriving at Ponape in the Caroline Islands on July 17.[82] From there the squadron temporarily relocated to the Mariana Islands prior to setting out again on August 14. A day earlier the light cruiser *Emden* and an accompanying collier had detached from von Spee in order to conduct commerce raiding in the Indian Ocean. A month later on September 14, the squadron arrived off German Samoa (recently captured by a New Zealand expeditionary force) with the intention of destroying any British or Australian warships in the vicinity, but with no enemy vessels present the Germans departed without incident.[83] On September 22, von Spee's ships bombarded the French colony at Papeete, sinking a French gunboat before arriving at Easter Island on October 12, where they were joined by the light cruisers *Leipzig* and *Dresden*, together with four additional colliers. The Germans subsequently proceeded toward the Chilean port of Coronel to attack a British cruiser squadron that had been observed farther to the south at Punta Arenas by German agents ashore; the operatives provided accurate details of the composition of the enemy force.[84]

Off Coronel in high winds and heavy seas at dusk on November 1, 1914, the East Asia Squadron clashed with elements of the British 4th Cruiser Squadron under the command of Rear Admiral Sir Christopher Cradock. In a hopelessly one-sided action, the crack gunners on board the German armored cruisers savaged their obsolete British counterparts within minutes. Soon afire from stem to stern, the armored cruiser *Good Hope* suffered a magazine explosion and blew up, while the similarly pummeled *Monmouth* was sent to the bottom shortly thereafter.[85] Subsequently pausing for twenty-four hours at Valparaiso, von Spee proceeded to round Cape Horn in an attempt to return to Germany itself. His efforts ended abruptly on December 8 in the vicinity of the Falkland Islands. Seeking to seize the vital enemy coaling station at Port Stanley, the Germans were surprised by a superior British force containing the fast battle cruisers *Invincible* and *Inflexible*. In the pursuit that followed, both of von Spee's armored cruisers and two of his light cruisers were run down and sunk, with the admiral and all of the crew on board *Scharnhorst* going down with their ship. In the Indian Ocean meanwhile, the light cruiser *Emden* had created mayhem by single-handedly sinking no less than twenty-five enemy steamers and two warships as well as attacking the port facilities at Penang and an oil refinery at Madras. On November 9 *Emden*'s luck ran out when in the course of the destroying the wireless station on Cocos Island she was ambushed by the light cruiser HMAS *Sydney*, and after a vigorous but unequal fight was beached on a coral reef and thereafter shelled into submission.[86]

The signal "*Emden* beached and done for" proved to be one of the few pieces of welcome news for the British and their allies throughout a frustrating and costly operation. A small but well-equipped and highly trained German force under skillful command had easily evaded its superior Japanese and Australian pursuers to reach Chilean waters without injury. As first lord of the Admiralty, Winston Churchill had knowingly dispatched a far weaker British cruiser squadron to stop the Germans in their tracks.[87] Churchill's obstinacy and von Spee's marked advantage in speed, gunnery, and tactics cost the lives of all 1,660 officers and enlisted men on board the *Good Hope* and *Monmouth*. And a single light cruiser was responsible for paralyzing sea commerce in the Indian Ocean, at one point steaming unsuspectingly within striking distance of the convoy charged with transporting the ANZAC expeditionary force to the European theater.[88] The sinking of *Emden* and the final destruction of the East Asia squadron in the South Atlantic removed Germany's conventional naval threat in the Pacific, but it did not spell the end of hostile activity nearer the Australian coastline. During the period from June 1917 to August 1918, the German commerce raiders *Wolf* and *Seeadler* operated in the vicinity of the Australian east coast, and, though their successes were limited, they tied up numerous Allied warships that had launched an ultimately unsuccessful campaign to locate these elusive predators.[89]

As part of the Australian efforts to track down the East Asia Squadron, on August 7, 1914, the commander of the RAN, Vice Admiral Sir George Patey, ordered a reconnaissance-in-force of Rabaul harbor by *Sydney* and three destroyers. No German ships were sighted in the course of the mission and the Australians were preparing to resume their search for von Spee when Pately's ships were detailed to attend to another urgent task. At the request of Whitehall, both Australia and New Zealand had been detailed to organize punitive expeditions to seize a number of Germany's Pacific island colonies.[90] Consisting of some 1,500 troops, the Australian Naval and Military Expeditionary Force required an escort to its primary destination of Rabaul, as did the New Zealand expedition to German Samoa, and the Australian warships were required to provide it. On September 11, the Australian force landed at Rabaul and, after encountering brief resistance, on September 17 obtained a surrender by the German governor of not only Rabaul itself but all of the German Pacific islands under his direct administrative control.[91] These included several groups and chains to the north of the equator, the most substantial being the Caroline Islands, the Marshall Islands, and the Mariana Islands. The subsequent fate of these German possessions was to provide Australia with a sharp lesson in the exercise of wartime realpolitik and further exacerbate Australian fears over Japanese intentions in the region.

The opening phase in the saga of the German Pacific islands coincided with Andrew Fisher's third term as prime minister after he defeated Joseph Cook in the September 1914 federal election. Initially the Japanese professed no interest in the German island possessions, a claim that was publicly acknowledged by the British foreign secretary on August 18. Five days later the Japanese declared war on Germany, and on September 2 Tokyo advised the British that the Imperial Japanese Navy would expand its Pacific coverage, including its participation in the search for von Spee.[92] On October 4, Japan commenced her occupation of all the German island groups to the north of the equator, a process that was completed within a single week. Although the Admiralty accepted the seizures as inevitable, especially given the general lack of British warships in the Far East at the time, the Foreign and Colonial Offices still encouraged the Australians to proceed with a proposed military expedition to occupy the islands as per the terms of the Rabaul surrender.[93] The expedition was publicly endorsed on November 18 by Australian defense minister George Pearce, who stated that Tokyo had agreed to a handover, but this was swiftly rebutted by the Japanese. Under pressure from Whitehall the Australian expedition was postponed and, on December 1, Japan informed Britain that, with the possible exception of Yap (in the Pelew Group), the remainder of the Japanese-occupied islands would not be vacated.[94]

Fisher's subsequent efforts to advance Australia's interests ran into a brick wall. The British brushed aside his request for an imperial defense conference to address the problem, citing their belief that any such undertaking could seriously jeopardize Anglo-Japanese relations. And pressure was being applied upon Fisher from other quarters. Without the prime minister's knowledge, Australia's governor general, Sir Ronald Munro-Ferguson, had been co-opted by the Colonial Office to convince the government to accept the Japanese occupations.[95] Furthermore, in May 1915 the Japanese government began to apply concerted diplomatic pressure upon Australia to become bound by the terms of a renewed Anglo-Japanese Commercial Treaty. Nevertheless the Australians pressed ahead with elements of their own security agenda. While the Naval Board continued to construct the strategic case for Australia's eventual occupation of the Northern Pacific islands, the government convened a Royal Commission to establish the legal basis for pursuing such claims at the cessation of hostilities. Other practical measures taken during 1915 included the reform of national defense planning by the army and the beginning of intelligence collection from the Japanese-occupied islands by Australian commercial trading companies, such as Burns Philp.[96]

As the year progressed it became increasingly obvious that Australia had no alternative but to acquiesce to the situation. In April 1915 the British confirmed to the Australians that in secret correspondence dated December 1, 1914, Japan had made demands upon the German islands that would be finally determined in a future peace settlement.[97] Faced with the growing need for Japanese naval assistance in the European theater, Whitehall was willing to tacitly accept Japan's activities as the necessary geopolitical price to be paid for securing such cooperation in the eventual defeat of the Central Powers.

Growing problems with illness led to Fisher's resignation as prime minister in October 1915. His successor, William (Billy) Morris Hughes, assumed office during an increasingly arduous period for the Allied cause. Any belief that the war in Europe would last but a matter of months had by now been thoroughly extinguished. The French and British were beginning to endure heavy casualties on the western front while British commerce suffered ever-increasing losses at the hands of the German U-boats. And in the Dardanelles, the Allied armies, which included the ANZAC expeditionary forces, were bogged down in a costly offensive campaign in which the prospects for a decisive strategic success against Turkey had all but vanished. Unlike Fisher, Hughes relished the challenges that lay before him. Though diminutive in stature, his razor-sharp mind, boundless energy, and superb oratorical skills had already paved the way for his emergence as a long-standing giant in Australian public life. Possessing an incendiary temperament, Hughes was never afraid to speak his mind. His private secretary John Paton recalled an incident during the Munich Crisis in 1938, when Hughes stated to a group of journalists that "if you paved the way from here [Inverell] to Broken Hill with Bibles, and if that man Hitler swore an oath on every one of them, I wouldn't believe a goddam bloody word he said!"[98]

With little prospect of the Japanese relinquishing control over their recent island acquisitions, Hughes too looked to his nation's defenses. Following in Fisher's footsteps, his administration continued the development of Australia's intelligence capabilities, introduced compulsory domestic military training for national defense, and formed the Australian Army Reserve. In their development of a postwar naval policy the Australians re-embraced the ideals of the 1909 Imperial Conference, which had called for the establishment of an Imperial Pacific Fleet.[99]

These reforms were taken with future Pacific geopolitics in mind, most particularly the specter of Japan carving out its own imperial destiny within the region. Although Japan had rejected German overtures to switch sides in the period from December 1915 to February 1916, there were increasing British and Australian fears that Tokyo was tiring of the Anglo-Japanese Alliance and that the Japanese were becoming more belligerent in their stance over the future course of affairs in both China and the Pacific.[100] Visiting Britain in March 1916 to discuss the progress of the war, Hughes stood firm against Japan's demands for equal trade under the umbrella of an Anglo-Japanese Commercial Treaty, believing that the Japanese would use this instrument to ultimately undermine and destroy Australia's restrictive immigration system. During his visit Hughes took the opportunity to make a series of rousing speeches in which he exhorted the fighting of a total war in order to finally crush the Central Powers.[101] Yet in the months to come it was the means by which the prime minister sought to wage such a conflict that came to overshadow the Pacific question, divide the Australian people, and jeopardize his own political survival.

The introduction of military conscription in Britain during May 1916 reinvigorated the issue in Australia. In his pursuit of a total war approach, Hughes supported the British decision and commenced a public campaign for its introduction. Conscription not only divided the nation politically and socially, but likewise resulted in the public airing of competing strategic viewpoints. Hughes and the proconscription lobby argued that Australia's future Pacific security could only be guaranteed by the defeat of the Central Powers in Europe. His anticonscription opponents countered this assertion by emphasizing the need to first and foremost safeguard the nation itself from the threat posed by Japan.[102] On October 28, 1916, the Australian people narrowly rejected the "Yes" case in the first of two national referenda. Along with twenty-four of his colleagues, Hughes defected from the Labor Party and continued to govern, first in coalition with the Liberals and from February 1917 as leader of the new National Party. But in retaining his leadership, the prime minister was left with a wafer-thin majority in parliament and was beset by the threat of civil unrest over the conscription debate. Widespread dissent among the Irish-Australian community, and especially within the Labor movement, over the British repression of the 1916 Easter Rising in Dublin further exacerbated his problems.¹⁰³ The consequence was that Hughes could not attend an Imperial Conference called for March 1917, in spite of the wish of the new British prime minister, David Lloyd George, to have him present as an ally in urging an all-out effort to win the war.

Conscription proved to be a millstone for Hughes. Despite his new National Party easily defeating the Labor opposition in the May 1917 federal election, the prime minister again failed, this time in a December 1917 referendum, to convince the Australian people to support his conscription policy. And it was through the prime minister's initial unsuccessful attempt in October 1916 that the Australians were denied a rare opportunity to impose some genuine leverage upon Whitehall. When Lloyd George had succeeded Asquith in December 1916, the British armies were suffering horrendous casualties in France and British merchant shipping was being systematically exterminated by submarines.¹⁰⁴ In such parlous circumstances Lloyd George was willing to grant the Dominions a means for direct participation in the formulation of war policy through the membership of the prime ministers in an Imperial War Cabinet. Hughes' absence at the March 1917 conference left Australia's interests unrepresented save for the New Zealanders successfully pushing the British to reconsider the formation of a postwar Imperial Pacific Fleet.¹⁰⁵ Yet at the same moment Whitehall's desperation to secure Japanese military assistance resulted in an agreement between both nations that Japan's claims to the North Pacific islands would be supported by Britain in any peace settlement. When this agreement came into force in May 1917, the Australians, who had been informed of the situation by Whitehall three months beforehand, made no protest.¹⁰⁶ This apparent acquiescence was not to persist for long once Hughes arrived in England in June 1918 to attend a fresh Imperial Conference.

By the time Australia's prime minister arrived in England, the last great German offensive on the western front was about to commence. Its eventual rebuttal in late July 1918 meant that the defeat of the Central Powers was close at hand. Hughes wanted an Australian say in the peace settlement to follow. In the words of Neville Meaney, Australia's foremost scholar in the field of Australian foreign relations during the Great War, Hughes first visited the United States and then had to come to England "to demand a peace of annexation and indemnity."¹⁰⁷ He desired no less than the economic restoration of the British Empire, Australia's future possession of Germany's South Pacific colonies, and the imposition of harsh material reparations upon the vanquished Germans. This placed Hughes squarely at odds with the idealistic liberal view of a new world order espoused by the president of the United States, Woodrow Wilson. Hughes had elicited only limited sympathy for Australia's position from Wilson when the two met at the White House on May 29.[108] There was little love lost between the two men, largely because of a prior dispute over the proposed American seizure of merchant ships that had been ordered by Australia the previous year. Hughes' response, in which he described the planned impounding as an "unfriendly act," was greeted with considerable anger by the U.S. government.[109] But this outburst from the Australian prime minister would pale in comparison with his behavior when he finally took his place at the big table alongside his Dominion counterparts.

As a member of the Imperial War Cabinet, Hughes' sole substantive achievement was to sponsor a successful resolution to amend the chain of communication between the Dominion leaders and Whitehall by removing the Colonial Office and the Dominion viceroys from the equation, thereby permitting a direct channel to the British prime minister. Hughes, however, was no team player. He took the British to task over Whitehall's prior agreement with the Japanese concerning the Northern Pacific islands, and more was to follow when Lloyd George returned to Britain in early November from a meeting of the Allied leadership in France. When Lloyd George briefed the Imperial War Cabinet as to the substance of the armistice terms on November 5, Hughes could no longer contain himself. The following day he flew at his hosts, accusing the British of betraying the Dominions by agreeing to Wilson's Fourteen Points without prior consultation. Hughes further charged that Lloyd George had not done enough to push the issues of German reparations and Dominion claims over conquered German possessions, and he further denounced the proposed formation of the League of Nations, which Hughes believed would usurp the rights of the British Empire.[110] Lloyd George responded vigorously in his own defense, denying all of Hughes' accusations. Hughes publicly repeated his claims on November 7, whereupon Whitehall issued a formal response two days later that stated that the Dominions were privy to the formulation of peace terms and would continue to be so advised.[111] Under growing pressure from his cabinet colleagues in Australia, Hughes grudgingly abandoned his public campaign and returned to the tent to plan for the approaching peace with his British and Dominion counterparts.

On November 11, 1918, the guns fell silent. The bloodiest war waged thus far in the industrial age was over, with millions dead on the battlefields, treasuries emptied, and the old European order crushed almost beyond recognition. Approximately 60,000 Australian troops had been killed and more than 100,000 wounded, which, given that Australia's population was under five million, represented one of the highest casualty rates of the combatant nations on both sides.[112] And whereas from December 1914 onward the Pacific had by-and-large remained so named, its geopolitical tectonic shifts proved to be as far-reaching as those that had demolished the European edifice. German influence had been swept from the region and the boundaries for a new Pacific order established in substance, if not yet by signature. Without a shot being fired, Australia's subcontracted third-party naval protecter was now the master of the northwestern Pacific. In the reckoning of William Morris Hughes, the barbarians were at the gates. Unless he and his learned colleagues could safeguard Australia's strategic interests at Versailles, those gates would be inevitably forced open. The stakes had never been higher, and, commencing with the 1919 negotiations, the strategic circumstances of the early 1920s were to determine the character of Australia's naval defense for more than two decades to come.

The course of the Great War laid bare the geopolitical conundrum Australia could not avoid in its strategic relationship with Great Britain. Regardless of whether the British wished to pursue an imperial-centric defense policy or its continental-focused alternative, the naval security of the British Isles themselves provided the mutual centerpiece. It proved impossible for Whitehall to divorce its imperial obligations from the machinations of European great-power diplomacy in peace, a state of affairs that had increasingly frustrated the semiautonomous Australian colonies from the 1880s and likewise aggrieved the subsequently federated Australian nation from 1901 onwards. With the onset of war in August 1914, the litany of preexisting negotiation and assurance between Britain and the Dominions concerning naval security was speedily flung aside. In order that the overwhelming bulk of the Royal Navy could lie in wait to intercept and destroy its German opponent in the North Sea, Australia would have to accept the seaborne protection of the military power Australia's statesmen feared more than any other. The primary lesson for those same statesmen, who were shortly to be responsible for the planning of the nation's future defense strategy, was unambiguous. A genuine community of strategic interest would only be achieved if Whitehall believed the Pacific to be of such vital importance to British national security that Britain could not afford to neglect its defense. And if the British Admiralty were to undertake such a task, the assembled Imperial Pacific Fleet would have to possess sufficient firepower to either deter Japan from creating mischief or defeat the Imperial Japanese Navy in battle should it seek to acquire a Pacific empire via hostile means.

3

Paris, Washington, and Singapore

1919–1923

Australia's titular head of state, Sir Ronald Munro Ferguson, had not been exactly supportive of the third Fisher Labor government during his term in office. In a March 1915 letter to the colonial secretary in Whitehall, the governor general didn't miss his mark when it came to Fisher's reluctance to accept the Japanese occupation of the German islands to the north of the equator: "This fool's paradise needs a rude awakening, and if a Japanese Naval Base near the Line should act as a solvent then it would be a blessing in disguise."[1] During the course of the interwar period, such a base would be established at Truk Atoll in the Caroline Islands. Labeled "the Gibraltar of the Pacific," this vast reef-protected lagoon could accommodate the entire Japanese Combined Fleet, along with several seaplane anchorages and five airfields that were to be constructed upon the islands within the lagoon.[2] Yet whatever additional apprehension was to occupy the minds of Australia's leaders through the eventual militarization of Truk was nothing compared with the rude awakening they were to experience in December 1941, when it came to the material cornerstone of their own defense policy. And it was through the particular events and circumstances to be explored in this chapter that Australia committed itself to a defensive strategy that was to assemble a breastwork of illusion and reassurance as its primary bulwark.

1919: The Paris Peace Conference

The Paris Peace Conference commenced on January 16, 1919. It had been established by the victorious Allied powers for two purposes, namely to impose sanctions upon a defeated Germany and to establish a new postwar order for the administration of international affairs. Though the victors were unanimous in their pursuit of the first objective, there was less unanimity in their views upon the second, described by the leader of the Japanese delegation Baron Makino Nobuaki as the opportunity to end the reign of "old diplomacy" through the formation of a League of Nations.[3] Headed by Prime Minister Hughes and Sir Joseph Cook, the Australian delegation entered the negotiations seeking to punish Germany via the imposition of heavy reparations and to keep the Japanese out of the South Pacific. This latter outcome, which the Australians regarded as the minimum prerequisite for the preservation of their nation's military security and the maintenance of its particular racial-based social character, was regarded by Hughes and his Paris-bound colleagues as nonnegotiable.

As had been the case since 1901, the initial obstacle to be overcome by Australia was achieving entry to the tent itself. When it came to the question of Dominion representation in Paris, a further complicating factor became the attitude of the broader assembly of Allied powers and most particularly the United States. These predicaments were partially resolved at the beginning of December 1918, when the Imperial War Cabinet conferred upon the Dominions the same rights of representation that had been mooted for other small powers such as Serbia and Belgium.[4] After learning about a French proposal that did not include Dominion representation, on December 31 Lloyd George reaffirmed British support for separate delegations. In spite of his objections to this plan, Woodrow Wilson agreed to a compromise after several days of intense discussions; New Zealand would be represented by one delegate and the other Dominions by two each. Aside from their self-representation for the first time at an international conference, the Dominions likewise possessed an avenue of influence in the form of the Imperial War Cabinet in its new role as the British Empire delegation.[5]

In dealing with the situation in the Pacific, the original Australian proposals documented Hughes' stubborn determination to get his own way. In August 1918 he had denounced the February 1917 Anglo-Japanese agreement over the future of Germany's North Pacific islands and denied that his government had ever consented to such a course of action. Armed with the case prepared by the Navy Board in support of Australia's occupation of all the German islands under the terms of their original surrender at Rabaul in September 1914, Hughes sought their unconditional annexation.[6] But Whitehall would not budge, and Hughes' cabinet colleagues in Melbourne rejected their prime minister's efforts to employ wholesale annexation as Australia's stated position. Acting Prime Minister Watt and his ministers, worried that Hughes' belligerence could strain relations with Britain and the United States (not to mention Japan), supported Hughes' stance in respect to German New Guinea but otherwise counseled prudence.[7] In an attempt to effect a compromise, on December 18, 1918, Prime Minister Borden of Canada urged the Imperial War Cabinet to have all German colonies that were not adjacent to Australia, New Zealand, and South Africa dealt with under a mandate system to be administered by the League of Nations. Hughes consented to Borden's concept, but Lloyd George remained uncommitted prior to discussing the matter with Wilson.[8] Unsurprisingly, Wilson wished that the entirety of the matter be determined by the new league, and there was thus no position upon the German colonies agreed upon by both Britain and the United States, nor within the British Empire delegation itself prior to the start of the conference in mid-January 1919.

Unlike Australia, Japan attended Paris as an acknowledged senior Allied power. Headed by Baron Makino, the Japanese delegation sought two primary outcomes: the possession of the North Pacific German colonies and the founding of a League of Nations that would remove the stigma of racial discrimination. Regarding the latter point, the Japanese press were especially insistent. Major journals such as *Asahi*, *Kokumin*, and *Yonozu* all called strongly for the application of racial equality, with the editorial in *Yonozu* expressing the view that it would be impossible for President Wilson to retreat from his ideals for a new world order.[9] Not all the members of the Japanese delegation were of a similar mind when it came to the potential success of their endeavors. In an article printed in the nationalist-oriented *Nihon Oyobi* on December 18, 1918, Prince Konoe Fumimaro urged Japan's rejection of a League of Nations unless economic imperialism and racial discrimination were to be eliminated within its covenant.[10] As for the subject of relations between Japan and Australia, the influential journal *Nichi Nichi* did not mince its words in a December 16 opinion piece: "Australia has prohibited landing of Asiatics there and Japanese have been denied the privilege of entering that country. During the War, Australia pretended to be friendly, as if the old feelings were swept away completely. When the War situation changed and the armistice was signed, the Australians began to agitate for checking the southward advance of Japan. By the export prohibition in New Guinea recently, one can see a portion of the anti-Japanese policy of the Australians.... This should not be lightly regarded by the Japanese."[11]

If the Japanese believed that the echoing of such sentiments would somehow act to curb the bellicose antics of Australia's lead negotiator in Paris, they quickly learned otherwise. Once the conference had gotten underway, the Japanese delegates along with their European and American counterparts were soon left in no doubt that commonly accepted diplomatic niceties did not sit well with the redoubtable Mr. Hughes. To the European diplomats especially, the Australian leader presented as a low-class philistine. Clemenceau dismissed Hughes as a "cannibal," while Wilson employed some homespun frontier badinage in decrying him as a "pestiferous varmint." Even Frederic Eggleston, a fellow member of the Australian delegation, came to regard him as a "criminal lunatic" possessed by an "unbridled bloodlust."[12] Hughes could certainly dish it out, especially when it came to Wilson. His dislike of the American president respected no boundaries, as John Latham, a senior member of the Australian contingent, was to discover. Informed by Hughes at breakfast one morning that the battleship returning Wilson to Europe had sunk with the loss of all on board, a genuinely shocked Latham expressed his dismay, whereupon Hughes replied, "Yes, Latham, but there is worse to come. It is not bloody true."[13] And well-schooled as he was in the general hurly-burly of Australian domestic politics, Hughes' familiarity with wrecking tactics would further infuriate his detractors as he sought to advance Australia's national and imperial interests by whatever means he deemed necessary.

This experience came to the fore during the preliminary determination of the mandates issue at the conference. In spite of President Wilson's opposition to a pre–League of Nations settlement, the Dominion representatives were invited to put their respective cases before the Council of Ten on January 24, 1919. Though Hughes supported Borden's concept for a mandate system, his rejection of its application to the islands in the South

Pacific reflected the prime minister's deep contempt for Wilson's internationalist initiative. A number of postwar Australian historians, including Charles Manning Clark, have described the members of the Australian delegation as "Empire Men," and Hughes personified this commitment to the imperial ideal.[14] His vision for the restoration of the British Empire as an economic and military superpower did not include the presence of a body that would compromise imperial security by restricting the freedom of action of the Royal Navy. Nor would he accept the negation of Australia's so-called White Australia Policy via the required removal of racial barriers under the terms of an international convention. And if Australia were to gain what he described as "the great rampart of islands" to Australia's immediate north through mandate instead of annexation, the nation's naval defenses would likely be compromised if the terms of the mandate demilitarized the territories in question.[15] In the latter instance, such a dilemma would be made considerably more difficult if the Japanese were simultaneously permitted to annex, and thereafter militarize, the former German possessions to the north of the equator.

Hughes presented Australia's arguments to the Council of Ten on January 24 by setting out the strategic crisis that would arise for his country if its demands were not met:

> Mr. Hughes said [that] . . . it was obvious that 5 million people could not hold, against powerful enemies, a country larger than the United States, with a coast-line as long as the distance between Australia and England. If there were at the very door of Australia a potential or actual enemy Australia could not feel safe. The islands were as necessary to Australia as water to a city. If they were in the hands of a superior power there would be no peace for Australia. . . . The security of Australia would threaten no one. No state would suffer if Australia were safe, Australia alone would suffer if she were not.[16]

Wilson remained unimpressed. With no specific formula yet devised to formally structure a mandates system, he admonished Hughes for Australia's lack of faith over the resolution of the issue by the League of Nations. Furthermore, the president maintained, there was a general sentiment throughout the world for an end to annexation as an acceptable means for nations to advance their own territorial interests.[17] His obstinacy over the issue's being resolved by the proposed league prompted Lloyd George to initiate a fresh round of behind-the-scenes negotiations in an effort to prevent the disintegration of the discussions altogether. In response, Prime Minister Jan Smuts of South Africa and Sir Maurice Hankey, secretary to the British Empire delegation, stitched up a three-tiered mandate proposal. Under their proposed C-Class Mandate, which was designed to apply to the Pacific, isolated territories with small populations were to be administered under the laws of the mandate holder but with similar safeguards for the indigenous populations as set out in the A- and B-Class Mandate proposals.[18] Wilson indicated his preliminary approval for such a scheme, but Hughes would not back down in his determination to gain the South Pacific islands by annexation. Clearly exasperated by the Australian prime minister's truculence, Lloyd George warned Hughes that if he persisted with his demands for annexation the Australians would receive no support from the Royal Navy in implementing such a policy.[19]

Still unwilling to compromise, Hughes resorted to the press to reinforce Australia's position. On January 30, the *Daily Mail* published a report that asserted that Dominion dissatisfaction over the controversy could threaten the stability of the British Empire itself.[20] On the same day, the Council of Ten reconvened to further consider the mandates question. Supported by Prime Minister William Massey of New Zealand, Hughes wanted to know the details of the proposal before Australia would agree to it. Neither he nor Massey had been consulted as to its specific contents. The substance of a subsequent acrimonious exchange between Wilson and Hughes was recorded in the official minutes of the meeting:

> President Wilson asked if he was to understand that New Zealand and Australia had presented an ultimatum to the Conference ... [that] they proposed to do what they could to stop the whole agreement.... Mr. Hughes said he did not know how he could put it better than he had done that morning. He would like to say that Clause 8 of that proposal—President Wilson enquired if Mr. Hughes had heard his question. Mr. Hughes replied in the negative. President Wilson then said he wanted to know if they were to understand that Australia and New Zealand were presenting an ultimatum to

that Conference.... Mr. Hughes replied that President Wilson had put it fairly well, that that was their attitude subject to the reservation which he had stated that morning.[21]

Once tempers had subsided, a compromise was thrashed out. In return for Wilson's consent that the Smuts-Hankey mandate structure be provisionally accepted, Hughes and his colleagues reluctantly agreed to any further reconsideration by the league if so required. One sticking point remained unresolved. The president realized that unless the mandates were extended to the North Pacific as well, Japan's occupation of the islands would be unfettered and this would likely compromise America's own strategic position.[22] Hughes too came to his senses in due course, realizing that a universal adoption of the mandate system would prevent the Japanese from militarizing their acquisitions. Begrudgingly satisfied that the operation of a C-Class Mandate would not impinge upon Australia's immigration and trade policies, he finally agreed to its implementation. After much discussion throughout the following month, Japan agreed to the imposition of the mandates to the north of the equator on precisely the same terms as sought by Australia, though not without some pointed bitterness in Tokyo. At a meeting of Japan's Advisory Council of Foreign Relations on February 3, Ito Miyoji stated that the "proposal of the mandate system was a betrayal of British friendship towards Japan... an act of deception taken without respect for the treaty of alliance between us, and without any prior consultation."[23] On May 7, 1919, the Council of Three (Britain, France, and the United States) formally allocated the Pacific mandates, with Japan being awarded the northern islands. New Zealand was awarded Samoa, and Australia was awarded the remainder of the German possessions south of the equator with the exception of Nauru, which was designated a British Empire Mandate under the joint administration of Britain, Australia, and New Zealand.

Japan's frustration and anger over the imposition of mandates would prove to be mild in comparison with its reaction to the determination of the racial discrimination issue. Australia's attitude to Japan's proposal for nondiscriminatory migration was clearly spelled out in a front-page editorial of the *Melbourne Herald* on February 14, 1919. Under the banner headline "White Australia at Stake," the Japanese initiative was characterized as part of "the general conflict now proceeding between

Wilsonism and realism," and that it was obvious that neither Britain nor America would agree to such a request.[24] Japan's delegates, however, had actively sought the assistance of the American delegation for the wording of a racial discrimination clause, presenting to Col. Edward House, Wilson's principal adviser, the following proposed wording: "The equality of nations being a basic principle of the League of Nations, the High Contracting parties agree that concerning the treatment and rights to be accorded to aliens in their territories, they will not discriminate, either in law or in fact, against any person or persons on account of his or their race or nationality."[25]

Though rejecting the clause in this form, House accepted a second version whereby aliens would instead be treated equally if the laws of the host nation so allowed. But when it came to the Dominions, any form of consent to a racial discrimination clause that would compromise their varying exclusionist policies was simply unthinkable. And in this instance it was the Dominions who were framing the British Empire case and not Lloyd George. Aware that any compromise proposal on Britain's part would undoubtedly provoke the same sort of internal imperial dissent that had so colored the mandates imbroglio, the British prime minister determined to let the Dominions have their way.[26] Thereafter, advancing the "No" case on behalf of the British Empire fell to William Morris Hughes, and Hughes was at his wrecking best in the negotiations that followed. He had informed Baron Makino on March 14 that Australia would not consent to the insertion of any such clause, whereupon the Japanese delegation scrambled to come up with something that would meet with the Dominions' approval.[27] Over the next eleven days they presented a series of modified proposals that slowly but surely removed any direct reference to racial discrimination. Meeting with the Dominion representatives on March 25, the Japanese finally made some headway when the other side agreed to "just" (as distinct from "equal") treatment in the covenant wording, but Hughes was having none of it in spite of efforts by Borden and Smuts to have him see otherwise.[28] Hughes subsequently advised Watt of these developments:

> These last few days several Conferences have taken place between Dominion representatives and one in which representatives of Britain, Dominions, and Japan took part. I have declined agree to

any form of words—the Japanese have modified their demands many times—and stated plainly that Australia cannot agree to what they want. It is rumoured here that unless they succeed Japan will not accept the Covenant. I do not know whether this is true or only bluff. Nor do I know whether Britain would agree if we did not. But in either or both contingencies I do not propose to agree even subject to Australian Parliament right to ratify. Fact is that tentacles of League of Nations will be so intertwined about Peace Treaty that Parliament will have no option but to accept or reject in globo—including probably mandates, indemnity, etc.[29]

At the League of Nations Commission meeting on April 11 the much-amended Japanese proposal gained an overwhelming body of support from those present. But President Wilson (who was in the chair) ruled that because the British Empire delegation had opposed it, the motion was defeated because it failed to achieve a unanimous vote.[30] The Americans thereafter blamed the British and the Australians for their obstinacy, yet they had abstained from the vote for equally partisan reasons. Advised that the adoption of the Japanese proposal would likely cost the Democrats critical votes in California because of ongoing tension with Japanese immigrants there, Wilson elected to place his domestic interests first, just as Hughes had done. Hughes had contributed to Wilson's discomfort by gaining sympathy for Australia's position in sections of the American press and threatening to personally campaign against the president in the United States itself.[31] Predictably, the Japanese reacted to this snub with great anger, especially through the press and a number of younger right-wing politicians. There were calls for Japan to walk out of the talks, abandon the league concept, and create its own Monroe Doctrine in the Pacific.[32] Perhaps most pointedly of all, the highly respected *Japan Times* recorded that this episode revealed the existence of "irreconcilable aspirations" between white and colored races that made Japan's membership in the league an irrelevance. Australia, Britain, and the United States were individually and collectively condemned by the nationalist Japanese media and by politicians, who accused Wilson of betraying his ideals and accused the British and the Australians of betraying their trustworthy wartime ally.[33]

The bitterness of the Japanese response created considerable alarm among Hughes' cabinet colleagues in Melbourne. Two of the Australian government's leading experts on Japanese affairs, Major Edmund Piesse and Keith Murdoch, warned Acting Prime Minister Watt that Australia's behavior in Paris would play into the hands of the Japanese nationalists and imperialists and most particularly those within Japan's armed forces. In a May 1919 letter to John Latham, Piesse set out his concerns: "The whole business in Paris seems to have gone badly for us, from our apparent lack of cordiality towards the United States to the barren victory over racial discrimination. How much better it would have been to accept the Japanese amendment in one of its least noxious forms and rely on the opportunities the Covenant of the League gives to protect ourselves from any unfavourable interpretation. As it is we have been perhaps the chief factor in consolidating the whole Japanese nation behind the imperialists."[34]

The exact extent to which Japan's rebuff at the conference contributed to the rise of the nationalist-militarists in Japan during the early 1930s remains a matter for debate among Australia's postwar historians. Yet it was the case that the events in Paris undoubtedly created a ready template for a "stab in the back" narrative the Japanese radicals could employ to their advantage in the years ahead, just as Adolf Hitler and the National Socialists were to do in Germany. This outcome was to be further fueled by the negotiations in Washington, where Japanese interests were to be yet again challenged by the Anglo-Saxon powers. With respect to the mandates issue, the award of the former German colonies in the Pacific established the frontiers between Japan and the West in the region for the next two decades and as such acted to frame the future naval strategies of the interested parties, including Australia. As noted at the outset of this chapter, the possession of the Caroline group gifted the Japanese with a most valuable site for a major fleet base and, along with her newfound gains in the Marshall and Mariana groups, provided the geographical ingredients for a forward defensive shield against any potential hostile American naval thrust toward Japan itself.

Aside from the Pacific, Australia's other major area of interest at the Paris talks was the question of German reparations. Prime Minister Hughes had been appointed by Lloyd George as the chair of the British Empire committee charged with determining the cost to the British Empire of German aggression, an appointment that eminently suited what Manning Clark described as Clemenceau's Carthaginian attitude toward German restitution.[35] Prior to the conference, Hughes had displayed his pro-Clemenceau credentials by delivering a series of Cato-like public statements on the matter, though he was to subsequently wield only limited influence over the final determination of the peace terms imposed upon Germany. Of particular interest to both the British and the Dominions was the fate of Germany's High Seas Fleet, which had surrendered following the cessation of hostilities and interned at Scapa Flow. On February 21, 1919, the *Melbourne Herald* set out the peace terms as they related to the destruction of the German ships and German naval power generally. There was a tempting hint that the Dominions may be gifted "some of the most modern British warships" should the Royal Navy be reduced to its prewar size.[36] It was the Germans themselves who settled the issue on June 21, when the crews of their big ships opened the seacocks and sent their charges to the bottom. With the bulk of the High Seas Fleet consigned to the murky depths of the Scapa roadstead, the Royal Navy seemingly possessed the wherewithal to make the assembly of an Imperial Pacific Fleet a feasible proposition.

1921–1922: The Washington Conference

Via telegram to Prime Minister Lloyd George on October 8, 1920, Prime Minster Hughes requested that his British counterpart call an Imperial Conference in June of the following year. Believing that vital imperial business had been allowed to stall in the aftermath of the Paris negotiations, Hughes made his concerns clear. "We ought not in fact, we dare not allow ourselves to drift along. The necessity for a clear understanding—policy—call it what will on certain matters vitally affecting Empire is urgent and obvious. We must at least try to evolve some workable scheme re foreign policy."[37] With the ready concurrence of the new colonial secretary, Lord Milner, Lloyd George agreed to the conference. Aside from the desire to sort out the issues of Dominion consultation and contribution to the formulation of imperial policies, naval defense in the Pacific and the renewal of the Anglo-Japanese Alliance due in July 1921 were high on the agenda.[38] Events across the Atlantic had likewise contributed to the desirability of such a meeting. During a tour of the United States in September 1919 to gain support for that nation's membership in the League of Nations, President Wilson had suffered a debilitating stroke that would seriously impair his capabilities for the remainder of his term in office. The U.S. Senate subsequently determined to reject ratification of the Treaty of Versailles and with it America's participation in the league. Instead the new Republican president, Warren Harding, opted for a separate peace with Germany, Austria, and Hungary and, pursuant to the Knox-Porter Resolution Harding was to approve in July 1921, formal treaties with each of these nations were signed a month later.[39]

With Harding taking office in March 1921, the days of Wilson's internationalism had come to an end. Under the umbrella of a renewed isolationist-oriented foreign policy, those on Capitol Hill came to cast their gaze upon the continuing viability of their nation's capital shipbuilding program. In August 1916 the Congress had passed the Naval Appropriations Act, which for a price tag of just over $500 million provided for the construction of ten new battleships, six battle cruisers, and additional screening craft.[40] Though thereafter suspended until 1918 because of priority being afforded to the construction of additional submarines and merchant shipping, the program was reinstated with an additional three battleships authorized for construction. An estimated sum of $1.5 billion for the completion of a vastly strengthened U.S. Navy proved to be too excessive for the liking of the nation's legislators. Led by Senator William E. Borah and sustained by vigorous lobbying on the part of the *New York World*, a public campaign was instituted to block further appropriations. Adopted by the Senate 74–0 and 330–4 by the House of Representatives on June 29, 1921, the Borah Resolution called for an international conference to reduce naval expenditures for a period of five years.[41] By calling such a meeting, the Harding administration was also presented with the opportunity to exercise one element of practical bipartisanship it shared with its predecessor. This was the removal of the Anglo-Japanese Alliance, an agreement regarded by many in Washington as a British permit for Japanese expansion in China and the Pacific, and by some even as an invitation for eventual hostilities between the United States and Britain.[42]

On the subject of the Anglo-Japanese Alliance, the Americans possessed a willing ally in Canadian prime minister Arthur Meighen, whose subsequent clashes with Hughes provided the majority of the fireworks at the June 1921 Imperial Conference. In spite of the British taking all administrative steps to ensure that the participants were fully briefed on all the issues for discussion, the results were colored by deferment rather than adjudication.[43] There was deadlock between the Canadians and the remainder of those present on the alliance question. Meighen maintained that its renewal would have adverse outcomes for Anglo-American relations (and therefore Canadian interests), whereas the Australian prime minister spoke of his nation being left at the mercy of an embittered Japan if the alliance were terminated.[44] The Canadians likewise rejected the idea of Dominion financial contributions toward an Imperial Pacific Fleet because, Meighen asserted, his parliamentary colleagues would refuse to sanction such a scheme. Hughes retorted by asking "by what right" did the Dominions who did not make contributions believe they were entitled to be involved in discussions concerning imperial foreign policy.[45] It was in the midst of these debates that a message arrived at Whitehall on July 8, 1921, from the American secretary of state Charles Evans Hughes extending an invitation from President Harding to attend a forthcoming arms limitation conference in Washington. Accepting the American request, Lloyd George and his Dominion colleagues resolved to defer consideration of both the Anglo-Japanese Alliance and the naval questions until the conclusion of the proposed discussions. Clearly unimpressed, Prime Minister Hughes described the failure of the Imperial Conference to determine these questions as delivering "a very small mouse, and one half-dead at that."[46]

From the outset, the Americans left the British in no doubt as to who would be running the agenda at the forthcoming negotiations. Attempts by Whitehall to organize a preliminary meeting in London, in part to meet the scheduling arrangements of the Dominion prime ministers, were firmly rebuffed. On the insistence of Meighen, Lloyd George consented to the same form of representation as undertaken in Paris, although both Hughes and Massey were originally content that the British represent Australian and New Zealand interests.[47] In Hughes' place, Australia's representative at Washington was to be the country's long-standing minister for defense, Senator George Pearce. Unlike the situation in 1919, the British were to enter the November conference in a weakened condition. Insurrection plagued the British Empire in both Ireland and the Middle East, while the pressing need for domestic social reform in Britain itself could not be ignored, given the potential for internal disorder if effective steps were not taken. Of particular importance to the British and Dominion governments was the question of war debt, and it was here that the United States held the whip hand. As Hughes reported to the Australian House of Representatives in April 1921, British indebtedness hovered in the vicinity of £7–8 billion, with much of the outstanding sum owed to the Americans. Furthermore, it was reported to the Imperial Conference on July 27 that the U.S. Treasury intended to suspend all debt negotiations with foreign nations until the conclusion of the Washington conference.[48] And most galling of all for the British Admiralty, the Royal Navy had been compelled by domestic economic circumstances to accept the imposition of a one-power standard, "an equality in fighting strength with any other Naval Power."[49]

Equipped with the third strongest navy afloat, the Japanese likewise came to Washington with serious financial questions hovering over the nation's ongoing capacity to expand its capital ship capabilities. Furthermore the Japanese delegation, led by Navy Minister Baron Kato Tomosaburo, held divided views regarding the minimum acceptable naval strength for the defense of Japanese interests in the Pacific. His deputy, Vice Admiral Kato Kanji, believed that Japan needed to possess a capital ship force that was 70 percent the size of the American and British contingents, whereas Baron Kato accepted a 60 percent ratio as sufficient.[50] At stake was the Imperial Japanese Navy's "Eight-Eight" program, which called for the construction of eight battleships and a similar number of battle cruisers, so that the core of the Japanese fleet would be less than eight years old. The cost to construct these ships was projected to absorb as much as 60 percent of Japan's annual budget outlays.[51] Though originally an ardent supporter of eight-eight, Baron Kato came to recognize the futility of continuing the program and made his views known to his department while he was present in Washington:

> Defence is not a monopoly of the military, nor is war the prerogative of the military alone. Neither can easily attain its aims without a general mobilization of the whole nation. . . . One cannot, very broadly speaking, make war without money. . . . Even supposing Japan's armaments were to rival those of America in strength, the nation could not, as it did in the Russo-Japanese War, fight on a shoestring. Where then would the money come from? The answer is that there is no country other than America that could oblige

Japan with the foreign credit required—and this is obviously not [to] be forthcoming if America were the enemy.... The conclusion is that a contest between Japan and America is unthinkable.... At all costs Japan should avoid war with America.... In view of this, I believe the true aim of national defense at present should be to maintain a military strength commensurate with the nation's resources and to nurture that strength while using diplomatic means to avoid war.[52]

With delegations from Italy and France also present, President Harding formally opened the proceedings in Washington on Armistice Day 1921. In the following address Secretary of State Hughes set out America's objectives for the conference: "(1) That all capital-ship building programs, either actual or projected, should be abandoned; (2) That further reduction should be made through the scrapping of certain of the older ships; (3) That, in general, regard should be had to the existing naval strength of the Powers concerned; (4) That the capital-ship tonnage should be used as the measurement of strength for navies and a proportionate allowance of auxiliary combatant craft prescribed."[53] From there Hughes addressed the specifics of the proposal as they applied to the various nations. For the present, consideration of the French and Italian positions was deferred because of the relatively small size of their respective fleets. When it came to the British, the Japanese, and the Americans themselves, the secretary of state advocated deep cutbacks to numbers of contemplated, under construction, and currently commissioned capital ships. The British delegation in particular was visibly shocked when Hughes called for the scrapping of nineteen commissioned and four proposed British vessels, one correspondent noting wirily that the secretary had sunk more British battleships than the admirals of the world had done in centuries.[54] Four days later the discussions commenced with the future of the Anglo-Japanese Alliance as one of the first matters on the agenda for negotiation.

A month later, on December 13, 1921, the representatives of the United States, Britain, Japan, and France signed the Four-Power Pact. Following ratification, the pact was formally proclaimed on August 21, 1923. In place of the Anglo-Japanese Alliance, the new treaty spelled out the obligations of the participants in the following terms under Article I:

> The High Contracting Parties agree as between themselves to respect their rights in relation to their insular possessions and insular dominions in the region of the Pacific Ocean. If there should develop between any of the High Contracting Parties a controversy arising out of any Pacific question and involving their said rights which is not satisfactorily settled by diplomacy and is likely to affect the harmonious accord now happily subsisting before them, they shall invite the other High Contracting Parties to a joint conference to which the whole subject will be referred for consideration and adjustment.[55]

In most respects the negotiation of the new agreement proved to be a fait accompli. As the Australian historian John McCarthy indicated in his summation, the British had little choice but to relinquish the Anglo-Japanese Alliance because of Whitehall's war indebtedness to Washington.[56] Reluctantly the Japanese followed suit. The participation of France was obtained in order to prevent the possibility of three-cornered disputes between the other parties. An oversight in the original declaration, however, meant that the Japanese home islands were not excluded from the provisions of the agreement, as was the case with the home territories of the other signatories. With the support of the Australian representative Senator Pearce, the Japanese sought to amend the agreement, and this was acknowledged in a supplementary treaty signed on February 4, 1922.[57] To ensure that the Four-Power Pact would be ratified by the U.S. Senate, the status of Japan's "insular possessions" was fully addressed within the amendment. These were defined as the southern Sakhalin islands, Formosa, the Pescadores, and all the islands previously allocated to Japan under the 1919 League of Nations mandate structure.[58]

Reactions to the termination of the Anglo-Japanese Alliance were mixed. Lord Balfour, who had played an integral role in the original drafting of the alliance in 1902, acknowledged the difficulties the Dominions would have found themselves in had Britain made common cause with Japan in a war against the United States, and the likelihood that the British Empire itself would have fractured under such circumstances.[59] Edmund Piesse, the director of the "Pacific Branch" of the Australian Prime Minister's Department and a member of the Australian delegation in Washington, interpreted the agreement as an implicit acknowledgment on Japan's part of the existence of the White Australia policy. Piesse also believed that if Australia could convince itself that Japan was no longer a threat during the stated ten-year term of the pact, existing plans for the defense of the continent could be abandoned.[60] The Japanese reactions reflected the divergence of opinion that colored Japan's attitude to the Washington negotiations as a whole. A correspondent from the journal *Jiji Shimpo* who covered the proceedings described the termination in sentimental terms: "A strong and healthy evergreen tree, which has symbolized peace in the Orient for over twenty years, had been felled, crumbling without any resistance when swept by a cold blast of wind."[61] Conversely, the head of the Imperial Japanese Army's representation in the Japanese delegation, Lieutenant General Tanaka Kunishige, expressed sentiments of disgust: "In short, the conference proved to be an attempt to oppress the non-Anglo-Saxon races.... It was a great victory for them [Britain and the United States] brought about by crafty British diplomacy."[62]

The most tangible reform that emerged through the formulation of the Four-Power Pact was the removal of a direct treaty relationship between Japan and a single great European power. Described by Hosoya Chihiro as the sinew of Japanese diplomacy, the superseded alliance had provided Japan with her most effective means of conducting international affairs with the West.[63] It was viewed by both Britain and Australia as exercising a practical restraint over Japanese expansionism. And it was for this reason that postwar historians such as McCarthy have considered the Four-Power Pact to be an inadequate replacement when it came to thwarting future Japanese ambitions in East Asia and the Pacific.[64] Yet for all its undoubted importance, the superseding of the Anglo-Japanese Alliance did not serve as the keynote subject for discussion at the Washington talks. This role was filled instead by negotiations surrounding the future of the capital ship. The outcomes contained within the eventual agreement known as the Five-Power Pact (better known as the Washington Naval Treaty) were to become pivotal aspects in determining both the scale and character of naval operations in World War II.

First signed on February 6, 1922, and finally proclaimed on August 21, 1923, the Five-Power Pact imposed the following limits upon the possession of capital ships, aircraft carriers, and auxiliaries by the signatory powers under Chapter I of the pact. All capital-ship-building programs were to be abandoned, and no new ships could be constructed except by way of replacement for existing vessels (Article III). The total capital ship replacement tonnage levels were as follows: United States and Britain (each): 525,000 tons, Japan: 315,000 tons, France and Italy (each): 175,000 tons (Article IV). No replacement capital ship could exceed 35,000 tons standard displacement, and the maximum allowable gun caliber was 16-inch (Articles V and VI). The total permissible tonnage levels for aircraft carriers were as follows: United States and Britain (each): 135,000 tons, Japan 81,000 tons, France and Italy (each): 60,000 tons (Article VII). New aircraft carriers were limited to 27,000 tons, although two carriers up to 33,000 tons could be converted from existing capital ships (either constructed or under construction) that were otherwise due to be scrapped (Articles IX and II). No vessel other than a capital ship or aircraft carrier could exceed 10,000 tons standard displacement or carry armament in excess of 8-inch caliber (Articles XI and XII). Under Chapter II, which provided the specific compliance regimes for each nation, a capital ship or aircraft carrier was only eligible for replacement at twenty years after the date of its completion (Part 3, Section I).[65]

The final agreement of the nations concerned was inevitably obtained through the outcome of some fairly intensive horse trading behind the scenes. Japanese objections were placated by permitting the Imperial Japanese Navy to retain both of its *Mutsu*-class battleships in exchange for the U.S. Navy retaining USS *Maryland* and two other *West Virginia*-class ships under construction. Thanks to both its prior scrapping of existing battleships (including the original HMS *Dreadnought*) and the relative age of its fleet, the Royal Navy gained consent to build two new *Nelson*-class battleships in accordance with treaty specifications.[66] As a result the British were left with twenty capital ships, the Americans eighteen, the Japanese ten, the French seven, and the Italians six. With the calculations for the new era of limitations being based upon replacement tonnage limits, the so-called 5–5–3–2–2 ratio came into effect. Under the provisions of Articles II and IX, four of the five signatories were to undertake aircraft carrier conversions: Britain (*Courageous* and *Glorious*), the United States (*Lexington* and *Saratoga*), Japan (*Akagi* and *Kaga*), and France (*Bearn*). And in exchange for a smaller fleet, the Japanese were able to obtain the agreement of the British, French, and Americans to the prohibition of any further fortification or improvement of a list of Pacific bases as outlined under Article XIX of the pact.[67] These included each of the North Pacific island groups that had been allocated to Japan by mandate, together with American bases in Guam and the Philippines and the British naval facility at Hong Kong.

Of equal importance would be the issues the negotiations in Washington were unable to resolve and which were not to be effectively tackled prior to the London Conference in 1930. Aside from imposing a standard tonnage and gun caliber ceiling, no other restrictions were agreed upon for the future construction of cruisers and destroyers. The consequence of this impasse was to be a continuing arms race in miniature for the remainder of the 1920s, as the contracting parties steadily expanded their cruiser fleets in particular. Submarines were likewise exempted, with the exception of provisions contained in a subsidiary agreement that governed the conduct of submarine warfare against merchant shipping.[68] More noticeable still was the failure of the conference to take any steps regarding the policing of naval aviation, though as of 1922 this science had yet to become a central plank in the evolution of fleet tactics as it would become in the 1930s. Until such time as the ongoing development of the airplane would reveal the full extent of its capabilities in an anti-shipping role, the battleship remained at the forefront of contemporary naval tactics. What the outcomes of Washington did substantially curb was the possibility of another giant surface engagement on the scale of Jutland in May 1916, which had involved more than 250 ships (including 58 capital ships) and approximately 100,000 men.[69]

The outcomes of Washington were generally greeted with enthusiasm by the British and American press and disappointment by the respective naval establishments of both nations. Editorials in leading newspapers such as the *Times* of London and the *New York Herald* summed up the majority of public sentiment in describing the talks as "a great day for all time in the history of the world" and "much the greatest [conference] of all time."[70] Taking the opposite view, the former first sea lord, Admiral Sir Rosslyn Wester-Wemyss, described the actions of the British delegation as "an act of renunciation unparalleled . . . in history."[71] Reaction from within the U.S. Navy was similarly critical, especially when it came to the relative strengths of the American and Japanese fleets in the Pacific. Senior officers such as Adm. H. S. Knapp believed that while limitations were justified, the United States had been far too generous to the Japanese and had thus jeopardized America's strategic position in the Pacific.[72] As for the reaction in Japan itself, criticism was in no short supply. Predictably, the nationalist-oriented journals in Japan such as *Kokumin* and *Nichi Nichi* had a field day, with Japan generally cast as the victim of an Anglo-Saxon conspiracy.[73] Within the Imperial Japanese Navy the consequences were to prove highly divisive. Already at odds over the 60 percent to 70 percent question, the divisions within the Japanese delegation became subsequently entrenched within the wider service, with serving naval officers dividing into the so-called "treaty" and "fleet" factions. This schism resulted in the dominance of the latter faction during the course of the 1930s and the eventual pursuit of closer naval ties with National Socialist Germany.[74]

Though reaction in the Australian press was similar to that in Britain and the United States, Prime Minister Hughes was cautious in his address to the Australian House of Representatives on July 26, 1922. While praising the Four-Power Pact as "a great thing for this young Commonwealth" and the Five-Power Pact as providing "the positive assurance of a substantial reduction in our Naval Estimates," Hughes reminded the chamber of their respective limitations: "They do not guarantee to us material support if we are attacked. They insure merely moral support and the public opinion of the people of the contracting countries."[75] On his return from Washington, Senator Pearce expressed positive sentiments regarding the behavior of the Japanese delegation and the desire of the Japanese to avoid the same fate as Germany:

> I frankly confess that I went to the Conference as one who suspected Japan and her intentions in regard to the Pacific. I think that suspicion had some grounds. I think it has been the policy of Japan to look out over the Pacific, perhaps quite legitimately; but while the Conference was proceeding the statesmen of Japan realised that the fate that overcame Germany—her moral isolation from the rest of the world—was a fate that Japan must, at all costs, avoid. I believe that the present policy of Japan—the policy that she put into practical effect at the Conference, and which her representatives displayed in every word and action—aims at avoiding that moral isolation at all costs.[76]

The RAN had not been spared within the disarmament formula that arose from the negotiations over naval limitations. Classified as a British ship under the terms of the Five-Power Pact, the battle cruiser *Australia* was scheduled to be scrapped under the terms of the agreement.[77] Of far greater consequence, however, was to be the impact of the settlement upon the then-existing proposals for Australia's maritime defenses. In May 1919 Lord Jellicoe, the former commander of the British Grand Fleet, had visited Australia to enquire into the issue and thereafter make recommendations for the future development of Australia's naval requirements. Jellicoe's mission was to set in motion a process whereby the primary naval defense of Australia would be entrusted to an ambulatory arrangement known as the "Singapore strategy."

1919–1923: The Genesis of the Singapore Strategy

During 1918 the Australian government and the nation's armed services began turning their minds to the question of postwar defense. At the planning level, a restructure of the Council of Defence was undertaken in March 1918, which was to be followed by reforms to the Navy Board as recommended in September 1918 by the findings of a royal commission. In their deliberations over the size and operational scope of a postwar RAN, the planners proceeded on the basis of Admiral Henderson's 1911 report, which had called for a fleet strength of fifty-two vessels and the construction of new facilities at Flinders (Port Phillip) and Cockburn Sound in Western Australia.[78] Of equal importance were the findings contained in a secret report by Commander W. H. C. S. (Hugh) Thring that had been completed in July 1913. In partnership with Captain Constantine Hughes-Onslow, Thring undertook a wide-ranging study that considered the means by which Australia could be threatened by the Imperial Japanese Navy and recommended the establishment of a series of advanced fortified bases in Papua New Guinea to guard against any form of direct threat to the Australian continent.[79] Thring likewise made a series of sage observations that set out the difficulties that were to occupy the thinking of Australia's interwar planners:

> Could Australia hope for help from England or any other power? A war between England and another European Power would give Japan a good opportunity to carry through her designs in the

East . . . it is unlikely that England could send adequate help to Australia. But even without such a war, the continual recurrence of "strained relations" in Europe makes it impossible for England to send to Australia a Fleet which could meet Japan's Battle Fleet on equal terms. . . . British ships stationed at the Cape [of Good Hope], in the East Indies, China and New Zealand would undoubtedly help; but in the case of a European war, would be largely occupied with other matters than the defence of Australia.[80]

The sticking point in pursuing the Henderson report in a postwar environment was the likely prospect that naval funding would be reduced in the immediate aftermath of the Great War. With this factor taken into account, together with the need to evaluate imperial defense on the basis of knowledge gained in the war itself, in August 1918 the Australian government chose to defer further consideration until such time as the situation had been reappraised by the British Admiralty.[81] Meanwhile, the Admiralty itself had been addressing the concept of a postwar Imperial Fleet. In response to a request from New Zealand at the 1917 Imperial Conference to do so, in May 1918 its planners produced a memorandum that outlined a series of controversial proposals. Central to these was the proposed formation of an Imperial Fleet that would be responsible for the defense of the British Empire as a whole, and the control of this force through a centralized command structure.[82] This did not receive a favorable response from the Dominion governments, yet discussions proceeded between Whitehall and the Dominions concerning the dispatch of an Admiralty representative to undertake a fresh appraisal of their individual defense circumstances. In a letter to the first lord on November 16, 1918, the Australian navy minister, Sir Joseph Cook, formally requested the presence of Lord Jellicoe, the former commander of the Grand Fleet, to undertake the task.[83]

Based upon his service career prior to May 31, 1916, Jellicoe presented as a most suitable candidate for such a mission. Following the massive engagement between the Grand Fleet and Germany's High Seas Fleet at Jutland on May 31, however, his reputation had taken a considerable beating. In the course of the battle three British battle cruisers had been blown up and sunk, with less than thirty survivors from a combined total of more than 4,300 officers and enlisted men on board. Two large armored cruisers were likewise destroyed, both of which foundered with all hands. Through the search for scapegoats that followed, Jellicoe was widely accused in both government and navy circles of having failed to exercise adequate control over the British capital ships and failing to pursue and destroy the smaller German fleet. Though he was appointed as first sea lord in November 1916, controversy continued to plague him, particularly regarding his perceived lack of action over the use of convoys to thwart German U-boat attacks.[84] After further maneuvers within Whitehall and the Admiralty, Jellicoe was subsequently dismissed from his post by First Lord Sir Eric Geddes on December 24, 1917. Admiral Sir Arthur Wilson, a highly esteemed figure in the Royal Navy who had briefly served as first sea lord before the Great War, regarded Jellicoe's removal as "a disgraceful concession to an unscrupulous Press agitation."[85] Nevertheless Geddes subsequently recommended Jellicoe's mission to the British War Cabinet on December 17, 1918.[86]

Before Jellicoe's scheduled visit in May 1919, the Australian government undertook further measures to strengthen the nation's defenses. The first of these was the creation of the Pacific Branch of the Prime Minister's Office, which commenced its functions in the same month as Jellicoe's arrival. Headed by Major E. L. Piesse, the office's principal task was to study the affairs of Far Eastern and Pacific nations "in so far as these may in the immediate or distant future affect the foreign relations or domestic affairs of the Commonwealth."[87] In reality the creation of the Pacific Branch was an expansion of Australia's intelligence capabilities with one specific nation in mind: Japan. Yet in a wide-ranging tour of Asia from September 1919 until March 1920, Piesse concluded that the Japanese were not a menace to Australian security, a view confirmed by his meeting with Japan's vice foreign minister in Tokyo on December 25, 1919.[88] Convinced otherwise, Prime Minister Hughes was to shun Piesse's advice and exclude him from the Australian delegation at the 1921 Imperial Conference. The second measure involved the recommendation of a subcommittee of the Council of Defence (COD) on January 20, 1919, for the creation of an Australian air corps. Since April 1918 both the Naval and Military Boards had been busy drawing up proposals for air arms that would suit their individual needs, and on August 13, 1918, the government approved a start-up budget of £3 million for three years, with the funding allocation to be determined by the COD.[89] Five months (and much interservice conflict) later, the subcommittee in question made a compromise decision, the details being deferred for consideration until the conclusion of the Paris Peace Conference.

Traveling on board the battle cruiser HMS *New Zealand*, Jellicoe arrived at Albany in Western Australia on May 15, 1919. Over the next three months he visited Melbourne, Hobart, and Sydney as well as Gladstone (Queensland), Newcastle (New South Wales), and the Northern Territory, the Solomon Islands, and Port Moresby.[90] For the purposes of his mission to Australia and the other Dominions, the Admiralty had provided Jellicoe with the following instructions in point form to guide his deliberations:

> 2. Whilst the Admiralty do not depart from their declared views as to what would be the most effective scheme of Naval Defence of the Empire, they cordially recognise that the main object of this invitation is the promotion of uniformity in naval organisations and training and types of naval material throughout the Empire with a view to efficient naval co-operation.
> 3. They therefore propose to depute Lord Jellicoe to visit the Dominions to advise the Dominion Authorities whether in the light of the experience of the War, the scheme of naval organisation which has been adopted or may be in contemplation between all the Naval Forces of the Empire.
> 4. Should Dominion Authorities desire to consider how far it is possible for the Dominions to take a more effective share in the Naval Defence of the Empire, he will give assistance from the naval point of view in drawing up a scheme for consideration.[91]

Upon his arrival in Australia, Jellicoe received a detailed letter from Acting Prime Minister Watt that contained the specific areas of inquiry that the Australian government wished to be addressed. As set out below, the relevant points clearly indicated Australian expectations regarding the nation's strategic position and the future composition of the continent's naval defenses:

> (a) *Naval strategical problems affecting Australian waters and the Pacific.*

(1) Probable routes of attack on Australia, with special reference to the occupation by a foreign power of Islands north of the Equator.

(2) Protection of Trade Routes. (a) To North America; (b) To Panama Canal and South America; (c) To Africa; (d) To Colombo; (e) To Singapore.

(b) *Future composition of the Australian Navy.*

(1) Probable composition of Imperial Fleet in Pacific.

(2) Suggested organised co-operation in Pacific Defence by Canada, New Zealand, India and Malay States.

(3) Suggested strength and future increase in number of R.A.N. ships, keeping in view probable financial resources available.[92]

In the process of completing his report on the Australian situation, Jellicoe was handicapped by a lack of guidance from the Admiralty when attempting to address the questions under subheading (b) of Watt's annexure. In spite of communications with London during the period from May to October 1919 to receive the required clarification, no advice had been forwarded. In his Australian report supplied to the Commonwealth Parliament on October 21, 1919, Jellicoe noted that he had been unable to make conclusions regarding "a definite standard of future [imperial] naval strength to Australia without considering the whole Pacific problem."[93] Nevertheless he employed his own detailed knowledge and experience in proposing his own version of the Japanese eight-eight scheme in an operational context, determining that a force of eight battleships and eight battle cruisers should form the core of an Imperial Pacific Fleet. With specific reference to the Australian navy, it was proposed that the RAN's individual strength be increased to two battle cruisers, eight light cruisers, an aircraft carrier, and further auxiliary vessels. And on the issue of basing, Jellicoe supported the establishment of a major naval base at Singapore for use in the defense of Australia, New Zealand, the Malay States, and British interests in the Indian Ocean.[94] During the course of the Australian leg of his mission he also noted the potential of base sites on the southeastern Australian coastline, including Sydney and Port Stephens, a large protected expanse of water some twenty-two miles to the north of the industrial port of Newcastle.[95]

Unbeknown to either Jellicoe or his hosts, the Admiralty had prepared a further memorandum in July 1919 on the subject of imperial naval defense prior to the completion of the Australian report. When the Admiralty were apprised of Jellicoe's preliminary conclusions following the submission of his report to the Australians, the criticism of the former first sea lord's actions was scathing.[96] In a memorandum dated October 31, 1919, Jellicoe was accused of acting well outside his stated terms of reference and that his hosts would come to assume that the report reflected the views of the Admiralty. A direction was made that he be immediately provided with the July appraisal and that the document "should form the basis of any recommendations he [Jellicoe] may make to the Canadian and South African Governments."[97] Within the fresh memorandum itself the concept of a centrally controlled Imperial Fleet in peacetime was largely discarded, whereas the concept of an ambulatory Imperial Fleet (with Dominion naval participation) remained. In the section addressing the selection and maintenance of naval bases, both Cockburn Sound and Sydney were suggested as suitable sites, in the latter case because Sydney would cover "the more important trade routes from attack from the north-eastward."[98] At the same instant the Admiralty planners stated that with Hong Kong's vulnerability as a forward base, "the Imperial Fleet should be provided with a secure base well to the southward of Hong Kong, and no more suitable position can be suggested than Singapore . . . an excellent strategical position for a fleet covering the vital Australian and East Indian routes."[99]

Having left Australia for New Zealand on August 16, 1919, Lord Jellicoe missed observing the reaction of Prime Minister Hughes to the staging of routine fleet exercises by the Imperial Japanese Navy in early October. Seemingly panicked by the maneuvers, Hughes requested the immediate deployment of British capital ships to the Pacific, a request that was brusquely refused.[100] Following the Admiralty's admonishment of Jellicoe later the same month, the planning of imperial naval policy began to descend into the kind of "drift" that would eventually motivate Hughes to seek an Imperial Conference for 1921. In December 1919, the Admiralty's May 1918 appraisal of imperial naval defense was replaced by the July 1919 version, but the new policy would not be granted official status until it had been fully examined by the Committee of Imperial Defence.[101] Two months later the Admiralty received Jellicoe's closing remarks regarding his mission, in which he defended his decision to provide specific advice as to the required strength of an Imperial Pacific Fleet to the Australian government. Jellicoe maintained that he exercised his personal knowledge in order to secure the support of the Dominions to contribute their "just share of the burden of naval defence."[102] Thereafter the course of policy deliberation surrounding both national and imperial defense in Britain and Australia became increasingly dominated by financial constraints and interservice conflicts for much of the remainder of 1920. The introduction of the so-called Ten-Year Rule by Lloyd George's government in August 1919, an attempt to regulate defense funding upon the assumption that there would be no major war for a period of ten years, was to serve as a catalyst for further steep reductions to British naval expenditures.

Within the explanatory notes for the Royal Australian Navy's 1920–1921 estimates it was explained that economies were required because of the enormous war debt incurred by the nation, and that the subject of naval defense as a whole had yet to be considered by the forthcoming Imperial Conference.[103] Similarly, Australia's new defense policy, announced in the House of Representatives by Prime Minister Hughes on September 9, was essentially a temporary measure to serve until such time as the talks in London had taken place. But in March 1921 a conference on board HMS *Hawkins* at Penang revealed the Admiralty's underlying intentions in the development of the Singapore strategy. Discussions between the commanders in chief of the Royal Navy's China, East Indies, and Australian squadrons considered the question of waging a naval war "between Japan and the British Empire alone."[104] In performing their task the participants acted on the basis of the following premises as outlined by the Admiralty: (1) "For the present and near future," financial and political considerations prevented the establishment of a fleet in the Pacific that was "in any way comparable with the Japanese fleet." (2) In the event of war with Japan, it would take at least two to three months for a relieving force to arrive in the Pacific theater, and that this period of time should be considered "the defensive period." (3) "The Conference regard Singapore as the key to the British naval position in the Pacific, and they are basing their proposals on the assumption that Singapore is made impregnable."[105] These premises provided the framework for the future strategic protection of Australia.

So the prospects, however tenuous, for the permanent regional presence of a mighty Imperial Pacific Fleet were finally exploded. As elaborated under the prior subheading, the 1921 Imperial Conference effectively exercised the wisdom of Pilate and placed the naval security of the British Empire in the ultimate hands of the U.S. Senate. With the signing of the Four-Power and Five-Power Pacts in February 1922, Whitehall no longer possessed a major alliance partner in the Asia-Pacific region and the Royal Navy was left to contemplate its status as a one-power standard force holding global responsibilities. The fate of the proposed naval base at Singapore, which had received preliminary approval from the Committee of Imperial Defence on June 16, 1921, similarly rested upon the deliberations in Washington.[106] And it was through the terms of the Five-Power Pact, which governed the militarization of bases and facilities in the Pacific and the Far East, that Singapore became the centerpiece of Britain's future imperial bulwark to the east of the Suez Canal. Isolated and unfortified, Hong Kong could no longer serve as a viable forward fleet base to counter any possible southern thrust by the Japanese fleet. Exempted from the negotiated restrictions, Singapore had by default become the new first line for Empire naval defense, and thereby the first line of defense for the Australian continent. Yet in spite of this critical shift in the strategic landscape, the British government remained reluctant to exercise decisive leadership in ensuring that Singapore was indeed made unassailable.

Throughout 1922 both Whitehall and the British armed services were heavily preoccupied with the effects of reduced funding. In February the government examined the findings of the Geddes Committee on National Expenditure, which had been instituted in August 1921 to consider sweeping budget reductions across the three services. While the review of these findings determined to lessen their proposed scale, Lord Balfour saw the whole question of expenditure priorities as a choice "between Scylla and Charybdis," the specter of naval and military inadequacy versus the threat of social dislocation and civil disturbance.[107] In their scramble for increasingly scarce finances, the Admiralty and the War Office reignited their pre-Washington efforts to emasculate the Royal Air Force. To be addressed in greater detail in the following chapter, the effects of this ongoing struggle were to have a marked impact upon the selection of defenses for the Singapore base in the latter 1920s. As for the development of the base itself, it was not until December 14, 1922, that the Committee of Imperial Defence finally approved the chosen site for its construction on Singapore Island.[108] These deliberations had been overshadowed by what became known as the "Chanak Crisis" in September 1922, where Lloyd George had attempted to secure Dominion support for a military campaign in the Dardanelles to prevent Kemal Ataturk's revolutionary forces from seizing Constantinople (Istanbul). The final refusal of Australia, Canada, and South Africa to heed Lloyd George's plea represented the most public departure from imperial solidarity since the Paris Peace Conference and previewed the difficulties Whitehall was to face in obtaining Dominion consensus for the Singapore strategy at the forthcoming 1923 Imperial Conference.[109]

Australian defense expenditure was likewise coming under heavy pressure. Convinced that the signing of the Washington agreements had removed the threat of war with Japan (at least for the short to medium term), the Australian public and their political representatives were receptive to a reduction in the service outlays. Along with the curtailment of all work on the Cockburn Sound base site as well as the retrenchment of personnel at other naval establishments, the cuts contained in the 1922–1923 Naval Estimates meant that, in the words of the Naval Board, the RAN "must deteriorate in defence value owing to the impossibility of maintaining it at full efficiency."[110] Neither was the outlook rosy for Australia's nascent air arm. The deliberations of the COD subcommittee in January 1919 resulted in the proposed founding of a centrally controlled air corps for the army and navy. The involvement of the two senior services, however, merely exacerbated the squabbles between them as they competed for the lion's share of the £500,000 allocated in the 1920–1921 Air Estimates.[111] In a policy memorandum dated April 6, 1922, the Air Council decreed that the majority of funding in the 1922–1923 Air Estimates package be spent on training and infrastructure rather than equipping the RAAF (which had been formally created on March 31, 1921) with modern aircraft.[112] Perhaps the severest boning of all was reserved for the Australian army. No longer visible as the elite force that had played such a crucial part in the final defeat of the Germans on the western front, the army stood to be shrunk to "the lowest possible cadre organisation," a skeletal framework through which a volunteer force could be raised if the necessity arose.[113]

In his summation of Australian defense priorities in this period, John McCarthy believed that it would have been interpreted as a sign of disloyalty to what he has described as the "imperial defence connection" if funding for the army or air force had exceeded the naval allocation.[114] The fundamental importance of McCarthy's assessment has been to highlight the growing divergence of views within the Australian political and defense establishments as to the best means of guaranteeing the nation's security. By 1922 an increasing number of politicians and military figures were convinced that the combination of an effective air arm and a mobile army offered a more affordable and practicable alternative to the naval status quo. This was the beginning of a major division in Australian strategic thinking between the supporters of the imperial "blue-water school" and those who believed in what McCarthy labeled as "Fortress Australia."[115] Though support for a powerful air arm crossed party and political lines, it was the Australian Labor Party that came to embrace in its party platform the idea of priority spending for national defense. Hughes too was an enthusiast when it came to the air weapon, but by the time of the staging of the 1923 Imperial Conference, Hughes was no longer prime minister. In the December 1919 federal election he had only held power by the skin of his teeth through a coalition with members of the recently formed Country Party, and he had been compelled since then to govern with a party whose representatives strongly favored reductions in defense expenditures. Subsequent to the December 1922 federal poll, the leader of the Country Party, Earle Page, refused to enter into a coalition with a Hughes-led government, and Hughes was duly replaced as prime minister by Stanley Melbourne Bruce.[116]

A steady and cautious man, Bruce was likewise interested in the potential of air power. Following a series of separate tests conducted in Britain and the United States where aircraft had bombed stationary target vessels, he sought the opinion of the first lord, Leo Amery, as to the potential influence of aircraft at sea. In response, Amery advised Bruce that while the future use of airplanes in narrow waters may result in a reevaluation of naval dispositions and operational methods, capital ships could not be sunk by air attack and that the battleship remained the focal point of any naval engagement.[117] Satisfied with Amery's response, Bruce prepared for the October 1923 Imperial Conference, which was to discuss the way forward for imperial defense in the wake of the Washington agreements.

For the British the development of Singapore remained the way forward. On February 15, 1923, Whitehall reaffirmed its support for the construction of the base, but with an eye to its financial viability as had been elaborated in the proposal presented at the 1921 Imperial Conference.[118] In the months leading up to the 1923 talks, questions were raised by naval experts and others as to the strategic value of a base at Singapore. Among these were Admiral Henderson and a British war correspondent, Colonel Charles Repington, who proffered his opinion in the *London Daily Telegraph* in July 1923: "It is of little importance where ships are distributed in peace. The only test is war. It is the tradition of the Japanese to seek the initiative, and begin when the flag falls or a little before. We must expect the loss of Singapore and Hong Kong before our Grand Fleet trails out there. . . . It is useless to send a battalion to Singapore when Japan has shown herself capable of capturing a first class fortress like Port Arthur, defended by 45,000 men."[119]

Defending the Singapore proposal in the House of Representatives on July 24 before departing for Britain, Bruce stated that "the provision of this base is condition precedent to a large fleet being stationed in Australian waters or the Pacific, and as such it must commend itself to the people of Australia."[120] Yet once the Imperial Conference had gotten under way, the Australian prime minister expressed his own doubts. In questioning Amery over the Admiralty's conclusions, he asked whether the chosen locality was strategically sound and how was it to be defended, adding that if there were any doubts over its final establishment, Australia would never have consented to the agreements made in Washington.[121] Amery's response was rich with reassurance. He informed Bruce that a permanent squadron (including capital ships) would be stationed at Singapore to repel the Japanese before the arrival of a relieving force, and that its distance from Japan meant that it was unlikely that a hostile invasion fleet would assault Singapore before Hong Kong had been captured.[122] Although still unsure of just how Singapore's inviolability could be guaranteed, especially in the event of a concurrent European conflict, Bruce took the matter no further. In concert with the representatives from New Zealand and India, he supported the continuation of the project and the Admiralty's assumptions that underlaid it.[123] In his explanation to the House of Representatives on July 24, 1924, Bruce outlined the strategic case for Singapore's importance: "The next guiding principle that emerges from the Conference resolutions is the vital necessity for the maintenance of the safe passage of our mercantile marine along the great sea routes to the East through the Mediterranean and the Suez Canal. Here, again, I stress the importance to Australia of the preservation of that vital artery in our Empire communications."[124]

After two years of postponement due to the Washington Conference, the Singapore "strategy" had at last become the official centerpiece of future imperial naval strategy in the Asia-Pacific region. But its acceptance had not been achieved without considerable reservations as to the viability of a project for which few concrete details had been supplied. Thus Australia entered the mid-1920s with the fate of the nation's defenses pinned to a plan that relied upon the construction (and defense) of a large modern facility in a period of escalating financial stringency. Whether it would be realized in accordance with Australian expectations remained to be seen, and the various steps undertaken throughout the remainder of the decade to prepare this supposed bulwark are explored at length in the following chapter.

―――

Five years had passed since the end of the Great War had ushered in a new world order, yet the security of the Australian continent remained far from assured. At Paris, the practical Pacific frontier between Japan and Australia had been driven south to the vicinity of the equator. In the process the wider effectiveness of Prime Minister Hughes' opposition to the Japanese push for racial equality in the new League of Nations had provided Japanese nationalists with one of the necessary emotive tools required to eventually transform Japan into a nationalist-militarist state. At Washington, Whitehall had forfeited an enduring alliance with the nation that Australia's leaders feared most, while simultaneously consenting to a naval arms limitation agreement that neutered any feasibility of a permanent large-scale British naval presence in the region. These circumstances, coupled with the severe downgrading of Australia's own defense capabilities in peacetime, propelled the protection of the Australian mainland into the clutches of the Singapore strategy, which imparted assurance and faith in place of substance and fact. Yet for the present, Japan presented as a friendly power as the Asia-Pacific, and the world at large, moved on from the horrors of 1914–18. Fresh prosperity loomed on the horizon, and with the League of Nations providing an alternative to war for the solving of international disputes, few in Australia or elsewhere could bring themselves to believe that a second Great War could arise in their lifetimes. In the passing of the next six years the peace would indeed endure, but for both Australia and the British Empire the price to be paid would be the steady degradation of the naval and military means to preserve it.

4

Not a Cloud in the Sky

1924–1929

In spite of its leaders' hopes that the 1923 Imperial Conference would deliver certainty for the future of imperial naval defense to the east of Suez, Australia was again left frustrated by continuing obfuscation from Whitehall and the British Admiralty. Though the decision to site a naval base at Singapore was affirmed, no definitive time scale for its construction had been provided. On the question of Dominion support for the project, only Australia and New Zealand had indicated their ready acceptance. After Lord Jellicoe's ambitious plan for an eight-eight capital ship deployment to the Pacific was swiftly dismissed by the Admiralty in October 1919, at the 1923 talks the British proposed that a squadron containing two capital ships be permanently deployed at Singapore to ensure its immediate security. Given, however, the reduction of the Royal Navy's capital ship force under the Five-Power Pact and the enforcement of a building holiday for these vessels, the likelihood that this deployment would proceed was minimal. This was reinforced by the stated opinion of the British Foreign Office at the conference that "there was not a cloud in the sky" when considering the possibility of conflict between Britain and Japan during the remainder of the current decade.[1] Accordingly there appeared little prospect that the British would solidify the Empire's defenses in the Asia-Pacific prior to the 1930s, yet upon the basis of a proposal raised by the Admiralty at the talks, an imminent symbolic gesture was in the offing.

The 1924 and 1925 Naval Visits to Australia

Since the days of Henry VIII the Royal Navy has proven its expertise in the staging of great peacetime pageants to reinforce its stature in the minds of the British people. Events such as the launching of capital ships and the staging of fleet reviews off Spithead were carefully choreographed occasions that demonstrated the willingness of British governments to spare no expense in the defense of the realm. Likewise, the deployment of squadrons to show the flag overseas played an important role in projecting British naval strength to the wider world. Be it through visits to the colonies and friendly powers or through the exercise of so-called gunboat diplomacy to aid the achievement of specific geopolitical aims, the message was the same, that Britain had the capacity to use its naval power wherever and whenever required. In the aftermath of the Washington Conference, however, the practical realization of global deployments on a large scale was at best doubtful. Nevertheless the Admiralty maintained its willingness to display the might of its biggest and most powerful warships, and it proposed such a course at the 1923 Imperial Conference:

> In connection with Naval Defence one matter of immediate interest came before the Conference, namely, the projected Empire Cruise of a squadron of modern warships. The First Lord of the Admiralty explained that the project was that two capital ships, the "Hood" and the "Repulse," together with a small squadron of modern light cruisers, should visit South Africa, Singapore, Australia and New Zealand, and return by way of British Columbia, the Panama Canal and Eastern Canada. The light cruisers would accompany the battle cruisers as far as British Columbia, but would return to England by way of the west coast of South America and Cape Horn. The Dominion Prime Ministers expressed their appreciation of this proposal, and assured the Conference that the ships would be most heartily welcomed in their countries.[2]

The choice of the giant battle cruiser HMS *Hood* as the flagship of what became designated as the Special Service Squadron would prove to be a masterstroke in public relations. Launched on August 22, 1918, and completed on March 5, 1920, *Hood* was the first (and last) of the four *Admiral*-class battle cruisers to be completed prior to the negotiation of the

Five-Power Pact. At 44,600 tons full displacement and some 860 feet in overall length, she dwarfed any other capital ship, British or foreign-built, then in service. The combination of her main armament, eight 15-inch guns, together with a maximum speed of 32 knots, made *Hood* arguably the most powerful warship afloat. Her price tag of £5,698,946 upon completion represented almost twice the sum of the entire budget for the Royal Australian Navy under its 1922–1923 Naval Estimates.[3] Yet appearances could be deceiving, and *Hood* suffered from the same inherent weakness that had been exposed among her predecessors at Jutland, namely the extreme vulnerability of British battle cruisers to plunging heavy-caliber shellfire. But she presented to the press and the public at large as a slim, stylish behemoth that was all but unsinkable. As the famed British author and broadcaster Ludovic Kennedy was later to remark, *Hood* encapsulated the symbolic power and prestige of the British Empire itself.[4]

Under the command of Vice Admiral Sir Frederick Field, the six ships in the Special Service Squadron departed Devonport on November 27, 1923. The squadron's first port of call was at Sierra Leone, to be followed by visits to Capetown, Durban, and Zanzibar. It reached Trincomalee (Ceylon) on January 26, 1924, and after a seven-day stopover at Singapore, arrived at Fremantle on February 27. Commencing with Fremantle, the Australian leg of the voyage included visits to Albany, Adelaide, Melbourne, Hobart, Jervis Bay, and Sydney. Departing Sydney on April 20, the ships proceeded to New Zealand, Fiji, and Hawaii, then paid visits to various ports in Canada, the United States, and the Caribbean before returning to Devonport on September 29, 1924. In the course of the "Empire Cruise" the squadron had steamed a total distance of 38,152 miles.[5] As part of their duties in Australia, elements of the force led by *Hood* provided a formal escort for the first flagship of the RAN, HMAS *Australia*, when she was scuttled off Sydney Heads on April 12, 1924, in accordance with the terms of the Five-Power Pact.

From a public relations perspective the visit by the Special Service Squadron to Australia was generally regarded as a success. The ships were warmly received in each port they visited, and there was an endless round of parades, receptions, speeches, sports, patriotic events, and enormous public interest in the ships themselves, most especially *Hood* and *Repulse*. One eyewitness in Melbourne described how "many families were making a day of it. . . . The Bay was dotted with sailing boats. . . . It was a wonderful sight [when the squadron arrived] . . . everyone cheering and the kids running up and down and the sirens of all the ships in the harbour going off."[6] But it was not all beer and skittles for the visitors and their hosts. Days after the arrival of the squadron at Fremantle, the recently elected Labour coalition government under Prime Minister Ramsay MacDonald decided to suspend the construction of the Singapore naval base. At a parliamentary reception in Fremantle for Vice Admiral Field and his staff, Mr. W. O. Angwin, the deputy leader of the Western Australian state opposition, criticized the selection of Singapore for the site of the facility, suggesting that Cockburn Sound was a better strategic alternative. Angwin was taken to task in a number of newspapers for supposedly showing disrespect for his British guests and embarrassing Field personally. An alternative viewpoint expressed in the *Perth Call* on March 7, 1924, vigorously defended Angwin's position and added its own for good measure:

> The whole truth about the naval base at Fremantle as everybody else knows, is that it was woefully bungled from start to finish, and it cost the country a huge sum of money, which we, as taxpayers, have to find. Now, as we are to share directly or indirectly in any expenditure for the defence of Australia, we are certainly entitled to demand the fullest information before we commit ourselves to more payments. Mr Angwin's criticism was based on these principles, and he was acting perfectly within his rights. . . . If the fleet were merely on a pleasure-jaunt, national questions might well be eschewed, but it is admitted that defence matters will be inquired into. Under the circumstances then we want our visitors to be fully informed and it's no use of merely throwing complimentary bouquets and telling them nothing of our side of the question. Nobody has yet explained why one British admiral's recommendation of the Cockburn Sound base has been turned down. We got no information, but we are asked to pay the bills.[7]

In a subsequent editorial in the *Hobart World* on March 24, the wider substance of the argument in favor of Australia's localized naval defense during the 1920s was clearly set out, and is worth quoting in some detail here:

When H.M.S *Hood* berths at the Ocean Pier [on] Thursday, people will have the opportunity to inspect one of the most expensive ships afloat. She costs about £6,000,000, or rather more than the total costs of all Tasmania's roads, and a good deal more than the building of all the state's railways. . . . When gazing at this great fighting machine, the average elector, who has to decide on methods of defence for his own country, will doubtless be worried when he remembers that a fierce argument goes on from day to day between experienced admirals as to whether these big costly ships . . . are the most efficient and reliable means of defending a nation from all the war perils that come by sea. . . . The resources of Australia, in their present stage of development, are not equal to the supplying of defence of our huge coastline and trade routes. . . . We are driven therefore by dint of sheer necessity to consider some other method of coastal defence from invaders who may feel inclined to run in close and bombard our cities. . . . This being so, there is all the more reason for Australians to congratulate themselves on their luck in being relieved of the liability for a goodly portion of the cost of a naval base at Singapore. . . . No matter how pacific our attitudes and intentions may be, we may be drawn into an international dispute entailing reliance upon our own efforts to repel an enemy lunge at ports and cities, although an invasion does not appear to be practicable to any possible enemy in the world today. Coastal trade-routes must also be kept open, but the policing of ocean routes is to everybody, but the thousands who flock to see Admiral Field's great flagship at the Ocean Pier need not be downcast because of that, because for Australia's particular purpose an efficient fighting defence fleet can be had that Australia can afford to maintain.[8]

Following an official announcement from the governor-general's office on March 18, 1924, that the Singapore base project had been abandoned, Vice Admiral Field found himself in an awkward predicament, especially as the Admiralty was firmly opposed to the decision. In his speech at a dinner hosted by the Commonwealth government in Melbourne on March 21, he emphasized the need for Australia to build up its cruiser and submarine defenses as well as to establish a naval base at Darwin.[9]

On the subject of Singapore, he sidestepped the issue at another function the following evening by stating that regardless of whether the base was built or not, Australia should look to developing its own naval means.[10] Certain aspects of his personal observations got him into hot water. In a subsequent retraction the squadron commander insisted that he had never insinuated that the money allocated to Singapore was better spent on the development of the RAF and that he had not meant to convey the impression that a base at Darwin was necessary if the construction of the Singapore facility was not proceeded with. Furthermore he denied that he had previously advocated the absorption of the RAN into an imperial fleet.[11] Yet to be fair to Field, he had been well and truly put on the spot by the actions of his political superiors in London, though his statements nonetheless were hardly music to the ears of those of his hosts who still regarded Japan's naval might as a mortal threat to Australia's security.

For all its success as a fly-the-flag endeavor, the presence of the Special Service Squadron sharply exposed the deepening divisions within Australia over which form of defense, national or imperial, should be given precedence. It could also be argued that the deployment of just two capital ships, even given the prestige afforded to *Hood*, already indicated the limitations imposed upon the Royal Navy's post-Washington capacity to send its big ships to operational areas beyond the North Atlantic and the Mediterranean. The following visit by a foreign fleet to Australian shores was, however, to dwarf the size of the British squadron. This was to be undertaken by the 4th and 5th Divisions of the U.S. Navy's Combined Fleet. Under the command of Adm. Robert E. Coontz flying his flag on board the heavy cruiser USS *Seattle*, the American fleet that arrived in July 1925 remains to this day the single largest assembly of naval vessels from one nation to have visited Australian waters. Spearheaded by its three most modern battleships, USS *Maryland*, *Tennessee*, and *West Virginia*, the USN had assembled eleven of its eighteen battleships, one heavy cruiser, six light cruisers, twenty-seven destroyers, two destroyer tenders, and eight fleet auxiliaries.[12] By any measure of naval power as it existed in the mid-1920s, this particular concentration of armored might had not been assembled for the purposes of a courtesy sojourn alone.

At times overlooked by postwar Australian histories, the precise nature of America's own Far Eastern strategic problem, which literally presented as an east-to-west version of the Singapore strategy, was as challenging as the British west-to-east conundrum when considered from a geographical standpoint. The renowned American naval historian Hector Bywater said of the Philippines that when "the United States relieved Spain of the Philippines, she gave hostages to fortune in a sense the American people never fully realised."[13] To secure the Philippines in the event of war with Japan would require the U.S. Navy to dispatch a relieving fleet from either San Diego or Hawaii. In the course of its voyage to Manila this force would have no option but to traverse the seas that bordered Japan's recently acquired island groups in the North Pacific if the fall of the Philippine archipelago was to be rapidly countered by naval means. The alternative was the stationing of a squadron or fleet in Manila Bay that was capable of withstanding an initial Japanese assault. Worse still for the Americans, the terms of the Five-Power Pact forbade any fortification of Guam, while the strength of Corregidor and the other fortifications covering the entrance to Manila Bay could be neither upgraded nor expanded.[14] Once it reached the vicinity of the Marshall Islands, an advancing American fleet would likely come under attack from the Imperial Japanese Navy, and, as will be highlighted in due course, Japan's primary defensive strategy was specifically configured to counter this eventuality.

In 1925 America's senior naval and military planners had yet to fully formulate a basic war plan. Prior to 1922 they had been conducting their assessments upon the basis of three possible war scenarios: war against Japan (ORANGE), war against the British Empire (RED), and war against the Anglo-Japanese Alliance (RED-ORANGE). By 1922 the Navy Department had determined that Japan alone was the most likely future opponent, and as a consequence the majority of the USN's most powerful battleships were based on America's western coastline.[15] The accessibility of the Panama Canal provided the capacity for the various portions of the Navy to carry out joint exercises in either the Pacific or the Atlantic, and likewise allowed for the rapid movement of ships between these operational theaters in wartime. In these respects the foundations for an American naval relief expedition were significantly sounder than was the case for its British counterpart. As commander in chief of the Combined Fleet, Admiral Coontz was particularly interested in obtaining information as to the logistics required for long-range operations, and a trans-Pacific voyage by two fleet divisions would provide important evidence for his deliberations.[16] And the very deployment of such a large force to the Antipodes would bluntly demonstrate to the Japanese that the U.S. fleet possessed the capability to pursue operations anywhere within the Pacific, including the Philippine archipelago, and do so in great strength.

The nationalist elements of the Japanese press quickly responded to this sizeable naval deployment as well as to the Pacific exercise that had preceded it. An article in *Shizuoku Shimpu* spoke for the majority of its counterparts in criticizing the Americans for carrying out war games in which it was assumed that relations had been severed with "a certain imaginary country."[17] Furthermore, the article alleged that the United States was attempting to push Australia and New Zealand into an alliance relationship with the Americans against Japan. Yet it wasn't just the Japanese who had misgivings over the presence of almost 25,000 U.S. personnel in Australian waters. In one of a series of memoranda to the Department of State in Washington, the American consul-general related that instances of anti-American feeling that could arise during the course of the forthcoming visit. Though he reported that "the average labouring man is not pro-American," and the "labour union soap box orators" were similarly unfriendly, the same could be said for some on the conservative side as well, as this excerpt from a letter sent to the consul-general illustrated:

> Australians as a body strongly resent the visit of the United States Fleet. We know perfectly well the aims of your government to spread sedition throughout the Empire in the hope of seeing it dismembered so that the United States should be supreme. . . . For a country that is extracting from the heavily taxed people of England the Shylock pound of flesh for debts contracted on behalf of your sister republic, France; a country that induced weak or corrupt English politicians to surrender British sea supremacy and insisted on the sinking of the H.M.A.S. *Australia*, for such a country to send a fleet here to vaunt the strength it won out of the miseries of the war-stricken peoples of Europe, is a piece of contemptible effrontery. . . . You will find that instead of exalting the worship of Americanism here as against British ideals will only engender feelings of bitterness between the two countries. For we will strive

our upmost to make the crews realise how much Australians detest the United States and its doctrines.[18]

Though a number of union leaders were to refuse their invitations to official functions, of more immediate concern for both countries was the capacity of Australia's ports to handle this armada, and the accommodation required for such a large number of American personnel. These problems were eventually solved by deploying the majority of the battleships to Sydney while the cruisers, destroyers, and most of the auxiliaries would visit Melbourne.[19] Following Whitehall's formal approval being received on November 26, 1924, both port cities prepared for the American presence with considerable enthusiasm. When the ships reached Australia on July 23, 1925, they received a reception similar to that afforded to the Special Service Squadron, but on twice the scale. The subsequent rounds of parades, speeches, balls, dances, sports, and pageants kept the visitors busy for fifteen days, and in that time there were only a few relatively minor instances of public ill-feeling toward the American sailors. The only political incident of any note was the nonattendance of the New South Wales Labor premier Jack Lang at the official functions, with the overwhelming majority of public commentary from both sides of politics being positive, as was the Australian and American press coverage in general.[20] The *Industrial Australian and Mining Standard* had some especially flattering words for the visitors:

> It is no exaggeration to say that the visit has done more to help Australia understand and to like America than could a century of skilful propaganda. . . . It has given us a larger concept of the problems of the Pacific, and has inspired us with gratifying recognition of the fact that when facing and attempting the solution of the problems we can rely on the sympathy of a friend whose views and interests are identical with ours. Above all, it has taught us that the British-speaking races have a kinship that is not only of flesh and blood, but of the heart and the soul.[21]

There was no doubt that the mission to Australia was a timely and valuable way of promoting better understanding between both nations, each of which had been ignorant as to the true character of the other's society and culture. Yet, little or no effort had been expended by either side in pursuing the question of a possible future military alliance or any other form of military relationship.[22] The primary attraction for the USN in sending a large-scale expedition to Australia and New Zealand appears to have been that a voyage to these localities was operationally advantageous. The patriotic speeches and news reports are to be found in Admiral Coontz' mission report to his immediate superiors, yet they occupy the last few pages of a lengthy and complex document. Clearly Coontz' main objective was to thoroughly test his command in its operational conduct of a long-range mission. His instructions concerning the logistics of the voyage paid testament to his thinking: "Before undertaking the cruise the Commander in Chief laid down the policy that the Fleet was to be self-sustaining and independent of ports visited insofar as fuel, provisions, consumable supplies and water are concerned."[23] The majority of Coontz' report addressed in great detail the consumption of fuel and other staples, the outcomes of tactical exercises, and other experience gained in operating effectively on the other side of the Pacific. Australia and New Zealand made ideal destinations because the distance was roughly analogous with that between the United States and the Philippines. To attempt such an exercise in the western waters of the North Pacific invited the potential risk of an international incident, as the Japanese would have likely sortied their own surface warships and submarines to shadow the oncoming American force.

The visit of the Special Service Squadron to Australia in 1924 had at best provided a temporary illusion. Since 1919 both Whitehall and the Admiralty had, through the combination of accident and design, sought to address the problem of imperial defense in the Far East and the Pacific by vacillating their way through a seemingly endless stream of inquiries, commissions, Imperial Conferences, acres of reports, and associated memoranda. And all they had to show for it thus far was a shallow commitment to build a naval base at Singapore and the staging of a year-long circumnavigation to somehow convince the wider world that a service beset by shrinking expenditures could still dominate the seas on a global scale. By contrast, the cruise undertaken by the U.S. Combined Fleet the following year can be viewed as a deliberate operative portion of America's ongoing planning for a future war in the Pacific. The lessons in fighting a distant naval war from the standpoint of command and control, logistics, and supply were to serve as the initial foundations for the USN's successful wartime prosecution of its "island-hopping" campaign that was to ultimately emasculate Japan's Pacific defenses. From the Australian perspective, many fine words had been said and written, but little apparent substance yet dwelled beyond the temporary spectacles of mighty warships at anchor in Sydney Harbour and Port Phillip Bay. Nor did these events bring a halt to the ever-growing divisions within Australia's political and armed service establishments over the nation's defense priorities. With their allocated expenditures now in constant retreat, the mid-1920s were a time of looming trepidation and crisis for the Australian armed forces. Just how much further their situation, and that of their British counterparts, could be permitted to deteriorate without causing irreparable harm was beginning to emerge as an issue of paramount future importance for both nations.

The Expenditure Squeeze and Interservice Tensions, 1923–1929

In 1919 the total defense expenditure for Great Britain amounted to just over £2.1 billion. In 1923 that sum had been reduced to £123 million; it would eventually bottom out at just under £111 million in 1932.[24] Unlike the situation that existed in the Japanese and American armed services, the British (and the Australians) were required to divide their defense funding between three entities instead of two. For the Royal Navy, the retention of an effective level of operational readiness required the careful fiscal balancing of three interrelated areas: the fleet itself, the infrastructure that constructed and supported it, and the research and development that would maintain the RN's status as a contemporary fighting force. If vital elements within any or all of these areas remained chronically underfunded, the invariable ill-effects to be experienced by the service in a future war would be incalculable. In the case of the Royal Australian Navy, the imposition of heavy cuts since 1918 had already reduced Australia's domestic naval defenses to the point of almost total ineffectiveness, a circumstance the RAN shared in common with its army and air force compatriots. And following the fall of the MacDonald Labour coalition government in November 1924, the possibility that Australia would be obliged to assist in the funding of the Singapore base represented yet another potential impost upon an already thinly stretched national defense budget.

Before turning to Singapore in detail, it is necessary to identify and illustrate the key post-Washington defense policies pursued in Britain and Australia, particularly those which by the end of the 1920s would leave the Australian continent almost entirely undefended in every respect. From the British standpoint the first of these in time sequence was the determination by the Conservative coalition government in August 1923 to place the future development of naval aviation under the joint administration of the Admiralty and the Air Ministry. The formation of the Royal Air Force in April 1918 was an attempt to improve wartime operational efficiency by combining the Royal Flying Corps and the Royal Naval Air Service within a single air arm. Following the cessation of hostilities, both of the senior services began a lengthy campaign to have military and naval aviation returned to their respective jurisdictions.[25] After exhaustive deliberation by separate subcommittees of the Committee of Imperial Defence, delayed by the Washington Conference and the subsequent fall of Lloyd George's Liberal-coalition government in October 1922, the survival of the RAF was not confirmed until July 1923. This was followed by further debate between the Admiralty and the RAF over the workings of what was to become known as the "Dual Control" system, which was announced in the House of Commons in August.[26] These deliberations, however, did not signal an end to the matter, which was only resolved in July 1924 with the formation of the Fleet Air Arm after the so-called Trenchard-Keys agreement apparently settled the outstanding differences between the two services. In spite of the settlement, the interservice bickering continued over the issue of manning ratios until a final determination was made in March 1928, almost a decade after the dispute had commenced.[27]

The imposition of the Dual Control regime was to have serious consequences for the subsequent role of aviation within the Royal Navy. Under this system the Admiralty was responsible for funding, operational specifications, and tactical control, while the RAF attended to training, technical development, and aircraft supply.[28] Each service possessed widely differing ideas as to how air power would be best employed at sea, though it must be recalled that naval aviation in the 1920s was still in its infancy. Though noted for his support of innovation in the RAF, the chief of the Air Staff, Lord Trenchard, did not regard flying at sea as different from any other form of flying. Furthermore Trenchard, who placed great emphasis on the initial development of infrastructure instead of material air strength, presided over a system that did not sufficiently invest in technological progress.[29] As will become apparent in later chapters, the inability of British carrier-borne aviation to progress beyond the role of a fleet support instrument in the late 1930s was to have critical repercussions once war broke out between Japan and Britain in December 1941. The FAA's limitations within a new form of naval war dominated by the aircraft carrier would be potentially disastrous for the Royal Navy's efforts to effectively perform its duties in the Far East, including the protection of the Australian continent and its vital external sea communications.

Within the Admiralty itself, opinions over the usefulness of the naval air weapon in the 1920s were likewise divided. Though some advocates perceived the eventual effectiveness of aircraft at sea, the vast majority of senior officers believed that reconnaissance and gunnery spotting were the most useful form of airplane participation in future naval combat.[30] In spite of these differences, the one point that attained widespread consensus among the Admiralty's senior officers during the course of the decade was that aircraft did not possess the wherewithal to sink capital ships. The following extract from the findings of the Bonar Law inquiry into the future of the capital ship (March 1921) demonstrated the starkly divergent views between the Royal Navy and the RAF regarding naval air power:

> Evidence put forward by the Admiralty showed that much improvement had been made in anti-aircraft defence, and considerable confidence was expressed that the danger from aircraft had diminished accordingly. On the other hand, the two witnesses from the Air Ministry—Air-Marshal Trenchard and Major-General Sykes—were emphatically of the opinion that within a period of say ten years, if money were allocated for the purpose, aircraft could be designed to operate from shore bases, and destroy any ship or fleet within their radius of action, unless protected by adequate air force. It must be remarked that the Air Ministry witnesses were unable to produce any conclusive facts to support their views, or to point to results of experiments or investigations as was done by the Admiralty.[31]

The second of the policy battlegrounds to exercise a debilitating impact upon the future of the Royal Navy was the decision of the Treasury to disallow the Admiralty's expansion program in the 1925–1926 Naval Estimates. Though the strength of the British fleet had been reduced to a one-power standard, the first sea lord, Admiral Sir David Beatty, and his planning staff were determined to gain every possible advantage within the limitations of the Five-Power Pact. This meant the establishment of a greatly increased cruiser force on the basis of the Admiralty's interpretation of the Ten-Year Rule, which meant that the fleet was being prepared for a war in 1929.[32] In submitting its proposals for the 1925–1926 fiscal year the Royal Navy did not enjoy the same environment that had existed in the decade prior to the Great War. With Germany no longer a threat, the Admiralty was compelled to emphasize the potential menace posed by Japan in order to convince Baldwin's government to allocate the required funding.[33] Given that the economic situation in Britain had become increasingly frail by 1925, Beatty's chances of securing the RN's position were unfavorable, and they were not to be assisted by the first sea lord's frequent bellicosity over the issue of reduced expenditure as a whole. His attitude toward the Exchequer was one of scarcely concealed contempt, describing his continuing frustration with the "Treasury myrmidons" who in his opinion were seeking to undercut the Royal Navy's fighting strength at every opportunity.[34]

The chancellor of the exchequer, Winston Churchill, regarded the Admiralty's submission as outrageous. In his response via memorandum on January 29, 1925, Churchill took the opportunity to illustrate just how broad the negative effects of adopting such a submission would be both at home and abroad:

> The First Lord wishes to present Naval Estimates to Parliament for the year 1925–26 of £69,241,477 gross and £65,500,000 net. This is described as an increase of £9,700,000 over the current financial year. As £580,000 of terminable Annuities fall in this year and are absorbed by fresh expenditure, it is really an increase of £10,280,000. . . . Such an event will excite national and worldwide attention. It must necessarily become the outstanding feature of our policy, and it will be taken at home and abroad as indicating the spirit and policy of the new Government. It will

play a prominent part in all the criticisms directed against us from every hostile quarter.... Such a policy would of course concentrate upon us a most formidable agitation at home. The whole force of the Opposition Parties would be directed to denouncing the militarism of the Government, which it could truly be stated had closed the doors on social reform. But more dangerous than this will be the discontent of the direct taxpayer.... Our League of Nations position will of course become ludicrous. It seems almost certain that the expansion of our Navy Estimates and the growth of our new construction will entail immediate rejoinders from Japan and still more from the United States.[35]

Responding to the chancellor's critique, the Admiralty fired its own broadside by asserting that Churchill was apparently "distressed at the idea that we should dominate Japan in her quarter of the globe."[36] The core assertion on the part of the sea lords was that the Japanese navy unquestionably commanded the North Pacific and the Far East and Britain could only respond to Japanese aggression by waging war in Japan's home waters. Further, the Admiralty charged that the strategic situation in the Asia-Pacific region "appears neither to arouse any comparable anxiety nor to wound our susceptibilities."[37] These submissions were made in vain. The rejection of the Admiralty's case was largely based upon the Exchequer's interpretation of the Ten-Year Rule, which Churchill and his colleagues regarded as applying to the year 1935 instead of 1929. With no present evidence of any hostile intent on the part of the Japanese, the employment of the rule on a sliding scale could not be easily contradicted.[38] Yet it was to become evident that the rejection of the Admiralty's submissions did exercise an adverse impact upon the Royal Navy's future operational capabilities. The refusal of the expansion program meant that the British shipyards were deprived of orders that would sustain their functionality, albeit at a reduced level, as the Admiralty had intended.[39] And with no replacements forthcoming, the Royal Navy ran the serious risk of being in possession of a large number of vessels that would be at best obsolescent if the international situation were to deteriorate in the short to medium term. Thus the outcomes from the 1925–1926 estimates imbroglio were indeed a reflection of Balfour's Scylla and Charybdis analogy, and given the economic downturn that was to follow, it is difficult to contemplate how a decision in favor of the Admiralty could have been justified in circumstances where no definitive Japanese threat was as yet foreseeable.

In the wake of the Exchequer's refusal to endorse the Admiralty's recommendations, the third of these policy issues arose from what Orest Babij has described as the navy's pursuit of an opportunistic agenda to sustain its primary functions from 1928 onwards.[40] After a further attempt to procure new cruisers was again rejected in 1927, on this occasion, because of further naval arms limitation negotiations at Geneva in the same year, the Admiralty determined to follow a far more cautious approach. Under the stewardship of a new first sea lord, Sir Charles Madden (1927–1930), the budgetary emphasis fell upon maintaining the Royal Navy's short-term readiness for war at the expense of long-term programs.[41] In order to keep the fleet's capital ships and cruisers in operational order, large cuts were undertaken in the areas of naval aviation, technological research and development, and the stockpiling of vital resources. With a new Labour administration under Ramsay MacDonald coming to office in 1929, the idea of attaining national security at the lowest possible cost complemented the Admiralty's decision to narrow the focus of its own spending. Over the following three years the stockpiling of the fleet's fuel oil and ammunition was to be substantially reduced, and in 1932 there were to be a series of short mutinies throughout British bases when the pay scales for seamen and noncommissioned officers came under review.[42] On the basis of this decline it is difficult to conclude at first blush that the effects of Madden's tenure as first sea lord were anything but deleterious for the future maintenance of British sea power.

Viewed in isolation, this would be an inescapable inference to draw. By failing to strike a balance in its own internal spending, it was undeniable that the Royal Navy went to war in September 1939 in a less-than-prepared state, and that previous cuts to projects such as the development of naval aviation would have fateful consequences. The decline of the naval shipbuilding industry due to an insufficiency of new orders was similarly damaging, especially when it came to the inevitable loss of a highly skilled workforce and the mothballing of expensive plant and equipment. Yet when considered in the context of Admiralty policy as a whole throughout the 1920s (as Babij suggests[43]), the negligence of the sea lords extended beyond Madden alone. In a letter to his wife in February

1922, Lord Beatty wrote that it "seems very hard that departments like Transport, Education, Housing, Labour, should not be attacked as vigorously as the services. But it is always the same. In time of peace we have no friends and no influential party supporters."[44] This headstrong intransigence on Beatty's part, and the Admiralty's continuing inability under his stewardship to appreciate the practical limits of its fiscal demands, was one of the main reasons the Admiralty lost much of its political clout in the mid-1920s. Nor had the Admiralty's cause been aided by its ongoing brawl with the RAF over the future of the air weapon at sea and the painting of a then-peaceful Japan as the emerging threat that would justify the expenditures Beatty and his colleagues sought. When these issues are considered, the extent of Madden's culpability cannot be accurately determined without first taking into account the substantial fallout he inherited through his predecessor's recklessness.

The slide of the Admiralty's fortunes under Madden's authority was to be replicated during the term of his successor, Admiral Sir Frederick Field, whose tenure is explored in the following chapter. On the other side of the world, meanwhile, Australia's Bruce-Page government contended with a similar range of problems to those experienced in Whitehall. On September 1, 1923, the Air Force bill passed into statute, but its passage through the Australian parliament had been anything but smooth. In its initial form the legislation permitted the deployment of the RAAF to imperial service overseas, which was unacceptable both to the opposition Labor Party and to many on the government benches. Opposing its adoption in that form, James Scullin, the future Labor prime minister, set out these objections to the imperial component: "The Bill has been drafted with the idea that our air force be sent abroad to fight. It is a Bill for the air defence of Australia. . . . The Government are asking us to surrender our political independence as well as the independence of Australia."[45] Labor's growing anti-imperial defense credentials were again on display in March 1924 when Prime Minister Bruce reported to the House of Representatives upon the outcomes of the 1923 Imperial Conference. During the course of Bruce's remarks, Matthew Charlton, the leader of the Labor opposition, interjected on more than one occasion that the Australian people did not agree with the prime minister's support for the Singapore project.[46] And in opposing the government's introduction of a comprehensive five-year defense plan, Charlton's deputy Frank Anstey outlined his party's objections to the majority of the funding being allocated for the purchase of two new heavy cruisers from British yards:

> In face of that desire to decrease armaments, the Government proposes to increase them. The Labour party accepts the statement of the Prime Minister that it is the desire of every man and woman in Australia to decrease armaments, and it proposes to act in accordance with that desire. Its members, therefore, will not vote for millions of pounds to be spent upon additional armaments against that desire. . . . While he [Bruce] admits that the people of to-day are anxious for peace, and that there is a revulsion of feeling against bloodshed, he points out that their aspirations, dreams, and desires may change. Not because of facts that confront us, not because of things as they are . . . because the Prime Minister fears that a monster man may arise, and that the people who are now anxious for peace will change their minds, the right honourable gentleman proposes that we should spend a large sum of money in providing additions to our navy. If there is any justification for what he says, we must ask ourselves, where is this enemy?[47]

Nevertheless both sides of Australian politics retained a strong unity ticket when it came to maintaining the White Australia policy. In September 1924 Bruce warned the Australian delegation attending the Fifth Assembly of the League of Nations that Australia would only consent to Article 36, which proposed the establishment of the Permanent Court of International Justice, if safeguards existed that prevented "such questions as White Australia to be referred to Court without our consent."[48] As the decade progressed, the international treaty regime (which both sides of Australian politics otherwise strongly endorsed) appeared to further strengthen the hand of collective security as the guarantor of world peace. Western Europe embraced the ideals of the 1925 Locarno agreements, which stabilized the frontiers of Germany, Belgium, and France. And in 1928 the signing of the Kellogg-Briand Pact, which renounced war as an instrument of national policy, included the agreement of both the United States and the Soviet Union, neither of whom at that time were members of the league. For the British Empire, the so-called Balfour Declaration, which arose through the deliberations surrounding the 1926 Imperial Conference, signaled a new era in the application of Dominion foreign policy. In the assessment of historians such as Denis Judd, the decision by Whitehall and the Dominion prime ministers to provide for the formulation of independent foreign policies laid bare the impossibility of contriving a joint imperial alternative.[49] By removing the existing "reserve power" capacity of the British government to exercise a veto over Dominion foreign policy, nations such as Australia were able to determine for themselves whether they wished to follow Britain's lead in international affairs, including the waging of war on its behalf.

The Balfour Declaration represented a watershed moment in the history of Australian foreign policy, for the Dominions had been presented with two clear alternatives: autonomy or continued subordination in the conduct of their foreign affairs. Before leaving for London in 1926 Bruce stated to the House of Representatives that prior to the Great War, Australian statesmen "allowed our foreign policy to be entirely formulated and controlled by British statesmen acting on behalf of the Empire as a whole. Obligations in foreign policy were then seldom in the minds of those in control of Dominion affairs."[50] There was clearly no desire for a repetition of these circumstances, but at the same moment Bruce and his government shied away from the alternate course. Instead the Australians acknowledged this shift in Empire policymaking, but eventually declined to sign its legal instrument in the form of the 1931 Statute of Westminster. As James Curran has remarked, Australia's leaders determined to carry on as if the statute did not exist.[51] Their objective remained as it had always been: the panacea of a unified imperial defense and foreign policy framework in which the Dominions had equal say with Whitehall. Bruce emphasized the situation that had existed in the Great War whereby "there emerged a new realisation of the obligations of the Dominions as part of the Empire and of the necessity for the Dominions to be consulted with regard to, and to have a voice in the framing of, the foreign policy of the Empire from which these obligations arose."[52] To the disquiet of Australia and New Zealand, which had likewise declined to sign the statute, the Balfour Declaration effectively reduced the device of the Imperial Conference itself to a means of consultation alone.

Though the declaration provided the Dominions with equal foreign policy status among one another, it still proclaimed that they were united in common allegiance to the Crown.⁵³ While these nations possessed the right to maintain neutrality in the event of Britain being at war, those that did make common cause with the British would do so with Whitehall calling the shots. Otherwise Australia could rely upon the moral authority of the League of Nations for its principal protection against external threat. In either case an effective local defense was a self-evident requirement, and given the vast distances involved the importance of air defense could not be ignored. Under the five-year defense plan drawn up in 1924, however, the most important of Australia's defensive capabilities received just one-fifth of the funding that had been allocated to the Royal Australian Navy.⁵⁴ Equally onerous for the future of an independent Australian air arm was the existence of an interservice feud that resembled in miniature the concurrent battle being waged between the RAF and the two senior British armed services.

Since the end of the Great War, debate over the future of military aviation in Australia had produced three possible scenarios: an independent air force, the control of air power by the army and the navy, or development through the establishment of civil aviation. Prior to 1923 the latter course presented as potentially viable, with the rapid conversion of civil aircraft for military purposes serving as a major attraction.⁵⁵ The government, however, determined to retain the Royal Australian Air Force as an independent service, which gained statutory authority with the passage of the Air Force Act in 1923. Like Lord Trenchard, the commander in chief of the RAAF, Air Marshall Sir Richard Williams, proved to be a feisty campaigner when it came to the preservation of his patch. He needed to be, as the formation of the new Defence Committee in 1926 contained many who opposed the need for an independent air service.⁵⁶ In August 1924 the RAAF had come under attack from the navy over the proposed formation of an Australian Fleet Air Arm and over which service would control the seaplanes on board the new seaplane carrier *Albatross*. Using his contacts within the RAF (including Trenchard himself), Williams eventually saw off the naval challenge and a compromise was reached with the navy in January 1929.⁵⁷ In the same year the Defence Committee concluded that a separate air force was not in keeping with operational requirements for Australian conditions and that the RAAF should be merged with the Australian army.

The final adjudication of this matter was left for the incoming Scullin Labor government that came into office in October 1929.

In July 1928 Air Marshal Sir John Salmond of the RAF arrived in Melbourne to review the status of the air force and make recommendations for its further development. Although highly critical of its operational readiness (which he regarded as nonexistent), Salmond was alert to the difficulties in building an air force up from scratch.[58] But his recommendation for the gradual expansion of the RAAF was about to fall on stony ground. At a meeting of the Council of Defence on July 8, 1929, Australia's lurching defense situation became clearly evident. Chairing the meeting, Prime Minister Bruce expressed his opinion that the forthcoming budgetary allocation be "sufficient to prevent serious and permanent detriment to the services, though it would allow for no expansion." In response, Lieutenant General Sir John Monash warned of the damaging consequences for service morale and stated that the reduction of estimates should be regarded as a necessary response to the developing economic crisis, but not "as a policy."[59] According to Major General Sir Cyril White, the situation with the army was approaching the point of no return. Because the government wished to retain the Citizen Forces, White warned, any further reduction "would amount for practical purposes to the abolition of the permanent forces, and it would thus become impossible to man the necessary coast defences in the Precautionary Stage [of any potential amphibious attack]."[60] Even with existing economies in place, the government representatives present informed the military attendees that the five-year program must be terminated in view of the rapidly worsening economic climate.

On November 12, 1929, Australia's military leadership came to experience the policy priorities of the first Australian Labor government since the Great War. In the discussions within the Council of Defence, two principal issues emerged. The first of these was the introduction of voluntary citizen military training in place of the compulsory scheme that had been formally discarded on October 31 by the incoming government. The second was a reconsideration of the maintenance of a separate air force organization.[61] While Prime Minister Scullin emphasized that the adoption of a voluntary training regime was the unanimous view of the COD, he was of the view that any decision on the future of the air force should be first examined by the Defence Committee. On the question of the Royal Australian Navy, Scullin was informed by the naval representatives present that pursuant to Admiralty advice, the "ideal strength" of the Australian fleet was two heavy cruisers and two light cruisers, and that Australia's two submarines should be returned to the Royal Navy.[62] Unlike the aforementioned cases, Scullin wished this issue to be resolved by the cabinet instead of by the Council of Defence. This course of action was to be in common with that of another conundrum the new prime minister had inherited, namely the ongoing trials and tribulations of the Singapore strategy.

The Singapore Project, 1924–1929

The decision by the MacDonald government in March 1924 to cancel the construction of a naval base at Singapore did not go down well with the Bruce-Page government in Australia. In a telegram to Whitehall on March 11, Stanley Bruce urged Ramsay MacDonald to reconsider his decision, stating that if the mobility of the Royal Navy was retarded by the lack of a major base in the Pacific it would not only imperil the British Empire but also deliver "a fatal blow to the League of Nations."[63] When introducing the Australian government's five-year defense plan (drafted in response to the cancellation of the Singapore base) to the House of Representatives on June 27, 1924, Bruce was even more pointed in his criticism of MacDonald's decision:

> I do not propose to discuss, at this time, the debatable question of the Singapore Base, but I would remind the House that there were two paramount questions that had to be considered by the British Government in framing their defence estimates for this year. One was the provision of a first class base in the Pacific, for the general defence of the Empire, and the other was an increase in the air defence of Great Britain, for the immediate defence of her own shores. We all know that the former was vetoed, while the latter was put into operation. That was an indication of lack of knowledge on the part of the people of Great Britain regarding the Empire and its far-flung dependencies. There is the danger that Empire defence may, in future, be relegated to the second place, Britain's own defence becoming her primary consideration.[64]

For the following eight months Australia's leaders and military planners stared over the proverbial strategic abyss. Without a secure major fleet base in the Asia-Pacific, the Royal Navy could not send a fleet to Australia's aid, and the Royal Australian Navy was utterly incapable of repelling any form of Japanese naval incursion. With the return to office of a Conservative coalition administration under Stanley Baldwin in November 1924, some but not all of Australia's fears were extinguished and Bruce indicated his future preparedness to make a contribution to the project in a telegram to Baldwin on December 4.[65] On February 27, 1925, the Committee of Imperial Defence formed a subcommittee to reexamine the sites that had been approved in December 1922 so as to consider how rapidly the base site should be developed and to consider a construction timetable for both the base and its defenses. This latter requirement included the examination "of deterrents as alternatives to heavy guns against attack by capital-ships; the scale of defence required; the strength of the Military and Air Garrison; and the approximate cost of the proposals recommended."[66] The subcommittee included Winston Churchill, who in the previous month had taken the Admiralty to task over its use of Singapore as the "peg" for the Royal Navy's offensive-minded strategy in the Far East, a strategic posture that was effectively sunk by Churchill's denial of the Admiralty's request for additional funding in the 1925–1926 Naval Estimates.[67]

Churchill, however, was seemingly prepared for the base's construction to proceed on the basis that it served defensive purposes only, as its supporters were keen to emphasize during the debate in the House of Commons that followed in March 1925. On March 19, the 1925–1926 Naval Estimates were passed by the House of Commons with the first lord, William Bridgeman, allaying fears that the Japanese would regard the project as a threat to their interests, stating that the base "was for purely defensive purposes against a danger which at present could not be foreseen."[68] On the other side of the coin, Ramsay MacDonald made clear in his continuing opposition to the Singapore project that the interests of Australia were not of paramount importance. Furthermore, MacDonald charged, Singapore defended the White Australia policy, which could instead have been examined by the International Court and resolved legally, rather than inviting a Japan-Australia military conflict that could involve the Empire as a whole.[69] In response, an editorial in the *Melbourne*

Herald labeled the former British prime minister's claims as ridiculous: "Australia regards Japan as her friend. . . . It cannot be part of a friend's duty to object to a purely defensive measure as the construction of the Singapore base—rather it is a matter of congratulation that Australia will cease to be utterly defenceless."[70] Some elements of the Japanese press were critical of remarks made by Lord Balfour in the House of Lords on July 1, 1925, which supposedly implied that Japan had hostile intentions toward Australia; the *Jiji Shimpo* warned that such statements had the capacity "to impair old [Anglo-Japanese] friendships."[71]

Bruce's revived interest in contributing to Singapore's construction was tempered by the need to fund Australia's five-year defense program. He duly informed the 1926 Imperial Conference that while his government was prepared to consider any question of contribution with sympathy, Australia's current defense plan was all that Australia could do at present to defend both her national and imperial interests.[72] Given the existing schedule for the planning and construction of the base, an Australian financial contribution could be safely deferred for another decade. An extract drawn from the draft minutes of a meeting of the Committee of Imperial Defence on December 13, 1928, revealed that the completion of the Naval Repair and Storage Base had been deferred until 1937, and the second stage of development of the base's defenses was "postponed for the present."[73] These were but a handful of the numerous base infrastructure developments that were not scheduled for completion before the mid- to late 1930s. From 1925 until 1929 much of the work was concerned with clearing the chosen site for the naval base and beefing up Singapore Island's existing oil storage capacity. In an article published in the *Melbourne Herald* on June 18, 1925, the progress made in the latter endeavor was highlighted at some length, but it was also observed that "the British Royal Air Force is not represented there [at the base site]."[74]

The absence of the RAF at that time was not surprising given both the programming for the establishment of the base's defenses and the assumptions upon which the schedule for construction had been drawn up. In March 1928 an interim report by a Chiefs of Staff subcommittee addressed the likely means of attack and defense, and did so "with a view to producing revised plans on the most economical scale possible compatible with the objects to be attained."[75] On the question of hostile ground assault, the subcommittee's stated assessment was unambiguous, and it would prove to be one of the worst miscalculations in military history:

> Continuous investigations, pursued during the last few years both at Singapore and at home, tend to confirm the opinion expressed by the Overseas Defence Committee in 1924 "that a hostile landing on the mainland of Johore, with the object of an attack on Singapore Island from that direction, would, owing to the difficulties of the terrain to be traversed and various other factors, be an operation of so difficult a nature, that the probability of an enemy attempting it on a large scale may be excluded." We regard a bombardment of the naval base and its resources, and the landing of raiding parties on Singapore Island, as the most likely form of attack.[76]

Based upon this adjudication the subcommittee's recommendation was for the initial construction of coastal artillery positions on the eastern shore of Singapore Island, with three 15-inch guns plus supporting 9.2-inch and 6-inch batteries to be installed over the following five years. When it came to the role of air power in the defense of the naval base, the committee considered that "it may be possible to express more definite opinions a year or two hence."[77] Its attitude on this point reflected a view expressed in the concurrent debate over the air weapon's participation in naval combat that the evolution of the airplane had yet to reach a point where a definitive judgment could be made as to its future effectiveness.

From the standpoint of aeronautical development in the late 1920s, this judgment is difficult to contradict. The vast majority of aircraft types, both operational and experimental, were little advanced over their Great War predecessors in general terms of construction and configuration. All-metal monoplane airplanes with far greater speed, range, defensive armament and load-carrying capabilities had yet to seriously enter into the calculations of aircraft designers and engineers. Yet in the opinion of Lord Trenchard, the Singapore defenses represented a test case. In his memorandum titled "The Fuller Employment of Air Power in Imperial Defence 1919–1929," Trenchard illustrated the potential of air attack against shipping and noted the opposition that his proposals had thus far encountered:

> This policy [the establishment of an air striking force] has in the past been strongly advocated in connection with the defence of Singapore, and has been as hotly contested. It has been argued that aircraft can provide no adequate defence or deterrent against surface ships; yet torpedo attack from the air is now recognised by the Admiralty as one of the most serious menaces to which warships are exposed, and the figures of effective hits in peace exercises during the last four years has averaged nearly 50 per cent, of the torpedoes fired, a far better result than that shown by any other form of torpedo carrier; while bombing, though still almost in its infancy, has already attained a percentage of hits against a moving ship greatly in excess of that attained under similar conditions by coast defence guns.[78]

While the Chiefs of Staff continued to debate the relative merits of coastal artillery versus air power, in October 1929 the Singapore project as a whole entered a new phase of uncertainty. With the return of Ramsay MacDonald as prime minister in June 1929 and the onset of the Great Depression, the outlook was grim for Britain's major imperial bastion to the east of Suez, only partially constructed as it was. In a meeting between the Fighting Services Committee and the new Labour chancellor of the exchequer, Philip Snowden, on October 22, 1929, Snowden determined that work on the Singapore base be slowed down "as much as possible" and that "all work that can be suspended, should be suspended."[79] With a fresh naval arms limitation conference due to commence in London in January 1930, extensive new cuts might be made to capital ship fleets, perhaps leading to the eventual abolition of battleships and battle cruisers. The chancellor was thus of the belief that "to continue the entire Singapore scheme in complete disregard of the possibilities of the [London] Conference would be indefensible."[80] Given the growing pall of gloom that hovered over the project during 1929, it was understandable that even the completion of new capital works would be greeted with a less-than-glowing response. At the opening of Singapore's new floating dock in the same year, the governor of the

Straits Settlements, Sir Hugh Clifford, remarked that he was unsure of whether he was presiding "over a christening or a funeral."[81]

Aside from the extreme financial difficulties that were encountered in the final years of the 1920s, doubts also remained over the geographical selection of the base site. In assessing Amery's advice to Bruce in 1923 as unsound, McCarthy noted that the then–first lord ignored the fact that Singapore was surrounded by land masses and narrow seas and similarly neglected to consider Japan's construction of aircraft carriers, which would permit the Japanese to attack the base at the outset of hostilities.[82] During the debate surrounding Singapore that followed the project's resurrection in November 1925, a Liberal member of the House of Commons, Lieutenant Commander J. N. Kenworthy, suggested that Sydney was a more strategically important locality than Singapore in the event of a Pacific war. And one of the points raised by W. O. Angwin at the reception in Fremantle for the visiting Special Service Squadron in February 1924 had been the suitability of a base in Western Australia because of its direct access to the Indian Ocean.[83] If the Japanese were able to seize control of the seas surrounding the island before a relieving fleet arrived, they could await the British at the southern entrance to the Strait of Malacca (or the Sunda Strait between Java and Sumatra) and pick off their opponent's ships, as they had done with the Russians at Tsushima. And while an active British naval presence at Singapore did provide cover for the Australian continent to the west of Darwin, it was difficult to envisage how a Japanese expedition targeting the eastern Australian seaboard could be intercepted unless the intercepting force was deployed with sufficient prior warning to reach the southwest Pacific in time.

An Australian parliamentarian named Walter M. Marks had painted a fairly stark picture for the House of Representatives in June 1922 as to what would likely occur if such a hostile expedition remained unmolested. Having recently visited Japan as a naval observer, Marks had been given the opportunity to view, at the invitation of the Imperial Japanese Navy, units of the Combined Fleet, including the aircraft carrier *Hōshō* and the partly converted carrier battle cruiser *Akagi*. He informed the House that, in his professional estimation, a force consisting of these ships could bring about Australia's rapid downfall via naval air power alone.[84] Marks also made the salient point that Japanese technological ingenuity and flying skill were not to be underestimated. This observation was as pertinent in its application to the defense of Singapore as it was to the security of Australia's coastal centers. The credibility of these assessments, however, was substantially diminished over time by Marks' penchant for making other predictions of a highly dubious character, including his pronouncement that Armageddon would take place in 1934. The Admiralty's planners had factored in the possible involvement of Japanese carrier-borne aircraft in a naval assault against Singapore Island, but by the end of the decade no allowance had yet been made for the possibility of attacks mounted by long-range land-based bombers. Unbeknown to the British, a brilliant Japanese aeronautical engineer, Honjo Sueo, was soon to design a remarkable airplane that possessed an operational range of more than three thousand nautical miles.[85] With its first flight as a prototype in 1934, the Navy Type 96 attack plane would render Singapore's first-line fixed defenses obsolete before the majority of the big guns were even installed.

The 1920s had drawn to a close with the skies still clear, but just below the horizon dwelled the overcast that was to precede an eventual descent into another global conflict. For a brief moment Australia's shores had played host to a symbolic display of British naval might and a subsequent demonstration of America's logistical capacity to wage a future war at long range in the Pacific. But these instances were to be quickly replaced by the realities of maintaining adequate levels of domestic and external security in an increasingly tenuous economic environment. With its own armed forces progressively cut to the bone, Australia was left with the promise of British naval intervention, yet concurrent reductions in British naval expenditure rendered such a prospect ever more doubtful. As for the material strongpoint of the Royal Navy's presence in the Asia-Pacific region, the majority of the Singapore base and its defenses remained upon the drawing board, and while the effects of the Great Depression persisted, the future completion of "Fortress Singapore" continued to be shrouded in uncertainty. If Japan were to become hostile within the following decade, nothing short of a fully rejuvenated British fleet could hope to successfully intervene against a southward thrust by the Imperial Japanese Navy. But with the combined effects of the Admiralty's commitment to short-term readiness, the progressive demobilization and closure of British shipyards and ancillary industries, and the likelihood of further naval limitation measures arising from the forthcoming London Conference in January 1930, a substantial renewal program in the near future had become well-nigh impossible. So for the balance of the 1930s an undefended Australia would have to depend upon a one-power standard fleet that was about to experience perhaps the lowest ebb of fortune in its lengthy and illustrious history.

5

The Onset of the Two-Ocean Dilemma

1930–1935

For seventy-five years since the onset of the Crimean War in 1854, the succession of theorists and strategists who separately considered the problem of Australia's external defense had come to broadly similar conclusions. The protection of the continent's vital overseas trade and communications, and indeed of the Australian mainland itself, stood to be compromised by what Frederic Eggleston had described in 1912 as Britain's "Two-Ocean Dilemma."[1] Should the British find themselves embroiled in a simultaneous global conflict against major European and Asian powers, Britain would be compelled to concentrate its sea power in the Atlantic. For the purposes of his study, Eggleston nominated Germany and Japan as the hostile parties; his contemporaries largely followed suit. Twenty years later a series of disparate events began to form the eventual basis for such a fear being realized. In September 1931 Japan's Kwantung Army was incited by ultranationalist officers within its garrison ranks to annex the northern Chinese province of Manchuria by force. On January 30, 1933, the prospects of a future European war received a significant boost when Germany's President von Hindenburg invited Adolf Hitler to form a cabinet. And in October 1935 fascist Italy's Benito Mussolini embarked upon expanding his existing North African empire by invading Abyssinia. By December 1935 the edifice of collective security and international arms limitation had been fatally weakened, and the laying of the foundations for the future Axis tripartite alliance was under way. Still recovering from the

Great Depression, Britain reluctantly contemplated the need for rearmament; its navy in particular was well short of adequate operational readiness. In Australia meanwhile, an increasingly vigorous debate was being waged over the direction of the nation's defense policy, with specific reference to what form of future threat should become the primary focus for Australia's military preparations.

"The Weakness of Our Present Position": The British Perspective, 1930–1935

"Desiring to carry forward the work commenced by the Washington Naval Conference and to facilitate the progressive realisation of general limitation of reduction of armaments," the London Conference in January 1930 represented the pinnacle of the interwar naval arms limitation process.[2] Under Part I, Article I of the negotiated agreement, Britain, Japan, and the United States agreed to defer replacement capital ship construction until 1937, exemptions being granted to France and Italy. The principal advances over the original Five-Power Pact related to the regulation of cruisers, destroyers, and submarines. Pursuant to Part III, Article 16, the following tonnage ratios were to be enforced by December 31, 1936:

Table 5.1. Tonnage Rates for Cruisers, Destroyers, and Submarines*

Country	Cruisers (greater than 6.1-inch caliber guns)	Cruisers (6.1-inch caliber or less)	Destroyers	Submarines
United States	180,000	143,500	150,000	52,700
Great Britain	146,800	192,200	150,000	52,700
Japan	108,400	100,450	52,700	52,700

* Measurement in standard (nonmetric) tonnage

"International Treaty for the Limitation and Reduction of Naval Armament," http:// www.navweaps.com/index_tech/tech-089_London_Treaty_1930.php, first viewed March 8, 2018.

With agreement reached on the scrapping and demobilization of existing capital ships, the ratio between the three leading naval powers was reduced to 15:15:9. Aircraft carrier design was further clarified by forbidding the fitting of flying-off platforms to existing capital ships. Both the French and the Italians refused to be bound by the tonnage ratios for cruisers, destroyers, and submarines and were therefore not included under Article 16.[3] What became known as the London Naval Treaty was finally signed by the five participating powers on October 27, 1930.

The outcome of the London negotiations was particularly unfavorable for the Admiralty, especially given its existing policy of keeping the bulk of the British fleet in a state of short-term operational readiness. With its allowable capital ship replacement tonnage unavailable until January 1937, it was imperative that the Royal Navy's existing battleships and battle cruisers be upgraded to meet modern standards.[4] Without the benefit of modernized propulsion, communications and fire-control systems, antiaircraft batteries, and other improved defensive measures such as antitorpedo bulges, the Admiralty's capital ships would be hard-pressed to compete within modern operational environments. Furthermore, the majority of British light cruisers commissioned in the early 1920s (particularly the "C" and "D" class vessels) were unsuitable by virtue of their size and endurance for operations in equatorial waters.[5] By contrast, both the Americans and the Japanese were to separately commence rebuilding programs for the majority of their respective capital ships. And with Admiral Sir Frederick Field succeeding Admiral Madden as first sea lord on July 30, 1930, the steady deterioration of the Royal Navy's all-important reserves of fuel oil and ammunition was to continue. Accordingly, it was difficult to conclude just how the Admiralty would respond to a crisis in the Far East if such a circumstance arose within the short term, especially given the incomplete nature of the Singapore naval base. The denial of access to adequate logistical facilities at Singapore, coupled with the defenselessness of Hong Kong as a forward base, made it virtually impossible for any British fleet or squadron to be deployed beyond the confines of the Indian Ocean.

Even if Field had been inclined to reverse the focus of Madden's cost-cutting policies, his appointment as first sea lord unfortunately coincided with a period of major crisis for both the British government and the economy it presided over. Reliant upon a coalition partnership with a fracturing Liberal parliamentary rump, Ramsay MacDonald's Labour administration found itself increasingly incapable of balancing the national budget in the midst of a currency crisis. The submission of the May Report in July 1931, which recommended steep public-sector cuts, proved to be the breaking point for Labour.[6] With subsequent deadlock within MacDonald's cabinet over May's recommendations, the prime minister resigned on August 24, and in a fashion similar to Hughes' experience in Australia during 1916–1917, MacDonald and a number of his ministers opted to form a national coalition with the Conservative and Liberal parties. In the subsequent general election of October 1931, the new National coalition trounced Labour, from which MacDonald and his colleagues had been expelled. During the course of the preceding month the nation had been shaken by industrial disturbances among the naval personnel at Invergordon and elsewhere.[7] Aware that the Royal Navy's fiscal fortunes were apparently approaching a critical juncture, First Lord Sir Austen Chamberlain issued a warning to the government in a memorandum dated September 30:

> Obviously, some powers including ourselves are below the strength permitted by Treaty in ships, and the appropriate quota of men or munitions. The Budgetary Limitation figures must clearly, then, be such as will not prevent such Powers from making good all their deficiencies. So far as this country is concerned, the only meaning that can be attached to the "ten years peace rule" as the basis for service estimates is that, in the event of the political horizon clouding over, increase of expenditure would be contemplated with a view to catching up arrears in preparedness for war. . . . Nor does it appear to the Admiralty that Budgetary Limitation should be accepted which would limit our right to adequate replacement of reserves or development of auxiliary services, even though, as a matter of economy, we are not at present taking such action. In this view, the slackening of the development of the Singapore base must be regarded as a domestic matter and not to be enforced upon us by a Budgetary Limitation figure; so must the delay in the building up of oil fuel reserves, and the completion of coast defences.[8]

Within the wastes of Manchuria twelve days beforehand, the first clouds had indeed begun to form. The establishment of a Japanese ultranationalist society known as Sakurakai (Cherry Blossom) in

September 1930 attracted the adherence of numerous middle-ranking officers from the Imperial Japanese Army, and especially from within the Kwantung Army based in the northern Chinese province.⁹ The garrison flexed its muscles in June 1928, when radicals in its ranks assassinated a Manchurian warlord by blowing up his personal train. No effective action was taken by the Japanese government to punish those responsible for this incident, which emboldened the miscreants to take further measures. On September 18, 1931, another explosion on the South Manchurian Railroad was employed as a pretext for the Kwantung Army to commence fighting the resident Chinese garrison. The Japanese were victorious and by November 1932 Manchuria had been totally annexed, renamed Manchukuo, and placed under a puppet government headed by the Manchu "emperor" Henry Pu-yi.¹⁰ Then on January 28, 1932, elements of the Kwantung entered Shanghai to end an economic boycott against Japan by Chinese nationalists, though this incursion was reversed in March through negotiations in the League of Nations, which led to the withdrawal of the Japanese troops involved.

Given the nature of the 1889 Meiji Constitution, it was unsurprising that the Japanese military provided fertile ground for the rise of nationalist-militarist sentiment. Under Articles XI and XII of the constitution, the armed services were directly subordinate to the emperor and not the civilian Diet.¹¹ Therefore a radicalized Japanese army and navy could justify their excesses on the basis that they were acting in the sovereign's interests, and Emperor Hirohito appeared loath to pull the services into line. Additionally, the introduction of a series of laws and regulations by the Diet prior to 1930, most notably the Peace Preservation Law (1925), had steadily eroded civil rights and liberties.¹² From 1927 onwards the suppression of communist, socialist, and liberal Western tendencies became the prerogative of the so-called "thought police," the Tokubetsu Kôtô Keisatsu (Tokkô for short).¹³ And as foreign influences began to come under the gun, so did Japanese politicians, industrialists, and those members of the senior army and navy commands who did not fall into line. For the supposedly heinous crime of supporting the ratification of the Treaty of London, Prime Minister Hamaguchi Yuko was shot by an assassin on November 14, 1930, and died from his wounds nine months later.¹⁴ Then, in what came to be known as the "May 15 Incident" (May 15, 1932), radical naval officers murdered Prime Minister Inuka

Tsuyoshi, his finance minister, and a prominent banker in an abortive attempt to seize power. The demise of liberal influence in Japan in the early 1930s was enhanced by the slide of the nation's economy with the collapse of textile exports to Britain and the United States, which resulted in considerable poverty in rural Japan that played into the hands of the nationalist-militarists, as it was to do in Germany.[15]

British reaction to these events assumed the character of the carrot and stick. At the diplomatic level, MacDonald's National government was far less hostile toward the annexation of Manchuria than was the United States (the "Stimson Note" of January 7, 1932), although the approach hardened in the aftermath of the Shanghai episode.[16] From the late 1920s both the British and the Japanese had recognized the threats to their own interests in China through the expansion of Chinese nationalist and Soviet influences. In response to the annexation of Manchuria, the British did little more than call on the Japanese to respect the "Open Door" policy in Manchuria, and following the incursion at Shanghai, no British sanctions (let alone military action) were forthcoming.[17] Even following the report by the British-sponsored Lytton Commission to the League of Nations, which rebuffed Japanese actions in Manchuria, leading to Japan's withdrawal from the League on March 27, 1933, Britain's attempts to achieve Anglo-Japanese rapprochement continued. The dispatch of the Barnby (September 1934) and Leith-Ross (September 1935) missions to Tokyo sought a nonaggression pact and the recognition of Manchukuo upon the basis of joint Anglo-Japanese economic ties within the annexed province. Though Japan's civilian government was favorably disposed toward these initiatives, the Imperial Japanese Army thought otherwise.[18] To the militant Japanese generals the presence of British industries within Manchukuo was unacceptable, and they viewed the approaches by Whitehall as merely propping up British commercial interests in China. Both missions thus failed to achieve their objectives in the face of Japanese military intransigence.

Simultaneously, Whitehall took less conciliatory steps by way of response to the Manchurian and Shanghai incidents. On March 23, 1932, the British cabinet abandoned the imposition of the Ten-Year Rule, which had been formally operating in ambulatory form since 1928.[19] Then on March 27, 1933, Britain's foreign secretary, Sir John Simon, announced an arms embargo against both China and Japan. Less than a month later on

April 10, Britain abrogated the existing Treaty of Commerce with Japan. In this case the measure was likewise motivated by disputes between both nations over the textile trade and the decision taken at the Ottawa Conference (July 1932) by which Britain and the Dominions elected to erect protectionist imperial trade barriers.[20] In terms of a material military response to the events in the Far East, the RN was in no position to intervene, a position the Chiefs of Staff clearly raised in their annual review of imperial defense dated March 17, 1932:

> The question of the defence of Imperial interests in the Far East is raised by the Chiefs-of-Staff with special reference to the present Sino-Japanese dispute, and they point out that in present circumstances we are unable to resist Japanese aggression in the Far East. It may be granted that recent events have demonstrated not only to ourselves but to other countries, and particularly, no doubt, to Japan, that we are not at the present time in a position to defend our interests and possessions in the Far East against Japan.... But when all this has been granted, what is the alternative? To have put Hong Kong and Singapore in a condition in which they could be temporarily defended would not have been sufficient, though this in itself would no doubt have involved very substantial expenditure.... It would seem, therefore, that as regards the Far East we must for the time being be content with applying such deterrents as may be available.[21]

"The weakness of our present position" as referred to in an assessment of the Far Eastern situation by the Committee of Imperial Defence dated April 17, 1933, contributed to the formation of the Defence Requirements Committee in October of the same year. Reports from the new committee, however, were delayed until July 1934 in order for the ongoing Geneva arms limitation negotiations to proceed without external prejudice.[22] Talks had commenced in 1932, and this latest round of negotiations sought to address the control of armaments beyond a solely naval sphere. A central component to the talks was the proposition that aerial bombardment be largely prohibited, to which the British Air Staff was strongly opposed. With reference to the imperial aspect, the RAF maintained that "it would be a serious disadvantage if air forces at or within reach of Singapore... were deprived of the right of attacking ships with bombs and torpedoes."[23] The major sticking point, however, was the obstinacy of the French when it came to British support for the rehabilitation of Germany as a European power. In any event, the withdrawal of Germany from the talks in October 1933 and a subsequent stalemate in negotiations led to the effective collapse of the initiative in July 1934.[24] As a consequence, the Defence Requirements Committee made recommendations that the three armed services be made ready for war over the following eight years. In dealing with the question of air defense especially, the overriding intention of the RAF planners was the establishment of a powerful deterrent force.[25] The course of this process was, however, to exercise a serious impediment upon the operational capabilities of the Royal Navy, as will become apparent in due course.

By endeavoring to support Germany's return to the European fold as an equal partner, Whitehall was in effect engineering the very global dilemma it sought to avoid. In so doing the British essentially fell into the same trap as those conservative German politicians who had facilitated the coming to power of the National Socialists, namely the belief that Chancellor Hitler could be curbed by the existing power elites. Events such as the Reichstag fire, the passage of the Enabling Act, and the persecution of the new regime's opponents during the course of 1933 clearly demonstrated Hitler's aggressive tendencies on the domestic stage. Likewise, his oft-stated determination to be rid of the constraints imposed by the Treaty of Versailles, together with Germany's withdrawal from the League of Nations in October 1933, illustrated to the world at large that dealing with the Third Reich in an international setting would likely be fraught with difficulty. With Hitler assuming the powers of head of state following Hindenburg's death in August 1934, the way had been cleared for the new Fuehrer's desire to proceed with large-scale rearmament. Of especial concern to Whitehall was the supposed potential of the Luftwaffe as a strategic bombing air force, in fact a hollow facade that in the words of A. J. P. Taylor, led the British to be "frightened by a ghost of their own making."[26] At sea, Whitehall sought to head off a naval arms race by concluding the Anglo-German Naval Agreement on June 18, 1935. Under the terms of the pact, the Kreigsmarine was permitted to construct a fleet that was 35 percent the tonnage of the Royal Navy, while there would be parity in submarine tonnage between Germany and the British Empire.[27]

If the resuscitation of the German navy presented a possible new threat to British maritime security in the Atlantic and a possible two-ocean dilemma, the situation in the Mediterranean significantly compounded the problem. Though considerably smaller than the British fleet, Italy's Regia Marina was equipped with a range of powerful modern warships and submarines.[28] For the present the British could take comfort from the presence of the French fleet (Marine Nationale) in the western Mediterranean, which would act as an available bulwark against Italian aggression, though no military action was undertaken by either Britain or France against Italy when the latter invaded Abyssinia in October 1935. Provided that French naval power in the Mediterranean could be effectively sustained, the Admiralty possessed a far greater capacity to deploy adequate naval forces to the Far East if so required. In the absence of such support, the Royal Navy would be hard-pressed to deliver upon its commitments to the Far East and the Pacific, including the defense of Australia, especially if Germany and Italy made common cause against the British Empire. Furthermore, this potential dilemma stood to be considerably exacerbated in the event war came about prior to the rejuvenation of Britain's sagging fighting capabilities at sea.

As of December 1935 the situation in Europe had become increasingly ominous for the future maintenance of the interwar peace. Though it had not yet taken any form of aggressive incursion beyond its borders, Germany's ambitions were unmistakable. In March of that year the German government formally repudiated the Treaty of Versailles, which coincided with Hitler's announcement that military conscription was to be reintroduced. His diplomatic interactions with other European nations were likewise alarming, with the practical conduct of foreign affairs being gradually placed in the hands of Nazi toadies such as the odious Joachim von Ribbentrop.[29] For their part, a number of significant figures in British and French politics were at least acquiescent if not sympathetic toward the dictatorships in Berlin and Rome. Though an attempted accommodation with Mussolini over Abyssinia through the abortive Hoare-Laval Pact (December 1935) was aimed at sundering the relationship between the Fascist and Nazi regimes, it was to nevertheless usher in a period where concessions to the continental dictatorships became the order of the day.[30] And though Ramsay MacDonald had been replaced as the leader of the national government by Stanley Baldwin in

June 1935, Whitehall still remained committed to the concept of collective security through the League of Nations.[31] Within a matter of months, however, the specter of the two-ocean dilemma would come to assume far more menacing proportions. In January of the following year Japan's withdrawal from the London naval limitations accords signaled the onset of a new naval arms race, while the global sinews of the future Axis relationship were to be woven more tightly in December 1936 with Germany and Japan signing the Anti-Comintern Pact.

Through the combination of Japanese aggression in China and the establishment of the Nazi government in Germany, both Whitehall and the British armed services were compelled anew to consider the future of the Singapore naval base. In 1930 the Committee of Fighting Services recommended that while there should be no change to the policy of "ultimately establishing a defended naval base at Singapore," the previously contemplated completion date (1937) under the "truncated scheme" should be abandoned in view of the then-existing financial situation.[32] But following the Japanese incursions in Manchuria and at Shanghai, the Committee of Imperial Defence recognized the necessity to complete the base's defenses, and in a memorandum dated July 11, 1932, the CID resolved to continue the development of fortified coastal artillery positions at Singapore. In spite of submissions from both the Air Staff and the Admiralty that air attack would eventually supersede the power of fixed batteries, the committee saw no reason in the short term at least to depart from the previously determined coastal defense policy:

> Whether eventually attack by sea-borne aircraft on ports may replace bombardment by warships we cannot tell. The evidence we have received, however, does not support the view that it would be sound to base our coast defence system on the assumption that this development is imminent. If aircraft have improved since the war, the same is true of naval gunnery. . . . The fact that many foreign nations have recently rearmed their coast defences with heavy guns, and are continuing to do so, is an indication that they do not take the view that bombardment is about to be succeeded by air attack. Since it is foreign nations whose attack we have to apprehend, we think that for an indefinite time to come our coast

defence system must provide against ship bombardment as well as attack by aircraft.[33]

When considering an arms embargo against Japan and China in February of the following year, MacDonald's cabinet noted that such a decision would entail the "dire risk of war," and that Admiralty intelligence indicated that a Japanese scheme to attack Singapore "is possibly ready now."[34] Three months later the CID recommended to Whitehall that additional measures be taken. These included the construction of a second airfield and the deployment of further garrison troops.[35] In making these proposals the Chiefs of Staff Sub-Committee issued a grim assessment of the consequences that would follow if real progress in the development of Singapore's defenses continued to be compromised:

> It is sufficient to mention that the Naval Base at Singapore is the pivot of our whole naval strategical position in the Far East; that, until provided with adequate defences, the Naval Base and its facilities are liable to capture or destruction by a *coup de main* before our main fleet can arrive on the scene; that its recapture would be a major operation of the greatest difficulty; that in the meantime, the important Naval Base at Hong Kong would be liable to share the same fate as Singapore; that British territory in the Far East, including the coasts of India, Australia, New Zealand, and the various Colonies and Protectorates, would be exposed to depredation, and that our trade and communications in the Eastern Hemisphere would be, to a large extent, at the mercy of the enemy. . . . Up to now, however, the question of the defences has not been tackled in earnest, with the result that the resources of the Naval Base offer an inviting objective for an enemy desiring to dislocate our entire system of Imperial defence in the Pacific before the arrival of the Main Fleet.[36]

The preparation of the annual review of imperial defense policy by the Chiefs of Staff Sub-Committee in November 1933 was similarly important, given that it represented the first such review following Hitler's appointment as chancellor in January. It also marked the first contribution by Admiral Sir Ernle Chatfield, who had replaced Field as first sea lord in the same month and was to emerge as a driving force in the subsequent reinvigoration of the Royal Navy. Central to the review became the delineation of the separate problems in Europe and the Pacific, which were outlined in the following terms: "The two problems of Europe and the Pacific, however, are different in kind. The problem in Europe may resolve itself into the fulfilment of obligations into which we have entered at various times with the object not only of maintaining the peace of Europe, but of ensuring, as is vital to our security, that the Low Countries are not again overrun by a great continental power. The problem of the Far East is the defence of our interests and possessions."[37]

It is noteworthy that one of the bases for the recommendations as to the deployment of the British fleet was based on the assessment of the Foreign Office and other intelligence sources that Germany would pursue a rapid policy of rearmament, even though Hitler had yet to assume the roles of both head of state and head of government. From the naval perspective, the Far East continued to be the dominant theater in terms of dispositions. According to Admiralty estimates, the minimum force requirement to repel the Japanese in the event of war would be twelve capital ships, five aircraft carriers, and at least forty-six cruisers, virtually the entire available British fighting strength in these classes.[38] But Chatfield and his colleagues also recognized the urgent need for modification of the capital ship component. It was proposed that four capital ships be laid up for modification in 1934–1935, and that up to the year 1940, three such vessels "will be continually absent from the Fleet for large repairs."[39] It was also acknowledged that considerable air reinforcements would have to be assembled at Singapore over the next seven years, and the air defenses of Hong Kong were likewise to be significantly augmented. Yet at the same instant, the assignment of relatively minor naval forces in the Atlantic and the Mediterranean was based on the premise that if war broke out in Europe the Germans, in light of their experiences from the Great War, would look to the east instead of attempting to inflict a crushing stroke against the French.[40] Based upon the ongoing assembly of the Maginot Line, which the chiefs of staff believed would be impregnable once completed, this assessment was to prove a costly error of judgment.

An analysis of the future situation in the Far East by the Foreign Office in March 1934 revealed further bases for British thinking on the imperial defense problem. In this instance the conclusions were governed by the assumption that friction between Japan and the Western powers would be primarily fueled by trade competition and, with particular reference to Australia, the question of Japanese immigration:

> If anything more is meant than a determination to capture fresh markets for Japanese trade, then it is difficult to imagine how any such plans of political expansion could take concrete shape. None of the numerous very detailed reports that come from British Malaya have ever suggested that the Japanese are a political danger.... It is of course conceivable that the Japanese might make a descent upon the Netherlands East Indies in order to secure a source of oil supplies for their navy, or might seize the Philippines, or the Japanese navy might appear off Australia and demand the opening of the northern territories to Japanese immigration. But in view of her very serious military preoccupations nearer home, the danger that Japan will embark on wild-cat military adventures further afield hardly seems one that needs to be seriously guarded against.[41]

Separated in time by a matter of four months, these reports demonstrated the notable difference of opinion between the British armed services and the Foreign Office when it came to the question of Japanese intentions. Whereas the chiefs of staff were of the belief that Japan's actions in China had set the scene for a lengthy period of instability in the Far East, the Foreign Office believed that the Japanese would be placated by active rapprochement from Whitehall regarding issues of trade and the future status of Manchukuo.[42] Should the British government accept the latter view, the proposed commitment of the bulk of the Royal Navy to the Asia-Pacific region could not be strategically justified. Yet at the same instant, the Foreign Office examination outlined the influence of the ultranationalists within the Japanese armed forces, the friction between Japan's army and navy, and that "the real masters of Japan must be some group or groups of nameless officers of no high rank."[43] If this analysis proved to be correct then it followed that any form of effective Anglo-Japanese reconciliation would be compromised, given that it was likewise concluded by the Foreign Office that the attitude of the militarists was distinctly pan-Asiatic and anti-Western in character. Above all, these contradictory statements highlighted the apparent muddle within British diplomatic thinking during this period of heightening anxiety.

By July 1935 the Chiefs of Staff Sub-Committee had become positively anxious over the present state of the Singapore project. As had been the case since 1923, sound funding was central to the progress of the base and its defensive works. Financial relief was at last in sight, and it emerged from an unusual source. Fiercely loyal to the British Empire, the Sultan of Johore gifted the sum of £500,000 for the accelerated completion of construction.[44] Following discussion, the CID Sub-Committee on Defence Policy and Requirements recommended that the majority of the sultan's gift be allocated to the installation of the base's primary coastal defenses, two batteries containing a total of five 15-inch guns. Further proposals approved the construction of a third airfield and the strengthening of Singapore's land-based air defenses to five squadrons. Furthermore, the completion of the delayed Stage 1 coastal defenses was scheduled to take place in early 1937, with Stage 2 projects to continue thereafter.[45] In December 1935 a report from Anthony Eden, minister for League of Nations affairs, advised of the risks entailed if Britain sought to proceed beyond the limitations of Article XIX of the Five-Power Pact and take similar defensive measures with respect to Hong Kong:

> What is there likely to be the effect on Japan if we decide to turn Hong Kong into a first-class naval base? At the worst Japan might decide that it is best to strike while we are still weak in the Pacific and the capture of Hong Kong is a relatively simple matter. . . . Japan might take no offensive action of any kind, but might nevertheless regard our action in creating a first-class base at Hong Kong as something even more dangerous for Japan than our activities at Singapore and as evidence of definitely hostile intentions on our part. A change for the worse in our relations with Japan would definitely follow. The development of Singapore as a naval base has all along been distasteful to the Japanese, whose feelings would no doubt have been stronger if the progress made had been faster. . . . It is not suggested that these possibilities should, in themselves, deter us from fortifying Hong Kong, because, if we are to retain our position as a Great Power, we must

be prepared to run risks and take all steps we think fit for the defence of our territories.[46]

And for that matter, the defense of Australia. Within the previous four years, ever more serious doubts had been openly voiced within the senior leadership of the Australian army regarding the reliability of existing British guarantees to protect the external security of the Australian mainland. Having been apparently shaken from its Far Eastern slumber by the emerging menace of Japanese militarism, the seeming determination of Whitehall to shore up Britain's imperial muscle to the east of Suez could not have come too soon for the cause of Anglo-Australian defense relations. To do otherwise invited what the British Navy League had described in 1930 as "but a sorry return for what they [Australia and New Zealand] had done, and is little short of a betrayal of their confidence."[47]

"As Defenseless as She Is Now": The Australian Perspective, 1930–1935

With limited capital reserves, with comparatively narrow industrial and manufacturing bases, and overly dependent upon commodity exports, Australia in January 1930 was heavily exposed to the ravages of the Great Depression. By 1932 the nation's unemployment rate would reach 29 percent, one of the highest levels in the world. Adopting the advice provided by a visiting delegation from the Bank of England in August 1930, the Scullin Labor government pursued a range of deflationary measures in a desperate effort to alleviate the prevailing economic crisis.[48] Steep cuts to government expenditure had become the order of the day, and the nation's military needs were not exempted from this process. In common with the situation that had existed in the 1920s, the discourse among Australia's political and armed service establishments was not motivated by any form of imminent external threat, but rather by the prioritization of limited funding among the three services. And during the period from 1930 to 1935 this discussion was to intensify, fueled as it were by the so-called "raids versus invasion" debate, which itself was sustained by a growing belief among a number of the civilian and military participants that the Singapore strategy would likely fail if Britain became embroiled in another European war.

Table 5.2. Australian Defense Expenditure
(from Consolidated Revenue), 1926–1936*

1926–27: £7,890,839	1931–32: £3,184,836
1927–28: £7,385,800	1932–33: £3,159,960
1928–29: £6,536,482	1933–34: £4,157,494
1929–30: £4,885,987	1934–35: £5,457,800
1930–31: £3,859,069	1935–36: £7,014,432

*Note: the above schedule does not include payments for War Services Debt 1914–18.

P. Hasluck, *Australia in the War of 1939–45: The Government and the People 1939–41* (Canberra: Australian War Memorial, 1952), 41.

Before addressing the substance of the raids-versus-invasion controversy, it is important that the subject be placed in its proper context. As set out in the 1930 defense appreciation below, the expected primary military threat to Australia remained the likely prospect of naval attacks mounted against the nation's external trade routes, and this assumption was to remain fundamentally intact prior to December 1941. The question of whether a raiding or invasion strategy would be chosen by a hostile power (i.e., Japan) was concerned with specific physical threats to the Australian mainland and its offshore islands. It therefore does not (and did not) immediately follow that some form of attack against the continent itself was the most likely form of threat when considering the problem of Australia's external defense as a whole.

The invigoration of the raids-versus-invasion debate in the early 1930s owed much to the participation of Frederick Shedden, a highly able senior official within Australia's Department of Defence. While in London, where he attended the Imperial Defence College in the late 1920s, Shedden had been approached by the then–Australian defense minister Sir Thomas Glasgow to prepare a paper on imperial defense and its relation to Australia.[49] In late 1929 he completed the work under the title "The Principles of Imperial Defence with Special Reference to Australian Defence." Something of a protégé of Admiral Sir Herbert Richmond, the commandant of the Imperial Defence College and a firm adherent of the Singapore strategy, Shedden embraced the concept of the "mere raid" theory in his thesis.[50] In his view the primary role assigned to the nation's armed forces was to be their contribution to imperial operations. As for the defense of

Australia itself, Shedden surmised that the Japanese would confine their focus to raids, hit-and-run operations by small naval squadrons or minor amphibious operations against isolated targets.[51] Upon this latter basis the deployment of localized land, sea, and air forces would be limited to the repulse of such attacks. In due course the paper was referred to the new Labor defense minister Albert Green and henceforth Prime Minister Scullin, neither of whom elected to provide any comment on its substance.[52]

This indifference to Shedden's paper was principally motivated by the preoccupation of the newly elected Labor government with the effects of the economic crisis. Nevertheless, the new administration was fervently in favor of international disarmament and peaceful dispute resolution through the League of Nations. Having superseded the system of compulsory military training with a volunteer-based regime on October 31, 1929, Scullin's cabinet turned its attention to the RAN. In November of the following year the government determined to return the navy's two existing submarines to the Admiralty and to decommission a range of surface units.[53] On the subject of the future of the RAAF as an independent air arm, a government announcement in June 1930 confirmed its retention as such but contained little else in the way of forward policy.[54] The general attitude of Scullin's colleagues to defense matters was amplified in a series of speeches and submissions during the course of the same year. In an address to the House of Representatives in April, the future Labor prime minister John Curtin reasoned that peace was only possible when the profit motive for armaments production had been removed, and that such an initiative could only be undertaken by the League of Nations, as distinct from the employment of an ad hoc treaty system.[55] Frank Brennan, Scullin's attorney general, was equally resolute when he addressed the Eleventh Assembly of the League of Nations in September: "Australia tells the world, as a gesture of peace, that she is not prepared for war. We have given practical proof of our earnestness. We have drawn our pen through the schedule of military expenditure with unprecedented firmness. We have reversed a policy which has subsisted in Australia for twenty-five years of compelling the youth to learn the art of war."[56]

Whereas the government had been largely unmoved by the substance of Shedden's advice, the same could not be said for the reception it received from the director of military operations and intelligence,

Colonel John Lavarack. In 1928 the Defence Committee had approved compiling a national security appreciation based on the assumption that the Singapore base was incomplete.[57] On the basis of the conclusion that a limited Japanese invasion of Australia could not be definitively dismissed as a threat, Lavarack was instructed to prepare plans for such a contingency. Shedden, who had been elevated to the position of secretary to the Defence Committee, provided his existing thesis to a meeting of the Defence Committee on March 6, 1930, where the 1928 appreciation was discussed. During the debate that followed, Lavarack was scathing in responding to Shedden's views. Believing that the latter had largely ignored the effects of the London negotiations upon the Royal Navy's capacity to execute the Singapore strategy, Lavarack provided a particularly damning commentary: "The despatch of a British battle fleet to the Far East for the protection of Imperial (including Australian) interests cannot be counted on with sufficient certainty, and the risk that it will be withheld, added to the risk of the non-completion, capture, or neutralisation of Singapore, results in a total risk that no isolated white community such as Australia would be justified in taking."[58]

With the Royal Australian Navy supporting Shedden's advocacy against the opinions of both the army and the air force, the stage was set for a major showdown over the allocation of scarce defense funding. No agreement could be reached during the four Defence Committee meetings that followed in March, with the result that equal cuts across all three services were proposed.[59] Matters came to a head on April 11, 1930, at a further meeting of the committee, and the minutes of that gathering bear this out. On the question of the relevance of the 1928 appreciation, the following conclusions were reached:

The Chief of the General Staff and the Chief of the Air Staff reaffirmed the following conclusions recorded in such appreciation:

I. Extensive raiding of trade routes is certain and must be provided against.

II. Raids on important centres are to be expected and must be provided against.

III. Attack on Singapore, if the British Fleet is delayed, is a possibility, but not until after Hong Kong has been effectively disposed of (this is an Imperial commitment).

IV. Invasion of Australia, but only on a limited scale, is within the bounds of possibility and not so improbable as to allow of it being definitely ruled out.

The Chief of the Naval Staff, whilst agreeing with the conclusions of the appreciation, is strongly of the opinion that the naval strength of the Empire is sufficient insurance against invasion. The Chief of the General Staff desires to add a comment on this opinion to the effect that he is of the view, that, invasion being the only means by which an enemy could obtain a decisive result, it is a vital danger which should be further provided against by land forces, and shore-based air forces. With this the Chief of the Air Staff agrees.[60]

These opinions were replicated when discussion specifically turned to the topic of invasion. In this instance, however, the chiefs of the General and Air Staffs pointedly referred to the potential inadequacies of a British response. They rejected the navy's opinion "owing to doubts regarding the effective British naval power that could be brought to bear in the Pacific, both in respect of the strength that could be despatched from European waters, and the guaranteeing of the inviolability of the Singapore base."[61] Arriving at the question of expenditure, all three service chiefs agreed that raids were the more likely of the two threats to be realized, and in considering this problem, both Rear Admiral William Munro Kerr and Air Commodore Richard Williams agreed that defense against raids be afforded funding priority. In this instance the chief of the General Staff General Sir Harry Chauvel was alone in advocating joint priority for defense against both raids and invasion.[62] And in dealing with Australia's contribution to imperial naval defense as a whole, both Munro Kerr and Chauvel agreed that a financial payment to the Exchequer be determined afresh. In providing his concurrence on this point, Chauvel noted that an agreed sum must not be such that it would prejudice the primary responsibility of the Australian armed services, namely providing local territorial defense.[63]

In expressing their opinions, both Chauvel and Williams alluded to the prospect of a two-ocean dilemma, while Munro Kerr seemingly ignored the issue altogether. The response of the government to the deliberations of the Defence Committee was to essentially ignore them, and in the expenditure reductions that followed, it was the army that bore the brunt of the cuts.⁶⁴ This pattern was to continue in 1931 as the government further committed itself to the push for general disarmament in the League of Nations. In October of that year the three services were instructed to prepare position papers for consideration by "the League of Nations for the purposes of limitation."⁶⁵ During the course of 1931, however, the Scullin administration itself had begun to fracture. Green was replaced as defense minister by Senator John Daley in February, who in turn was succeed by J. B. (Ben) Chifley shortly thereafter. This revolving door largely paralyzed any further consideration of defense policy, as the Labor government followed a path parallel to that of its British Labour counterpart in the same year. In Scullin's case, a furious brawl with the state Labor government of New South Wales over the issue of due repayments to British bondholders split his cabinet. Spiraling unemployment and the influence of the Communist Party in the trade unions, which led to a stream of strikes and riots, did not assist matters.⁶⁶ Forced to the polls in December 1931, Labor was trounced by the United Australia Party (UAP), a combination of former National Party and dissident Labor members, in coalition with the Country Party.⁶⁷ The incoming coalition government was headed by Joseph Lyons, a previous Labor premier of Tasmania, who had defected to the new conservative party.

For assistance in dealing with matters of foreign affairs and defense, Prime Minister Lyons was aided by the presence of several old hands from the 1920s, including John Latham (external affairs) and Senator George Pearce (defense). In January 1932 the government reaffirmed its adherence to the basic imperial defense principles of the Bruce-Page administration and the following month announced a revised policy for the purposes of the forthcoming Geneva Conference. With Shedden as the secretary of the cabinet committee that determined the policy, it was decided that the army and the Royal Australian Air Force would be configured to defend against raids only, a decision that did not sit well with the new chief of the general staff, Major General Julius Bruche.⁶⁸ The major armed services problem occupying the minds of the new government was, however, the future of the RAAF. Abolition of the independent air force struck a positive chord within the cabinet, and the wider international push to abolish offensive military aviation at the Geneva Conference served as a powerful incentive.⁶⁹ Yet, as was the case with the general outcomes of the conference itself, the proposal fell flat on its face.

Fearing that this course of action would weaken imperial defense as a whole, the British Air Ministry and the RAF opposed it, and in May 1932 Lyons' cabinet dropped the initiative, a decision confirmed by Pearce in September of that year.[70] It appears that the refusal of the RAF to countenance the Australian proposal was motivated by a review of the 1928 Salmond Report by the Air Ministry, which concluded on May 31 that the RAAF could play a key role in the defense of Singapore, but for the present this conclusion was not further agitated.[71]

While performing his duties as Australia's delegate to the Geneva Conference, Latham also spent periods in London and attended a meeting of the Committee of Imperial Defence on June 9, 1932, where the question of resuming work on the Singapore base was discussed. He informed those present that, speaking on behalf of Australia, "he would be very glad" to see the project proceed because of the importance of Singapore to the security of the Dominions in the Pacific.[72] Later that year on November 8 the CID addressed Paper 372C, titled "Defence of Australia," together with other related material. Stanley Bruce, the former prime minister and Australia's new resident minister in London, was present at the meeting. Within this and other papers presented, the general assumption of the British chiefs of staff was as follows: "Provided that the British Fleet arrives in time and finds a properly equipped base at Singapore, Australia has nothing to fear beyond sporadic attack. If, for any reason, the main fleet is unable to reach Singapore, or if the base is seriously damaged by naval or air bombardment before its arrival, then Australian interests become exposed to attack on a considerable scale."[73] In the attached CID Paper 249C, which had been originally authored in 1925, the assumptions were more specific as to the minimum prerequisites for a workable Singapore strategy:

(a) The establishment of a Naval Base at Singapore capable of the maintenance of capital ships of the most modern type.
(b) The addition of a squadron of battle cruisers to the British Fleet in the Far East which would be based on that port; and
(c) The arrival of the British Main Fleet at Singapore within 42 days of the outbreak of war.[74]

It was decided by the committee that in-depth analysis of Paper 372C be deferred until the Australian government had had the opportunity to study it. Events in Australia meanwhile were to mark the gradual turn of the tide in bipartisan political support for disarmament through the League of Nations. By January 1933 the strength of the Australian armed forces had reached a new low. There were fewer than 28,000 trained troops, and the RAAF possessed twenty-eight "first-line" aircraft, all of which were obsolete. As for the RAN, its commissioned strength amounted to two cruisers, one destroyer, a depot ship, a sloop, and a motorboat.[75] Fresh concerns were likewise being raised over the Singapore strategy. At a meeting of the Military Board on March 29 it was noted that Paper 372C merely restated the 1925 appreciation (Paper 249C) with the exception of the removal of the battle cruiser component and weakening the so-called "period of relief" by declining to set out a definitive timeframe in which the British fleet would be sent to the Far East.[76] And at a meeting of the Committee of Imperial Defence on April 6, Bruce attempted to press home to his hosts the increasing gravity of the Australian situation. Noting the deteriorating circumstances in the Far East due to Manchuria and Shanghai, he warned that unless the Singapore project was expedited, Australia would have to allocate more funding to its own defenses, thus reducing Australia's warship contribution (two proposed new 10,000-ton cruisers) to imperial defense.[77] Back in Canberra, the government finally determined to take the bull by the horns. On October 5, Pearce announced an increase of more than £1,000,000 in the 1933–1934 Defence Estimates, the start of a three-year expansion program.[78]

Aside from echoing Australia's concerns over the Singapore project, which he was to do again in August 1933, Bruce had also taken Whitehall to task over another familiar Anglo-Australian malady: lack of consultation. In early March he had communicated Canberra's displeasure concerning Britain's decision to impose its arms embargo against China and Japan without first consulting the Dominion governments.[79] Yet it must be again emphasized that none of the problems being grappled with by Australia's political and military leaders, be they among themselves or with the British, were motivated by any fear of an imminent Japanese military threat in Southeast Asia or the Pacific. Indeed it was rapprochement with the Japanese that became the order of the day for the Lyons government when John Latham undertook a mission to Asia in April 1934, the first endeavor of its kind conducted by Australia to foreign countries. Commencing on April 1 with a visit to Macassar in the Celebes, the mission visited other centers in the the Netherlands East Indies, Malaya (including Singapore), French Indochina, Hong Kong, Japan, and the Philippines, with the last stop being at Menado on June 2. Trade issues were the principal object of discussion in most of the localities visited, though discussions with representatives of the Japanese Foreign Office did touch upon security issues.[80] Latham was well-received in Japan, with the Japanese foreign minister, Hiroya Koki, noting that Australia's proposal to appoint a trade commissioner to Japan "would be warmly welcomed." Overall the tenor of the visit to Japan was friendly and constructive; the British foreign secretary, Sir John Simon, praised the Australian initiative in the House of Commons on June 14.[81] Upon his return to Australia, the minister for external affairs urged Lyons to recognize Japan's control in Manchuria in order to reinforce regional stability:

> It appears to me that the policy of non-recognition of Manchukuo is going to meet increasingly greater difficulties as time passes. So far as one can judge there is not the slightest probability that Manchukuo will cease to exist. Certainly China can do nothing to interfere with the present position, and it does not appear to be at all likely that any other power would undertake the military operations which alone could alter the existing position. It is quite certain that Japan will never agree to the abolition of Manchukuo as an independent or quasi-independent state unless Japan is decisively beaten in war and forced to yield on what is regarded as perhaps the major point in present-day Japanese policy. Accordingly it appears to me that consideration should be given to the possibility of discovering some formula which would enable both Japan and the League to "save face" and get rid of what threatens to be a permanent source of poison in the relations between Japan and other countries. It is most improbable that any conceivable formula would satisfy any of the Chinese factions, but that could not be helped.[82]

Lyons took Latham's advice with him to a meeting of the British Commonwealth prime ministers in London in May 1935. On the basis of Latham's findings, Lyons counseled the prudence of such a move, but both the British and the Canadians thought otherwise because of the involvement of the League of Nations and the attitude of the United States.[83] At the same meeting Lyons informed his British hosts that Australia was content to leave the conduct of European diplomacy in the hands of the British government. With the recent escalation of continental tensions in mind, the prime minister "did not think Germany was so belligerently inclined as she was sometimes regarded, but he was not happy at the situation which had arisen as between Italy and Abyssinia, but here again he was content to leave matters in the hands of the Government of this country."[84] In Canberra the Australian government persisted in its attempts to highlight the need for the Western powers to seek an ongoing accommodation with the Japanese for the maintenance of regional security. Newly installed as minister for external affairs in 1934, Senator Pearce believed that Whitehall's persistent failure to recognize Japan's supremacy in the Far East, a "hard fact" in Pearce's analysis, would only further alienate Tokyo.[85] Lyons adopted a similar approach when, during discussions with President Roosevelt in Washington in July 1935, he raised the question of a possible Pacific pact involving Japan and the United States. In a subsequent discussion with Pearce, the U.S. consul-general in Sydney, Jay Pierrepont Moffatt, recorded the Australian viewpoint:

> He [Pearce] barely completed the usual amenities than he came to what was on his mind. This was that I would find that in matters of politics there was a feeling that America was indifferent to Australia's welfare and could not be counted on to come to her aid in case of need.... This had led Australia at large to feel that she could not count on American help in case of Japanese attack, a feeling which personally he did not share, but which none the less existed. This feeling was colouring Australia's policy vis-à-vis Japan. The Government remained suspicious of her ultimate intentions, but with British naval strength reduced below the safety point, and with American aid discounted, there was no policy open to her other than trying to be friendly with Japan.[86]

Latham's mission to the Far East had initiated a course of diplomacy that, as Pearce related above, was his nation's only practical means for shoring up its external security. It was to be followed in October of the same year by a similarly important episode in the ongoing saga of the internal Australian discourse over naval and military policy. In part motivated by Bruce's expressions of concern to the Committee of Imperial Defence in 1933, the CID's secretary, Sir Maurice Hankey, accepted an invitation to visit Australia. Ostensibly coming to mark the centenary of self-government in Victoria, the true purpose of Hankey's mission was, like Jellicoe's before him, to conduct a thorough investigation of the nations defenses.[87] Prior to his departure from England, Hankey had discussed the visit with Stanley Baldwin, then lord-president of the council, with particular reference to the Singapore project. Realizing that his hosts would ask him whether a British fleet would indeed be dispatched in the event of war with Japan, Hankey sought a guarantee from Baldwin to this effect. Baldwin was not prepared to issue such a guarantee, instead promising that Singapore's facilities would be advanced so that a fleet could attend in a major emergency, subject to a buildup in British naval strength pursuant to the outcomes of the forthcoming London Naval Conference in 1935.[88]

Seemingly satisfied with Baldwin's response, Hankey arrived in Australia on September 26, 1934. Prior to sailing from Sydney en route to New Zealand on November 17, he visited numerous defense facilities and ancillary industries, attended seven meetings of the Defence Committee, and held discussions with the nation's political leaders, including Archdale Parkhill, who had succeeded Pearce as minister for defense on October 12.[89] On the basis of his inquiries, which were assisted throughout by the presence of Frederick Shedden as his personal adviser, Hankey submitted an extensive report to Parkhill on November 15. Subsequent to his Australian visit, Hankey attended a joint Australia–New Zealand defense conference on November 23–24 in which a number of the aspects covered in his Australian report were reiterated. In drawing up his appreciation, he was guided by the contents of the Salmond Report (1928) together with the previous CID Papers 249C and 372C; his findings essentially updated and consolidated these three reports. As one of his initial remarks, he made it clear that financial circumstances permitting, Stage 1 of Singapore's defenses would be completed by the end of 1936, thereby providing "a considerable deterrent to attack."[90] With specific reference to the Royal Australian Navy, he stated that "it is imperative, from the point of view of public opinion, that the Commonwealth should maintain a naval force that can cooperate with the Royal Navy."[91]

Turning to the military situation, Hankey noted that his consideration of Australian army requirements exceeded the previous parameters of CID Paper 372C. He acknowledged the existence of "a strong school of thought originating in but by no means confined to Australian army circles" that rejected the strict application of the mere raid theory to Australian defense policy, and he took some trouble to address the specific concerns of those in the invasion camp. Specifically addressing the prospect of a two-ocean dilemma, Hankey's assurance was to the point. Even if confronted with a simultaneous conflict in Europe and the Far East, the current capital ship ratio between Britain and Japan (15:9) still permitted "a numerically superior battle fleet to be sent to the Far East."[92] Further referring to the threat of invasion, Hankey addressed the debate in the following terms:

> The correct solution appears to lie between the two extreme theories. . . . In strict logic my mind rejects the theory that Australia lies open to invasion so long as there exists a British fleet superior to that of Japan. But I have considerable sympathy with those who reject the extreme application of the "mere raid" theory to Australian Defence. National safety cannot be calculated on too narrow a margin. Public opinion, which is always ill-informed on these matters, cannot be ignored, and, in the absence of visible military and air defence in different parts of the Commonwealth, public opinion in time of war might demand the retention of the [Australian] fleet in Australian waters.[93]

By proposing a mobile land force of 35,000 and a sufficient air force to repel all but a full-scale Japanese invasion, Hankey's report represented a pragmatic means to conciliate the raids-versus-invasion debate. Yet at the same time he had not shrunk from his ultimate belief that the Singapore strategy was the best (and only) available means of ensuring Australia's external security. His report received a mixed response. Once the visit had been concluded, it did not take long for the various armed services combatants to dust off their cudgels and echo the arguments put forth at the Defence Committee meeting of April 15, 1930. The chief of naval staff, Vice Admiral George Hyde, supported Hankey's stance on imperial defense by arguing that Australia's primary commitment must be to naval defense (and naval expenditure). Air Commodore Williams essentially had a bet each way, supporting the Singapore strategy but doubting whether a sufficient fleet would be sent, while believing that the RAAF's first priority was to defend against raids.[94] Again it was the army officers who were most pronounced in their opposition. Major General Bruche insisted that while Hankey's findings be treated with respect, it was up to Australia's armed service advisers to take the major responsibility for furnishing advice.[95] Colonel Lavarack, Bruche's designated replacement as chief of staff, went further. After publishing an article in the 1933 *Army Quarterly* that criticized the viability of the Singapore strategy, he said of Hankey's advice that "there is little better reason for following British advice on local defence than there would be for following Australian advice on the defence of London against air attack."[96]

Joining the debate on the side of the army and the RAAF in 1935 was former prime minister William Morris Hughes. In his book titled *Australia and War Today: The Price of Peace*, Hughes set out the danger of a two-ocean dilemma in typically blunt fashion, emphasizing the potential impossibility of receiving British naval assistance in the event of a second world war:

> To-day a very different story must be told. Australia still relies on the British Navy, despite its reduced strength and the plain warning of British Ministers and naval experts that it is no longer able to guarantee the safety of Britain, or even to protect its food-supplies. Yet her dependence is more complete than at any time during these last thirty years, for her own defences are, despite marked improvements during the past twelve months, but pale shadows of what they were ten or twelve years ago. . . . In Europe the nations are armed to the teeth and the tension is such that war may break out at any moment. The situation in the East is highly unstable. Fleets without bases are as useless as guns without munitions; or armies without food.
>
> At the present time there are no bases in the Pacific from which a powerful British Fleet could operate. Singapore base is not yet completed. When it will be completed, or whether it can be held

after completion is a matter for speculation. No other base is available. . . . While we may be quite sure that Britain will do everything possible to help us if need arises—and I do not suggest for a moment that she could not and would not do a great deal—we cannot expect that the British people in the present disturbed state of Europe, would agree to the dispatch to the other side of the world of such powerful squadrons as would be necessary if Australia were attacked by a first-class Power, when this would leave themselves open to attack from any one of the great naval Powers of Europe.[97]

Following Hughes came a published essay titled "Japan and the Defence of Australia," authored by Edmund Piesse under the pseudonym "Albatross." Drawing upon his extensive experience dating back to his service in military intelligence during the Great War and thereafter as head of the Pacific Branch of the prime minister's office, Piesse proffered a similarly bleak outlook. On the prospect of a potential two-ocean dilemma, his assessment was particularly stark: "The danger of war in Europe grows month by month. Australia cannot ignore the probability that if war does occur no British Naval forces could leave European waters that would be of any use in defending Australia, still less in defending trade routes in the Pacific, Indian and Southern Oceans. What, for instance, would be done with the fleet if Japan and Germany were allied against Britain?"[98]

As Hughes had done, Piesse pointed to the fact that the Royal Navy was "over-age and under strength," and he specifically referred to the threat posed to Australian cities and ports by Japan's growing aircraft carrier strength.[99] Nevertheless he considered the threat of blockade to be greater than that posed by invasion. When it came to the issue that would cause Japan to become hostile, Piesse nominated the White Australia policy as the most likely source of trouble, though he freely admitted that there was no existing evidence that Japan sought to annex Australia by force of arms.[100] Given the serious prospect that Australia may be left alone to defend itself, he urged that the preparation of the nation's armed services be afforded top priority: "Short of war, Australia might be very embarrassed in her relations with Japan if Japan has armaments capable of use against Australia and Australia remains as defenceless as she is now."[101]

The final contribution to the debate in 1935 came from the man who had initially coined the term "two-ocean dilemma" in his 1912 essay. In a commentary published in the Melbourne *Herald* on December 31, 1935, Frederic Eggleston noted that with the conclusion of the Anglo-German naval agreement earlier that year, "she [Britain] must surely have abandoned all thought of transfer of any substantial part of her fleet to the Indian or Pacific Oceans."[102] Like Hughes and Piesse before him, Eggleston referred to the incomplete nature of the Singapore base and added the further observation for good measure: "Singapore is such a danger spot that it is not likely that any substantial British force will be immured there."[103] While recognizing that his views would not find favor within Australia's naval establishment, he believed that he undoubtedly enjoyed the support of both the army and the air force. And in concluding his assessment, Eggleston raised one of the core ideals that had resided in the mindset of Australia's leaders since the middle days of the six independent colonies: "Australia has different interests from those of any European power and should think out the policy required to protect them."[104]

Almost six years had passed since the signatories to the Five-Power Pact had reassembled in London to further advance the cause of comprehensive naval disarmament across the globe. As 1936 commenced they were again assembled in the British capital, but the hopes of January 1930 were by now a distant memory. Within a month both Italy and Japan were to withdraw from the treaty process, the latest blow to the interests of collective security, which had already suffered the exit of Germany, Japan, and Italy from the League of Nations and the effective collapse in July 1934 of the Geneva disarmament initiative. Manchuria and Abyssinia stood as recent markers for a new era of annexation via aggression, and National Socialist Germany was soon to embark upon a campaign of annexation via duplicity and blackmail. Similarly recovering from the ravages of the Great Depression, the Western democracies appeared powerless to prevent a gradual slide to war. This malady was personified by the lack of readiness on the part of the Royal Navy to fulfill its role as the first-line defender of both Great Britain and the wider British Empire, pending the fulfillment of a hefty rearmament program. And this was a task that would be complicated by the need to restart and re-equip the shipyards and ancillary armaments facilities that had been heavily impacted by the Great Depression. If one added to this the inevitable reconstruction of the German navy under the terms of the Anglo-German naval agreement, and the presence of Italian naval power in the Mediterranean, it was only a matter of time until the Empire east of Suez became a secondary consideration in the minds of Whitehall and the Admiralty.

Isolated and defenseless, Australia possessed few options for securing its security interests. Its most promising strategy in the short-to-medium term was to further solidify relations with Japan, especially while the Japanese were preoccupied with their situation in North Asia. The Australians had to buy the necessary time for the strengthening of their national defenses, and likewise for the stiffening of British imperial defenses in the region. But which should be afforded priority? After six years of debate between the national and imperial lobbies, the Lyons government still maintained its support for the latter, but it was not without challenge. Given the still-antiquated state of the Australian armed services in 1935, the newly installed leader of the opposition Labor Party, John Curtin, was poised to take the opposite view and make the nation's naval and military ill-preparedness an issue at the scheduled 1937 federal election. As for the assurances that had been provided by Sir Maurice Hankey, the latest of many regarding Britain's willingness to send substantial naval assistance in the event of a crisis, these stood on increasingly shaky ground. Over the next five years Australia would come to sound out the prospects of American assistance in various forms, including the acquisition of modern aircraft for the Royal Australian Air Force, and would persist in its inquiries of Whitehall as to the impregnability of the Singapore base and just how long it would take the "Main Fleet" to arrive there. Would the protection be worth the premium paid, in this case the cornerstone of Australia's homeland defense, and thus the survival of the Australian nation at a future time of imminent peril?

6

Something Less Than Fools

January 1936–August 1939

Rear Admiral Sir Herbert Richmond and Admiral Sir Richard Webb were both senior officers serving in the Royal Navy during the 1920s. Each served a term as commandant of the Royal Naval College, Richmond from 1922 to 1923 and Webb from 1926 to 1929. Richmond subsequently held the same post at the Imperial Defence College and was a keen supporter of the Singapore strategy. When asked by his Australian protégé Frederick Shedden to support the latter's 1929 paper on imperial defense, Richmond reassured Shedden that there was no doubt that a British fleet would be sent to the Far East and that the chances of a future war between the Empire and a German-Japanese alliance were of "a highly improbable nature."[1] Webb held precisely the opposite opinion. On the occasion of an address to the Royal United Services Institution in 1930, he made his assessment plain: "We are not only an Oceanic power in the widest sense, but also a European country with all Europe's complicated troubles and responsibilities at our door; that being so, to imagine that we are going to uncover the heart of the Empire and send our fleet thousands of miles into the Pacific with only one base, Singapore, for our supplies and damaged ships is to write us down as something less than fools."[2]

As the international situation grew increasingly ominous with the passage of years in the latter half of the 1930s, the wisdom of Admiral Webb's thoughts echoed ever more loudly within the corridors of the Admiralty and Whitehall. With time running short before the onset of hostilities in Europe, the glaring inadequacies of Britain's imperial naval defenses were no longer a matter for procrastinated inquiry; the various material ills that fettered the Royal Navy were undisguisable, as were the far wider deficiencies within Australia's armed services. Just restoring the Royal Navy's status as a one-power standard fleet required a rejuvenation of enormous size and expenditure, but even more ships were needed to ensure that the Singapore strategy could be successfully executed in the event of war with Japan. Pending this reconstruction, the dispatch of a large British fleet beyond Suez was no longer a realistic strategic option as Britain confronted the expansionist ambitions of the dictator regimes in Rome and Berlin.

Preparations and Anxieties: January 1936–April 1937

When signed by the participants on March 25, 1936, the second London Naval Treaty marked the critical turning point in the course of naval limitations since 1922. Quantitative measurements of the signatory fleets in the form of numeric ratios for capital ships and tonnage ratios for all other classes of naval vessel were to be superseded by a scheme of qualitative limitation. As described in a short memorandum to the Australian minister for defense dated January 23, 1936, the underlying principle of qualitative limitation was that a limit in size "prevents inordinate expenditure on the unit, and restricts individual power within the limits of ingenuity of design. The natural tendency to build a 'bigger and better' type indulged in before the [previous] War is thus avoided."[3] In seeking to avoid a repetition of Fisher's *Dreadnought* moment in 1906, the outcomes of the conference implicitly acknowledged a collective belief that while general naval rearmament could no longer be avoided, it could at least be controlled. Tonnage and armament ceilings were prescribed for individual warships within a series of designated classes. The size of a new capital ship was limited to 35,000 tons and its main armament limited to 14-inch caliber. Aircraft carriers were restricted to a maximum displacement per carrier of 22,000 tons, and future cruisers were reduced to 8,000 tons with 6.1-inch main armament.[4] Within Article 25 of the treaty, however, there was a provision whereby a signatory was entitled to "meet the requirements of his national security" and construct vessels beyond the agreed limits if nonsignatory nations proceeded to build ships that exceeded the stated size and armament ceilings.[5]

Both Japan and Italy were nonsignatories to the new treaty. In the latter instance the Italians had been angered by the economic sanctions imposed by the League of Nations following Mussolini's invasion of Abyssinia. The Japanese, however, had given due notice of their preparation to withdraw from the treaty process as required under the 1930 agreement. Japan's exit from the talks themselves was largely prompted by the inability of her delegates to persuade the other parties to permit the IJN numeric parity in battleships with Britain and the United States, a point of Japanese grievance since the days of the Washington negotiations.[6] The British response to the 1936 agreement came on March 3, twenty days before it was formally signed. In a statement to the House of Commons, Prime Minister Baldwin announced that two new capital ships were to be laid down in early 1937 following the expiration on December 31, 1936, of the existing "building holiday" imposed on such vessels. Provision was also made for the construction of a small carrier, five new cruisers, and the continued replacement of destroyers, submarines, and other small craft.[7] The specifications revealed by Baldwin did not, however, represent the complete picture of the Admiralty's anticipated rearmament program. As disclosed in a cabinet memorandum dated February 1, 1937, the minister for the coordination of defense, Sir Thomas Inskip, outlined the full schedule: seven new capital ships in 1937–1939, four new aircraft carriers (1936–1942), five new cruisers and three new submarines per year, new destroyer flotilla leaders (1936–1937), and the modernization of seven existing capital ships.[8]

Conducting its deliberations prior to Baldwin's statement to the House of Commons, the Committee of Imperial Defence's Defence Requirements Sub-Committee had determined that the only means of restoring the Royal Navy's operational strength was by way of constructing a two-ocean fleet. The number of ships involved in the committee's rearmament plan was, as McCarthy and other historians have remarked, insufficient to meet this objective.[9] The modification of seven capital ships meant that as many as eight of their existing compatriots would likely remain unmodified for naval operations at the outset of hostilities. The addition of seven new battleships would thus do little to revitalize an effective two-ocean presence while one-third of Britain's available capital ships were ill-equipped for deployment in a modern wartime setting. Yet regardless of the scale of rearmament being proposed, the British shipbuilding industry was, as of January 1937, in no position to accelerate construction, because of the immediate need to reactivate facilities and retrain workforces.[10] Furthermore, the Admiralty was exposed to similar difficulties in another field of development and production, namely that of naval aviation. In a memorandum by the secretary of state for air dated January 14, 1937, the planned first-line strength of the RAF as of April 1939 was to be expanded to 2,422 aircraft, of which 1,681 were to be bombers; this figure was based upon an estimated first-line strength of the Luftwaffe in the vicinity of 2,500 aircraft.[11] The assembly of a state-of-the-art Fleet Air Arm for the RN would prove to be impossible prior to September 1939 because of the consequential low priority assigned to the production of carrier-borne aircraft.

While Baldwin's government had been reluctantly compelled to pursue a policy of general rearmament, British diplomacy was still aimed at achieving separate rapprochements with Japan, Italy, and Germany. In spite of the recent failures of the Barnby and Leith-Ross missions to achieve a settlement of Anglo-Japanese relations regarding China, another opportunity presented itself in October 1936 through an approach by Japan's ambassador to the United Kingdom, Yoshida Shigeru. Though the so-called Yoshida Memorandum was initially rejected by the British Foreign Office, a Japanese economic mission was nevertheless dispatched to Britain and the United States on April 28, 1937, and discussions with the British were to commence following the conclusion of the 1937 Imperial Conference.[12] The difficulties in achieving a successful outcome stemmed from the Foreign Office's wariness of entering into an agreement that might compromise Anglo-American relations, and the attitude of the Japanese militarists. As noted in a memorandum prepared by the Australian Department of External Affairs for consideration at the Imperial Conference, it was doubted that the radicals in the Imperial Japanese Army would accept any agreement because "the alleged antagonism and obstruction of Great Britain to Japanese aspirations" formed a crucial plank in their justification for Japanese rearmament.[13] The potential for a future settlement was further compromised through an abortive coup by an extremist faction of the Imperial Japanese Army on February 26, 1936. Though the rebellion was crushed and a number of its ringleaders were subsequently executed, the "February 26 Incident" ushered in a period of instability within the Japanese government that would persist until the appointment of Prince Konoe Fumimaro as prime minister in June 1937.[14]

In their dealings with the Italians, the British were impeded by the effects of the Abyssinian crisis, which had resulted in economic sanctions against Italy imposed by the League of Nations. The specter of a military alliance between Italy and Germany spread considerable alarm within Whitehall, and the primary objective of British diplomatic interaction with Mussolini's regime was to prevent the establishment of this union.[15] Efforts in this regard were not assisted by the outbreak of the Spanish Civil War in July 1936, which led to the direct involvement of Italian and German troops and aircraft in support of the Falangist cause. Though a nonaggression agreement would be eventually finalized between the parties in April 1938, Mussolini was not to be swayed from Hitler's side.[16] As for confronting National Socialist Germany itself, British intentions were made clear in Whitehall's response to the remilitarization of the Rhineland on March 7, 1936. This action constituted a violation of the terms of the treaties of Versailles and Locarno, yet no military response from either Britain or France was forthcoming. Instead the British sought to hose down the possibility of French and Belgian sanctions against Germany and resolve the issue through negotiations with the German government.[17] This response was to herald what eventually became a general policy of appeasement toward Germany. It was the belief of a number of senior British (and Australian) conservative politicians that constructive consultation with Germany would only be possible once the restrictions of Versailles were removed, and Hitler's regime was likewise viewed by some as the lesser of two evils when compared with Stalin's tyranny in the Soviet Union.[18]

The prospect of Germany acting as an eastern bulwark against Bolshevism certainly served as an enticement to those who supported better relations between Britain and the Third Reich. In the west, however, the chief rampart against Hitler's designs was the French army, and France in the mid-1930s was no longer the great military power that had gone to war in August 1914. The Popular Front government that had come to office in 1936 initiated a wide-ranging nationalization of French industry, with ultimately disastrous outcomes for the nation's rearmament schedules, most especially within the French aviation industry.[19] In the field the French generals were still welded to the tactics of the Great War, imagining they were shielded by the supposedly impenetrable Maginot Line. Immediately following the Rhineland's remilitarization, a concerned

Whitehall supplied a guarantee of assistance to the French government under the terms of the still-existent Anglo-French Alliance.[20] The British knew full well that the collapse of French arms would open the door for Hitler to subvert or conquer all of Western Europe, which in turn would lead to a direct armed threat against Britain itself. In addition, the recent crisis in the Mediterranean had demonstrated the importance of the French fleet to the Admiralty's capacity to wage war beyond the Atlantic. Almost three-quarters of the Royal Navy's available strength had been deployed to the Mediterranean to cover any hostile Italian naval activity, a scale of expedition that would be almost impossible should Britain find herself at war with both Italy and Germany.[21] A powerful French naval presence would not only resolve this conundrum but also provide the Admiralty with greater scope in assembling a force to steam to the Far East if so required.

The necessity for French naval support added a further variable to what was becoming an increasingly conditional assurance to the Australian government that a British fleet would be sent to Singapore. At the Commonwealth prime ministers' meeting in May 1935, Prime Minister Lyons had been informed that along with the necessity for French assistance, "sufficient cover" could not be dispatched until 1940 at the earliest, provided there were enough capital ships and cruisers then in operational service to send.[22] In spite of this advice the Australian government retained its belief in the integrity of the Singapore strategy as the debate within Australia over its viability evolved into a partisan political issue. Prior to the second half of 1936, domestic criticism of the strategy had been largely confined to senior officers within the nation's armed services and civilian commentators with expertise in the fields of defense and foreign affairs. Chief among the former was the now Major General John Lavarack, who had succeeded Major General Bruche as the Australian army's chief of staff in April 1935, and Lieutenant Colonel Henry Wynter, the director of military training and a long-standing skeptic of the Singapore project since the mid-1920s. At a meeting of the Defence Council on August 24, 1936, the defense minister, Archdale Parkhill, observed reprovingly that Lavarack's views were "implications of a highly political nature and the subject is one solely for the United Kingdom and Commonwealth Governments."[23] When elements of Lavarack's and Wynter's criticisms were employed by the leader of the Labor opposition,

Prime Minister Andrew Fisher (1908–1915). In his three terms as Australian prime minister, Fisher experienced firsthand the problems of reconciling national and imperial defense priorities, which would eventually compromise Anglo-Australian defense relations in World War II.
National Archives of Australia

Senator George Pearce, Australia's long-standing minister for defense.
National Archives of Australia

The feisty William "Billy" Morris Hughes. As Australian prime minister from 1915 to 1923, Hughes regarded Japan as the major threat to Australia's external security, and played a major role in derailing Japan's attempt to add racial equality language to the covenant of the League of Nations at the Paris Peace Conference in 1919. *Australian National Archives*

Stanley Bruce, Australian prime minister, 1923–1929. Having assented to the implementation of the "Singapore strategy" at the 1923 Imperial Conference, Bruce took the British to task in July 1939, when, as high commissioner to London, he learned that concrete Admiralty plans to deploy a fleet to Singapore were nonexistent. *Australian National Archives*

Admiral Lord Jellicoe, RN. Jellicoe's survey mission to Australia in 1919 aroused the anger of the Admiralty when he recommended the establishment of an Imperial Pacific Fleet. *U.S. Naval Institute photo archive*

Admiral Robert E. Coontz, USN (*center*). *U.S. Naval Institute photo archive*

The visit of the U.S. Navy's Combined Fleet to Sydney, 1925. The voyage to Australia was used by Admiral Coontz to experiment with procedures in long-range, self-sufficient fleet operations on the other side of the Pacific. *U.S. Naval Institute photo archive*

Robert Menzies, prime minister of Australia, 1939–1941.
Australian National Archives

Sinking of the Italian cruiser *Bartolomeo Colleoni* on July 19, 1940, by HMAS *Sydney*. *Sydney* was sunk with all hands on November 19, 1941, by the German auxiliary cruiser *Kormoran* off the coast of Western Australia.
Australian National Archives

A CAC Wirraway multirole aircraft en route to Singapore, 1940. Converted from a training aircraft, the Wirraway was Australia's front-line fighter plane at the outset of the Pacific War, but was easily outclassed in combat by the far superior Japanese Zero (Zeke). *Australian National Archives*

Prime Minister John Curtin (1941–1945) (*front right*) and Frederick Shedden (*left*). In spite of their differences over Australian defense policy in the 1930s, Curtin and Shedden (secretary to the Department of Defence) forged an effective wartime partnership. *Australian National Archives*

Merchant ships burning and sinking in Darwin Harbour during the Japanese air attack, February 19, 1942. *Australian National Archives*

Sinking of the Japanese carrier *Shōhō* at the battle of the Coral Sea, May 5–11, 1942. *U.S. Naval Institute photo archive*

One of the three Japanese midget submarines that attacked Sydney Harbour on May 31, 1942, on display outside the Australian War Memorial.
Australian National Archives

Sinking of the USS *Hornet* at the battle of Santa Cruz, October 26, 1942. Though suffering heavy casualties throughout the Solomons campaign, the USN emerged victorious, and Australia's external security was finally assured as a result of the lengthy war of attrition for possession of Henderson Field on the island of Guadalcanal. *U.S. Naval Institute photo archive*

John Curtin, in the House of Representatives during November 1936 the government took swift action. Believing that these critiques indicated disloyalty on the army's part, Parkhill ordered an inquiry by the Military Board, which resulted in Wynter's demotion from his post.[24]

Curtin's adherence to the cause of national defense was an attempt on his part to assemble an electorally viable Labor defense policy on behalf of a party that found itself deeply divided over its response to the various international crises of the day. Splits were evident in Labor's response to the Abyssinian crisis, and even more so when it came to the Spanish Civil War.[25] In this instance the Irish-Catholic conservatives leaned toward Franco, the socialists supported the Republicans, and an isolationist rump opposed any Australian involvement whatsoever. Curtin's response to the imposition of sanctions on Italy due to Abyssinia reflected the isolationist viewpoint: "Australia is different and distinctive in character from countries of the old word, and we should occupy a distinctive place in the conflicts of the world. . . . We should not be dragged willy-nilly into every European dispute. We should be the sovereign judges of what we should and should not do."[26] Nevertheless he clearly grasped that his party would be likely trounced by the UAP government at the polls in 1937 if a credible policy position on defense was not formulated, and the occasion of the 1936 Labor Interstate Conference provided the platform to rectify this. Aside from declaring the party's "greatest abhorrence of war and Fascism," the Labor position was entirely devoted to the creation of an effective national self-defense capability. Central to this initiative was the development of Australia's logistical base in areas such as munitions, transport, and fuel reserves, with the first line of continental defense to be provided by the Royal Australian Air Force.[27]

The marked contrast between government and opposition defense policies came to the fore during debate in the House of Representatives in November 1936 concerning the 1936–1937 Defence Estimates. Initiating a new three-year program, the total defense vote amounted to £8,783,070, the largest sum invested in the Australian armed services since 1918.[28] Speaking in favor of the proposed funding, Defense Minister Parkhill echoed the views of the Admiralty that naval expenditure must take into account the global responsibilities of imperial naval defense. This had been reflected in the Naval Board's expenditure submission, which was again based on Admiralty advice that the RAN's best contribution to the imperial system was through the purchase of new cruisers.[29] In making his case, Parkhill emphasized the point that "no dominion is capable of providing absolutely for its security by its own efforts alone." By way of reply, Curtin warned against Australia's reliance upon Singapore as the nation's primary safeguard: "That is our case. The dependence of Australia upon the competence, let alone the readiness, of British statesman to send forces to our aid is too dangerous a hazard upon which to found Australia's defence policy."[30] On the subject of local defense, however, there was a commonality of purpose between both parties concerning the development of the RAAF. The formation of the Commonwealth Aircraft Corporation in October 1936 significantly advanced the cause of localized aircraft production, with the provision of considerable American financial assistance in the form of a 25 percent holding in the enterprise by General Motors–Holden. This initiative had been taken in the face of stiff opposition from the British Air Ministry, whose policies regarding the supply of aircraft to Australia shall be revisited shortly in greater detail.[31]

Responding to Curtin's demand for far greater independence in the conduct of Australian foreign policy, Lyons was prepared to follow the British lead in Europe, and he communicated this intention to his hosts at the 1935 prime ministers' conference. In a cable to Whitehall following the events in the Rhineland the prime minister supported Britain's efforts to find a peaceful solution: "Commonwealth Government concurs wholeheartedly in United Kingdom attitude and endeavour to find a formula as to present status of Rhineland which would be acceptable to Germany without undue loss of prestige and pending the negotiations for a general settlement with German proposals as basis of discussion. . . . We suggest that any proposal should have the appearance of being based upon Hitler's proposals rather than upon Germany's breach of Locarno Pact."[32]

A second instance of loyalty toward Britain and the wider Empire came about in May 1936, when the Lyons government adopted a trade diversion policy that exposed American and Japanese importers to license fees and tariff preferences on their goods. At the conclusion of his statement announcing the move in the House of Representatives on May 22, the responsible minister, Sir Henry Gullett, noted that attempts to make a "friendly arrangement" with the Japanese government over the exclusion of Japanese textile imports had been unsuccessful.[33] Given that Lyons' plan for the creation of a Pacific pact required cooperation from both Japan and the United States, the implementation of trade diversion stood out as a foolish provocation, and the policy was rescinded in December of the following year.

Though Lyons' advocacy had previously failed to gain British support at the prime ministers' conference, the Australian pursuit of a Pacific pact was to form the key plank in the nation's foreign policy platform at the forthcoming Imperial Conference. In explaining the necessity for a regional nonaggression pact to the House on September 29, 1936, Attorney General Robert Menzies confirmed (in answer to a query from Curtin) that an agreement could be reached that would act within the spirit of Article XVI of the League of Nations Covenant, given that Japan and the United States were nonmembers, and could do so without infringing any of the covenant's vital provisions.[34] While the future of this proposal was further complicated by Japan and Germany entering into the Anti-Comintern Pact in November 1936, the Australian government remained committed to supporting its cause. The issue was to fall under the broader umbrella of achieving imperial cooperation on a global basis, including the relationship between the British Empire's foreign policy and the League of Nations and the approach to be taken in dealing with the European dictator powers. For these purposes the Australian delegation was well-prepared with position papers to discuss the problems at hand.[35] A February 1937 memorandum prepared by the Department of External Affairs displayed considerable foresight in plotting the oncoming dangers of German expansionism in particular:

> Probably German ideas of foreign policy are in a state of flux and they do not quite know what they want, and their actions since 1933 have been opportunist in taking advantage of a difficult economic and political situation both international and as regards individual states. Apart from the return of colonies, there are still some German demands such as the status of Danzig, Memel, Luxemburg, the union of Austria and Germany, the revision of frontiers and German minorities, particularly in Czechoslovakia, which are likely to come to the front at any time and which may not only increase the prevailing tension, but cause a general conflagration.[36]

Notwithstanding the unique importance of each of the diplomatic situations for which the Australian government had requested advice from the British, the common contextual thread shared by all was their impact upon the practical application of the Singapore strategy. Among the no less than twenty defense papers prepared for the Australian delegation, Paper No. 4 set out two questions relating to the nation's most fundamental strategic concern:

> 10. (1) *Strategical appreciation of defence against invasion*
> The Commonwealth Government would be glad to be furnished with a strategical appreciation of the danger to Australia of invasion and the defence against same, in the light of the Naval situation and the security of the Singapore Naval Base and the line of communications thereto—(a) For the period up to 1942; (b) After 1942.
> It is desired to know whether, in certain circumstances (the reasonable probability of which might be indicated), it would be possible for Japan to undertake major military operations with an object and on a scale amounting to invasion, against Australia. The probable form and scale of such an attack might be stated. It is also desired to know the probable period of warning that might be available for completing preparations for defence after the first obvious indication of a threat of war.
> (iii) *Strategic assumptions*
> The Government in the light of the strategical appreciation of the defence of Australia against invasion, which is sought in Paper No. 4, would like advice on the validity of Assumption (c)—"The arrival of the British Main Fleet at Singapore with a minimum of delay after the outbreak of war in the Far East."
> (Note: The phrase "minimum of delay" connotes some period comparable with the terms used in C.I.D. Paper 249-C, Part I, Paragraph 8 (C) viz, "The arrival of the British Main Fleet at Singapore within 42 days of the outbreak of war.")[37]

The choice of 1942 as a dividing line in defense preparations had been based upon a request by the Commonwealth in Paper No. 3. It sought advice regarding the completion dates for individual armed service programs under the umbrella of Australia's overall defense program. Relying upon previous advice, the submission noted that "the United Kingdom Government is working on plans for the completion by 1939 of its defences against any risk from Germany, and the British position in the Far East *vis-à-vis* Japan is unsatisfactory until 1942, owing to the time required for new naval construction."[38] This extract represented the biggest hurdle confronting the Australian delegation when it journeyed to London. In submitting their arguments to Whitehall, Lyons and his colleagues were burdened with the knowledge that the Far East was being steadily relegated to second priority behind Europe in British strategic thinking. Unless they could press home the need for adequate resources to be sent to Singapore, and likewise be given some priority for the purchase of defense material from Britain so that the nation's domestic defenses could be strengthened, Australia would be left helpless at a time it could least afford it. But to do so, the prime minister and company were committed to running that by-now most tenuous of arguments, namely that the Pacific and Far East were as important to Britain as the British Isles themselves. With Hitler already casting impatient glances in the direction of Austria and beyond, it would not have been unremarkable for at least some senior members of the Australian delegation to have had thoughts of snowballs and Hades in mind when contemplating the likelihood of this view being afforded a favorable response.

The 1937 Imperial Conference

The Imperial Conference opened on May 14, 1937, two days after the coronation of King George VI. To pursue Australia's interests, Prime Minister Lyons was accompanied by the minister for defense, Sir Archdale Parkhill, the treasurer, Richard Casey, and Stanley Bruce in his capacity as Australian high commissioner in London. The secretary of the Department of External Affairs, Lieutenant Colonel W. R. Hodgson, and Frederick Shedden as first assistant secretary in the Department of Defence, were among the delegation's most senior advisers. To confer with the Dominion delegations, Whitehall had assembled a heavyweight lineup led by Prime Minister Stanley Baldwin, with all relevant government departments represented at ministerial level. In November 1936 the British had indicated to Canberra that both foreign affairs and defense were the major topics for discussion at the conference, but included a rider that such conversation would be of a general nature only.[39] This was backed up on March 3, 1937, by the suggestion from Whitehall that subjects for discussion be categorized as either general or "technical," with topics in the latter category being dealt with at a subordinate level outside the confines of the conference itself. The suggestion was subsequently followed throughout the proceedings, and, as Paul Hasluck later observed, the conference never got to examine in depth "those vital questions of survival which were facing the British Commonwealth and each of its members."[40]

The first of the foreign policy issues to be addressed was the future relationship between the British Empire and the League of Nations. In the view of all the delegations bar New Zealand, reform of the organization's covenant was necessary because the league had failed to settle the Sino-Japanese, Chaco, and Abyssinian crises.[41] The Australians argued also that the integrity of a unified imperial approach toward foreign policy and defense could be compromised by strict adherence to the league's articles: "The future cohesion of the Empire would in a large measure depend upon the extent to which British foreign policy could command the confidence and support of the Dominions. If that policy were based purely on European considerations, then the Dominions might well be unwilling to co-operate."[42] Yet the creation of a conference policy platform for presentation as a remedy to these problems was stymied by differences between the delegations over the best means for achieving effective reform. At the same instant, the league's existing means to foster collective security could not be publicly disowned by the conference members because of the far broader diplomatic instability that would have inevitably followed. Instead, the conference framed a series of general principles emphasizing the conduct of Empire foreign policy in a manner consistent with the principles of the covenant, but it simultaneously reserved the right "to adopt such measures of defence as are deemed essential for their [the Commonwealth members'] security, and for the fulfilment of their respective international obligations."[43]

When the conversation turned to the European situation on May 21, an Australian proposal (with South African support) for rethinking existing British foreign policy in Europe fell flat on its face. In preparing several preconference position papers dealing with this topic, the Department of External Affairs had proceeded on the basis that

Whitehall was seeking at all costs to avoid any simultaneous threat from Germany, Japan, and Italy.[44] The Australian solution to this problem was to split Berlin and Rome by what Christopher Waters has characterized as a policy of proactive appeasement.[45] By Britain agreeing to Anschluss between Germany and Austria, it was hoped that the Italians would be perturbed by the existence of a shared border between themselves and Germany in the Brenner Pass, and thus be encouraged to reenter the British fold. Furthermore, granting Germany a freer hand in Eastern Europe would resolve issues of German expansion before Hitler sought to achieve his aims by resorting to force of arms.[46] British foreign secretary Anthony Eden vigorously rejected this approach in a speech the following day and again on June 3, where he stoutly defended Britain's opposition to any Anschluss unless the majority of the Austrian population desired it.[47] The foreign secretary also noted that as France had separate agreements with nations such as Czechoslovakia, any proposal to give Hitler a free hand would likely damage relations between London and Paris. Lyons quickly backed down, and on June 1 he cited Australia's declared principle of seeking friendship with all nations when urging his fellow Dominion representatives to support British foreign policy in Europe.[48]

By contrast, Australia's case for a Pacific pact was received by Whitehall with cautious interest. At the fourth meeting of the principal delegates on May 22, Eden welcomed Prime Minister Lyons' initiative, noting that such agreements "might play a part in producing a *détente* and he would do nothing to discourage any attempt to consolidate the situation in any part of the world."[49] Eden's response to the Australian proposal did, however, identify several reservations. He believed that the conference must be sure "that a Pact of Non-Aggression would contribute to that end before we embarked upon it, because after all a simple Pact of Non-Aggression only repeated what was already contained in the Kellogg Pact, and to reaffirm Treaties might only have the effect of casting doubt on their validity." Additionally, the foreign secretary, in noting the desirability of American participation, cautioned the Australians that the effectiveness of such an agreement may not extend beyond moral value alone.[50] Responding to Eden's request for further particulars, the Australian delegation prepared a supplementary memorandum that emphasized the expired Four-Power Pact as a structural model. By way of buttressing their proposal, the

Australians specifically noted that "any pact of mutual assistance for the Pacific, having a military character, is neither practicable nor desirable, as a Pact of this nature would command little support, and would only add to the commitments of the British Commonwealth."[51] Agreeing that the future implementation of such a pact was "a desirable objective," the conference resolved that the matter be given further consideration, with steps to be taken (in secret) to sound out the views of other interested parties such as China, the Netherlands, and the Soviet Union.[52]

Discussion of the Singapore strategy commenced at the seventh principal delegates meeting on May 26 with an address from the first lord of the admiralty, Sir Samuel Hoare. At the outset Hoare acknowledged the public airing of doubts over the Admiralty's capacity to dispatch a fleet to the Far East. His response was to reiterate the view that the very existence of the Empire itself depended upon this capability, and that the Singapore base was "now happily" approaching its scheduled completion date.[53] In a direct retort to Australian critics of imperial defense, Hoare bluntly asserted that a full-scale Japanese invasion of the continent could not be successfully resisted by any level of ground and air defense that the Australians could conceivably assemble. Turning to the likely strength of a British fleet presence, he said that as of May 1937 the Royal Navy was capable of sending an "adequate fleet," but he alerted his audience to the difficulties that would emerge over the following three years:

> Looking ahead we appreciate that there will be a period, from the Spring of 1938 to the Summer of 1939, when we could only retain forces in Home Waters barely adequate to meet the naval forces of Germany and must rely on being assisted by the French Navy. We could still send to the Far East a Fleet, but it would be, from a purely material point of view, slightly inferior to the full Japanese naval strength. By the adoption of a defensive policy and, relying on the superior fighting qualities of the British race, this Fleet should achieve its object of assuring the Dominions from serious aggression ...
>
> But let us look further ahead and contemplate the time when the battleships now building in other European countries have been completed. A study of comparative numbers at once shows that after 1940, or thereabouts, from the standpoint of Capital ships alone, the despatch of a fleet to the Far East would be a most

hazardous undertaking unless our battleship strength is increased above the number of 15 ships. The problem of maintaining the standard necessary in the years beyond 1940 is one therefore that will call for effort and expenditure of unprecedented magnitude...

These forecasts are based on our own new construction programmes and on the present known intentions of Germany. Thanks to the Anglo-German-Naval Agreement of 1935, whereby Germany voluntarily restricted herself to a limited of 35 per cent of British naval strength, we can face the future, as far as the German Navy is concerned, with equanimity. Japanese intentions are, on the other hand, still shrouded in oriental mystery.[54]

Responding briefly on Australia's behalf, Sir Archdale Parkhill made one specific point. He emphasized the opinion of the British chiefs of staff that in the event of a world war, "no anxieties or risks connected with our interests in the Mediterranean can be allowed to interfere with the despatch of a fleet to the Far East." On the wider substance of Hoare's remarks, Parkhill expressed his general satisfaction but indicated that he wished to study the British appreciation more closely before delivering a response, as he likewise wished to do with the suggestion from the chiefs that Australian ground and air units be stationed at Singapore.[55]

A follow-up briefing from the first sea lord, Admiral Lord Chatfield, took place a few days later on June 1. While noting the danger posed by a hostile Italian fleet in the Mediterranean to Britain's line of communications between Europe and the Pacific, Chatfield reinforced Parkhill's observation from the gathering on May 26 by asserting that potential base losses in the Mediterranean were recoverable, whereas similar losses in the Pacific were not.[56] Of specific relevance to Australian concerns, he set out the time factors and strategic considerations that would govern both the dispatch and operations of a fleet sent to Singapore:

In addition to the passage time for the Fleet, either via the Mediterranean or via the Cape, 10 days had to be allowed for the necessary preparatory measures such as docking, fuelling and storing the Fleet prior to its sailing for the Far East. 15 days had also to be added for possible delays due to weather and for re-fuelling en-route. The net result was that the Fleet might not arrive at Singapore before either 53 or 70 days after the order to sail, according as to whether it proceeded via the Suez Canal, or the Cape. These times made no allowance for delay in giving the orders to the Fleet to sail, due to political or other factors . . .

In the best case, war with Japan might not start until we had fully developed our naval resources and while the Germans, on the other hand, were maintaining a defensive attitude. In the worst case, we might not have had time fully to develop our naval resources, and the Germans for their part might have assumed a vigorous offensive against our trade in the Atlantic . . .

Once war with Japan has broken out, our policy must be governed by the consideration that, until the issue with Germany has been settled, we cannot count on being able to support anything more than a defensive policy in the Far East.[57]

In the further course of his remarks, Chatfield provided an extremely detailed picture of the benefits and problems associated with the execution of the Singapore strategy. He emphasized the need for the arrival of a British fleet at the earliest possible moment if Britain was at war with Japan alone, or the dispatch of ground and air reinforcements to Singapore well prior to Japan's entry if Britain was already engaged in a war with Germany. Upon its arrival, Chatfield envisaged the presence of a British fleet as the linchpin in denying the Japanese ready access to the commerce and resources of the Asia-Pacific, an enterprise best undertaken with "the sympathy and assistance of America."[58] At the same time he did not attempt to evade the negative impacts that a war in the Atlantic may have upon the Royal Navy's strategic flexibility. In doing so he placed further meat on the bones of Hoare's fleet readiness time frames by carefully explaining the urgent need for the Admiralty's aging capital ships to be progressively withdrawn from service for modifications, which would take two years on average to complete.[59] On the state of Singapore itself, Chatfield conceded that aspects of the defenses such as available antiaircraft batteries were still weak, but he was confident that the coastal artillery was strong enough to repel any direct assault. But his otherwise comprehensive appraisal of the fortress' capacity to withstand attack was entirely predicated upon his belief that a large Japanese expedition with aircraft carrier support would attack Singapore Island directly. He made no mention of any possible ground attack by way of the Malayan peninsula and believed it was "very unlikely that shore-based air attacks could be made except as part of successful major operations."[60]

Questions relating to the defense of Australia itself against raids or invasion were subsequently addressed by the Chiefs of Staff Sub-Committee of the Committee of Imperial Defence. In preparing their appreciation as to the scale of anticipated raids against eight nominated targets (including Sydney and Melbourne), the subcommittee assumed three categories of attack: a landing in force to capture the designated locality, landings by small raiding parties to destroy military targets, or light air attacks by carrier-borne aircraft.[61] Aside from these brief generalities, much of the assessment as to the likelihood of such attacks was dealt with under a more rigorous assessment of the invasion issue. In this instance the subcommittee provided a detailed list of proposed dispositions prior to 1941 in the event of war with both Germany and Japan. With reference to non-capital-ship classes, the appreciation judged that at the likely "low ebb" point in 1939, the Royal Navy would be able to deploy up to four aircraft carriers, seven heavy cruisers, forty-eight light cruisers, and five destroyer flotillas for both the Far East and general trade protection.[62] Referring to the anticipated availability of the fleet's capital ship force, the subcommittee detailed the period from summer 1937 until spring 1940 in a table (table 6.1) that included the likely strength of the German fleet and the number of British ships that were scheduled to be laid up for lengthy modernization.

"In war, the fate and future of overseas territories has always been decided by the outcome of the war in the main theatre. In a Far Eastern war the fate of British Commonwealth territories in the East will be decided on the outcome of the struggle between the British Commonwealth and Japan for the control of sea communications."[63] From this starting point the subcommittee assessed the threat of a Japanese invasion to be a highly improbable undertaking so long as Singapore was secure and the Royal Navy was strong enough to send a fleet capable of containing the Imperial Japanese Navy. Nevertheless it was conceded that dispatching ships beyond Suez would be conditioned by numerous variables if Britain found itself already at war with Germany before the

Table 6.1. Heavy Ship Strength Available to Meet the German Fleet and Nine Modernized Japanese Heavy Ships

Period	German Fleet	British Home Fleet	British Far Eastern Fleet	Out of Action (modernize)
Summer 1937 to Spring 1938	3 *Deutschlands*	*Hood* *Repulse*	2 *Nelsons* *Warspite* (fully modernized) *Malaya, Royal Oak* (partly modernized) *Barham* 4 *Revenges* (unmodernized) Total: 10 ships	*Renown* *Valiant* *Queen Elizabeth*
Spring 1938 to Summer 1939	3 *Deutschlands* 2 *Scharnhorsts*	*Hood* *Repulse* *Malaya* *Barham*	2 *Nelsons* *Warspite* *Royal Oak* 4 *Revenges* Total: 8 ships	*Renown* *Valiant* *Queen Elizabeth*
Summer 1939 to Spring 1940	3 *Deutschlands* 2 *Scharnhorsts* 2 – 35,000 ton battleships	*Hood* *Repulse* *Renown* 2 *Nelsons*	3 *Warspites* *Malaya* *Royal Oak* *Barham* 4 *Revenges* Total: 10 ships	

"Questions Raised by the Australian Delegation," report by Chiefs-of-Staff Sub-Committee, June 9, 1937, TNA (UK): CAB/21/2525 XC17491, 8.

commencement of hostilities with Japan. The subcommittee estimated that should Australia became the target of a large-scale Japanese invasion, the force required for this task would involve no less than two divisions and at least 400,000 tons of shipping (forty to seventy ships), and that such an expedition could not be mounted until such time as the British fleet had been destroyed and Singapore itself was captured.[64] A crucial omission in these calculations was any reference to the scale of

Italian naval opposition in the Mediterranean beyond a repetition of the pledge that operations against the Italians would not be allowed to interfere with the commitment of forces to the Far East. And in assessing the degree of air support available to an invading Japanese force, the chiefs of staff noted that "if she [Japan] relied on ship-borne aircraft, she could not hope for air superiority."[65]

Addressing the House of Representatives on August 27, 1937, Prime Minister Lyons reported the Australian government's satisfaction with the outcomes achieved at the Imperial Conference. With reference to foreign affairs, he expressed his approval that both Britain and the Dominions were committed to "making a definite contribution to general world appeasement, but also [to] clearly indicating fundamental principles for which the Empire stood."[66] Similarly he applauded the positive response to Australia's initiative for a peaceful settlement in the Asia-Pacific region through the negotiation of a Pacific pact. On the vital questions relating to the Singapore strategy, he advised that Singapore itself was so powerful a fortress that "its capacity to fulfil its function should be undoubted."[67] Lyons further outlined the advice the Australian delegation had received on the strategic aspects of dispatching a fleet to the Far East and proceeded to detail the future strengthening of Australia's armed services. The RAN was to be maintained "at a strength which is an effective and fair contribution to Empire naval defence," the RAAF would continue its expansion under the existing Salmond scheme, and "as a further deterrent to invasion, the Australian Field Army is organised in seven nucleus divisions, and increased provision is being made in the new programme for its maintenance on an efficient basis."[68] Yet in spite of the prime minister's public confidence, there could be no disguising the fact that the integrity of Australia's imperial naval security was now entirely dependent upon a complex set of assumptions and conclusions that placed the sending of an adequate British fleet at the mercy of circumstances to be played out in the European sphere. Time was now the central factor, and in Europe it would soon be running very short indeed.

"The Ante-chamber to a Wise Man's Hell": July 1937–September 1939

On July 7, 1937, an "incident" manufactured by radicals within Japan's Kwantung Army at the Marco Polo Bridge outside Peking heralded the outbreak of the Second Sino-Japanese War. Inside a matter of weeks the Chinese Nationalist forces under Chiang Kai-shek had been driven from most of their great eastern cities as the Japanese began to thrust into China's vast hinterland. No military response was forthcoming from the Western powers. Instead, the Western signatories to the Nine-Power Pact signed at Washington in 1922 arranged a November conference in Brussels to discuss the issue. Both the British and the Australians did not support the imposition of sanctions on Japan for its conduct, and no sanctions were imposed by the common agreement of the delegates present.[69] True to its stated principle of not resorting to arms in an effort to achieve a settlement, the conference concluded "that a prompt suspension of hostilities in the Far East would be in the best interests not only of China and Japan but of all nations and that with each day's continuance of the conflict, loss in lives and property is bound to increase and the ultimate solution of the conflict to become more difficult."[70] With that the delegates effectively folded their tents and went home. Nor was there any military response on the part of the British or the Americans following the sinking of the gunboat USS *Panay* and the shelling of the gunboat HMS *Ladybird* on the Yangtze River in the vicinity of Nanking on December 13, 1937. The same day marked the onset of the so-called "Rape of Nanking," an episode of unfettered barbarism that involved the massacre of perhaps as many as 300,000 Chinese civilians by Japanese troops during a six-week orgy of raping and looting within the captured city.

President Roosevelt's call for a "moral embargo" of Japan in early 1938 by American exporters was the only Western reaction of any substance to the continuing belligerence of the Japanese in China. From the British perspective, Whitehall's reluctance to impose sanctions reflected the policy of appeasement the new prime minister, Neville Chamberlain, sought to apply in Europe. After succeeding the retiring Baldwin on May 28, 1937, Chamberlain favored a policy of ongoing negotiation with Germany and Italy without the necessity for preconditions. This caused friction within his government and the subsequent resignation of Foreign Secretary Anthony Eden in February 1938, who was replaced by Lord Halifax.[71] Nevertheless Chamberlain pushed on with the support of a number of his senior ministers and other influential civic and business personalities, and he pursued the policy during the Anschluss in March 1938. What followed thereafter in Europe has been exhaustively explored by postwar historians, and the further events that marked the way toward Germany's eventual invasion of Poland in September 1939 are only addressed in relation to their impact on the course of the Singapore strategy. In Japan, tentative discussions commenced in July 1938 between Foreign Minister Ugaki Kazushige and the British ambassador, Sir Robert Craigie, in an effort to settle Anglo-Japanese differences. As had been the case in both 1934 and 1935, these discussions were subject to opposition, in this instance by a cabal within the Japanese Foreign Ministry that favored the strengthening of the existing Anti-Comintern agreement with Berlin in preference to a stitched-up settlement with London.[72]

Thanks to a deadlock of opinions within the Konoe government over the direction of policy toward Britain and British interests in China, the Ugaki-Craigie talks went nowhere. The desire of army leaders such as War Minister Itagaki Seishiro to expel British influence from China clashed with moderates led by the navy minister, Yonai Mitsumasa, who were opposed to upgrading Anti-Comintern with the Germans.[73] Following an incident at Tientsin on June 14, 1939, where the British and French concessions were blockaded by Japanese troops as retribution for the failure of the British to surrender the suspected assassins of a pro-Japanese official, anti-British feeling erupted in Tokyo. Prior to negotiations between Ambassador Craigie and the new foreign minister, Arita Hachiro, on July 15 to resolve the matter, mass anti-British demonstrations attracted upwards of 60,000 participants.[74] The incident was not resolved until August, when the suspects were eventually handed over (and subsequently executed), but by then another complication had raised its head. During the course of their offensive operations in China, the Japanese had engaged in skirmishes with Soviet forces along the Manchukuo border. After the sinking of a Soviet gunboat on the Amur River in June 1937 and a two-week fight at Chang-ku Feng from July 30, 1938, hostilities escalated with a Japanese incursion into Outer Mongolia at Nomonhan on May 11, 1939. But following their defeat at the hands of the Soviets in July, the Japanese were compelled to withdraw into Manchukuo.[75] With Whitehall attempting to conclude an agreement with the Soviets, the threat that Japan may join the Axis motivated the Australian government to urge Britain to confine any Anglo-Soviet accord to Europe alone.[76] British efforts in this regard were eventually stymied by the signing of the Molotov-Ribbentrop Pact on August 23, 1939.

Negotiations with France and the United States prior to September 1939 over the situation in the Far East did not greatly assist Whitehall and the Admiralty. Anglo-French staff-level talks on the subject in June 1939 raised the topic of cooperation, but with just a single light cruiser, twenty-five aircraft, and 50,000 colonial conscripts based in Indo-China, any potential French contribution beyond the borders of France's Asia-Pacific colonies was negligible.[77] Nor was much progress made with Washington. In their advice supplied to the Australians at the Imperial Conference, the British chiefs of staff were of the opinion that no specific assistance could be relied upon from the United States in spite of Roosevelt's earlier assurance to Prime Minister Lyons that America would make common cause with the British in the Pacific if hostilities arose.[78] The major sticking point in the staff-level talks that took place during January 1938 and May 1939 was the nature of the Singapore strategy itself. The Americans had no preexisting plans to dispatch their ships beyond the Philippines and were loath to make any commitment to do so unless the British themselves provided more than a symbolic naval presence in the Far East.[79] In any event the calculated period of relief involving an American fleet amounted to at least four months, and the undertaking of such an expedition would be wholly dependent upon the course of events in the Central Pacific. Furthermore, the Americans advised the British that while they would fight for the Philippines, a large U.S. fleet was not to be based in Manila Bay, as it was expected that Japanese force of arms would initially prevail in the Philippine archipelago.[80]

At Singapore, meanwhile, a crucial change in British thinking was taking place. Since 1936 the general officer commanding (GOC), Major General William Dobbie, had come to the conclusion that a Japanese overland attack against Singapore was indeed feasible. He instructed his head of intelligence, Colonel Arthur Percival, to draw up an appreciation detailing the likely points of Japanese attack:

> In November, 1937, having, as G.S.O.I. Malaya, made a careful study of the problem of the defence of Singapore, I prepared on the instructions of the General Officer Commanding (Major-General, now Lieutenant-General Sir W. G. S. Dobbie) an appreciation and plan for an attack on that place from the point of view of the Japanese. In this appreciation it was pointed out (a) that, as a result of

the political situation in Europe, it was unlikely that the British Fleet would be able to reach Singapore in 70 days, (b) that in consequence, a more deliberate form of attack could be undertaken. The plan recommended consisted of preliminary operations to seize the aerodromes in South Thailand and in Kelantan, the Island of Penang and the naval and air facilities in Borneo, followed by the main operation to capture Singapore itself.[81]

Percival's appraisal and a follow-up report by Dobbie himself early in 1938 represented a fundamental repudiation of the views expressed by the Overseas Defence Committee in 1924. For the first time, it had been officially acknowledged that Malaya may be targeted by a Japanese advance before any assault took place against Singapore Island, and Dobbie authorized the construction of a defensive line in Johore to counter a possible amphibious landing at Mersing, seventy miles to the north of Singapore.[82] Most of the work was complete in July 1939, when Dobbie was relieved as GOC by Major General Lionel Bond, who in April 1940 was to recommend the erection of ground defenses along the Malayan-Siamese frontier.[83] The inclusion of the Malayan peninsula in the defense plans for Singapore would alter the focus of the Singapore strategy once war broke out in Europe, with the requirement for additional ground and air forces to hold Malaya becoming yet another variable in the strategy's expanded parameters.

Amidst much pomp and ceremony, the Singapore base was formally opened on February 14, 1938. It had cost the British taxpayer a staggering £60,000,000 to build, and in the light of alterations to the projected strength and availability of the anticipated fleet that was to follow, value for money remained something of a moot point. With Chatfield's replacement by Admiral Sir Roger Backhouse as first sea lord in September 1938, the by-now moribund concept of the "Main Fleet" was informally superseded. In collaboration with Admiral Sir Reginald Drax, Backhouse developed a plan for the deployment of a flying squadron consisting of approximately five capital ships and an aircraft carrier with screening cruisers and destroyers.[84] While a formation of this size was insufficient to meet the full Japanese Combined Fleet in battle, it would nevertheless serve as a powerful deterrent to any lesser-scale Japanese naval thrust into the South China Sea and the adjacent Indonesian archipelago.

Furthermore, the presence of a flying squadron at either Trincomalee or Singapore spelled trouble for Axis raiders attempting to interdict British and Australian lines of communication in the Indian Ocean.[85] But even with this revision to a scale of deployment that presented as a far more feasible option, no consequent reduction of the fifty-three-to-seventy-day "period before relief" was forthcoming. Instead, as of August 1939 the period in question had been extended to not less than 180 days, meaning that the interim defense of Singapore, and now of Malaya as well, could no longer be regarded as a short-term exercise.[86]

If one aspect of the Singapore strategy remained constant throughout the final years of the 1930s, it was the procession of assurances from London to Canberra that Britain would honor its naval commitments. Publicly satisfied and privately doubtful, Prime Minister Lyons had returned home from the 1937 Imperial Conference with an election campaign to fight, in which he proclaimed the UAP government's support for imperial defense upon the basis of the assurances he had been provided with: "The Government's policy aims at preventing the enemy reaching our territorial waters. We consider a policy of isolation from Great Britain suicidal. Only by close co-operation between a strong Australian navy and the fleets of the Empire can we hope to prevent the enemy coming within striking distance of Australia."[87] Labor's John Curtin was equally resolute in pursuing an opposite course: "Our position renders it impracticable that we can exercise any decisive influence, either as a police or as a salvage corps, in the problems of Europe. We make that perfectly plain. The Labor party's policy involves, first, a paramount obligation to defend Australia, and secondly, no compulsion to be exercised upon any citizen for service on foreign battlefields."[88] But try as he might, including the claim in his policy speech that when "we defend Australia we defend not only these seven million British subjects, but also three million square miles of British territory and one thousand millions of British investments," he could not shrug off the twin tags of disloyalty and isolationism.[89] In a concluding pitch to the voters on October 21, 1937, Lyons reminded his listeners that "a vote for our opponents means a vote for isolation from the rest of the Empire."[90] On polling day, October 23, the influential *Sydney Morning Herald* summarized the competing election policies in similar terms: "Whereas Mr Lyons would strain every nerve and tendon to keep our coasts inviolate and our vital overseas communications intact in the event of war again breaking loose upon the world, Mr Curtin would leave the seas open to our enemies, deprive us of the right to any succour from Great Britain and her navy, and wait for invasion to prove that a fool's paradise is only the ante-chamber to a wise man's hell."[91]

Lyons' UAP–Country Party coalition was returned to power with a comfortable majority, but minus two of its most experienced members after George Pearce and Archdale Parkhill lost their seats.[92] Their departure came at a difficult time for Australian foreign affairs, with the need to maintain friendly relations between Australia and Japan in the midst of the Sino-Japanese War and to exercise as much influence as possible within British policy circles to support the cause of appeasement in Europe. In the latter case the Australian high commissioner, Stanley Bruce, wielded a considerable amount of personal influence with Neville Chamberlain and conversed with him at critical moments during the Munich crisis in September 1938.[93] The Australian government steadfastly supported appeasement in Europe until the sudden death of Joseph Lyons on April 7, 1939, and thereafter under his successor Robert Menzies. The policy was maintained all the way to September 1, 1939, when Menzies made a final plea to Chamberlain in which he urged that Poland cease being unreasonable in its attitude to German "proposals" or the Poles would lose public support in other nations, including Australia, if they failed to agree to negotiations.[94] Yet, as shall become apparent shortly, each of the major European crises from January 1938 until September 1939 were inevitably linked in Australian minds with the situation in the Asia-Pacific region, where trade and commerce had become a source of unwelcome friction between Australia and Japan and within Australia itself.

This was to prove a thorny path for both nations. The discovery of a large iron ore deposit at Yampi Sound in Western Australia during the 1920s stimulated Japanese commercial interest in a joint-venture exploration and mining operation with British companies. Initially there was little anxiety from the Australian government, which had sought advice from Whitehall on the matter.[95] But a report from Australia's trade commissioner in Tokyo in October 1937 alerted the government to instances of Japanese commercial infiltration into areas such as Portuguese Timor and the Netherlands East Indies, and that Japanese interest in Yampi was part of this Japanese "foothold" policy.[96] As negotiations began to drag out, the government changed its mind, and in May 1938 a general embargo upon iron ore exports from Australia was implemented. In spite of Lyons and his ministers claiming that the action had been taken to safeguard Australia's domestic resources for its own use, the Japanese were having none of it. Making a strong case that the Australian decision had not been based upon geological facts, they argued that Japan had been deliberately targeted and warned that the embargo could damage relations between both countries.[97] In an effort to soothe economic tensions, the Australians took steps to supply other forms of iron-based products. Since January 1938, trade union boycotts had affected the export of scrap metal to Japan on the grounds that would be used in munitions production.[98] Attorney general Robert Menzies undertook successful legal action on behalf of the government in late 1938 to overturn the boycotts, and supplies of pig-iron and other metal products resumed in February 1939. For his efforts in engineering this act of economic appeasement, Menzies acquired the lifelong moniker "Pig-Iron Bob."[99]

One of the principal difficulties for the Australians in conducting negotiations with the Japanese was that Australia possessed no independent representation with the major powers beyond the British Empire. Instead, the Australian government had been relying on liaison appointments within British embassies to facilitate contact and obtain information, and as of January 1939 the government saw no reason to change this approach. Menzies summed up support for the policy, noting "that if each Dominion begins separately to accredit diplomatic representation to foreign powers, grave divisions in our foreign policies will begin to appear and a serious blow will have been delivered at British unity."[100] Throughout the first five months of 1939, however, the government began to change its views as it recognized that surrogate diplomacy did not help where Australian and British regional interests differed. This change in attitude was, however, tempered by the realization that establishing separate representation meant that other powers would seek the same accommodation with Australia.[101] Nevertheless on April 26, 1939, Prime Minister Menzies in a radio broadcast spelled out the necessity for a new policy: "The problems of the Pacific are different. What Great Britain call the Far East is to us the near north.... I have become convinced that, in the Pacific, Australia must regard herself as a principal providing herself with her own information and maintaining her own diplomatic contacts with foreign Powers."[102] Moves to establish legations in Washington and Tokyo were taken, but neither had been fulfilled as of September 1, 1939, in the latter case due to fallout from the recent Tientsin crisis. Better news was to be had from Washington, where discussions between Stanley Bruce and President Roosevelt in May 1939 indicated the likely preparedness of the United States to intervene in the Pacific if the Japanese provoked hostilities.[103]

While Australia was attempting to beef up its diplomatic stocks abroad, increasingly urgent efforts were being made to mobilize the nation's military resources at home. From an administrative perspective this involved Frederick Shedden taking charge of the preparation of the structures and policies required by government to function in wartime; these were compiled in the form of a Commonwealth War Book.[104] From early 1938 there had been an increase in Defence Council meetings to iron out problems in administration and rearmament programs, as Shedden made plans for the composition of a small War Cabinet to succeed the Defence Council in the event of war. On the expenditure front, Lyons informed the House of Representatives on April 27, 1938, that an accelerated rearmament program costing £43 million would be required over the next three years.[105] In spite of calls from the Labor opposition for a scaling back of defense expenditure following the Munich crisis, Lyons determined that the programs should continue, with further expansion in some areas. With increased funding the militia was to be increased to 70,000 through use of the voluntary system, coastal and antiaircraft defenses upgraded, and defense production increased.[106] Benefiting from the largest share of the defense vote, the Royal Australian Navy had been enhanced since the doldrums of the early 1930s, when it had virtually ceased to exist as a recognizable fighting force. In September 1939 the RAN could field two modernized heavy cruisers and three modern light cruisers as its primary strength, reflecting the long-standing influence of Admiralty policy that regarded cruisers as Australia's most effective contribution to Empire naval defense.[107]

Controversy proved to be the persistent companion of the RAAF during its buildup in the period from 1937 to 1939. Following a series of training fatalities and criticism of flying standards, the chief of the British air staff, Air Marshall Sir Edward Ellington, visited Australia in June 1938 to investigate. Of central interest to Ellington was securing local support for the basing of Australian squadrons in Singapore, a course he promoted by suggesting a wider role for the service than simply localized coast defense.[108] But the chief impact on the air force came through Ellington's observations of RAAF command and administrative structures, which placed him at odds with the Australian chief of air staff, Air Vice Marshall Williams, and the Australian Air Board. In the imbroglio that followed, the government removed Williams from his post on January 16, 1939.[109] Meanwhile the RAAF had experienced endless frustration in obtaining aircraft ordered from British firms. In spite of incurring the displeasure of the British Air Ministry over the formation of the Commonwealth Aircraft Corporation and a subsequent decision by the Australians to acquire a manufacturing license for the NA-16 trainer from North American Aviation, an order was placed for Bristol Blenheim light bombers in 1936.[110] This was amended twice the following year with, the Bristol Beaufort eventually chosen with a scheduled delivery date of July 1939. Recognizing that this date would not be met because of the low priority afforded Australian-bound aircraft in the British aircraft industry and British export policies that favored other nations at Australia's expense, in November 1938 Prime Minister Lyons announced the intended purchase of fifty Lockheed Hudson aircraft from America. In September 1939 the RAAF possessed 164 airplanes, none of which could be classified under any then-relevant operational definition as a first-line fighter or bomber.[111]

Notwithstanding the state of Australia's domestic defenses, the thought uppermost in the minds of Australia's leaders during 1938 remained the reliability of the Singapore strategy. Aside from Lyons (and later Menzies), the majority of questions being asked came from Stanley Bruce and the irrepressible William Morris Hughes, recently appointed by Lyons as minister for external affairs. In March 1938 Chamberlain repeated British assurances as to the strength of Singapore itself, and at a meeting of the Committee of Imperial Defence on March 4, the "period before relief" for Malaya (not just Singapore) was officially set at seventy days.[112] Following Munich, in early November Bruce held discussions with the Admiralty and was informed by the first lord, Earl Stanhope, that seven battleships had been earmarked for deployment to Singapore, although their departure may be delayed due to the need to neutralize Germany's pocket battleships if the latter were at sea. Bruce was further informed that Australia's expressed desire for the presence of a capital ship in the Far East prior to hostilities could not be met until the commissioning of the new *King George V*–class ships in 1940; a prior request for the loan of a battleship to the Australian navy had been likewise declined.[113] In the House of Commons on December 7, 1938, Chamberlain offered a broad assurance to the Dominions that "I am sure I shall be rightly interpreting the wishes of the people of this country if I say that, if any other part of the British Commonwealth were attacked, we should without hesitation go to its aid."[114]

Bruce was unconvinced. In a cable to the first sea lord on March 14, 1939, the commander of the RAN, Vice Admiral Sir Ragnar Colvin, informed Admiral Backhouse that he had attempted to refute Bruce's advice to the Australian government that the British would be unable to send capital ships to Singapore if Britain was already engaged in a war in Europe. He advised Backhouse that the loan of a capital ship to be based in the Far East would be a beneficial inducement for Australia to purchase or construct a battleship of its own, but he warned that Bruce's summation may have serious repercussions in Australia: "Danger in effect of Bruce's views lies in Australia turning to military self-dependence, which though in my opinion illusory and impossible, is attractive to uninstructed public opinion."[115] Through the auspices of a defense conference organized by New Zealand held at Wellington on April 14, further evidence of Australia's growing reservations over British assurances, and the effect upon New Zealand opinion, was communicated to Whitehall by the British high commissioner to New Zealand, Sir Harry Batterbee:

> It became evident that underlying all the strategical and other discussions were doubts not indeed of the intention but of the ability of Great Britain to despatch a fleet of capital-ships to the East in time to prevent the fall of Singapore, and doubt of the security of Singapore itself before the arrival of the fleet. These doubts were clearly felt by the New Zealand Delegation and, though the Australian Delegation, being led by Vice-Admiral Sir Ragnar Colvin, did not express that feeling, he assures me that the Commonwealth Government feel them as strongly or even more so. Holding such views, the New Zealand representatives were more sympathetic to

measures calculated to increase their own domestic security than those aiming at the general defence of the Empire.[116]

For both the British and Australian governments, the Wellington Conference represented an unwelcome distraction. Although called primarily to discuss the defense of the South Pacific region against Japanese attack, the British wished to keep any reference to Singapore as brief as possible, as did the Australian government, which was of the view that public discussion of the subject may increase opposition within Australia to the potential dispatch of her armed forces overseas.[117] But even before the conference got under way, there was ample evidence that Whitehall's position on Singapore was fast descending into the realms of speculation alone. In response to Colvin's cable of March 14, Backhouse had replied that "there has never been any doubt that a force of Capital Ships would have to be sent to the East in the event of War with Japan. What is uncertain is [the] strength of the force as this would necessarily depend on situation in Europe. In any case I feel sure that force sent will be sufficient to safeguard communications in Bay of Bengal and Indian Ocean, and act as strong deterrent to any Japanese expedition against Australia."[118] On the same day, in a discussion with Major General H. L. Ismay, secretary of the Committee of Imperial Defence, Australia's acting high commissioner was informed that at a meeting of the CID on January 24, 1939, as few as two capital ships had been proposed for deployment to Singapore.[119] Chamberlain again attempted to reassure Lyons on March 20 that a fleet would be sent, and he repeated the assurance to Menzies on June 29.[120] By now, however, the language emanating from both Whitehall and the Admiralty had abandoned any notion of precision when it came to the size of a dispatched force, preferring instead to respond with the qualification that the force's composition would be governed by events in European waters.

At a meeting held at the Dominions Office in London on July 11, 1939, Australian disquiet over the Singapore strategy could no longer be contained. The minutes of the meeting disclosed the moment when Stanley Bruce vented his concerns to Lord Chatfield, then minister for coordination of defense. When Chatfield suggested that war with Japan may not start for some time, and that it may be a more sensible strategy to knock out the Italian fleet first, Bruce pulled the trigger: "The High

Commissioner for Australia said that, supposing events moved along the lines suggested by Lord Chatfield and we found ourselves at war with Japan, what did His Majesty's Government propose to do? Did they, or did they not, intent to send a fleet to the Far East, and if so, of what size? Had a decision already been taken on this point and was it being kept secret? Or alternatively, had no decision been reached?"[121] While denying that any decision had been kept secret from the Australians, Chatfield admitted "that no definite decision had been reached, and no definite plan had been formulated, in view of the fact that the position was still indeterminate." He then informed Bruce that the Admiralty was loath to abandon the Eastern Mediterranean "until the very last moment," though he added "there was no question that in the event of war with Japan, we would abdicate our position in the Far East without fighting."[122] With this final baseline commitment, peacetime Anglo-Australian discussions concerning the Singapore strategy ceased abruptly as the subsequent attention of both nations became consumed by the rapidly escalating crisis between Germany and Poland.

Stanley Melbourne Bruce occupies a unique place in the history of Australian defense and foreign policy. As Australia's prime minister at the 1923 Imperial Conference he was told that a flotilla of two or three capital ships would be permanently stationed at the yet-to-be-constructed Singapore naval base. And as Australia's high commissioner to the United Kingdom sixteen years later, he learned firsthand that his nation's primary means of defense was effectively nonexistent. In the course of his lengthy association with the narrative of the Singapore strategy in peacetime, Bruce had witnessed the steady evolution of a facade. For her security Australia was now reliant upon the supposed impregnability of "Fortress Singapore" itself and the dispatch of a fleet as a definite maybe, just as the lights in Europe were about to go out. On August 30, 1939, the following cable was dispatched from the Australian government to the secretary of state for Dominion affairs: "In the present international situation the Commonwealth Government desire to place the ships of the R.A.N. and their personnel at the disposal of the United Kingdom Government, but find it necessary to stipulate that no ships (other than H.M.A.S. *Perth*) should be taken from Commonwealth waters without prior concurrence of Commonwealth Government."[123] Two days later, the first German troops crossed the Polish frontier, and with the expiration of a British ultimatum to Berlin on September 3, Prime Minister Menzies informed his nation that "in consequence of a persistence by Germany in her invasion of Poland, Great Britain had declared war on her and that, as a result, Australia is also at war."[124]

In 1804 Horatio Nelson said of the Treaty of Amiens that "we made use of the Peace, not to recruit our Navy, but to be the cause of its ruin."[125] On September 3, 1939, the Royal Navy went to war against Germany following twenty years of peace, through which it had suffered the unavoidable consequences of international disarmament and domestic economy, and the avoidable harm inflicted by unstable Admiralty policymaking prior to 1933. On its own, Germany's Kriegsmarine presented a solid challenge to the Anglo-French navies, and if Mussolini determined to join Hitler on the battlefield, the considerable strength of the Italian Regia Marina's surface fleet would require a large-scale Anglo-French naval commitment to subdue it. Given that it was entering hostilities in an incomplete state of combat readiness, the Royal Navy faced the very real prospect that all its available capital ships and carriers would be tied up in European waters for months, if not years. From the rubble of the meeting at the Dominions Office on July 11, one assurance had remained for Australia's leaders: the Mediterranean would be sacrificed if necessary in order to preserve the Empire in the Far East. How long that commitment would last was anyone's guess. Until such time as the European Axis surface fleets had been neutralized, no realistic prospect existed for a squadron or fleet to be sent to Singapore. All now depended upon a decisive result at sea in favor of the Allied navies while Japanese eyes were still focused upon China. What would evolve into the largest and most complex war at sea yet seen was about to begin, and Britain's capacity to dominate the seas as it had largely done since Nelson's time was by now at best a matter for serious conjecture.

7

Conduits

September 1939–December 1941

Prior to Japan's entering into hostilities against the Western Allies in December 1941, a grim, relentless conflict was to be waged in the protection and interdiction of the combatants' seaborne lines of supply and communication. This war of attrition would extend across much of the globe and in so doing would assume a variety of operational guises to meet differing geographical and strategic circumstances. For island nations such as Britain and Australia, the preservation of these vital conduits governed their ongoing participation in the war itself, and likewise their own survival. Yet while Australia strove to provide as much material support as possible for the Allied cause in the European and Mediterranean theaters, the minds of its political and military leaders were never to be free of a dread prospect: that Japan would seek to exploit the entanglement of the European war and strike out with military force in pursuit of its own ambitions for dominance in the Asia-Pacific region. And hinging upon the success or failure of Britain to master the European Axis naval forces would be the Royal Navy's ability to muster sufficient firepower to decisively repel the Japanese threat.

September 1939–July 1940

For the initial protection of the Indian Ocean sea lanes, the Admiralty could call upon three cruisers based with the East Indies Station at Colombo and Trincomalee, together with the carrier *Eagle* and four cruisers based at Singapore as part of the China Station.[1] The first substantial threat to shipping in the region emerged in late September

1939 through the presence of the German pocket battleship *Graf Spee*, which sank the British tanker *African Shell* off East Africa during a brief sojourn to the east of the Cape of Good Hope. In response, the Admiralty assembled a number of hunting groups to track down the enemy warship, and on November 13 *Graf Spee* was cornered off Montevideo by the British cruisers *Exeter* and *Ajax* and the New Zealand cruiser *Achilles*. After a brisk fight off the mouth of the River Plate, *Graf Spee* retired to Montevideo; she re-emerged from the Plate on November 17 and was promptly scuttled by her crew.[2] Thereafter the Indian Ocean remained largely free from enemy operations until May 3, 1940, when the disappearance of the merchant ship *Scientist* and the subsequent discovery of mines laid off Cape Agulhas pointed to the activities of a German auxiliary cruiser in the area. The vessel in question was *Atlantis*, and thanks to her various disguises she would become a considerable thorn in the Admiralty's flesh in the Indian Ocean over the following eighteen months. Meanwhile the sinking of the liner *Niagara* by a mine off Auckland on June 19, 1940, betrayed the presence of a second raider, *Orion*, which had likewise laid mines off the southeastern Australian seaboard before escaping unscathed into the Pacific.[3]

Aside from these incidents, the only other episode of note in the Pacific prior to July 1940 was the pursuit of the Italian merchant ship *Romolo* by the Australian armed merchant-cruiser *Manoora*; the enemy vessel was scuttled by her crew to the north of the Solomon Islands on June 12.[4] Since November 1939 the major concern for both the Australian government and the RAN had been ensuring the safe passage of three separate convoys tasked with conveying the Second Australian Imperial Force (AIF) across the Indian Ocean to the Middle East.[5] Refusing a request from the chief of Australia's naval staff, Admiral Colvin, that additional escorts be supplied by the Australia Station, the Menzies government instead sought assistance from the Admiralty. Two extra cruisers were provided, and in company with the battleship *Ramillies* they accompanied the first of these convoys (U.S. 1), which arrived intact at Suez on February 12, 1940.[6] The two subsequent convoys likewise reached their destinations without incident. Colvin's request had been denied because the government was reluctant to weaken the operational capabilities of the Australia Station. Nevertheless the Australians were prepared to release five destroyers for overseas service, and as the Allied position in Europe began to deteriorate, further transfers were approved. By May 1940 the Australia Station had been reduced to the light cruisers *Perth* and *Adelaide*, two armed merchant cruisers, and three sloops.[7] And with the collapse of French resistance in June, the government sought to provide additional assistance to the Admiralty by authorizing the deployment of the heavy cruisers *Australia* and *Canberra* for operations in the Atlantic and the Mediterranean.

The scuttling of the *Graf Spee* provided one of the few bright moments for the Admiralty throughout an otherwise frustrating and costly opening eleven months of the war at sea. Torpedoed by her quarry in the course of an offensive antisubmarine sweep on September 17, 1939, the carrier *Courageous* was sunk with the loss of more than 500 of her crew. Her sinking was followed by that of the battleship *Royal Oak* and most of her 1,200-strong company on October 14 after it was torpedoed by the U-47 within Scapa Flow itself. And only the gallant self-sacrifice of those on board the armed merchant-cruiser *Rawalpindi* to the north of the Shetland Islands on November 23 had prevented the German battle cruisers *Scharnhorst* and *Gneisenau* from breaking out into the North Atlantic.[8] In the course of the Norwegian campaign from April 9 until June 8, 1940, the Royal Navy suffered a series of embarrassing reverses. Though three German cruisers and ten destroyers were sent to the bottom, two British cruisers and seven destroyers shared the same fate, along with the carrier *Glorious*, which was inexplicably ambushed by the aforementioned German battle cruisers on the afternoon of June 8 and sunk with the loss of more than eight hundred lives. A further six of the RN's destroyers were sunk and many others damaged during their participation in Operation "Dynamo" at Dunkirk from May 26 until June 4, by which time the collapse of French resistance had been all but secured by Germany's seemingly irresistible armored blitzkrieg.[9]

Worse was to follow. With Italy joining the fray on June 10, 1940, the Royal Navy became burdened with a fresh opponent at precisely the wrong moment given the inevitability of France's capitulation. As part of the armistice terms agreed between Germany and France on June 22, Clause Eight directed that the Marine Nationale "shall be collected in ports to be specified, demobilised, and disarmed under German or Italian control."[10] Determined to deny the two Axis powers any access whatsoever to the French capital ships, Winston Churchill ordered Force H under the command of Vice Admiral Sir James Somerville to neutralize the French Mediterranean fleet based at Mers El Kébir. Having failed to negotiate a peaceful solution between the parties on July 3, Somerville executed what Churchill later described as "a most hateful decision, the most unnatural and painful in which I have ever been associated."[11] In the bombardment that followed from three British capital ships, three of the four French capital ships present were sunk or crippled; 1,300 French officers and enlisted men were killed. Six days later, the RN's Mediterranean Fleet under the command of Admiral Sir Andrew Cunningham jousted for the first time with units of the Regia Marina in an inconclusive gunnery engagement off the Calabrian coast. As the Admiralty braced itself for an indeterminate lone stand against its Axis opponents, it did so with the knowledge that as of July 1940 more than two million tons of British merchant shipping (806 ships) had been sunk by U-boats, surface raiders, aircraft, and mines, while Britain itself was facing the prospect of an imminent German invasion.[12]

For the British, a number of sobering lessons from the fighting thus far were apparent. The course of events off Norway and Dunkirk had clearly identified the substantial risks entailed when squadrons and fleets were compelled to operate in waters above which the enemy enjoyed air superiority. Though the losses inflicted by the Luftwaffe upon the Royal Navy in the Norwegian campaign were relatively confined, the British ships had been repeatedly forced to vacate coastal waters due to their general lack of effective antiaircraft armament and the paucity of available fighter cover.[13] Even at Dunkirk, where the RAF fighter presence over the combat zone was far more substantial, evacuation operations were at times impossible in daylight thanks to the sheer weight of the enemy's aerial firepower.[14] Elsewhere, a series of flaws in British prewar operational doctrine and preparation had been ruthlessly exploited, most particularly in the fields of antisubmarine warfare (ASW) and commerce protection. The sinking of *Courageous* exposed the policy of conducting offensive aircraft carrier sweeps against U-boats as an ill-considered blunder. And with two million-plus tons of shipping already sent to the bottom (most lost to submarine attack), it was clear that substantial reforms in convoy protection were urgently required.[15] Unless more specialized escort vessels could be provided, better ASW tactics developed, and interservice cooperation between the Admiralty and the RAF vastly improved, Britain ran the risk of being eventually starved into surrender. Given the almost total emasculation of French naval support and with the looming threat of a German aero-amphibious assault across the Channel, the disposition of substantial British naval power beyond the European theater in the foreseeable future was beyond the bounds of serious contemplation.

In the Far East meanwhile, the roller coaster of Japanese politics was pushing Japan ever closer to the brink of war with the Western powers. The resignation of Prime Minister Hiranuma Kiichirō and his cabinet on August 23, 1939, had been prompted by the signing of the Molotov-Ribbentrop Pact, which was resented by Tokyo.[16] His replacement, General Abe Nobuyuki, was instructed by Emperor Hirohito's advisers to pursue cooperative relations with Washington and London, but instability within Abe's cabinet led to his resignation and replacement by Admiral Yonai Mitsumasa on January 14, 1940. Throughout the following six months there was heated debate within the Yonai administration as to whether Japan should join Germany and Italy in a formal military alliance.[17] With the pro-German militarists eventually gaining the upper hand, Yonai's cabinet collapsed on July 16 following the resignation of the war minister, General Hata Shunroku. This led to the resurrection of Prince Konoe Fumimaro as prime minister and a distinctly pro-Axis attitude on the part of the new government. Convinced that Japan must follow the European Axis and wage war against Britain, in early July the Imperial Japanese Army produced the so-called "Army Plan," which involved a pre-emptive strike against British possessions in Southeast Asia, including Malaya and Singapore.[18]

Since the outbreak of hostilities in Europe, Whitehall's policy toward Japan had been one of conciliation wherever possible, given Britain's ill-preparedness to wage war in the Far East. With the collapse of Holland in May 1940 the British accepted Tokyo's proposal that the existing status quo be maintained in the Netherlands East Indies, an initiative that was likewise accepted by France and Germany.[19] This was followed, however, by the adoption of a far less conciliatory posture on Japan's part when on June 19 Tokyo demanded the withdrawal of the British garrison from Shanghai and the closure of both the Hong Kong frontier and the Burma Road, the key supply route to China itself. Over the following two months Whitehall consented to these demands given that Britain was in no position to do otherwise, as a report to the British War Cabinet from the chiefs of staff dated July 27 outlined:

> We are all agreed that, committed as we are in Europe and the Middle East, we must do everything short of sacrificing our vital interests to avoid an open clash with Japan. We have already advised, for example, that we should make considerable concessions to Japan, including the closure of the Burma Road, as part of a general settlement. We are also agreed that in present conditions and with our existing resources we cannot afford to regard a Japanese occupation of Indo-China or Thailand as a casus belli. Any direct Japanese attack on British territory must of course involve us in hostilities but we are agreed in doubting whether the Japanese themselves are likely to make such an attack in the near future, since we think they must be anxious to avoid war with the British Empire if they can gain their ends without it.[20]

The British had been reduced to walking a policy tightrope in their relations with Japan. On the one hand, Whitehall and its military advisers were seeking to avert war with the Japanese for as long as possible, yet on the other, Britain could not survive without American military aid, which had been made possible by the repeal of certain prohibitive sections of America's Neutrality Act in November 1939. The sticking point between both nations was the recognition of Japan's current position in China, a prerequisite on the part of the Yonai government for any future Japanese conciliation with the United States.[21] Though Washington was committed to keeping Tokyo out of an active military alliance with Berlin and Rome in order to guarantee the safety of America's Pacific interests, this did not include any acknowledgment of the legitimacy of Japan's conquests in China. Furthermore, in April 1940 the American secretary of state, Cordell Hull, in response to Japan's publicly announced intention to seek relations of "co-existence and co-prosperity" with the Netherlands East Indies, warned that any attempt by a foreign power to forcibly annex the Indies "would be prejudicial to the cause of stability, peace and security" in the Pacific as a whole.[22] And though he privately understood the reasons why Whitehall felt compelled to close the Burma Road for a period of three months, Hull annoyed the British on July 17 in a public statement where he lamented the closure as an obstacle to world trade.²³ Washington's escalating concerns over Japanese ambitions had been made clear in May with the transfer of the bulk of the Pacific Fleet to Pearl Harbor as a deterrent measure. This was followed up in July by the formal commencement of American economic sanctions via restrictions on the export of aviation fuel and high-grade steel products to Japanese interests.²⁴

A settlement between Japan and the Western powers also occupied the minds of the Australian government, which had been reluctant to send military forces overseas until Japan's future intentions within the region were clarified. In a cable to Stanley Bruce in London on September 5, 1939, Prime Minister Menzies laid out the government's concern: "As we see the position at present, our task for some time will be the completing of training of forces for Australian defence. Until [the] position of Japan has been cleared up, it would be useless even to discuss the sending of [an] expeditionary force, and in any event we have grave doubts as to just how [the] war is to be carried on, and the ultimate use of our troops."²⁵ On the question of granting concessions to the Japanese, the Australians were of the opposite mind to the British when it came to the closure of the Burma Road. They feared that if the road was closed and China subsequently collapsed through lack of foreign military aid, the Japanese would be free to redeploy their forces on a large scale in the Pacific.²⁶ Nevertheless, both governments adopted a united approach by jointly approaching the U.S. government to discuss the current frailty of the British Empire's position in the Asia-Pacific region. In a meeting between Secretary of State Hull, British ambassador Lord Lothian, and the recently installed Australian minister to the United States, Richard Casey, on June 28, 1940, both Lothian and Casey informed Hull that the British Empire could no longer resist Japanese demands to the point where hostilities between Britain and Japan became inevitable. Hull's response to his guests' advocacy for a comprehensive settlement was lukewarm at best, doubting that Japan was capable of reaching an agreement on terms that Washington would accept.²⁷

The secretary of state likewise dismissed a second proposal presented by the British and Australian representatives. It was suggested to Hull that the deployment of part of the American fleet to Singapore would present a powerful deterrent to any southward advance that the Japanese may envisage. Hull rejected this course of action on the basis that

America's Atlantic seaboard would be left defenseless as a result, and it was hardly surprising that he did so when the ABC-1 war plan did not even provide for an immediate naval expedition to relieve U.S. forces based in the Philippines.[28] That same day the Australian government received a cable from Lord Caldecote, the secretary of state for Dominion affairs, which seemingly confirmed its worst fears regarding the fate of the Singapore strategy:

> The security of our imperial interests in the Far East lies ultimately in our ability to control sea communications in the South Western Pacific, for which purpose [an] adequate fleet must be based at Singapore. Since our previous assurances in this respect however, the whole strategic situation has been radically altered by the French defeat. The result of this has been to alter the whole of the balance of naval strength in home waters. Formerly we were prepared to abandon the Eastern Mediterranean and despatch a fleet to the Far East relying on the French Fleet in the Western Mediterranean to contain the Italian Fleet. Now if we move the Mediterranean Fleet to the Far East there is nothing to contain the Italian Fleet which will be free to operate in the Atlantic or reinforce the German Fleet in home waters using bases in North West France. We must therefore retain in European waters sufficient naval forces to watch both the German and Italian Fleets, and we cannot do this and send a fleet to the Far East.[29]

Stanley Bruce, Australia's high commissioner in London, was particularly aggrieved that what he described as the "complete reversal of the United Kingdom's naval policy in the Far East" had been communicated with little or no information as to future British strategy. In a memorandum to Menzies on July 3, Bruce informed the prime minister that he had made his displeasure known to Whitehall, especially in light of a separate request within Caldecote's communique that sought the deployment of an Australian division in Malaya.[30] In a memorandum prepared for the Australian and New Zealand governments the previous November, Churchill had again assured both that in the event of a serious Japanese threat to their respective homelands, the Mediterranean would be forfeited and a fleet sent to their aid.[31] His assessment had also included a summary as to how the Admiralty would respond to such a crisis: "However, should Japanese encroachment begin, or should Great Britain pass into a state of war with Japan, the Admiralty would make such preparatory dispositions as would enable them to offer timely resistance either to the serious attack on Singapore or to the invasion of Australia and New Zealand. These dispositions will not necessarily take the form of stationing a fleet at Singapore, but would be of a character to enable the necessary concentrations to be made on the eastward in ample time to prevent a disaster."[32]

Largely upon the basis of Churchill's appraisal, on November 24, 1939, the Australian government gave its approval to the overseas deployment of Sixth Division AIF.[33] This decision showed the Menzies government's general readiness to comply with British requests for military assistance, albeit on occasion with significant reservations. Australian consent was also obtained for the establishment of the Empire Air Training Scheme (EATS), an initiative through which Dominion pilots and aircrew would be trained, chiefly in Canada and Australia, for eventual service in the RAF. Various conditions were imposed by the government upon the command and disposition of troops abroad, and an agreement was reached with the Admiralty that all RAN ships were to be redeployed to the Australia Station should Japan enter the war.[34] In spite of its opposition to the external dispatch of Australian forces as a matter of party policy, the Labor opposition under John Curtin invariably acquiesced with the government's decisions in this respect. The line was drawn, however, over Menzies' proposal in May 1940 to introduce compulsory military service for home defense, which Labor vehemently opposed.[35] This policy was part of a specific suite of measures with which the Australian government sought to aid the British during the period of the French military collapse. These included the diversion of a shipment of forty-nine Hudson bombers to the RAF, the supply to Britain of two-thirds of Australia's small-arms ammunition stocks, and a commitment to wage an increased war effort within Australian industry.[36]

On June 26, 1940, three days prior to the receipt of Caldecote's cable, Menzies and his cabinet rubber-stamped the dispatch of three existing RAAF squadrons to Singapore. Three months previously, on March 21, the Australian government had been advised by Whitehall that two RAF bomber squadrons were to be withdrawn from Singapore, and a subsequent request was forthcoming for an RAAF squadron to be deployed in their place. In his reply to the British on June 13, Menzies upped the offer to three squadrons.³⁷ Following the receipt of Caldecote's advice, however, both the Australian and New Zealand governments approached British requests for troops with greater caution. Bruce's strident rejection of a major change in policy in the absence of an adequate appreciation by the British chiefs of staff was answered by the production of such a document on July 31, 1940. Its preparation was justified in a covering note to the British War Cabinet that stated that "the Commonwealth Government [of Australia] and the New Zealand Government are becoming somewhat restive and are reluctant to despatch further troops until they have received the military appreciation of the situation in the Far East."³⁸ What followed was to be the blueprint for the future face of the Singapore strategy:

> In the absence of a Fleet our policy should be to rely primarily on air power. The air forces required to implement that policy, however, cannot be provided for some time to come. Until they can be made available we shall require substantial additional land forces in Malaya, which cannot in present circumstances come from British or Indian resources. . . . In the light of the above conclusions, we recommend:—(i) The Commonwealth Government should be asked to provide, and to equip as far as possible, the rough equivalent of one division for the defence of Malaya.
>
> (ii) Preparations should be set in train in Malaya to receive a second Commonwealth reinforcing division, in anticipation of it been found possible to make this available from some source at a later date.
>
> (iii) As soon as possible and at the latest by the end of 1940, two squadrons of fighters and two of G.R. land planes should be despatched [from Australia] to the Far East, and the squadrons now in Malaya should be re-equipped and brought up to establishment.³⁹

If one thing could be said for the planners and policymakers in London, at least they were consistent in their indeterminacy. The defense of Singapore, and all of Malaya as well, had been placed in the hands of an air force that would supposedly exist at some point in the future.

In the meantime, the bulk of Australia's remaining troops were to be the means by which this deficit in air power was to be overcome. Thus indeterminacy had become the agent for operational irresponsibility, a state of affairs that would be illustrated by the course of forthcoming events in Greece and Crete. In November 1939 Churchill had told the Australians that a British fleet would arrive in ample time to prevent a disaster. Upon receipt of the July 31 appreciation, Australia's political and military leaders would have been legitimately excused for believing that the disaster was already a foregone conclusion.

August 1940–July 1941

While the issue of Singapore's defense was being determined anew, Germany's auxiliary cruisers had returned to prey upon Australia's sea communications on both sides of the continent. In August 1940 the armed freighter *Turakina* en route to Wellington from Sydney was attacked and sunk by *Orion* in the Tasman Sea. On the night of October 28–29, mines were laid between Sydney and Newcastle by *Pinguin*, with further mines subsequently laid off Hobart by the same vessel, while the captured Norwegian ship *Starsbad* laid a series of fields in Bass Strait.[40] In early December *Orion* returned in company with *Komet*, this time to the north of the Solomon Islands. Both ships sank a total of five steamers carrying phosphate in the vicinity of Nauru, and on December 27 *Orion* shelled the island itself, inflicting severe damage upon the local phosphate works.[41] None of these sorties were successfully intercepted by Australian or New Zealand warships. Similarly, in the Pacific the status of New Caledonia in the wake of the French capitulation had become a matter of concern for the Australian government in particular, given that the Japanese may attempt to occupy both New Caledonia and the New Hebrides if an administration loyal to the Vichy government held control. With authorization from de Gaulle's Free French government-in-exile (in London), a ship was dispatched to Noumea with a replacement governor, escorted by the Australian light cruiser *Adelaide*. The ships arrived on September 19, and the pro-Vichy officials were removed from their posts without incident.[42]

In the Indian Ocean meanwhile, *Pinguin* had followed up her activities off the eastern seaboard by sinking another three merchant ships before disappearing into the Southern Ocean, with the heavy cruiser

Canberra conducting a fruitless search for the shadowy raider. *Atlantis* was likewise active, and on November 11, 1940, she intercepted the steamer *Automedon* near the entrance to the Sunda Strait. Before sinking her prize, an inspection by the raider's crew uncovered a number of highly sensitive documents that had not been destroyed. Included among these was the July 31 appreciation by the chiefs of staff regarding the defense of Singapore, which was in due course forwarded to the Japanese intelligence services.[43] During the period from January to May 1941, both *Pinguin* and *Atlantis* were joined in the western Indian Ocean by the pocket battleship *Admiral Scheer*, which had broken out of the North Sea the previous October. The warship's visit proved to be fleeting, sinking three ships before retiring to the South Atlantic after being spotted by a reconnaissance plane on February 22, and thereafter returning to Germany itself on April 1, while the two raiders helped themselves to another six Allied merchant ships.[44] They suffered a blow, however, on March 4 when a German supply ship and the raider's oiler, *Ketty Brovig*, were scuttled after being pursued by *Canberra*, and this was followed up on May 5, when *Pinguin* was intercepted by the British heavy cruiser *Cornwall* and blew up after a brief exchange of fire. By the end of July 1941, the activities of the German raiders since September 1939 had netted a total of fifty-four merchant ships (235,931 tons) in the Indian and Pacific Oceans.[45]

The ease with which the *Admiral Scheer* had broken out into the Atlantic highlighted a frustrating period for the Admiralty in which Germany's warships, auxiliary cruisers, and U-boats were virtually coming and going at will. In December 1940 the heavy cruiser *Hipper* arrived at Brest, thereby becoming the first of the Kriegsmarine's warships to utilize a French Atlantic port as a base for operations. She was joined in March 1941 by the battle cruisers *Scharnhorst* and *Gneisenau*, which had just completed a joint raiding mission that claimed sixteen Allied merchantmen.[46] Attempts by the Royal Navy's Home Fleet to intercept the German ships had been hereto unsuccessful, but the Admiralty's luck changed on May 21, when a reconnaissance flight over Grimstadfjord on the Norwegian coast revealed the battleship *Bismarck* and the heavy cruiser *Prinz Eugen* undertaking refueling operations. What followed was one of the most dramatic sea chases in history as British hunting groups sought to run down the giant battleship before she could reach a

French port. In the course of the pursuit, the great Homeric moment of the Second World War at sea was played out at dawn on May 24 between the German vessels and the British capital ships *Hood* and *Prince of Wales*. Shortly after the start of the action, *Hood* was struck by one or more shells that detonated her magazines, causing the pride of the British Empire to vanish in a vast pillar of fire and smoke with the loss of all but three of her 1,400-strong crew. Thanks to the subsequent intervention of torpedo bombers from the aircraft carrier *Ark Royal* that crippled her two days later, *Bismarck* was finally brought to bay on May 27 and overwhelmed by the battleships *King George V* and *Rodney*.[47] The effects of her sinking upon future German naval strategy were profound, as Grand Admiral Raeder later recalled:

> Hitler's attitude toward any suggestions or proposals advocated by me was now completely different. Where before this he had given me a relatively free hand as long as government policies and the other armed services were not involved, he now became extremely critical and very apt to insist on agreement with his own personal views. He had previously preferred not to be worried with too much advance briefing about the sorties of the large ships, as he always felt anxious about them, but now he issued directives to me that radically restricted the movement of these major units. He forbade their [future] sorties into the Atlantic.[48]

By July 1941 the British had also succeeded in getting the upper hand against the Italian surface fleet in the Mediterranean. A major blow had been struck on November 11, 1940, when twenty-one torpedo bombers from the carrier *Illustrious* attacked the Regia Marina's fleet base at Taranto, sinking the battleships *Littorio*, *Caio Duilio*, and *Conti de Cavour*.[49] Then, in what proved to be the decisive clash at sea between the combatant fleets, the two sides met off Cape Matapan on March 28, 1941. In a high-speed engagement, Admiral Cunningham's Mediterranean Fleet gained the advantage after torpedo-bombers flying from the carrier *Formidable* damaged both the battleship *Vittorio Veneto* and the heavy cruiser *Pola*, causing the Italian commander, Admiral Angelo Iachino, to order retirement. In the subsequent pursuit the slower British battleships *Warspite*, *Barham*, and *Valiant* caught up with the crippled *Pola* and, by way of a radar-guided gunnery ambush at night, sank *Pola*, her fellow heavy cruisers *Zara* and *Fiume*, and two destroyers.[50] This defeat effectively neutralized the Regia Marina as a major surface threat for the remainder of the war, but the Mediterranean as a whole was still anything but secure. Since January 1941 life had become ever more difficult for both the Mediterranean Fleet and Force H with the arrival in theater of the Luftwaffe's elite Fliegerkorps X antishipping unit. *Illustrious, Formidable, Valiant,* and *Warspite* were all damaged by dive-bomber attacks, and during the evacuation of Commonwealth forces from Greece (April 29–May 3) and Crete (May 14–29) the dive-bombers likewise meted it out to Cunningham's cruisers and destroyers. In the operations at Crete the British lost three cruisers and six destroyers, with another six cruisers and seven destroyers badly damaged.[51]

Nevertheless, from the strategic perspective, British naval success in the Mediterranean coupled with the sinking of *Bismarck* prompted Churchill to start reconsidering the postponed deployment of British naval forces to the Far East. In a letter to President Roosevelt dated May 28, 1941, he positively assessed the effects of *Bismarck*'s destruction in this regard: "Her [*Bismarck*'s] removal eases our battleship situation, as we should have had to keep *King George V*, *Prince of Wales*, and the two *Nelsons* practically tied to Scapa Flow to guard against a sortie of *Bismarck* and *Tirpitz*, as they could choose their moment and we should have to allow for one of our ships refitting. Now it is a different story. The effect upon the Japanese will be highly beneficial. I expect they are doing all their sums again."[52]

These events in the Atlantic and the Mediterranean had attracted attention from elsewhere. Admiral Yamamoto and his staff planners were to take considerable note of the Taranto raid in particular during their assembly of the Japanese attack plan for Pearl Harbor, whereas Admiral Kimmel was similarly aware of the outcomes but chose not to proceed with changes to the harbor's existing screening measures.[53] Having already been exposed to the dangers of air attack in the Norwegian campaign and at Dunkirk, the Admiralty had again elected to risk operations in waters below enemy-controlled airspace in the absence of adequate carrier-borne or land-based fighter cover. The events off Crete in particular pointed toward an even greater catastrophe should the Royal Navy come up against the carrier- and land-based elements of the

Japanese naval air arm. And while the integrated air-surface tactics employed at Cape Matapan and against *Bismarck* proved to be successful, it would be a different story in the event of a confrontation with the massed aerial firepower wielded by Japan's First Air Fleet. At the same moment the Admiralty had still to implement a means to stifle the principal threat to Great Britain's security, namely the ongoing slaughter of Britain's all-important merchant shipping. During the period from August 1940 to July 1941 a staggering 1,175 ships (5,029,472 tons) had been sent to the bottom, the vast majority falling victim to U-boat attacks.[54] And as of June 22, 1941, the Royal Navy's convoy protection responsibilities were to grow in size as Hitler's Operation Barbarossa rolled across the Soviet frontier. Germany's invasion of Russia likewise heightened the prospects of a fresh Japanese military adventure in the Far East.

Since July 1940 the possibility of a hostile Japanese thrust through Southeast Asia had grown with each passing month. Upon the pretext of mediating a border dispute between Thailand and the French colony of Indo-China, the Japanese had demanded access to northern Indo-China for their armed forces. Under heavy pressure from Berlin, the Vichy government agreed to this partial annexation on August 30.[55] On September 27 the militarists gained their greatest prize thus far when Japan signed the Tripartite Pact with Germany and Italy. In the same month, Japanese forces commenced their move into northern Indo-China. This was followed by Tokyo's announcement of a new policy relating to Indo-China on January 30, 1941, which held that Japan would take military action if necessary to prevent an escalation of the border dispute with Thailand.[56] A series of naval exercises by elements of the Japanese fleet was undertaken near Hainan, and on July 28 Japanese forces began entering southern Indo-China. At a meeting of the Imperial Liaison Conference on June 11, the navy chief of staff, Admiral Nagano Osami, justified the latest annexation: "We must build bases in French Indo-China and Thailand in order to launch military operations."[57] With the signing of a nonaggression pact between Japan and the Soviet Union on April 13, 1941, Japan's leaders found themselves in a position where they could undertake a southern thrust with the risk of a concurrent war with the Soviets largely neutralized. On June 30 the army chief of staff, General Sugiyama Hajime, informed a meeting of the Liaison Conference that "there are several possible timetables and methods for moving south; but for the purpose of survival and self-defence, we are thinking of going as far as the Netherlands East Indies."[58]

In response to Japan's entry into the Tripartite Pact, Whitehall began to abandon its policy of appeasement in the Far East. On October 8, 1940, London informed Tokyo that the closure of the Burma Road would not be extended beyond three months. This was followed in December by the British providing a £10 million loan to the Chinese Nationalist government and the strengthening of military ties between London and Chunking.[59] For the present, a façade of diplomatic cordiality persisted between Britain and Japan, and in a February 1941 meeting with the Japanese ambassador, Churchill reiterated his desire for good relations between both nations.[60] Such an outcome, however, hinged upon a settlement to the Sino-Japanese conflict that would satisfy the United States, and since July 1940 Washington had been imposing ever-greater export sanctions against the Japanese. The passage of the National Defense Act by Congress in July provided President Roosevelt with the power to curtail exports, and in the same month the first embargoes of steel products and aviation fuel had taken place. Further restrictions were imposed in September upon scrap iron and steel, and the export of other metals, ores, and manufactured products were progressively sanctioned in December 1940 and January 1941.[61] Though negotiations between Washington and Tokyo commenced in April 1941, little progress was made as both sides sought to stall for time. There was little of it to spare, for with the final Japanese annexation of Indo-China in July, Roosevelt ordered the freezing of Japanese assets in the United States and simultaneously proclaimed an economic embargo upon Japan that included the supply of all crude and refined oil and all associated petroleum products.[62]

Further efforts to coordinate future strategic policy between the British and American navies had commenced in September 1940 with some preliminary Anglo-American staff conversations in London. When formal talks convened in Washington in January 1941 the main disagreement over strategy emerged through the Admiralty's insistence that a portion of the American fleet be assigned to the defense of Singapore, which the American delegation emphatically rejected.[63] Otherwise both parties agreed in principle that a de facto policy of "Europe first" be adopted, and a solution to the Singapore impasse was similarly included in the ABC-1 staff agreement of March 27, 1941:

The Atlantic and European area is considered to be the decisive theater. The principal United States military effort will be exerted in that theater, and operations of United States forces in other theaters will be conducted in such a manner as to facilitate that effort.... If Japan does enter the war, the military strategy in the Far East will be defensive. The United States does not intend to add to its present military strength in the Far East but will employ the United States Pacific Fleet offensively in the manner best calculated to weaken Japanese economic power, and to support the defense of the Malay barrier by diverting Japanese strength away from Malaysia.[64]

In the Far East meanwhile, the British had begun facilitating multinational talks concerning the coordination of British, American, Dutch, Australian, and New Zealand naval forces within Southeast Asian waters in the event of war. On November 18, 1940, Whitehall had appointed air chief Marshal Sir Robert Brooke-Popham as commander in chief, Far East command, which encompassed the defense of Singapore, Malaya, Burma, Hong Kong, and British Borneo.[65] Under Brooke-Popham's stewardship, preliminary talks had been held at Singapore in December 1940 and February 1941. At the major planning conference held from April 21 to 27 it was evident that reaching agreement on even operational matters would be difficult because of the varying scenarios under which the major powers, Britain and the United States, may enter hostilities.[66] The conference eventually recommended that Japan be opposed with force in the event of one of the following circumstances: (a) a direct act of war by Japanese armed forces against American, British, or Dutch territory; (b) a movement of Japanese forces into Thailand west of the meridian of Bangkok or south of the Kra Isthmus; or (c) the occupation of Portuguese Timor or the Loyalty islands off New Caledonia. The "ADB Plan," as it came to be known, was rejected in July by the American chiefs of staff, principally on the grounds that its broader operational proposals for localized forces in the region were too dependent upon maintaining the strategic integrity of Singapore.[67]

In the wake of Whitehall's July 1940 U-turn regarding the principal mode of defense for Malaya and Singapore, Australian anxieties over the credibility of British assurances were further exacerbated. In forwarding to the Australian government on August 11, 1940, a full summary of the July 31 Far Eastern appreciation by the British chiefs of staff, Lord Caldecote provided a sobering assessment of the situation. As circumstances stood at present, a British fleet had to be maintained in the eastern Mediterranean, and in the absence of a fleet, air power would be required to secure the most important British interests in the Far East.[68] In a separate cable, Caldecote included a secret message to Menzies from Winston Churchill:

> I do not think myself that Japan will declare war unless Germany can make a successful invasion of Britain. . . . In adopting against the grain a yielding policy towards the Japanese threat we have always in mind your interests and safety.
>
> Should Japan nevertheless declare war on us, her first objective outside the Yellow Sea would probably be the Dutch East Indies. Evidently the United States would not like this. What they would do we cannot tell. They give no undertaking of support, but their main Fleet in the Pacific must be a grave preoccupation to the Japanese Admiralty. In this first phase of an Anglo-Japanese war we should of course defend Singapore which if attacked, which is unlikely, ought to stand a long siege.
>
> We are about to reinforce with more first-class units the Eastern Mediterranean Fleet. This fleet could of course at any time be sent through the Canal into the Indian Ocean or to relieve Singapore. We do not want to do this even if Japan declares war until it is found to be vital to your safety. Such a transference would entail the loss of Middle East and all prospects of beating the Italians in the Mediterranean would be gone. We must expect heavy attacks on Egypt in the near future and the Eastern Mediterranean Fleet is needed to help in repelling them. If these attacks succeed the Eastern Fleet would have to leave the Mediterranean either through the Canal or by Gibraltar.
>
> No one can lay down beforehand what is going to happen. We must first weigh events from day to day and use our available resources to the utmost. A final question arises whether Japan having declared war would attempt to invade Australia or New Zealand with a considerable army. We think this very unlikely because Japan is first absorbed in China, secondly would be gathering rich

prizes in the Dutch East Indies, and thirdly would fear very much to send an important part of her Fleet far to the southward leaving the American Fleet between it and home.

If however, contrary to prudence and self-interest, Japan set about invading Australia or New Zealand on a large scale, I have the explicit authority of Cabinet to assure you that we should then cut our losses in the Mediterranean and proceed to your aid sacrificing every interest except only the defence position of this island on which all depends.[69]

Churchill's message to Menzies had betrayed the desperation of Britain's strategic circumstances in August 1940. With the Luftwaffe pounding the British Isles and the ongoing assembly of a German invasion fleet across the Channel, the offering of such a strategically tenuous assurance all but confirmed that for the moment at least, Australia was on her own. Yet following the receipt of this message, the Australian War Cabinet proceeded to debate the overseas deployment of a second division, the 7th Division AIF, in the knowledge that its absence would invariably weaken the nation's domestic defenses. This discussion took place in a pall of gloom following an air crash near Canberra on August 13 that claimed the lives of Brigadier Geoffrey Street (minister for defense), James Fairburn (minister for air), Sir Henry Gullett (minister for science and industry), and General Sir Cyril White, chief of the Australian general staff.[70] Shaken by the loss of such key personalities, the War Cabinet was divided in its views as to whether the Seventh Division should be sent to Malaya, India, or the Middle East. Though the Australian chiefs of staff agreed with their British counterparts and recommended that the division be sent to Malaya, the War Cabinet decided otherwise.[71] Following a further request from Whitehall, and with the consent of the new chief of the general staff, Lieutenant General Sir Vernon Sturdee, on September 23 Menzies and his colleagues determined that the 7th Division should go to the Middle East. Four days later Australia went to the polls, and in a tight race the UAP held on to office with the support of two independents. A subsequent attempt by Menzies to form a national government was quickly rejected by the Labor Party, though Curtin supported the formation of a bipartisan Advisory War Council, which held its first meeting on October 29, 1940.[72]

Alarming news soon followed. Prior to Brooke-Popham's appointment as CIC Far East, a conference had been held in Singapore in October 1940 involving British, Australian, and New Zealand military planners. Following the conference, the Australian chiefs of staff prepared a lengthy report in which they detailed a litany of weaknesses they had observed when studying Malaya's air and ground defenses firsthand. Recommending to the government that sufficient forces be retained in Australia for dealing with localized raids, the chiefs argued that a brigade from the 8th Division AIF be deployed to Malaya on a temporary basis until the division was sent to the Middle East.[73] Dismayed by this advice, Menzies decided that only direct contact with Churchill and the British War Cabinet would make Whitehall see reason when it came to properly equipping the Far East with aircraft and troops. After obtaining an invitation to sit as a member of Churchill's cabinet, the prime minister informed the War Council of his decision on November 25.[74] Departing Australia by flying boat in late January 1941, Menzies paused for a brief stopover in Singapore to confer with Brooke-Popham and inspect the situation for himself. He was impressed by neither and believed that neither Brooke-Popham nor his subordinates possessed a clear grasp of their operational predicament. On the basis of what he had observed, the prime minister pushed on to London via the Middle East with a reinforced resolve to obtain modern fighter aircraft and more ground resources for Malaya and Singapore.[75]

The mission was a failure. Though Menzies proved to be extremely popular with the British public thanks to his speeches and tours of the blitzed areas of London and other cities, his presence in the British War Cabinet became a progressive irritant for Churchill. It had not started on the best of terms due to a spat between the two leaders the previous September, when Menzies had taken issue with the British for employing the Australian heavy cruiser *Australia* in an operation against the Vichy French at Dakar without first informing the Australian government.[76] He was subsequently persuaded by Churchill to commit the 6th Division to Greece as part of an Allied expeditionary force, a decision that was endorsed by the Australian War Cabinet on February 26, 1941. Only the onset of a German offensive in North Africa on March 31 prevented the 7th Division from being dispatched to Greece as well.[77] The Germans commenced their invasion of Greece on April 6, and with the aid of overwhelming air superiority they quickly crushed the Allied defenses, forcing the evacuation of British and Commonwealth forces. Hot on the heels of this fiasco fell a massive German airborne assault against Crete, which necessitated yet another costly amphibious withdrawal. These disasters seriously weakened Menzies' political standing in Australia itself. Otherwise he was the author of his own misfortune in Britain through his active association with political opponents of Churchill, the substance of which is still keenly debated among Australian historians.[78] Menzies returned to Sydney on May 24, 1941, with little chance of being granted a return visit by Churchill (who had learned of his guest's dabbling in domestic intrigues) and with no specific commitments from Whitehall to supply the extra resources so desperately needed in the Far East.

Churchill had in fact authorized the deployment of additional troops and aircraft to Singapore on February 16, 1941, but the Australians regarded the addition of just two RAF squadrons as completely inadequate.[79] Furthermore, the Australian government had only recently learned that the British chiefs of staff had downgraded their existing assessment of aircraft numbers required in Malaya from 586 to 336. What the Australians remained unaware of, however, was Churchill's refusal to accept this modified total as binding.[80] In Menzies' absence, meanwhile, acting prime minister Arthur Fadden and his colleagues were being reassured by the CIC Far East that the position in Malaya and Singapore was far from hopeless. At a meeting of the Australian War Cabinet on February 14, Brooke-Popham spoke enthusiastically of the new Brewster Buffalo fighter planes that were to equip the RAF and RAAF squadrons, and he similarly praised the close-support attributes of the Australian Wirraways.[81] His audience was not entirely convinced. When questioned in detail, Brooke-Popham admitted to shortages in numerous areas, including munitions, antitank and antiaircraft defenses, yet he was confident that Singapore could withstand a nine-month siege and would not be abandoned by Whitehall. He was likewise convinced that while the Japanese possessed more aircraft, they were largely inferior to the available RAF types.[82] His dismissive attitude (and that of many of his subordinates) toward Japanese aviation, often expressed with racial overtones, was a thoroughly idiotic misjudgment, one that would prove fatal for many British and Australian pilots who were to enter combat under the belief that they were flying the superior machines.

In spite of Whitehall's indeterminate postponement of any fleet deployment to the Far East, the Australians persisted in addressing the issue. In a cable to Stanley Bruce on December 3, 1940, Menzies instructed Bruce to make a request to Churchill and the Admiralty that, in view of the recent success at Taranto, three or four capital ships be based at Singapore "without prejudice to the security of other areas where they may now be located." The prime minister also recommended an alternative disposition in the form of a battle cruiser and an aircraft carrier being based at Ceylon if the larger concentration could not be assembled. By way of response, Menzies received a virtual cut-and-paste of Churchill's August 11 assurance, with an updated strategic appreciation that discounted any fleet movement to the Far East until such time as the Regia Marina had been effectively knocked out of the fighting.[83] On February 12, 1941, Acting Prime Minister Fadden jumped on the merry-go-round when he pointed out to Whitehall that the naval planning at the December 1940 Singapore Conference was incomplete in virtually every respect. The same could be said of the contents of the reply he received from London eleven days later.[84] At a meeting with the vice chief of the naval staff, Rear Admiral Tom Phillips, at the Admiralty on March 8, 1941, Menzies finally acknowledged the apparent futility of pursuing the naval problem with any hope of success. As the minutes of the meeting recorded, the prime minister "was of the view that in the general reference to reinforcing our position in the Far East with capital ships, we have only been deluding ourselves."[85]

While Menzies was toiling away in London, a welcome soother for Australian nerves arrived in March 1941 in the form of the American heavy cruisers *Chicago* and *Portland,* accompanied by five destroyers. The task group visited Sydney on March 20 and Brisbane on March 25, with both visits being greeted with great public enthusiasm; the parade of USN personnel in Sydney drew an estimated crowd of half a million people. This warmth was echoed by Fadden in his greeting to the Americans at a luncheon at the Sydney Town Hall: "We welcome you as our cousins. We welcome you as a people from the other side of the Pacific, who have extended to us not only the hand of friendship, but also the hand of practical support and cooperation. Nothing in the life of Australia has so stirred, inspired, and thrilled that nation as has this visit of part of the great United States Navy, synchronising with the wonderful actions and works of President Roosevelt."[86]

The dispatch of this task group to the South Pacific (it likewise visited New Zealand, Fiji, and Tahiti) was to fulfill two objectives: a demonstration of strength to Tokyo and, in the words of the noted American naval historian Samuel E. Morison, "to hearten our antipodean friends who felt forgotten and virtually abandoned by Mother England."[87] What was not heartening for the antipodeans, however, were certain developments in the Anglo-American strategic relationship during the first six months of 1941. In the course of the Anglo-American staff conversations in February and March (at which the Australians were present as observers), the Australians were considerably alarmed by the refusal of their hosts to recognize the critical strategic importance of the Singapore base.[88] More alarming still was the mooted transfer of a portion of the Pacific Fleet to the Atlantic. In a cable dated May 2 to the Department of External Affairs, Minister Casey noted his fears, stating that he had "no hesitation in saying that the proposal for a transfer of a large portion of the United States Pacific Fleet would leave British countries and interests in considerable peril."[89] His spirits were lifted two months later following a private conversation with the Secretary of the Navy, Frank Knox. Knox informed Casey that the USN would shortly begin to take over convoy escort duties from the Royal Navy in the Atlantic, thereby freeing up British ships for service elsewhere. As Casey interpreted the ABC-1 agreement, at least six British battleships would be theoretically available for deployment to Singapore "on the United States becoming belligerent, and on the threat of war in the Far East."[90] The problem, as ever, was matching expectation with outcome, and given the prior conduct of the Singapore strategy in this respect, the portents were not exactly favorable.

August 1941–December 1941

During the latter half of 1941 the Royal Navy successfully targeted the activities of Germany's auxiliary cruisers in the South Atlantic. The destruction of a German supply ship was followed up on November 22 with the sinking of *Atlantis* by the heavy cruiser *Devonshire*.[91] In the Indian and Pacific Oceans, losses to raider activity amounted to less than a dozen ships since July, but in the late afternoon of November 19 the Germans struck back in devastating fashion. On a return passage to Fremantle, the Australian light cruiser *Sydney* came across a suspicious merchant ship that identified herself as the Dutch vessel *Straat Malakka* when challenged by signal lamp. For reasons that remain unknown, *Sydney* closed to within two kilometers of the vessel, whereupon the latter ditched her disguise and opened fire upon the Australian cruiser.[92] The ship in question was in fact the auxiliary cruiser *Kormoran*, which had been operating in the Indian Ocean since early 1941. *Kormoran*'s opening salvo at point-blank range succeeded in knocking out *Sydney*'s bridge and forward guns; further fire from her guns and torpedoes fatally crippled *Sydney*, which was last seen limping away ablaze to the east. Return fire from the cruiser was sufficient to disable the *Kormoran*, resulting in her subsequent scuttling, and the survivors of her crew were rescued on November 24.[93] All 645 members of *Sydney*'s crew were lost in the action, the worst single disaster suffered by the Royal Australian Navy to this day, and it was not until 2008 that the wrecks of both ships were finally discovered off the coast of Western Australia.

The loss of *Sydney* with all hands was greeted with great shock across Australia, for she had previously served with considerable distinction in the Mediterranean, sinking the Italian light cruiser *Bartolomeo Colleoni* off Cape Spada on July 19, 1940, and participating in a number of other successful surface operations.[94] Attacks by German U-boats operating in the Mediterranean during November 1941 likewise inflicted serious blows against the Royal Navy. Just thirty miles from Gibraltar on November 13, the aircraft carrier *Ark Royal* was struck by a single torpedo from U-81 and sank before help could arrive. Virtually all on board were rescued, a fortunate outcome that was not to be repeated some twelve days later. Off Crete on November 25 the battleship *Barham* blew up after being hit by several torpedoes from U-331, with more than eight hundred lives lost. In the following month it was the Italians who inflicted more pain upon the battered Mediterranean Fleet when semisubmersibles penetrated Alexandria Harbour on the night of December 18–19, 1941, and crippled the battleships *Queen Elizabeth* and *Valiant* with explosive charges.[95] Aside from reducing the British naval presence in the Eastern Mediterranean to a handful of cruisers and destroyers, these events were to have a marked impact upon the Admiralty's recently resurrected planning for future operations in the Far East.

Following the Atlantic Conference at Newfoundland from August 10–15, 1941, Churchill outlined his plans for naval dispositions in the

Indian Ocean by way of correspondence with both the first lord and first sea lord on August 25:

> It should be possible in the near future to place a deterrent squadron in the Indian Ocean. Such a force should consist of the smallest number of the best ships. We have only to remember all the preoccupations which are caused us by the *Tirpitz*—the only capital ship left to Germany against our fifteen or sixteen battleships and battle-cruisers—to see what an effect would be produced upon the Japanese Admiralty by the presence of a very small but very powerful and fast force in Eastern waters.... The most economical disposition would be to send *Duke of York* as soon as she is clear of construction defects, via Trinidad and Simonstown to the East. She could be joined by *Repulse* or *Renown* and one aircraft-carrier of high speed. This powerful force might show itself in the triangle Aden-Singapore-Simonstown. It would exert a paralysing influence upon Japanese naval action.... I do not like the idea of sending at this stage of the old "R" class battleships to the East. ... They might, however, be useful for convoy should we reach that stage, which is not yet by any means certain, or even, in my opinion, probable. I am however in principle in favour of placing a formidable, first-class squadron in the aforesaid triangle by the end of October, and telling both the Americans and the Australians that we will do so.[96]

Responding in writing to the prime minister's observations on August 28, Admiral Pound dismissed Churchill's idea that *Duke of York* could be worked up on her outward voyage as impossible, and he rejected any deployment of the other *King George V* ships beyond the European theater. His suggested alternative was to deploy the battleships *Rodney* and *Nelson* along with *Renown* and *Ark Royal* at Trincomalee or Singapore over a staggered period from November 1941 to April 1942, and he justified his approach in the following terms:

> (a) *Nelson* and *Rodney* will eventually form part of the Eastern Fleet, when it is possible to form one, which is dependent upon the availability of cruisers and particularly of destroyers.

(b) *Nelson* and *Rodney* will give the best backing to the "R" class when the Eastern Fleet is formed, and the combination will form the most homogeneous we can provide as regards speed.

(c) Until we can form a fleet in the Far East which is capable of meeting a Japanese force of the strength they are likely to send south, it is necessary to deter Japanese action in the Indian Ocean. By sending capital ships to escort our convoys in the Indian Ocean we hope to deter the Japanese from sending any of their battleships to this area. By sending a battle-cruiser and aircraft-carrier to the Indian Ocean we hope to deter the Japanese from sending their 8-inch gun cruisers to attack our trade in the area. It is not considered that the substitution of one of the *King George V* class for one of the above would give sufficient added security to justify the disadvantages which her absence from the home area would involve, as her speed is inadequate to run down a Japanese 8-inch gun cruiser.

(d) Depending on the situation at the time, and if war with Japan had not broken out, it may be found desirable to send *Nelson*, *Rodney* and *Renown* and the aircraft-carrier to Singapore in the first instance, as they would thus form a greater deterrent. If war eventuated they would have to retire to Trincomalee.[97]

In reply to Pound on August 29, Churchill vigorously justified his scheme to employ a *King George V*–class battleship as a deterrent against Japanese naval aggression by citing the Admiralty's own attitude toward *Tirpitz* in the Atlantic as a measure of just how effectively a single ship could impact upon an opponent's naval strategy:

It is surely a faulty disposition to create in the Indian Ocean a fleet considerable in numbers, costly in maintenance an manpower, but consisting entirely of slow, obsolescent, or unmodernised ships which can neither fight a fleet action with the main Japanese force nor act as a deterrent upon his modern fast, heavy ships, if used singly or in pairs as raiders. Such dispositions might be forced upon us by circumstances, but they are inherently unsound in themselves. . . . The potency of the dispositions I ventured to suggest in my minute is illustrated by the Admiralty's own extraordinary concern about the *Tirpitz*. *Tirpitz* is doing to us exactly what a *K.G.V.* in the Indian Ocean would do to the Japanese Navy. It exercises a vague general fear and menaces all points at once. It appears, and disappears, causing immediate reactions and perturbations on the other side. . . . It is very likely that she [Japan] will negotiate with the United States for at least three months without making any further aggressive move or joining the Axis actively. Nothing would increase her hesitation more than the appearance of the force I mentioned, and above all, a *K.G.V.* This might indeed be a decisive deterrent.[98]

Aside from his inflated opinion as to the impact of a single battleship upon Japanese thinking, Churchill's summation of Japan's broader intentions proved to be substantially correct. For this particular game of diplomatic musical chairs, the band had kicked in from the very moment the Roosevelt administration imposed its sanctions regime on July 26. As of April 1, 1941, the Japanese oil supply amounted to approximately twenty million barrels. By September 30 this had been reduced to fifteen million, and on September 6 the Imperial Conference set a deadline of six weeks for further negotiations.[99] In early August there had been some grounds for hope that a compromise between Japan and the United States could be achieved when Premier Konoe proposed a summit conference with President Roosevelt. These proved to be short-lived, as the Americans saw little point in the exercise given that Japan was highly unlikely to accede to any demand to cease her military activities in China. When the Liaison Conference's deadline was reached on October 12, Konoe saw no further way forward. He resigned two days later and was succeeded as premier by General Tojo Hideki. In order to finalize Japanese military preparations, Tojo extended the deadline for negotiations until November 25 at the latest. On November 10 the Imperial Army and the IJN reached what became known as the "Central Agreement" for Japan's war objectives:

1. Simultaneous landings of amphibious forces in Luzon, Guam, the Malay Peninsula, Hong Kong, and Miri, British North Borneo. All except the last to be preceded by air attacks.

2. Carrier air attack on the United States Pacific Fleet at Pearl Harbor.

3. Rapid exploitation of initial successes by the seizure of Manila, Mindanao, Wake Island, the Bismarcks, Bangkok, and Singapore.

4. Occupation of the Dutch East Indies and continuation of the war with China.[100]

Whereas the Americans were well aware of Tokyo's intentions through their decryption of the Japanese diplomatic ciphers, they remained unaware as to both when and where the first blows would fall and of the true extent of the looming fuel crisis for the Japanese navy. At a meeting of the Liaison Conference on October 23, Admiral Nagano bluntly stated the IJN's position. "The Navy is consuming 400 tons of oil an hour. The situation is urgent. We want it [the decision for peace or war] decided one way or the other quickly." He was backed up by the army chief of staff, General Sugiyama, whose impatience was undisguisable. "Things have already been delayed one month. We cannot devote four or five days to study. Hurry up and go ahead!"[101] Nagano had also given thought to the likely scale of British naval deployment to the Far East. On November 5 he advised the Liaison Conference that the probable composition of a British fleet would amount to a single battleship and a dozen cruisers deployed to Singapore.[102] By December 1, 1941, however, he had reconsidered the situation. During the course of the Imperial Conference in which the decision for war was undertaken, Nagano informed those present that because Germany and Italy "have become somewhat less active, and particularly because the Italian Navy has become passive, the British Navy has recently acquired reserve power and is gradually adding to its strength in the Orient."[103] As for the situation in Malaya and Singapore, the Japanese were by now well aware of the critical weaknesses in British land and air defenses. Much of the information had been gleaned by agents and fifth columnists and, in the final weeks before the outbreak of hostilities, high-altitude overflights from Indo-China that confirmed the limited number of aircraft present at RAF aerodromes.[104]

The capture of Malaya and Singapore had been assigned to the Japanese 25th Army under the command of General Yamashita Tomoyuki. Yamashita's chief of intelligence, Colonel Tsuji Masanobu, was concerned about the presence of aircraft at Kota Bharu, a small port town situated on the far northeastern Malayan coastline, just to the south of the

Malayan-Thai frontier.[105] Kota Bharu was one of three designated landing areas for the 25th Army, the others being at Singora and Patani in southern Thailand. Stationed there was 1 Squadron RAAF, which had been one of the original squadrons dispatched to Malaya in June 1940 as part of Australia's assistance package for Whitehall. As of the beginning of December 1941, four Australian squadrons were deployed in Malaya and Singapore as well as substantial elements of the 8th Division AIF. The dispatch of a brigade from the 8th had been agreed to by Prime Minister Menzies the previous year, but by December Menzies was no longer in office. He had returned to Australia in May to face a deeply divided coalition cabinet, and his second offer of national government to the Labor opposition was rejected on August 26. Two days later Menzies announced his resignation. He was succeeded as prime minister by Arthur Fadden, who was informed in a congratulatory cable from Churchill that Australia would no longer be afforded representation in the British War Cabinet.[106] Fadden's administration lasted barely over a month. On October 3 the two independents who provided the government with a majority in the House of Representatives voted against the supply (budget) bills, and Fadden was forced to tender his resignation.[107] With the support of the independents, John Curtin was able to form a government and was sworn in as prime minister on October 7.

Having spent the better part of the previous decade drifting between skepticism and rejection when it came to his views on the Singapore strategy, Curtin soon came face-to-face with his gravest fears. Chairing a meeting of the Advisory War Council on October 16, 1941, at which the commander in chief Far East was present, he learned from Brooke-Popham that of the 336 first-line aircraft expected to be available for Burma, Malaya, and Borneo, there were at present some 180 machines, which represented an increase of just 62 over the past five months. When Curtin observed that shortages in most areas had not been made up since April, Brooke-Popham informed him that he had made all representations to Whitehall "short of resigning," and that the British chiefs of staff were allocating as many resources as possible given the demands of other theaters.[108] If this wasn't enough to test Curtin's patience, he had shortly to deal with a problem he had inherited from Fadden. The Australian 9th Division, which had been raised in England in late 1940 from British-based elements of the 6th Division, had been holed up under siege in

Tobruk for the better part of six months, and the general officer commanding Australian forces, General Thomas Blamey, wanted his troops relieved on the grounds of growing ill-health, a claim disputed by the British. Fadden had formally requested their withdrawal on September 15, a request Churchill acquiesced to with ill-concealed disgust.[109] Some extra prodding from Curtin was required, which produced a cable from Churchill that not only curtly informed the Australians that the troops were being withdrawn but also provided unexpected good news regarding another well-worn issue:

> 1. Tobruk: Relief is being carried out in accordance with your decision which I greatly regret.
>
> 3. Admiralty dispositions have been to build towards the end of the year, H.M.S. *Rodney*, H.M.S. *Nelson* and four *R's* based mainly on Singapore. This, however, was spoiled by the recent injury to H.M.S. *Nelson* which will take three to four months to repair.
>
> 4. In the interval, in order further to deter Japan, we are sending forthwith our newest battleship *Prince of Wales* to join H.M.S. *Repulse* in the Indian Ocean. This is done in spite of protests from the Commander in Chief Home Fleet and is a serious risk for us to run. The *Prince of Wales* will be noticed at Capetown quite soon. In addition the four 'R' are being moved as they become ready to eastern waters. Later on H.M.S. *Repulse* will be relieved by H.M.S. *Renown* which has a greater radius.
>
> 5. I agree with you that the *Prince of Wales* will be the best possible deterrent and every effort will be made to spare her permanently. I must, however, make it clear that the movements of the *Prince of Wales* must be reviewed when she is at Capetown because of the danger of *Tirpitz* breaking out and other operational possibilities before the *Duke of York* is ready in December.[110]

Churchill had finally gotten his way with the Admiralty. Following a brief hiatus after his discussions with Admiral Pound in August, the prime minister determined on October 17 that *Prince of Wales* must be sent to the Far East, albeit with a recall option in place.[111] Both capital ships were to be accompanied by the aircraft carrier *Indomitable*, but the carrier suffered damage in a grounding at Jamaica prior to her departure and was sidelined for repairs. After stopovers in South Africa and again at Ceylon, Force Z arrived at Singapore on December 2, 1941. Churchill's decision had been made on advice from the Foreign Office that *Prince of Wales* would act as a powerful deterrent to Japan entering the war in the first place.[112] This was a different conception from that which the prime minister had envisaged in his original discussions with Pound. In their August correspondence, Churchill saw the presence of a modern battleship in the Indian Ocean as deterring Japanese naval activity to the west of the Malay Barrier. Yet the view that a single modern battleship would somehow make the Japanese back away from undertaking war with the Western powers was another matter entirely. Bearing in mind the strength wielded by the Japanese fleet, this determination was thoroughly ludicrous, a throwback to nineteenth-century gunboat diplomacy whereby militarily unsophisticated opponents could be easily cowed by the presence of an ironclad off their shores. It displayed the same inherent arrogance toward the Japanese that clouded British estimations of the effectiveness of Japan's aerial capabilities, and it was to prove equally costly once hostilities had commenced.

Time was now running short. On November 7 Curtin and the Advisory War Council entertained Alfred Duff Cooper, Churchill's newly elevated minister in the Far East. Duff Cooper's brief was to ensure the coordination of activities between the numerous strands of British colonial administration and Whitehall, which would be overseen by an existing Defence Council in Singapore.[113] Having outlined the scheme to those present, Duff Cooper ran into heavy weather when the conversation turned to material defenses, as the minutes of the meeting recorded:

The Minister for External Affairs [Dr. Herbert Evatt] asked what were the real plans of the United Kingdom Government in relation to Far Eastern and Pacific Defence. Mr. Duff Cooper said that it had always been the intention of the United Kingdom Government to reinforce the Far East and they were prepared to abandon the Mediterranean altogether if this was necessary in order to hold Singapore. Mr. Hughes thought that the abandonment of the Mediterranean was a very remote possibility. He doubted if public opinion in the United Kingdom would ever support this. His view was that such a policy did not have a firm basis and ignored the foundations of the Imperial structure which had roots in the Mediterranean as well as the Far East.... Mr. Duff Cooper in replying to [an earlier question by] Mr. Spender, said he did not agree that the United Kingdom Government was unconcerned about the defence of Singapore. Mr. Menzies said that Mr. Churchill had always told him of the importance he attached to the defence of Singapore, but Mr. Menzies doubted if Mr. Churchill was, in fact, fully seized of its vital significance.[114]

The Australian government reacted with shock on November 22 after Whitehall informed them that Brooke-Popham was to be relieved from his post in December.[115] Though a number of postwar Australian histories have been highly critical of his competency as a commander (when it came to Brooke-Popham's attitude toward Japanese aviation in particular, this criticism was thoroughly merited), he proved to be a capable strategist when required. In conjunction with the newly appointed general officer commanding, Malaya Command, the now Lieutenant General Arthur Percival, Brooke-Popham had devised Operation "Matador," a pre-emptive strike into Thailand in the event of an imminent Japanese invasion. Once it had been established that Japanese landings were imminent, British troops would advance over the Thai frontier toward Singora and Patani and, ideally, challenge the Japanese as the latter were in the process of disembarking from their troopships. Meanwhile the ships themselves were to be subjected to continuous airstrikes mounted by the RAF from its airfields in northern Malaya, with Brooke-Popham anticipating that much of the enemy's forces would be destroyed before they reached the beaches.[116] And unlike any other senior British military commander in the twentieth century or thereafter, the Air Chief Marshal had been granted the sole authority to commence hostilities in the absence of approval from Whitehall, as the contents of a cable from the secretary of state for Dominion affairs to John Curtin on December 5 disclosed:

1. The position is that we have now received an assurance of armed support from the United States. (a) If we find it necessary either to forestall a Japanese landing in Kra Isthmus or to occupy part of the Isthmus as a counter to Japanese violation of any other part of Thailand; (b) If the Japanese attack the Netherlands East

Indies and we go at once to support the latter; (c) If the Japanese attack us.

2. We have accordingly instructed the Commander-in-Chief, Far East, that he should take action . . . without reference to us if either (a) He has good information that a Japanese expedition is advancing with the apparent intention of landing on Kra Isthmus, or (b) The Japanese violate any other part of Thailand.

3. The Commander-in-Chief, Far East, has also been authorised in the event of a Japanese attack on the Netherlands East Indies to put into operation without further reference to us the plans already agreed with the Netherlands East Indies.[117]

For "Matador" to succeed, the British would have to reach the invasion areas within twenty-four hours, and this meant that accurate air reconnaissance was an absolute priority. On December 5 two Japanese convoys were sighted to the south of Cape Cambodia steering west into the Gulf of Siam. Further flights by RAF flying boats in the vicinity resulted in the loss of two aircraft, one of which was subsequently confirmed to be the victim of escorting Japanese fighters.[118] Poor monsoonal weather now intervened, with aerial reconnaissance rendered impossible until the morning of December 6. Meanwhile *Repulse*, which had left Singapore the day before for a short cruise to Darwin, had been recalled following the receipt of the first sighting report.[119] In the early afternoon of December 6, two RAAF bombers made separate sightings of Japanese formations from 185 miles to 360 miles east of Kota Bharu, all three steaming due west. Bad weather prevented further sightings until 1345 hours the following day, when unidentified transports were seen less than fifty miles from Patani. At dusk another aircraft made a further observation of a small force approximately 110 miles east of Kota Bharu, and it was fired on by a Japanese warship.[120] Because of communication difficulties, Brooke-Popham did not receive this latest information until 2100 hours that evening. Given that "Matador" needed at least twenty-four hours for the troops to reach the landing areas in Thailand, he ordered the postponement of the operation given the proximity of the approaching convoys to the Malayan coast. The airstrikes, however, would proceed once confirmation had been received that the Japanese ships had indeed arrived at the invasion sites.[121]

At approximately 0030 hours Malayan time on the morning of December 8, 1941 (December 7 in Hawaii), the beachfront at Kota Bharu came under fire from several Japanese destroyers that had arrived offshore; three transports were likewise sighted. Apprised of this activity, Brooke-Popham ordered immediate retaliation from 1 Squadron RAAF and the deployment at first light of an additional five bomber and one night-fighter squadrons to target enemy shipping in the vicinity. At 0200 hours, eight bombers began an intense round of low-level sorties against their nearby targets.[122] Shortly thereafter the first Japanese bombs were falling on Ford Island Naval Air Station at Pearl Harbor. At 0430 hours seventeen Japanese bombers hit Singapore City and several adjacent RAF aerodromes. These events heralded the beginning of a momentous day in what was to become one of the most wide-ranging and complex offensives ever undertaken in military history.

In an address to the House of Commons on April 11, 1940, Winston Churchill had described in broad terms how the Admiralty would seek to maintain Britain's naval superiority: "When we speak of command of the seas, it does not mean the command of every part of the sea at the same moment, or at every moment. It only means that we can make our will prevail ultimately in any part of the seas which may be selected for operations, and thus indirectly make our will prevail in every part of the sea."[123] By the beginning of December 1941 this strategy had resulted in partial success, particularly as was applicable to the neutralization of the German and Italian surface fleets. Otherwise, the menace posed by Germany's U-boat arm was yet to reach its peak, and the Royal Navy's vulnerability to land-based air attack had cost the British dearly, especially within the Mediterranean theater of operations. Yet in spite of the grievous losses suffered, the vital Allied supply and communications conduits remained unbroken. While Australia's overseas sea routes in the Indian and Pacific Oceans had suffered far less attrition than the carnage generated in the Atlantic, the blows already inflicted by Germany's auxiliary cruisers served as a powerful reminder that the Australian continent's geographical separation from the war in Europe did not equate to a reduction in vulnerability to hostile interdiction. With Japan's entry into the conflict, however, the whole nature of the nation's naval defense was transformed. Not only were its links with the outside world now under more immediate threat, but the Japanese, unlike their German and Italian counterparts, possessed the means and methods to directly threaten the Australian mainland itself, and unless Australia's reliance upon third-party protection was effectively fulfilled, the opportunity for Japan to do so would not long be delayed.

8

The Far East

December 1941–April 1942

> *Dr H. V. Evatt, Minister for External Affairs,*
> *to Mr F. K. Officer, Chargé d'Affaires in Japan*
> *Canberra, 9 December 1941*

You are instructed to inform the Imperial Japanese Government immediately that a state of war exists and has existed between His Majesty's Government in the Commonwealth of Australia and the Imperial Japanese Government as from 5 o'clock in the afternoon, 9th December 1941.

Evatt

—Doc. 174 in W. J. Hudson & H. J. W. Stokes,
Documents on Australian Foreign Policy 1937–49.
Volume V: July 1941–June 1942, 289

Two decades had passed since the conference between senior British and Australian naval representatives on board HMS *Hawkins* at Penang in March 1921 resolved that the keystone to the Royal Navy's future presence in the Asia-Pacific region was the establishment of an impregnable base at Singapore.[1] As of the early hours of December 8, 1941, Singapore's defenses were anything but unassailable. The Admiralty had conceded as much in prior discussions with Winston Churchill when the first sea lord advised that any force sent as a deterrent to Japanese aggression would have to be withdrawn to Trincomalee in the event of hostilities.² Churchill too considered the Indian Ocean the most viable setting for basing a small but powerful squadron to deter the Imperial Japanese Navy from conducting raiding activities that would threaten the sea lanes from India and Australia. So in the absence of a substantial British naval presence, the first line of defense for Malaya and Singapore was to be provided by land-based air power, and should this prove to be ineffective, the peripheries of the British Empire in the Far East stood to be consumed by an unprecedented military catastrophe.

The Bottomless Battleship: December 8, 1941–February 15, 1942

Prior to first light over the Malayan peninsula on the morning of December 8, the efforts by 1 Squadron RAAF to destroy the small Japanese invasion flotilla situated off Kota Bharu had met with considerable success. Flying in conditions that varied between clear moonlit skies and sudden rain squalls, the squadron's Hudson bombers succeeded in sinking the large fast transport *Awagisan Maru* (9,794 tons) and heavily damaging two other transports.³ Repeated bombing and strafing runs sank a number of landing barges packed with troops and inflicted casualties upon enemy forces that had already landed on the beachfront. In accordance with Brooke-Popham's plan for concerted follow-up strikes against the invasion convoys at dawn, six more squadrons attempted to intercept enemy shipping in the vicinity of Kota Bharu and Patani. Due to rainstorms and thick low clouds in the designated target areas, only three of these formations made fleeting contact with the enemy, with no further damage observed.⁴ A strike against Japanese transports in the vicinity of Patani by eleven Blenheims of 62 Squadron RAF proved fruitless in the face of determined fighter opposition, though none of the attacking bombers were lost. Just at 0900 hours a shot-up Beaufort bomber assigned to perform reconnaissance over the Singora-Patani roadstead crash-landed at Kota Bharu, with photographs revealing approximately sixty enemy aircraft occupying the airbase at Singora.⁵ Shortly thereafter the Kota Bharu airfield was strafed by fighters, the first of numerous Japanese strikes that were to hit RAF bases in northern Malaya during the course of the day.

Grave misfortune was to follow. Away to the northwest the airbases at Sungei Patani and Alor Star were similarly subjected to persistent bombing and strafing attacks. At the latter the luckless 62 Squadron was caught on the ground as it prepared to take off for a further strike against enemy shipping at Patani, with all but two of its bombers destroyed or severely damaged.[6] Other bomber and fighter squadrons suffered serious losses when attacked while refueling and rearming, while the few Buffalo fighters that were able to get airborne found themselves badly outclassed by the Japanese navy Zekes and army fighters operating from the captured Thai airbases. And as a result of confusion on the ground regarding the presence of Japanese troops near the Kota Bharu airbase, the facility was evacuated late in the afternoon, along with satellite airfields at Gong Kedah and Machang.[7] By nightfall Air Vice Marshal Pulford had ordered the evacuation of Alor Star and the withdrawal of the battered squadrons from northern Malaya.[8] This enforced retreat came hot on the heels of another opening day catastrophe for Allied land-based air power in the Far East, in which most of the U.S. Far Eastern Air Force's first-line strength had been targeted at Clark Field, sixty miles to the northwest of Manila. In spite of ample warning of the earlier Japanese attack against Pearl Harbor, the combination of command indecision and false alarms resulted in the majority of the base's P-40 fighters and B-17 bombers being assembled on the runways when a large Japanese formation arrived overhead at 1230 hours local time. Virtually unopposed, the fifty-four bombers and their Zeke escorts proceeded to devastate the base with great precision, leaving less than fifty airworthy aircraft available for subsequent operations.[9]

Within twelve hours the two major concentrations of Allied air power in the Far East were largely neutralized. The decision to abandon the airbases in northern Malaya gifted the Japanese air superiority over the landing areas, and they were to take full advantage of extensive air support for their ground forces. An attempt by the British to launch a limited ground incursion into Thailand in accordance with "Matador" was soon abandoned, and in a matter of days the Japanese had begun advancing down both sides of the Malayan peninsula toward Singapore.[10] At Singapore meanwhile, the onset of another disaster was taking place in the late afternoon of December 8. Aware since morning of the enemy landings and air attacks, Admiral Sir Tom Phillips determined that Force Z should depart Singapore as soon as possible and fall upon the Japanese transports off Singora at dawn on December 10. He proposed to do so on the understanding that Force Z would be provided with air reconnaissance one hundred miles to the north of his ships from daylight on December 9, searches as far north as Singora on December 10, and fighter protection during the course of the planned attack by Force Z at dawn that morning.[11] Shortly following the departure of the ships from Singapore, Pulford informed Phillips via signal that while reconnaissance could be provided the next day, further observation was uncertain and fighter cover over Singora was impossible. Phillips elected to proceed with his mission, and *Prince of Wales*, *Repulse*, and their four escorting destroyers steamed to the east of the Anambas Islands to avoid Japanese air searches.[12] On the morning of December 9 the admiral signaled *Repulse* with his intentions regarding the forthcoming action: "This is your opportunity before the enemy can establish himself. We have made a wide circuit to avoid air reconnaissance and hope to surprise the enemy shortly after sunrise tomorrow, Wednesday. We are sure to get some useful practice with high-angle armament, but whatever we meet I want to finish quickly and so get well clear to the eastward before the Japanese can mass too formidable a scale of air attack against us. So shoot to sink."[13]

While Force Z soldiered on northwards for the balance of the day, a series of heavy Japanese raids against the airbases at Butterworth and Kuantan further crippled Air Vice Marshal Pulford's remaining fighter and bomber strength in Malaya. After just two days of fighting the RAF could no longer exercise any form of control over northern and central Malaya, and within the next few days all the remaining British, Australian, and New Zealand aircraft were to be progressively relocated to airfields in Johore and on Singapore Island itself.[14] At sea, Phillips' impending presence was being awaited by powerful elements of the Japanese Second Fleet consisting of the battleships *Kongō* and *Haruna* along with nine cruisers and seven destroyers under the overall command of Vice Admiral Kondō Nobutake. Unbeknown to Phillips, Force Z had been under observation by a Japanese submarine for much of the afternoon, and just before dusk his ships engaged the attention of enemy reconnaissance aircraft.[15] With the advantage of surprise seemingly lost, the British admiral ordered retirement to Singapore at 2055 hours that evening when his ships were unknowingly within ten miles of Kondō's force. On the basis of the earlier sightings, a large formation of enemy aircraft from the 22nd Air Flotilla was dispatched to locate and attack the British ships by moonlight; no contact was made, and the aircraft returned without loss to their airfields in Indo-China.[16]

Shortly before midnight on December 9 a signal was received from Singapore advising that a Japanese landing was under way at Kuantan, 150 miles to the south of Kota Bharu. In spite of the risks, Phillips decided to alter course and intercept the enemy transports at first light. By dawn the ships were off Kuantan, and after a close inspection of the shoreline by one of the escorting destroyers, it was found that the original report had been false.[17] After investigating some small vessels in the vicinity, the squadron was recommencing its passage southward when at 1020 hours it came under notice from an enemy reconnaissance aircraft. Forty minutes later, *Repulse* was subjected to a high-level bombing attack from a small formation of "Nells," which scored a hit amidships. They were soon joined by further formations of Nells and "Bettys" armed with torpedoes, and *Prince of Wales* was struck at least twice by torpedoes, which severely damaged her port propellers and caused flooding that knocked out much of the electricity supply for her antiaircraft batteries.[18] *Repulse* successfully evaded attack until 1220 hours, when she was struck in quick succession by five torpedoes; she rolled over and sank ten minutes later with the loss of more than five hundred of her crew. *Prince of Wales* suffered two more hits from torpedoes before capsizing and sinking at 1320 hours; 320 of her complement were lost, including Admiral Phillips and Captain John Leach, who both went down with the ship. Just three of approximately eighty Japanese bombers were downed by antiaircraft fire during the action, with friendly fighter support in the form of 453 Squadron RAAF not arriving overhead until 1325 hours, by which time the last of the enemy aircraft were out of interception range as they departed the scene.[19]

Winston Churchill was aghast when news of the engagement reached Whitehall: "I was thankful to be alone. In all the war I never received a more direct shock. As I turned over and twisted in bed, the full horror of the news sank in upon me. There were no British or American capital-ships in the Indian Ocean or the Pacific except the American survivors of Pearl Harbour, who were hastening back to California. Over all this vast expanse of waters Japan was supreme, and everywhere we were weak and naked."[20] The previous evening the prime minister and his War Cabinet colleagues had discussed the proposed dispersal of Force Z from Singapore. Most of those present agreed with Churchill that the ships should join the remnants of the U.S. Pacific Fleet, a course of action that would serve as "the best possible shield to our brothers in Australasia."[21]

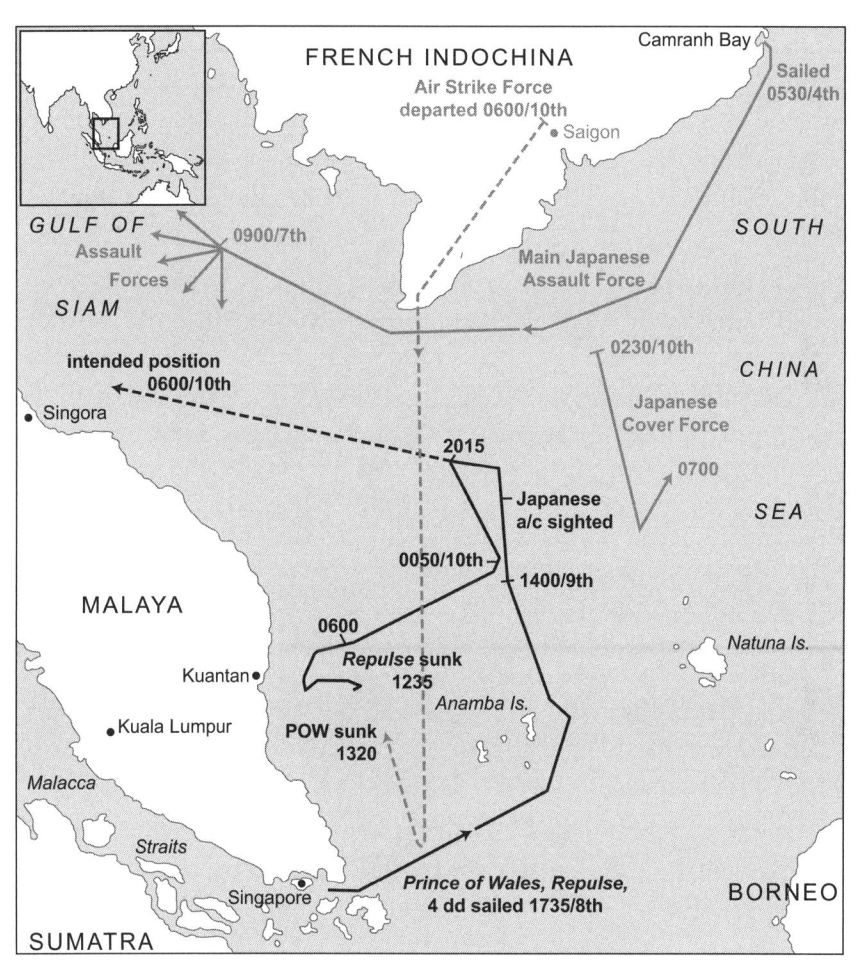

Sinking of HMS Prince of Wales *and HMS* Repulse, *December 10, 1941*

But with the ships still in transit to Singapore, a final decision had been deferred until the following day. It was typical of the whole sorry saga that such a critical adjudication was undertaken on the run as it were, one of several factors that effectively condemned Phillips' command well before his ships had cleared the Singapore roadstead for the last time.

In their separate analyses of the fate of Force Z, two of Britain's most eminent postwar naval historians, Captain Russell Grenfell and Captain Stephen Roskill, both concluded that Admiral Phillips had little choice but to execute his sortie against the Japanese invasion convoys. Roskill concluded that "the Admiral could not possibly ignore such a threat to the base on which our whole position in his theatre depended. The only conclusion that can reasonably be drawn is that, after the tremendous events of the 7th of December had transformed the whole war and rendered all previous strategic considerations obsolete, it was inevitable that his ships should in the end, if not immediately share the fate of all the other Allied forces in the area."[22] Grenfell's analysis as to Churchill's operational rationale for the presence of Force Z at Singapore is particularly insightful, and is worth repeating in its entirety here:

> The major error into which he [Churchill] seems to have fallen is indicated by his obvious obsession, noticeable in most of his minutes, memoranda, and telegrams during this period, with the idea of raids by individual ships and not engagements between squadrons. He thought in terms of the Japanese raiding the British communications in the Indian Ocean and of the British Far Eastern ships raiding the Japanese communications somewhere else, though he did not say where. He clearly failed to realise that the main issue at stake was an organised struggle for the command of the sea. What we should and did have to face in the south-west Pacific were not the sorties of so many Japanese *Bismarcks* but the embattled challenge of a superior Japanese fleet.[23]

And for that matter, a superior Japanese naval air arm. Brooke-Popham was not the only senior Allied commander to underestimate Japanese naval aviation to his ultimate cost. General MacArthur had not been overly concerned about the possibility of Clark Field being targeted by Japanese bombers flying from Formosa because he believed that none of the Japanese fighters in service had the range to provide an escort.[24] The hundred or so Zekes that escorted the bombers and subsequently strafed the remnants of the blitzed Far Eastern Air Force rapidly exploded his misconception. This ignorance of Japanese aerial prowess ultimately played a pivotal role in Admiral Phillips' decision to launch his sortie. As Grenfell records, Phillips believed that attacks by torpedo-carrying aircraft would follow the pattern already established in Europe, that no such airstrike would take place at a range of more than three hundred miles.[25] Yet there was ample evidence available at the time as to the capabilities of the Naval Type 96 Nells, which since August 1937 had been bombing Chinese targets up to a range of 1,250 miles from airfields on Kyushu, a factor apparently ignored or overlooked by many Western military experts.[26] While Roskill's sentiments are understandable, they must be balanced against the fact that one of Britain's few modern battleships and her valuable consort were lost in circumstances where the chances of success were so outweighed by the evident risks that the operation was doomed to amount to little more than a costly forlorn gesture.

Churchill's reaction to the sinking of *Prince of Wales* and *Repulse* was reflected in Australia when news of the disaster was published the following day. Across the nation, newspaper reports and editorials gave full vent to the dramatic circumstances of the episode itself and the direct consequences for Australia's defense that may follow as a result. The specter of a pending threat to the Australian mainland did not escape the attention of many in the press, as exemplified by the following editorial in the *Sydney Daily Telegraph* on December 12:

> The loss of the *Prince of Wales* and *Repulse* following swiftly the Japanese attack on the U.S. Pacific Fleet in Pearl Harbor, places Australia in imminent danger of bombardment from enemy warships and sea-borne planes. . . . Until British naval reinforcements reach the Pacific, until the U.S. Fleet has made new dispositions to meet the changed situation, Australia must rely upon her own defences to ward off attacks. Readjusted U.S. naval strategy may also bring us closer to the firing-line. . . . Sydney's strategic importance on the widespread Pacific battlefield would at once be enormously increased. It would become a focal point for Japanese attacks. Instead of expecting "irritation" raids, therefore, we must

prepare ourselves for stronger assaults, designed to reduce Sydney's military and naval value.[27]

Though acknowledging the seriousness of the situation, the *Melbourne Argus* placed the episode in a broader strategic context. "Nothing that happened off the coast of Malaya has markedly reduced the war potential of the Allies which is so immensely greater than that of our foes that we need only fully avail ourselves of it to make victory certain," proclaimed its editorial on December 11.[28] In his public response to the events of Kuantan, Prime Minister Curtin struck a similar chord. Noting that the disaster corroborated his long-standing stance regarding "the necessity for maximum air defence, which is imperative to the efficiency of land and sea forces, however strong they might be," he issued a rallying call for Australians to wage a total war:[29]

> We are now faced with the reality. The enemy's striking power has given an initial momentum that only a maximum effort on our part can arrest.... The Commonwealth is facing what I have described as a new war in the Pacific, and the new problems call for the prompt execution of our plans. Full implementation of the steps already announced by the Government is now demanded.... There must now be an end of all holiday plans. Every gallon of petrol must be saved; every ton of coal must be used for essential services.... No longer can there be 'Business as usual' in Australia. There must be absolute concentration of war production and war interests.[30]

Behind the scenes, the situation prompted the Australian government to press upon Whitehall the necessity for a coordinated strategic mechanism whereby Australia's interests would be fully represented and there would be fresh Admiralty dispositions in the Far East and more reinforcements for Singapore upon an urgent priority basis.

On December 8, 1941, Sir Earle Page, the Australian government's special representative in the United Kingdom, advised Curtin that Australia's minimum requirements for a coordinated Allied command structure in the Asia-Pacific theater should be: (1) that the Australian government should have "full knowledge of all essential facts, developments, and trends of policy," (2) that the government "should obtain this knowledge in time to express its view before decisions are taken," and (3) that the government "should have the opportunity through its accredited representative of presenting to and discussing with the War Cabinet, important committees such as the Defence Committee, and the Prime Minister or senior Ministers any suggestion as to new policy or views on the policy under consideration that Australia might from time to time choose to submit."[31] Three days later the government submitted a proposal to Whitehall that as a first step, a supreme Allied coordination body be set up at Singapore in conjunction with Air Chief Marshal Brooke-Popham's headquarters. On December 13, Stanley Bruce advised Curtin that in both his and Page's opinion, the British were unable to grasp either the gravity of the military situation in the Far East or the need to form an effective unified command as rapidly as possible.[32] With Churchill then in transit to Washington to meet with Roosevelt, the Australians were increasingly concerned as to the likely fate of the nation's views and interests in the grand strategy that both men were to formulate. In a cable to Richard Casey on December 16, "Doc" Evatt acknowledged Casey's doubts and impressed upon him the need for separate Australian representation in such discussions:

> I want you to press and insist that in every conference between representatives of Associated powers this Government must have the opportunity of separate representation even though it may appear impracticable at first sight. Your particular [recent] message shows danger that our own point of view may be regarded as of subsidiary importance. On the contrary our point of view must be continually stressed or our great needs will be overlooked. It is obvious that in some respects the views of the United Kingdom representatives will differ from our own both in relation to supplies and forces. This Government is far from satisfied with the results of the policy of subordinating our requirements to those of others. The result of such a policy is that this country's defence have been largely neglected.[33]

On December 29 Churchill advised Curtin that due to the gravity of the situation, he and Roosevelt had formulated an agreement regarding Pacific and Far Eastern strategy in the absence of other Allied representation. Churchill explained that the proposed "South-West Pacific" theater would extend from Burma to the Philippines and would include

Port Darwin. A multinational command would be led by General Sir Archibald Wavell based in Surabaya, with American, British, Dutch, and Australian naval forces placed under Adm. Thomas Hart, USN. Overall political authority was to be jointly controlled out of Washington and London.[34] Curtin barely had time to digest these new arrangements prior to receiving a cable from Casey the following day that warned the prime minister that the British and American planning staffs had determined to gerrymander Australian interests by excising the entire continent from the contemplated South-West Pacific theater. It had been proposed that an "Australia Area" be established, including Australia, Australian New Guinea, the Bismarck Archipelago, Solomon Islands, New Hebrides, New Caledonia, and Fiji, which would be Australia's primary defensive responsibility.[35] Yet in the tradition of imperial defense, Australian forces would be required for service under Wavell's command, thereby placing additional pressure on Australia's domestic defenses, such as they were. Curtin responded vigorously. He informed Churchill on New Year's Day 1942 that the contemplated changes to the original agreement were completely unacceptable. "It appears to us," Curtin cabled, "to be an outstanding paradox, following declaration framed to express unity of our aims and efforts that a plan should be put forward which viewed defence situation in Pacific in such a piecemeal manner."[36] In a joint Anglo-American declaration on January 3, 1942, the formation of the American, British, Dutch, Australian Command (ABDACOM) was announced, its structure and geographic coverage reiterating the contents of the initial proposal.[37]

The sinking of *Prince of Wales* and *Repulse* had prompted the Australians to immediately seek an urgent reappraisal of the Far Eastern position by the British chiefs of staff. In reply, the secretary of state for Dominion affairs informed Curtin that the speed of the Japanese advance was hindering the completion of this process. Aside from advising the Australians that there was no immediate large-scale threat to Australian security, Lord Cranborne provided few other details.[38] Elsewhere, the Singapore conference on December 18 produced a general naval plan of localized defense for the waters between Singapore and the Philippines involving British, American, Australian, and Dutch cruisers and destroyers, and American and Dutch submarines. The conference acknowledged the importance of keeping open the sea and air routes to Northern

Australia as part of the wider plan to keep the Japanese confined to the north of Singapore and the Netherlands East Indies.[39] Five days later, the Australian government received the completed British COS evaluation, the contents of which were scarcely encouraging:

(A) *Future British naval strategy*

(1) We must ensure sea communications in the Atlantic first, those in the Indian Ocean second. Limited United States Naval support can be expected in the Atlantic where our mutual interests coincide and from the United States Asiatic Fleet—but *not* elsewhere.

(2) Simultaneous withdrawal of capital ships from both the Eastern and Western Mediterranean is unsound.

(3) There is not one base which would be acceptable to both the United States and ourselves as affording sufficient protection to the interests of each at which our own and United States Forces equal or superior to the Japanese can be assembled.

(4) Apart from the question of fighter protection we ourselves cannot provide a balanced fleet at Singapore at once. Therefore unsound to send capital ships there at present.

(5) To produce the required fleet ourselves it will be necessary to withdraw capital ships from the Eastern Mediterranean. This withdrawal can only be offset by maintaining sufficient air striking forces at Malta and Cyrenaica to make, in conjunction with our submarines, operation of Italian heavy ships against our supply routes too hazardous.

(6) Pending assembly of a fleet in the Indian Ocean we must expect Japanese raiding forces in that Sea. But until the Japanese secure Borneo or an area to the South for the establishment of shore bases for aircraft within range of the Sunda Straits routes, escorted convoys should be able to reach Singapore.

(7) When a fleet *has been* assembled in the Indian Ocean, its action will depend on the conditions prevailing. It may have to relieve Singapore or repel a threat to Australia and New Zealand or operate for a time from its Indian Ocean base.[40]

In the resulting analysis by the Australian chiefs of staff that was forwarded to Churchill in Washington, the Admiralty's proposed strategy was taken to task. By way of summation, the Australian COS recorded that "the present situation is that we [the British] intend to base an unbalanced fleet in the Indian Ocean during the next two months, which will be inferior to the Japanese fleet, and during the period of formation we intend to use important portions of it, e.g., carriers in waters under Japanese naval and possibly air control." Furthermore the chiefs cautioned against dispersing then-available Allied naval assets "in an attempt to defend widely dispersed interests," recommending instead the concentration of available naval forces into a fleet that could match and defeat the enemy in a major action, a result that in their judgment would deprive the Japanese of the initiative.[41] Churchill responded bluntly on January 4, 1942. "The whole naval situation has been upset by the losses of the United States Fleet at Pearl Harbour and our own naval losses. At the moment there can be no question of providing a combined fleet capable of dealing with the main Japanese Fleet. . . . It may be extremely difficult to bring on a fleet action except in areas where the Japanese have superiority and where the whole course of action might be altered to our disadvantage by air attacks." Of the Australian COS themselves, Churchill observed that their conception of naval warfare when it came to engaging the Japanese fleet "is far from being a correct one."[42]

Better news, however, was finally forthcoming from Washington. After Roosevelt and Churchill had given further consideration to the Australian situation, on January 12, 1942, Churchill advised Curtin that an "Anzac Area" would be created along the geographic boundaries of the earlier-proposed "Australia area," and the primary command responsibility for its defense lay with the U.S. Pacific Fleet. Australian, New Zealand, British, and American warships operating in the Anzac Area were allocated the following assignments:

(a) To cover eastern and northeastern approaches to Australia and New Zealand;

(b) To safeguard, by all practicable escorting and covering operations, convoys in the Anzac Area;

(c) To support the defence of islands in the Anzac Area with particular emphasis on its key points, to attack adjacent enemy key points;

(d) To correlate operations with forces in the A.B.D.A. Area and with United States Pacific forces.[43]

For the second time in its relatively brief existence as a federated Commonwealth, Australia's third-party naval defense had been subcontracted with no Australian participation in the decision-making process. Yet this was to be a change with far more profound implications for the future of Australian defense and foreign policy than had been the case in 1902, as shall be enlarged upon in the following chapter. But as of January 12, 1942, the Anzac Area, ABDACOM, and other initiatives that had recently been contrived in Washington were paper solutions to a crisis that paid no heed to artificial boundaries and proposed command structures. Since the sinking of the British capital ships a month before, all that presently stood between the Japanese and their total conquest of Southeast Asia were a relative handful of Allied cruisers, destroyers, and submarines that would be compelled to operate together as a multinational force for the first time. At the same moment the Australian government remained preoccupied with the deepening ruin of the military situation in Malaya, and its attempts to have Britain strengthen Singapore's air and land defenses before it was too late were becoming a source of ill-disguised bitterness between Canberra and Whitehall.

If Malaya and Singapore were to be saved, a massive buildup of air support was an urgent requirement. Bringing this factor to Churchill's attention via cablegram on December 16, 1941, Curtin reminded his British counterpart of the previous British evaluations that had recommended 336 aircraft as the minimum number needed to put up an effective defense. By way of their fresh appreciation communicated to the Australians on December 23, the chiefs set out an air reinforcement schedule. Six medium bomber squadrons were to be redeployed from the Middle East, along with fifty-one Hurricane fighters in packing cases that were currently at sea. In response to further Australian pressure, Churchill undertook to procure another four Hurricane squadrons, which would be ferried from the Middle East on board the aircraft carrier *Indomitable*.[44] The crated Hurricanes arrived at Singapore on January 13, 1942, and after a week of assembly and testing they were thrown into action over Singapore City for the first time on January 20. A dozen of the new fighters intercepted an unescorted raid by twenty-seven Japanese bombers, shooting down eight and driving off the remainder. The effect on civilian morale especially was electrifying. An RAAF pilot later recalled that "morale skyrocketed 100 per cent, and the sun shone again and the birds sang. . . . That evening at all the night spots the gay topic of conversations was 'Hurricanes.' The miracle had happened. The Hurricanes were here and their world was saved."[45] But as Stanley Bruce had warned Curtin in late December, these reinforcements were only regenerating the RAF's original strength rather than expanding it. The next day the Japanese bombers were back, this time with fighter escort, and within a fortnight most of the surviving Hurricanes had been withdrawn to Sumatra as Singapore's airfields came under increasing air and artillery bombardment.[46]

Likewise addressed in the December appreciation was the dispatch of the British 18th Division and the Indian 17th Division, along with much-needed antitank and antiaircraft equipment. But, as pointed out by Casey in his cable to the Department of External Affairs on December 24, 1941, only a single battalion from each division had been definitely allocated to Singapore; the final destinations for the remaining troops having were yet to be determined.[47] Ever since the withdrawal of the Australian garrison from Tobruk the previous October, relations between the British and Australian prime ministers were at best strained, and Curtin's "America" speech of December 27 had certainly fanned the flames.[48] In a series of cables exchanged between the pair prior to January 20, 1942, Churchill rejected Curtin's assertions that Malaya was a repetition of the debacles in Greece and Crete and reminded him that he (Churchill) had played no role in the security assurances provided to Australia at the Imperial Conference in 1937.[49] On January 22 Page advised Curtin from London that a meeting of the Defence Committee the previous evening had discussed General Wavell's latest assessment of events in Malaya. With the Japanese fast approaching the Johore Strait, it was suggested that the bulk of the British and Indian reinforcements should be diverted to Rangoon and that Singapore itself should be evacuated. Discussion regarding these options had been undertaken with the knowledge that an Indian brigade and two Australian battalions staging a rear-guard action were at present cut off in southern Johore.[50] Cabling Churchill the following day, Curtin's response to both suggestions was blistering:

> Page has reported that the Defence Committee has been considering evacuation of Malaya and Singapore. After all the assurances we have been given, the evacuation of Singapore would be

regarded here and elsewhere as an inexcusable betrayal. Singapore is a central fortress in the system of Empire and local defence.... We understood it was to be made impregnable and in any event it was to be capable of holding out for a prolonged period until the arrival of the main fleet.... Even in an emergency, diversion of reinforcements should be to the Netherlands East Indies and not Burma. Anything else would be deeply resented and might force the Netherlands East Indies to make a separate peace.... On the faith of the proposed flow of reinforcements, we have acted and carried out our part of the bargain. We expect you not to frustrate the whole process by evacuation.[51]

Much of the basis for Curtin's disquiet had been provided by reports received from Vivian Bowden, Australia's official ministerial representative in Singapore. Since the outbreak of hostilities with the Japanese, Bowden had advised Canberra of all manner of inadequacies. In his estimation the British colonial authorities were incapable of understanding the seriousness of the situation, the bureaucracy was a shambles, and the governor, Sir Shenton Thomas, was unwilling to make changes consistent with a functional wartime civil administration.[52] When it came to the military, Bowden was equally scathing. He described the defeat of the RAF as "assuming landslide proportions" in late December, and he believed that the dispatched air and ground reinforcements would do nothing to alter the outcome.[53] And on January 23 he alerted the Australian government to perhaps the most disturbing revelation of all. "Keith Simmons [General Keith Simmons, general officer commanding fortress] reveals to me that all fixed defenses [on] Singapore Island are directed seawards. None are directed towards mainland."[54] Four days beforehand, Churchill had learned the same news from Wavell: "I do not write this in any way to excuse myself. I ought to have known. My advisors ought to have known and I ought to have been told, and I ought to have asked. The reason I had not asked about that matter, amid the thousands of questions I put, was that the possibility that Singapore had no landward defences no more entered into my mind than that of a battleship being launched without a bottom."[55]

One man who did know the truth had already made his last desperate plea for others to see sense. Brigadier Ivan Simson, Singapore's chief engineer, spent months imploring Lieutenant General Percival to authorize the construction of pillboxes, machine-gun nests, and the like upon the northern shoreline of Singapore Island facing Johore, and was constantly rebuffed with no accompanying explanation. On December 26 he made one final effort. Percival's response in again refusing Simson's request was that to erect such structures would be bad for the morale of both civilians and troops. Taking his leave, Simson responded, "Sir it is going to be much worse for morale if the Japanese start running all over the island."[56] Since the initial Japanese landings, the long British retreat down the Malayan peninsula had been one muddle after the next and, in Bowden's opinion, could be laid squarely at the feet of Percival as general officer commanding: "He appeared for instance to have no answer to Japanese infiltration tactics but to retreat, and I do not remember his proposing any counter-offensive action. Other incidents have suggested lack of decision. If Singapore is to be held I feel that high qualities of leadership, resource and determination will be necessary and I cannot feel confident that these will be found in the present General Officer Commanding Malaya."[57]

After the last of the Allied forces had crossed onto Singapore Island on January 31, 1942, the causeway was blown up and Percival's exhausted troops prepared to repel the expected enemy landings. By now Singapore had been under constant air attack for the past month, and such preparations as there were became constantly frustrated by air and artillery strikes. Following a massive daylight bombardment on February 8, Japanese barges crossed the Johore Strait to assault the island's northwestern shore. Though the Australian defenders in that sector gave the initial enemy waves a bloody nose, they were too few in number to prevent the Japanese from establishing a beachhead.[58] Once ashore the battle rapidly became a repetition of Malaya, with the Japanese outflanking their opponents at every turn. By capturing Singapore's reservoirs a matter of days later, the invaders eventually secured Percival's surrender on February 15. The fall of Malaya and Singapore resulted in the capitulation of 130,000 British, Australian, and Indian troops, including the majority of the 8th Division AIF. Under the title "The Fallen Bastion," the February 17 editorial in the *Sydney Morning Herald* proffered the following summation of the disaster:

It would be a cowardly burking of the facts to conceal that there have been few more serious miscalculations in all British history than those which have led up to the fall of Singapore.... Its real causes are rather to be sought in the attitude of mind which produced the constant official assurances on behalf of the highest Service officials in the Empire that Singapore was virtually impregnable and that its resistance, with the possibility of American help, would act as an effective deterrent to any major Japanese movement farther south. Now, not only has Singapore fallen, but the Japanese have shown that it was perfectly feasible, with Singapore still intact, for them to strike heavily in all directions from Sumatra to Wake Island and from the Philippines to the Solomons and Gilberts.... It is not too much to say that we have been taught to rely on a naval Maginot Line which the Japanese rapidly masked and outflanked with combined naval, air, and sea attacks our Service heads believed to be impossible, despite our lessons from Germany in three-dimensional warfare. Outmoded conceptions of naval strategy held in both Great Britain and America have led us to underrate the whole Japanese danger and are, therefore, at least partly responsible for the inadequate appreciation on the part of the Services of the efficiency of the Japanese Army and Air Force.[59]

"The War Comes to Australia": February 16–April 9, 1942

The *Herald*'s description of Singapore as a naval Maginot Line encapsulated the sequence of aero-amphibious operations through which the Japanese were able to commence the conquest of the Netherlands East Indies while Singapore itself was still to fall. By January 6, 1942, the invaders had secured the key strategic airfields and oil centers on the western and northwestern coastlines of Borneo. Four days later another small amphibious force seized the oil facilities at Tarakan, and the conquest of Borneo was thereafter completed with the capture of Balikpapan on January 24 and Banjermasin on February 16. Meanwhile Japanese parachutists had seized the port at Menado in the Celebes on January 11, and with further naval landings at Kendari (January 24) and Makassar (February 9) the Celebes similarly fell under Japanese control, as had the island of Ambon on January 30.⁶⁰ On February 15 the airfields and refineries at Palembang in southern Sumatra were occupied via a combined airborne-amphibious assault. Only at Balikpapan and Palembang did the Japanese encounter anything approaching serious resistance. Off Balikpapan on the night of January 24, three American destroyers and a Dutch submarine got loose among the invasion convoy, sinking four transports and two small escort vessels. And in the estuary of the Musi River to the east of Palembang from February 14–15, the Japanese transports and barges were mauled by RAF and RAAF bombers and fighters, with one transport and numerous barges packed with troops being sunk.⁶¹ But these successes did not significantly impede the Japanese timetable, which had targeted Java as the centerpiece of their Indies conquest. Yet before Java could be assailed directly, the IJN's strategists deemed it necessary to knock out Darwin, the main Allied point of supply for the remaining ABDA ground, air, and naval forces assembled in the area.

At dawn on February 19, 1942, a total of eighty-one aircraft were launched from the decks of four of the First Air Fleet's carriers situated in the Banda Sea. Earlier that morning, fifty-four Betty bombers belonging to the 21st and 23rd Air Flotillas had departed their new base at Kendari. The initial formation from the carriers was sighted by observers on Melville and Bathurst Islands, but due to confusion at the local RAAF headquarters, an alert was not sounded until just before 1000 hours, when the first enemy aircraft were virtually overhead.⁶² With the Zekes quickly disposing of four P-40s on patrol over the town, the accompanying bombers reduced the port facilities to flaming rubble. The American destroyer *Peary* and two other naval vessels were sunk along with five merchant ships, ten others receiving varying degrees of damage.⁶³ Following the retirement of the carrier-borne aircraft at 1040 hours, Darwin's RAAF station became the principal target for the inbound land-based bombers ten minutes later. The attackers devastated the facility, destroying or damaging some fifteen aircraft on the ground and wrecking many buildings and other infrastructure. Approximately 230 military personnel and fifteen civilians were killed in the attacks, with another 250 wounded. The Japanese lost just five of their carrier-borne aircraft.⁶⁴ On March 3 the Australian mainland was subjected to further attacks at Broome and Wyndham on the northern coast of Western Australia. In the strike against Broome, nine fighters flying from

Koepang destroyed twenty-four Allied aircraft, including sixteen flying boats that were strafed while at anchor in the town's harbor.[65]

News of the raid on Darwin was greeted with a mixture of shock, dismay, and fear throughout Australia. Under the banner headline "The War Comes to Australia," the editorial in the *Sydney Morning Herald* on February 20 proclaimed that any remaining complacency within the nation as to its isolation from the firsthand impact of the war had been thoroughly extinguished:

> Opening shots in the Battle of Australia were fired on the mainland yesterday, when Japanese aircraft made two heavy raids on Darwin. The whole continent may be said to have vibrated to the shuddering crash of their bombs, for, although an attack had been long expected, and our island territories had already been assailed, the first direct impact of war on home soil, soil on which an invader has never yet set foot necessarily sent a shock throughout the length and breadth of the land. The news that blood has been shed and damage wrought in Darwin means to Australians everywhere that their country is at last exposed to the ordeal which countless other communities have endured during two and a half years of merciless war—ordeal by bombing. How soon the sufferings of our northernmost port may be shared in fact, as they are now in spirit, by other coastal cities, we do not know. . . . We may as a people have needed some such grim development to awaken us finally to the realities of war. Too many in our midst have trusted despite all warnings that the storm might yet somehow pass Australia by. . . . Now the eyes of the blindest will be opened. . . . The fall of Singapore, the culmination of a series of disasters each bringing danger nearer to this country, left Java as the last bastion between us and the Japanese, and as we saw yesterday, they have not waited to attack it before striking at our mainland.[66]

Java was doomed. Within two days of Darwin being blitzed, Japanese airborne and amphibious forces had largely secured the island chain stretching to the east of Java with landings at Timor and Bali. In the course of the Bali landings, an attempted interception by elements of the ABDA cruiser and destroyer force was beaten off in the Badung Strait.

On February 18 the main Western Attack Force (Vice Admiral Ozawa Jisaburō) departed Indo-China on its passage to Batavia, while the following day the Eastern Attack Force (Rear Admiral Nishimura Shōji) left its anchorage at Jolo to advance on Surabaya.[67] Each of the transport convoys was screened by a detached group of cruisers and destroyers, and the Western Attack Force possessed direct air support in the form of the light carrier *Ryūjō*. Should its assistance be required, the First Air Fleet was presently operating to the south of Java, while the bulk of the land-based 21st and 23rd Air Flotillas were similarly available. To face this sizeable armada, the ABDA Combined Striking Force had been divided into two. The Western Striking Force, commanded by Captain Harry Howden RAN, consisted of the Australian light cruiser *Hobart*, the British light cruisers *Danae* and *Dragon*, and three destroyers, two British and one Dutch.[68] The main Eastern Striking Force, under the command of Rear Admiral Karel Doorman RNN, fielded the British and American heavy cruisers *Exeter* and *Houston*, the Dutch light cruisers *Java* and *De Ruyter*, the Australian light cruiser *Perth*, and eleven destroyers, five American, three British, and three Dutch. Possessing limited land-based air support and harried by persistent bombing that had greatly fatigued his ships' crews, Doorman's squadron steamed northward from Surabaya on the afternoon of February 27 to intercept the Japanese Eastern Attack Force, which had been spotted in the area.[69]

Thanks to their complete superiority in catapult-launched spotter seaplanes, the Japanese were able to interpose the heavy cruisers *Nachi* and *Haguro*, belonging to the Eastern Covering Group (Rear Admiral Takagi Takeo), between Doorman and Nishimura's transports.[70] Takagi's cruisers were supported by the light cruiser *Naka* and six destroyers from the Eastern Attack Group, as well as the light cruiser *Jintsu* and seven destroyers from the Second Destroyer Squadron (Rear Admiral Tanaka Raizō). The action commenced at 1616 hours with a long-range duel between the respective heavy cruisers, *Houston* suffering from the prior loss of her rear 8-inch turret to a bomb hit.[71] While the cruisers dueled, the Japanese destroyers launched a mass attack with "Long Lance" torpedoes, all of which missed their intended marks. At 1715 a plunging shell from *Haguro* penetrated a boiler room on board *Exeter*, crippling the British cruiser and causing her to swerve away. This maneuver caused chaos in the ABDA formation that was magnified minutes later when the Dutch destroyer *Kortenaer* was sunk by a Japanese torpedo. In an effort to protect *Exeter* with a smokescreen, the British destroyers *Electra* and *Encounter* engaged Tanaka's force, with *Electra* being surrounded and sunk by the Japanese destroyers.[72] At length Doorman was able to collect his wayward ships and steam southward. Further brief skirmishes followed, after which the five American destroyers broke off to fuel at Surabaya. Still determined to get at the troop transports, Doorman reversed course at 2100 hours. Twenty-five minutes later the British destroyer *Jupiter* was sunk when Doorman's ships ran into a Dutch minefield. At 2300 *De Ruyter* and *Java* exchanged fire with Takagi's cruisers, and at 2320 the Dutch cruisers were struck in quick succession by torpedoes, both ships sinking almost immediately with most of their crews and their luckless force commander.[73]

With the sinking of *De Ruyter* and *Java*, the final disintegration of ABDACOM's naval forces was under way. To the south of Java that same day the aircraft tender *Langley* had been bombed and sunk by Japanese aircraft. Further to the west the ABDA Western Striking Force withdrew through the Sunda Strait the next morning after a fruitless attempt to intercept the Japanese Western Attack Force on February 26.[74] While Howden's ships retired to Colombo unscathed, other Allied vessels attempting to run the Sunda Strait were not so fortunate. At 2255 hours on the night of February 28, the cruisers *Houston* and *Perth* came across Ozawa's troop transports and their cruiser and destroyer escorts in Bantam Bay. Both ships immediately attacked, and in the wild brawl that followed, four Japanese transports were sunk or beached before *Perth* was sunk at 0005 and *Houston* followed suit at 0033.[75] The Dutch destroyer *Evertsen* managed to evade the mayhem, but she too was located and forced ashore by gunfire just before dawn. On March 1 *Exeter* and the destroyers *Encounter* and *Pope* left Surabaya for the Sunda Strait; they were spotted by two Japanese cruiser forces at 0935 and after a one-sided fight all three of the Allied ships were finished off by the cruisers' gunfire and air attacks from *Ryūjō*.[76] From Doorman's Eastern Striking Force, only four of the American destroyers were able to evade destruction. Japanese ships operating to the south of Java likewise sank a number of small vessels attempting to reach Australia, including the Australian sloop *Yarra*, which was sunk on March 4 while gallantly defending a small convoy against three enemy cruisers and two destroyers.⁷⁷ With the landings on Java meeting little resistance, the Netherlands East Indies administration capitulated on March 9, 1942.

Japan's conquest of the Netherlands East Indies placed northern and northwestern Australia at imminent risk of a Japanese airborne or amphibious assault should the Imperial General Headquarters in Tokyo have desired to alter the set objectives for their southern offensive. Even though no such change of plan eventuated, the presence of roughly two-thirds of the Imperial Japanese Navy's carrier and surface strength within the waters of the Indonesian archipelago presented another equally dire threat to Australia's defenses. On January 6, 1942, the Australian and British governments had reached an agreement to recall the Australian Sixth and Seventh Divisions from the Middle East and redeploy the troops to the Netherlands East Indies.⁷⁸ On January 23 Curtin made it clear to Churchill that none of the Australian troops were to be redeployed to Burma. The following day Roosevelt waded into the issue, informing Casey that Burma was of greater strategic importance when it came to the allocation of reinforcements.⁷⁹ On February 12 the Australian government consented in principle to the allocation of one division each in Java and southern Sumatra, but formal approval was to be withheld pending a review of the situation when the transiting troops were closer to their destination. A major point of concern for the Australians had become an adequate escort for the troop convoys and the prospects of Japanese interception before the ships reached Fremantle.⁸⁰ Following the fall of Singapore, Curtin received advice from Generals Wavell and Sturdee that Java could not be held. In requesting of Churchill on February 17 that the 6th and 7th Divisions should be diverted to Australia, Curtin forwarded the following assessment from the Australian chiefs of staff:

> (I) As General Wavell does not consider Java can be held, Australia and Burma become of primary importance as the only position in which forces can be concentrated for an ultimate advance against the enemy.
>
> (II) That, if possible, all Australian forces now under orders to transfer to the Far East from the Middle East should be diverted to Australia.... They would prefer that all these forces should be concentrated in Australia but are mindful of the fact that the strategic

position of Burma may necessitate some reinforcement there until other troops are available from elsewhere.[81]

During the period from February 17 to March 10, 1942, the Indian Ocean was festooned with shipping carrying out the so-called "Stepsister" transfer of the Australian divisions from the Middle East. Though there were several convoys for the larger ships, much of the traffic proceeded independently and without escort.[82] With the proximity of the Japanese warships, especially the carriers of the First Air Fleet operating south of Java, any redeployment of the troopships toward Burma invited a catastrophe. This outcome remained a possibility until February 23 as the Australian and British governments squabbled over the destination of the two divisions. Immense pressure was applied to senior Australian officials in London and Washington to have Curtin recognize the strategic importance of protecting the Burma Road. After the offer of a trade, two American divisions to Australia in exchange for the AIF to Burma, was rejected by Canberra, Churchill took drastic action.[83] On February 22 he advised Curtin of his unilateral decision to divert the lead convoy:

> We could not contemplate that you would refuse our request and that of the President of the United States for the diversion of the leading division to save the situation in Burma. We know that if our ships proceed on the course to Australia while we were waiting for your formal approval they would arrive either too late at Rangoon or even be without enough fuel to go there at all. We therefore decided that the convoy should be temporarily diverted to the northward. The convoy is now too far north for some of the ships in it to reach Australia without refuelling. These physical considerations give a few days for the situation to develop and for you to review the position should you wish to do so. Otherwise the leading Australian Division will be returned to Australia as quickly as possible in accordance with your wishes.[84]

Curtin responded forcefully the following day:

> It appears that you have diverted the convoy towards Rangoon and treated our approval to this vital diversion as merely a matter of

form. By doing so you have established a physical situation which adds to the dangers of the convoy and the responsibility of such diversion rests upon you.... We feel a primary obligation to save Australia not only for itself but to preserve it as a base for the development of the war against Japan. In these circumstances it is quite impossible for us to reverse a decision which we made with the utmost care and which we have affirmed and reaffirmed.[85]

Churchill at last backed down and advised Curtin that increased escort would be provided for the convoy as it steamed to Colombo and then to Australia.[86] But Whitehall persisted in its efforts to have at least a portion of the 6th Division retained at Ceylon for garrison duties. After further communication between the two governments, on March 2 Curtin agreed that Ceylon's importance to Australia's security required the addition of two brigades from the 6th Division to augment the island's land defenses.[87] Because Ceylon was the major refueling and assembly point within the Indian Ocean for shipping in transit to and from Australia, Canberra could not reasonably reject a contribution to its defense, and Curtin displayed the qualities of a pragmatic negotiator in agreeing to this request.

Good fortune had favored the Stepsister operations during late February and early March 1942, as the Japanese remained preoccupied with intercepting and sinking shipping that was fleeing from the port of Tjilatjap in southern Java. A blunt reminder of the danger that lurked nearby came in the form of a large airstrike mounted against Tjilatjap on March 5 by the First Air Fleet, which sank or damaged seventeen vessels and left the docks and the town afire.[88] By late March, however, the roadsteads at Colombo and Trincomalee were occupied by a large number of warships belonging to the Admiralty's newly arrived Eastern Fleet. In spite of the recent loss of three capital ships and a carrier and the crippling of two other capital ships, Churchill had not retreated from his previous preference for a fleet operating in the Indian Ocean when the necessary resources became available. In correspondence with Curtin on January 19, he briefed the Australian prime minister on the forthcoming deployment. "We are sending two and possibly three of our modern aircraft-carriers to the Indian Ocean. H.M.S. *Warspite* will soon be there, and thereafter H.M.S. *Valiant*. Thus the balance of sea-power in the Indian and Pacific Oceans will in the absence of further misfortunes turn decisively in our favour, and all Japanese overseas operations will be deprived of their present assurance."[89] On March 29 the modern carriers *Formidable* and *Indomitable* and the battleship *Warspite* were present in Ceylon as part of the hastily assembled command, which had been assigned to Admiral Sir James Somerville.

The assembly of the Eastern Fleet on short notice had been prompted by recent Ultra intercepts that indicated that the Japanese were preparing for some form of offensive naval activity in the Indian Ocean. To meet the enemy threat, Somerville had divided his ships into two forces. Under his direct command, Force A contained the three aforementioned warships along with the heavy cruisers *Cornwall* and *Dorsetshire*, two light cruisers, and six destroyers. Commanded by Vice Admiral Sir Algernon Willis, Force B fielded the old light carrier *Hermes*, the four unmodified "R"-class battleships *Resolution, Revenge, Ramillies,* and *Royal Sovereign*, three light cruisers, and eight destroyers.[90] Though the Eastern Fleet represented the largest disposition of carriers and capital ships within a single fleet yet undertaken by the Admiralty outside of the Atlantic, it suffered from the same handicap the Russian fleet had conveyed to Tsushima in 1905. The big ships assembled in Force B were almost completely ill-equipped to fight in a major action in a broad ocean setting due to their chronic lack of speed, endurance, and antiaircraft armament. If Somerville chose to operate both forces in tandem, he would run the risk of compromising Force A's effectiveness as a strike weapon by the need to provide Force B with air cover. And as far as Force A was concerned, this was limited enough. *Formidable* and *Indomitable* contributed a total of forty-five torpedo bombers and thirty-three fighters, barely enough to meet the force's own reconnaissance, strike, and combat air patrol requirements. Nevertheless both Somerville and the Admiralty believed that a Japanese foray would be a primarily surface-oriented affair, with perhaps a single carrier provided for air support.[91]

Supplied with Ultra intelligence that a Japanese force would be likely to the south of Ceylon on or about March 30–31, 1942, the majority of Somerville's ships departed Colombo and Trincomalee on March 29. The Eastern Fleet had been primarily assembled to act as a fleet-in-being, which would "limit and check" (in Somerville's words) expected enemy raiding operations by either the force of its presence alone or its capacity to neutralize small-scale incursions.[92] In this role it was charged with the overall protection of what at the time was a very busy Indian Ocean, given the Stepsister activities in combination with normal wartime transportation schedules and heavy shipping movement in the Bay of Bengal due to the Japanese invasion of Burma. Under the assumption that his fleet would be encountering a smaller Japanese formation, Somerville intended to lay a trap some 250 miles to the south of Ceylon on the night of March 31. With a potential rerun of Cape Matapan in mind, he intended to launch a night attack by Force A's torpedo bombers, which if successful would bring the big guns from the nearby Force B into play.[93] No contact took place, however, and the Eastern Fleet steamed away westwards to refuel at the RN base at Addu Atoll. While engaged in refueling and resupply at Addu, Somerville received the first sighting report of an enemy presence on the afternoon of April 4: "At 1630, I received a report from a Catalina southeast of Ceylon that a large enemy force was in position 00-40N, 83-10E at 1605F, course 315 degrees. Shortly after this report was confirmed by a message from [RAF] 222 Group which gave the course as 330 degrees. This positioned the force 155 degrees from the Dondra Head [Ceylon], 360 miles, the distance from Addu Atoll being 85 degrees 600 miles. There was no indication as to the composition of the force."[94]

At dawn the following morning, Easter Sunday, approximately seventy-five Japanese bombers and fifty escorts struck at Colombo's port facilities and airfields. Forewarned by radar, the RAF had scrambled thirty-six fighters to intercept the incoming strike, and a large air battle rapidly developed.[95] With Colombo's roadstead virtually cleared of shipping, the attackers sank the destroyer *Tenedos* and hit two other vessels, but otherwise inflicted little serious damage. In the melee above the harbor the RAF fighters downed a Zeke and six Vals but lost nineteen of their number in reply; a flight of torpedo bombers from *Hermes* that were seeking to relocate to Trincomalee were likewise dispatched by the Japanese fighters.[96] Having departed Addu Atoll with Force A just after 0010 that morning, Somerville was attempting to position his ships for another interception when a blip on *Indomitable*'s radar at 1344 identified the presence of a large group of northbound enemy aircraft some eighty miles to the east of her position. Fifteen minutes later, more than fifty dive bombers descended upon the heavy cruisers

Cornwall and *Dorsetshire*, which were steaming from Colombo to rejoin Force A. Subjected to a lethally accurate storm of hits and near misses, both ships were sunk in fifteen minutes, two-thirds of their crews being subsequently rescued.[97] By 1900 that evening Somerville was aware that the enemy fleet contained at least two carriers; more accurate reports were not forthcoming, however, after two of his shadowing aircraft were shot down by Zekes. Nevertheless the British commander attempted to re-lay a trap for the morning of April 6, but when the Japanese again failed to materialize, he ordered retirement to Addu.[98]

Delayed by a day in returning to his forward base after receiving a message from Colombo advising that a large Japanese fleet was operating between Ceylon and Addu Atoll, Somerville learned the truth of the situation when he stepped ashore on April 8. He had unknowingly been attempting to intercept Vice Admiral Nagumo Chūichi's First Air Fleet, with five of its six large aircraft carriers present.[99] Escorted by four fast battleships, three cruisers, and eleven destroyers, Nagumo's carriers had departed Staring Bay in the Celebes on March 26. Under the requirements of the Japanese Naval Staff's Operation C, the First Air Fleet was to execute another Pearl Harbor–style attack against Colombo and destroy the Eastern Fleet, thereby removing any large-scale British naval presence from the eastern half of the Indian Ocean. At the same time, the Second Expeditionary Fleet under Vice Admiral Ozawa Jisaburō was ordered to attack Allied shipping in the Bay of Bengal so that the left flank of the current Japanese advance through Burma would be secured. For this purpose Ozawa's command consisted of *Ryūjō*, five cruisers, four destroyers, and five submarines. As of yet Somerville remained unaware of Ozawa's activities to the north, but he was under no illusion as to what course of action he would undertake next. Once refueling was completed, Force A was to steam to Bombay and Force B would proceed to the port of Kilindini in East Africa. During the afternoon Somerville received similar orders from the Admiralty instructing him to avoid Ceylon when withdrawing his ships. In the early morning darkness of April 9, 1942, the Eastern Fleet departed Addu, and shortly thereafter the respective fleet forces went their separate ways.

Almost all of them, that is. Previously detached from Force B, *Hermes*, two escort vessels, and a group of eight fleet auxiliaries had departed Trincomalee on the evening of March 8 following a reported sighting of

Nagumo's ships by a patrolling flying boat. Early the next morning they were sighted by a Japanese reconnaissance plane fifty miles to the southwest of Trincomalee.[100] In the meantime, thirty bombers with another strong escort had attacked Trincomalee and the Royal Navy's base at China Bay at first light. In a repetition of the Easter Sunday raid, minimal damage was inflicted; a second air battle resulted in the loss of a Zeke and three Kates, with the RAF losing a total of eleven fighters.[101] While this attack was under way, a separate strike by eighty dive-bombers was closing in upon the unfortunate *Hermes* and her consorts. With no fighters of her own to call upon, the veteran carrier proved an easy target for the attackers. The Japanese flyers similarly disposed of the Australian destroyer *Vampire*, the sloop *Hollyhock*, and two fleet auxiliaries. Shortly following the return of both strikers to their parent carriers, Nagumo was surprised by a strike mounted by nine bombers flying from Colombo, which dropped bombs in the near vicinity of *Akagi* before being chased off by the combat air patrol.[102] Thereafter the First Air Fleet departed to the northwest, pausing at Singapore before returning home to Japan. Meanwhile Ozawa's ships, aircraft, and submarines had succeeded in cutting a swathe through the undefended Bay of Bengal, sinking a total of twenty-eight Allied steamers and nuisance-bombing targets on the Indian coastline, in a combined naval arms operation lasting nine days.[103]

The failure of Nagumo's search planes to locate the bulk of the Eastern Fleet permitted one of the great escapes in modern naval history. In a cable to John Curtin on April 15, 1942, Winston Churchill wrote that due to "the very considerable detachment which the enemy has presumed to make from his main fleet for the Indian Ocean and the Bay of Bengal makes it undesirable for us to seek a fleet action for time being, but these conditions will change rapidly in the next few months."[104] On the latter point Churchill was to be proved correct, but the change would not come in the manner that he had anticipated. As for the "undesirable" fleet action, Curtin's reply addressed the issue in more candid terms:

> I wish to let you know with what uneasiness we learnt of the sinking by air attack of the *Dorsetshire* and *Cornwall* which is now followed by the sinking of the *Hermes*. These unfortunate happenings have been the subject of prolonged and anxious discussion by War Cabinet and Advisory War Council, and they raise such vital

questions that we feel constrained to ask you for full information as to the cause of them, and for an appreciation of the United Kingdom, United States and Japanese position in regard to aircraft-carriers, types of aircraft carried and views held as to the relative efficiency of the aircraft and personnel. We would also ask for a statement of the United Kingdom's immediate and long-range policy for combating the Japanese naval forces.... We share with you the anxiety at the repeated naval losses which have been sustained through lack of air support, and I should be grateful to have information and advice on this vital matter as early as possible.[105]

Curtin received an answer of sorts in a cable from Evatt on May 28 as part of a general Allied strategic appreciation: "Policy for the time being is to retain the fleet-in-being [Eastern Fleet] as a deterrent whilst the Americans contain as much of the Japanese Naval Force in the Pacific as their means allow."[106] In due course the Admiralty was to conduct a series of reviews that finally paved the way for the substantial re-equipment of the Fleet Air Arm with modern American carrier aircraft throughout 1943, and eventually led to the superseding of the battleship by the aircraft carrier as the primary weapons platform within the Royal Navy. Yet by the time that the prime minister had received the aforementioned response, conditions had indeed changed in the Far East. With the conclusion of Operation C on April 9, the vast majority of Japanese warships situated to the west of the Philippines subsequently decamped to the east. Those that returned over the following years largely did so to be in closer proximity to their by-then dwindling fuel supplies.[107] The redeployment undertaken by the Imperial Japanese Navy similarly transferred the geographical setting of the principal seaborne threat to mainland Australia from Darwin to the eastern seaboard. Thereafter the naval war in the Far East became dominated by the submarine as the climactic tussle for supremacy at sea between Japan and the United States, upon which Australia's survival would come to depend, was to be played out in the Pacific.

Just as the Japanese threat to the western half of the Australian continent had reached its zenith, it had abruptly passed away. Japan's Far Eastern rampage had cost Australia an infantry division captured, several fighter and bomber squadrons decimated, and a cruiser together with various other smaller warships and numerous merchant vessels sunk. The scars of Japanese aerial prowess were seared upon Darwin and Broome, and nothing stood in the path of the enemy carrying out follow-up amphibious assaults against these ports should Admiral Yamamoto and his colleagues have been so minded. Yet upon the broad Australian land mass, Darwin and Broome remained isolated outposts, sundered by enormous distance from the centers of population, industry, and agriculture that lay far away to the east. To bring about Australia's downfall through isolation, bombardment, or invasion, her most important eastern and southeastern coastal centers would have to be targeted. So with the Royal Navy presently nowhere to be seen in force to the east of Bombay, it was indeed time for Australia to look to America.

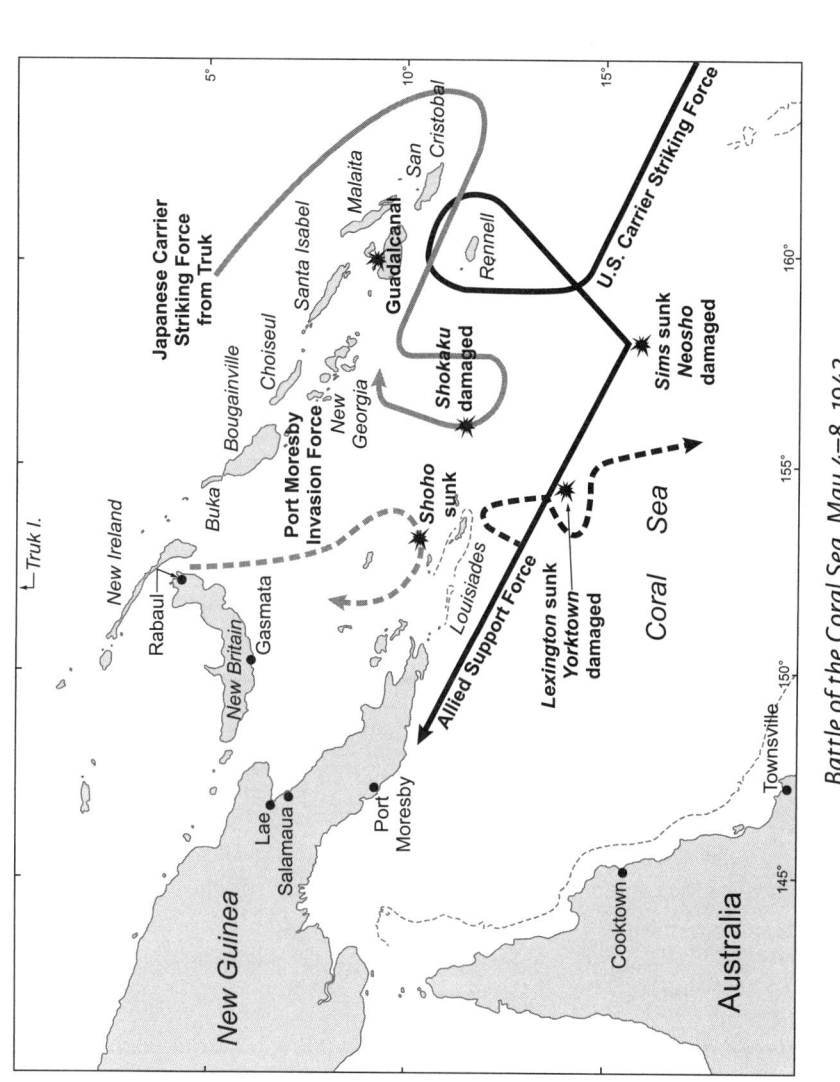

Battle of the Coral Sea, May 4–8, 1942

9

The Pacific

December 1941–December 1942

Without any inhibitions of any kind, I make it quite clear that Australia looks to America, free of any pangs as to our traditional links or kinship with the United Kingdom.

—John Curtin, December 27, 1941

The largely abortive clash between the Eastern Fleet and the First Air Fleet, the first and last of its kind between fleet-scale British and Japanese naval forces, was the first occasion in history where two forces possessing aircraft carriers had opposed each other. But while Nagumo's dive-bombers had targeted detached elements of the British fleet, there was no direct exchange of air strikes between the respective carrier formations. This would occur for the first time when battle was joined in the Coral Sea from May 4 through 8, 1942, and the combatant carrier air groups were to play the principal role in what emerged as a pivotal moment for the protection of Australia and a perceptible swing in the tide of affairs within the Pacific as a whole. The events in the Coral Sea marked both the conclusion of a lengthy period of military recovery for the United States following Pearl Harbor, and the beginning of a consolidation in which major steps would be taken toward the defeat of the Imperial Japanese Navy. And it was through these periods that Australia sought to develop almost from scratch a military partnership with America that would guarantee the former's security. This came none too soon, for as the politics played out in Washington, London, and Canberra, the Japanese were committing themselves to seizing

Australia's Mandated Territories, the outer breastworks of the continent's northeastern defenses.

Infamy's Aftermath: December 7, 1941–May 9, 1942

When the last of Nagumo's flyers departed Hawaiian airspace on the morning of December 7, 1941, the smoke and ruin they left behind concealed a costly strategic failure. While the attack itself had been brilliantly contrived and executed, the Japanese had effectively planted the seeds of their own naval destruction. With the heart of the U.S. Pacific Fleet's battleline crippled for many months, the U.S. Navy was now compelled to wage war in the Pacific with the aircraft carrier as the centerpiece for its strategic operations. When equipped with the massive resources of the Fifth Fleet from mid-1943 onwards, the American carrier task groups would proceed to crush Japan's Pacific defenses with overwhelming levels of concentrated aerial firepower. Yet in the immediate aftermath of the strike against Pearl Harbor, no such future was even remotely contemplatable as the Japanese proceeded with their plans to neutralize American defenses and lines of communication to the west of Oahu. Less than two hours after the events in Hawaii, thirty-four bombers of the 24th Air Flotilla flying from bases in the Marshall Islands struck Wake Island, destroying more than half of a recently arrived Marine Corps fighter squadron on the ground.[1] At 2130 hours that evening, Midway Island was subjected to shelling from a pair of enemy destroyers. And following an intense air and surface bombardment, Guam was rapidly overrun on December 10. In the Philippines that same day the Japanese exploited their earlier hammer blow against Clark Field through further air attacks targeting airfields in the vicinity of Manila and through a devastating raid upon the American naval base at Cavite on the shores of Manila Bay.[2]

The Japanese timetable in the Pacific was dealt a humiliating if temporary blow the following day. Under the command of Rear Admiral Kajioka Sadamichi flying his flag in the light cruiser *Yūbari*, a small invasion flotilla including two troop transports had been assigned the task of capturing Wake. As it approached within five miles of the island, the force came under fire from coastal batteries and four surviving Marine fighter planes, which between them sank two destroyers and damaged Kajioka's flagship and several other vessels.[3] Kajioka retired his ships to Kwajalein, but the Japanese returned on December 22 with a heavily increased escort, including the carriers *Hiryū* and *Sōryū*. After the garrison was subjected to heavy air raids, the landings went ahead on December 23 and the island fell after several hours of bloody fighting. Though a relief expedition in the form of Task Force 14 (Rear Adm. Frank Fletcher) containing the carrier *Saratoga* was less than five hundred miles to the northeast of Wake that evening, the acting commander of the Pacific Fleet, Vice Adm. William Pye, ordered its retirement.[4] With the conquest of Guam and Wake, the Pacific bridge between Hawaii and the Philippines had been rapidly severed. In the Philippines themselves the first Japanese landings at Aparri and Vigan in northern Luzon on December 10 secured bridgeheads and airfields for supporting the major invasion force, which arrived in Lingayen Gulf on December 22.[5] With no effective air cover, the American and Filipino forces fell back toward the Bataan Peninsula. Elsewhere the Japanese landed troops to the south and east of Manila, and on New Year's Day 1942 the city fell to the invaders: the second major colonial metropolis to be captured within seven days following the capitulation of Hong Kong on Christmas Day 1941.

Australian reaction to the attack against Pearl Harbor was colored by the brazenness of the strike against an unexpected target. The reports of the episode in the *Sydney Morning Herald* on December 9 typified this response in stating that "the attacks on the Philippines and Guam were expected, but that on the main American bases in Hawaii was so audacious that the element of surprise was greater than might have been expected, or perhaps even than was justifiable."[6] At the same moment, comment in Australia's print media such as that put forward in the *Herald* and the Brisbane *Courier Mail* emphasized the preparedness of the Allied forces in both the Pacific and the Far East to deal with the Japanese onslaught. "It is an eventuality long foreseen, the showdown against which the British forces in Malaya, the American forces in the Philippines, and the Dutch forces in the Indies have been steadily built up over the last two years," reported the *Courier Mail*, an assumption that would be rapidly disproved.[7] Turning to the question of future naval strategy, the *Herald*'s military correspondent proffered the following assessment:

> It is impossible at this stage to say what the basic naval strategy of either side will be. That of the American Navy may be to seek out

the Japanese Fleet for a major engagement or it may be to establish a blockading cordon, drawing ever tighter. In the first phases, the determining factor will be the degree to which Japan has split up her naval forces and damaged those of her opponents in her initial surprise attacks.... If Japan cannot neutralise the two pivotal points of our wider strategy by knocking out Singapore and Pearl Harbour at an early stage (and we do not believe that this is practicable), then, she must cope with the problem of concentrating on her southern drive, while her flank is exposed to attack by the main American forces. In the outcome, much will depend upon the offensive powers of Singapore and the Philippines. Naval realities in the South China Sea will determine the shape of the struggle at sea.[8]

While the Australian print media speculated as to what would happen next, the Australian government confronted the problem of establishing a first-time strategic relationship with the United States. Aside from the participation of both nations at the various Singapore Conferences, prior to December 1941 there had been little in the way of formal discussions regarding such a future partnership, though mutual diplomatic representation at the ambassadorial level had been in effect since July 1940.[9] In the days following Pearl Harbor, Canberra pursued a number of specific topics with Washington, including the need to further reinforce Singapore and reminding the Roosevelt administration of Australia's extremely limited military capacity to defend vital island bases in the South Pacific.[10] Discussion regarding the new Asia-Pacific theater and command boundaries was likewise undertaken, and the initial steps to create a Lend-Lease structure for Australia's needs were outlined. On a broader strategic scale, Prime Minister Curtin urged President Roosevelt to press for active Soviet involvement as soon as possible so that the war could be prosecuted in the near geographical vicinity of Japan itself.[11] Yet in advancing Australia's interests within the overall pattern of contemplated Allied grand strategy, Curtin and his colleagues were to be beset for many months with a range of difficulties similar to those that had plagued Canberra's efforts to conduct business with Whitehall since September 1939.

Though the proposed Lend-Lease arrangements were promising, the Australians were largely disappointed in their attempts during

December 1941 to gain favorable outcomes elsewhere. On December 20 Casey reported to Canberra that the Americans were at best only paying lip service to the strategic importance of Singapore, and subsequent cables revealed the futility of seeking American naval support for the embattled bastion. As for the disposition of the Pacific Fleet, Casey reported on December 17 that it would be concentrated for the present in Hawaiian waters.[12] And although Roosevelt was briefly receptive to the idea of diverting U.S. Army Air Corps reinforcements to Australia from deployment to the Philippines, the original decision to send the aircraft to Luzon was confirmed to Canberra on December 27. In the same instant it was also confirmed that no carrier deployments would be undertaken in the vicinity of either Singapore or the Australian mainland.[13] This latter news was a blow for Curtin, who since mid-December had sought to present a picture to Washington that emphasized Australia's military frailties, though Frederick Shedden had cautioned that such an approach could backfire: "[There is] a chance that the Americans might feel that their participation in the defence of this part of the Pacific is rather a hopeless task until they can gather their strength and assess the situation. I think, however, that this is a risk which has to be taken because if we approach this matter in a realistic manner there appears to be little we can do ourselves in regard to the defence of these two centres [Rabaul and New Caledonia]."[14]

When it came to the question of the broader strategic picture, Australian interests were not well-served thus far. The high point came with at least the prospect of American agreement on the appointment of General MacArthur as supreme commander of a Southwest Pacific command, which was supported by Canberra, but older problems and obstacles prevented any substantial progress otherwise.[15] In spite of Evatt's urgings, Australia was not permitted independent representation in the strategic planning process jointly overseen by Roosevelt and Churchill. And in a discussion with Roosevelt on December 17, Casey reported that his host had suggested that the war "had to be regarded from a geographical rather than a national point of view."[16] As discussed in the previous chapter, the preliminary outcomes from the Arcadia Conference were not greeted with enthusiasm by the Australians when it came to the division of Allied command boundaries and responsibilities. Prior to this, however, Curtin had certainly caused an uproar when he delivered his New Year's message to the nation via the *Melbourne Herald* on December 27, 1941. His direct appeal to the United States, which is addressed in substance in the following chapter, infuriated both Churchill and Roosevelt and has been the subject of detailed analysis and controversy within Australian historical circles and the wider national forum ever since.

When specifically applied to the situation in the Pacific Ocean, Curtin's remarks were underpinned by the lack of any meaningful British naval presence within that theater as a whole. With only limited support available from the Australian and New Zealand navies, the USN bore the full burden of confronting the Japanese fleet, and under a rejuvenated command from December 31, 1941, onwards it began taking steps to do so. The new commander in chief of the U.S. Navy, Adm. Ernest J. King, favored counterattacks against the Japanese as soon as practicable, and his newly installed commander of the Pacific Fleet, Adm. Chester Nimitz, devised a multipronged strategy. Separate task forces, each containing a single aircraft carrier with a cruiser and destroyer screen, were to attack various targets in the Central Pacific with the aim of disrupting further potential enemy advances to the south of the Gilbert Islands.[17] The first of these forays was undertaken by Task Force 11 (Vice Adm. Wilson Brown) against Wake, but it was recalled on January 23, 1942, following the sinking of the force's oiler by a Japanese submarine. On February 1 Task Force 8 (Adm. William F. Halsey) pounded targets in the Marshalls, while Task Force 17 (Rear Adm. Frank J. Fletcher) struck islands in both the Marshall and Gilbert groups. This was followed on February 21 by an abortive attempt by Task Force 11 to strike Rabaul, while Wake and Marcus Islands were subjected to attacks from Halsey's and Fletcher's formations on February 24 and March 4 respectively. The largest strike came on March 10, when aircraft from the carriers *Lexington* and *Yorktown* (Task Force 11) flew from the Gulf of Papua over the Owen Stanley Range to attack Japanese invasion shipping concentrated at Lae and Salamaua on the northeastern coastline of New Guinea.[18]

Though these operations collectively yielded minimal results, a six-thousand-ton transport sunk at Kwajalein being one of the larger blows inflicted, they provided the task forces and their air groups with invaluable combat experience. With the majority of the Japanese fleet then engaged in operations to the west of the Philippines, the only opposition came from the land-based air units, and this proved to be ineffective.

Something larger, however, was required in order to seriously rattle Tokyo's cage. Such an episode was played out on April 18, 1942, when the Americans produced their own piece of audacious strategy. Under the command of Lieutenant Colonel James H. Doolittle, sixteen Army Air Corps B-25 bombers alighted from the carrier *Hornet* more than six hundred miles to the east of Japan and proceeded to bomb targets in Tokyo, Nagoya, Osaka, and Kobe. Once again the material damage inflicted was slight, but the shock among Japan's military leadership was anything but. In a May 2 letter to Admiral Koga Mineichi, Admiral Yamamoto expressed his dismay: "About the raid on the eighteenth of last month, one has the embarrassing feeling of having been caught napping just when one was feeling confident and in charge of things. Even though there wasn't much damage, it's a disgrace that the skies over the Imperial Palace should have been defiled without a single enemy plane being shot down. It provides a regrettably graphic illustration of the saying that a bungling attack is better than the most skillful defense."[19]

Yamamoto's prior confidence would doubtless have been stoked by the first major breach of Australia's outer northeastern defenses in January 1942. The seizure of the Admiralty Islands and base and airfield sites on the northern coastline of New Guinea was necessary to consolidate Japan's defensive perimeter in the Southwest Pacific, and at its heart lay the vital base at Rabaul. The capture of Rabaul likewise provided Yamamoto with a springboard to undertake further offensive operations against the Solomon Islands, Papua, and the Australian mainland. Due to the paucity of available Australian forces, Rabaul was defended by just 1,400 troops.[20] From January 20 to 22, the base was pounded by land-based and carrier-borne airstrikes that destroyed most of the few RAAF aircraft present and several coastal strongpoints; the landings took place in the early morning hours of the following day. The defenders were rapidly overcome and the Japanese followed up this success with landings in New Guinea at Lae and Salamaua on March 8, which were virtually unopposed.[21] Across the Owen Stanley Range, Port Moresby stood as the last prominent Allied base to the immediate northeast of the Queensland coast. As the first reports of Rabaul's capture reached Australia, the *Sydney Morning Herald* seized upon its fall to declare that a line in the sand had been reached regarding Australia's lack of representation in the formulation of Allied strategy: "Accordingly, now that war threatens our very homes, we have an undeniable right to representation on bodies responsible for high strategy which includes supply of the fighting front. . . . No nation having its soil and people closely menaced by a powerful enemy can be expected, nor has its Government the right, to leave crucial decisions on which its survival depends, to the judgment of executives on which it is not directly represented. However strong the ties of kinship, that argument must be maintained."[22]

The capitulation of Rabaul could not have come at a more fragile time for Australia's political and military leaders. In Malaya the Commonwealth land forces were within days of being driven off the peninsula, and the Japanese were commencing their thrusts into the Netherlands East Indies. With the enemy now encroaching upon the continent from the northeast, the Australian government was still fighting to achieve some form of worthwhile representation in the wider strategic decision-making processes, a course of action unassisted by continuing friction between Curtin and Churchill in particular. And to defend the continent itself, Australia's effective military resources were nonexistent. A new strategic partnership with the United States was not something that could be conjured up overnight without the necessary administrative, logistical, and financial nuts and bolts being put in place first. This problem raised its head in early February 1942, with questions over which nation would bear the financial burden of establishing the material infrastructure for the basing of American forces in Australia.[23] Lend-Lease was likewise an absolute necessity if Australia's available armed forces were to be properly equipped to withstand the Japanese. But in spite of the positive early negotiations with Washington, the adoption of Lend-Lease became bogged down after February over questions of postwar economic outcomes. Of these, the issue of imperial preference in Australia's trading relationships became a particular sticking point.[24] Nevertheless, some progress was being made with discussions over economic assistance and the setup of a USN purchasing authority in Australia to further streamline the supply of necessary stores and equipment. By May 3 a final agreement was pending between the Australian, American, and British governments for a joint Lend-Lease structure that made allowance for Australia's frail economy.[25]

These steps were a positive indication that the Americans were beginning to appreciate the value of Australia's strategic position in the Pacific.

On February 17, 1942, Casey reported to Canberra that Roosevelt was impatient to end the reverses and make a stand in an area that could be securely held and resupplied. In a conversation with Harry Hopkins, the president's senior confidant, Hopkins informed Casey that Australia and New Zealand were the only locations that met Roosevelt's specifications.[26] Australia's situation had been similarly aided by the appointment of Admiral King as the USN's new commander in chief, for King was campaigning in Washington to secure adequate naval resources for operations in the Pacific.[27] Yet there was no escaping the demands of the bigger picture, and the Americans were in agreement with the British when it came to the diversion of the returning Australian ground forces to Burma. In a secret cable to Curtin on February 21, Roosevelt urged the prime minister to secure what he (Roosevelt) described as the "left flank": China, Burma, and India.[28] When Curtin refused to budge, Roosevelt accepted the outcome with regret, but he made it known to Casey that Australia's decision would have no negative bearing upon the dispatch of American reinforcements and material aid to Australia. In the course of his remarks, Roosevelt emphasized the potential for the success of future combined operations in the Pacific by pointing to the aerial victory achieved by Task Force 11 in the vicinity of Rabaul the previous day.[29]

With the arrival in Washington of Australia's minister for external affairs in mid-March 1942, a line was drawn under the two months of friction that had clouded Australia's relations with Britain and the United States. After meeting with Harry Hopkins, Evatt advised Curtin that "Hopkins stressed the need of starting from scratch again with Churchill in order to re-establish friendliest feelings, and he will advise the President to approach Churchill on the same lines."[30] On April 1 the Australians achieved their biggest diplomatic coup to date with the first meeting of the newly constituted Pacific War Council in Washington. To Evatt's obvious delight, Roosevelt displayed a keen interest in Australia's military position and the measures necessary to safeguard her interests: "General Council discussion was on the whole satisfactory, and the proceedings took much the form of a War Council meeting in Australia. I am certain that that machinery established is regarded by the President as being his own rather than Churchill's and that he is anxious to make a success of it."[31] Prior to departing for London, Evatt informed Curtin that the two primary purposes of his visit to Washington, the establishment of the functioning Pacific Council and securing agreements for the flow of aircraft and other munitions to Australia, had been successful. It was recognized by Evatt, however, that while the new council did give Australia a voice when it came to the consideration of strategic issues, others would call the big plays. It was to be the Combined Chiefs of Staff who would "exercise a general jurisdiction over grand strategic policy and over such related factors as are necessary for proper implementation, including the allocation of forces and war materials."[32]

On March 17, 1942, General Douglas MacArthur arrived in Australia to take command of the Southwest Pacific Area. Apparently once described by Roosevelt as one of the two most dangerous men in America (alongside the populist senator Huey P. Long), MacArthur's recent service record had been less than stellar.[33] In concert with his "Bataan Gang," as his personal staff was known, he had presided over the destruction of the Far Eastern Air Force in circumstances that have never been fully explained, while the ground defense of the Philippines had proven to be a shambles from the outset. Ever the consummate showman, MacArthur was used to getting his own way. His relationship with Australia's political and military leaders would soon provoke what David Horner has described as one of the most contentious issues in Australian political and military history.[34] At the center of the controversy would be MacArthur's personal relationship with Curtin and the extent of his influence over the governance of Australian domestic affairs. In the weeks following his arrival, friction developed over the proposed extent of his powers to command Australian forces in the field, with Evatt forced on April 7 to deny that any conflict existed between the American and his Australian counterparts.[35] With assurances from Washington that MacArthur's command structure did not preclude Australian generals from communicating directly with their government, and that Australia could refuse the use of its forces "for any project which it considered inadvisable," Curtin consented to the new arrangements:

> You have come to Australia to lead a crusade, the result of which means everything to the future of the world and mankind. At the request of a sovereign State you are being placed in Supreme Command of its Navy, Army and Air Force, so that with those of your great nation, they may be welded into a homogeneous force and

given that unified direction which is so vital for the achievement of victory. Your directive, amongst other things, instructs you to prepare to take the offensive. I would assure you of every possible support that can be given you by the Government and people of Australia in making Australia as a base for operations, in assisting you to muster the strength required to wrest the initiative from the enemy and, in joining with you in the ultimate offensive, to bring about the total destruction of the common foe.[36]

MacArthur's mission had already been aided by the agreement between Washington and Canberra on March 12 to establish a unified American-Australian air command in the Southwest Pacific Area.[37] But his determination to employ Australia as a base for an immediate counteroffensive against the Philippines vanished shortly after his arrival. Virtually all the 25,000 American military personnel in Australia at the time belonged to nonfrontline combat units, together with approximately 260 aircraft, most of which were unserviceable.[38] Once he ascertained the extent of Australia's domestic defensive capabilities, MacArthur quickly concluded that massive reinforcements would be required if Australia itself were to be saved. By May 1942 the position had improved somewhat with the arrival of major elements of the American Army's 41st and 32nd Divisions and the return of 7th Division AIF from the Middle East. Alongside a small handful of RAAF bomber and reconnaissance squadrons, the available American contribution had risen to three fighter and eight bomber groups, with more than two hundred of these aircraft being located in Queensland.[39] MacArthur likewise exercised authority over the Anzac Area cruiser force commanded by Australian rear admiral J. G. Crace, which included the heavy cruisers *Australia* and *Chicago*, the light cruiser *Hobart*, and the American destroyers *Perkins* and *Walke*. But he remained far from satisfied, in Curtin's words "bitterly disappointed," as to the level of reinforcement that had been thus far received, and in late April he requested that the American chiefs of staff dispatch an aircraft-carrier task force to strengthen his command. In support of his requests, MacArthur pointed to the recent concentration of Japanese forces in the Admiralty Islands as a signal that a new southern push through New Guinea and the Solomon Islands could extend to Australia as well.[40]

Thanks to the efforts of the ingenious Commander Joseph J. Rochefort and his Hawaii-based codebreakers, the Japanese JN25 command-level cipher had been penetrated. On the basis of Rochefort's assessment, on April 29 Admiral Nimitz determined that two of his carrier task forces would await the Japanese in the Coral Sea.[41] Steaming from Noumea, Task Force 17 under Rear Admiral Fletcher fielded the carrier *Yorktown*, five cruisers, and five destroyers. Proceeding from Hawaii under Rear Adm. Aubrey W. Fitch was Task Force 11, the carrier *Lexington*, and four destroyers, which would amalgamate with Fletcher's command. Likewise reassigned from MacArthur's authority was Admiral Crace's cruiser force, redesignated as Task Group 17.3. With Nimitz exercising authority over the naval elements of the Allied forces, MacArthur was responsible for supplying land-based air reconnaissance and combat support.[42] For their part, the Japanese had contrived Operation "MO," a multilayered expedition to seize Port Moresby and Tulagi (at the southern tip of the Solomon Islands chain), as well as Nauru and Ocean Island to the north of the Solomons. Under the overall command of CIC Fourth Fleet, Vice Admiral Inouye Shigeyoshi, the invasion forces (Rear Admiral Goto Aritomo) included the Tulagi Invasion Group, consisting of a transport, two destroyers, and a number of smaller craft, and the Port Moresby Invasion Group, which contained a dozen transports, six destroyers, and four converted minesweepers. Direct air and surface support for the Port Moresby Group was provided by the light carrier *Shōhō* and four heavy cruisers, with additional cover from elements of the 25th Air Flotilla based at Rabaul. And to guard against any incursion by Nimitz' carriers, a mobile force (Vice Admiral Takagi Takeo) consisting of the carriers *Shōkaku* and *Zuikaku* with a cruiser and destroyer screen, was to provide distant cover for the invasion forces.[43]

Based upon the information in his possession, Nimitz had concluded that the Japanese assaults would commence on or about May 3, 1942. After Fitch's and Fletcher's task forces rendezvoused to the west of the New Hebrides on May 1, the following day was taken up with refueling operations.[44] Fletcher departed northward toward the Solomons on the evening of May 2 and had drawn within 250 miles of Tulagi the next day when he received word at 1900 hours that Japanese landings were under way. Steaming north at high speed, *Yorktown* launched forty dive-bombers and torpedo-planes to attack Japanese shipping off Tulagi early on the morning of May 4. Three small craft and a number of barges were sunk at the cost of three aircraft lost, and on the basis of overoptimistic claims by the aircrews involved, Fletcher retired to rejoin Fitch.[45] In response to requests for help from the Tulagi invasion force, Vice Admiral Takagi's carriers to the north of the Solomons were immediately dispatched southwards to intercept their American counterparts, while Rear Admiral Gotō's Port Moresby force departed from Rabaul the same day.

On May 5 several bombers flying from Port Moresby located and unsuccessfully attacked *Shōhō* near Bougainville, but aside from an air raid mounted from Rabaul against Moresby itself, no other action took place as Fletcher and Takagi sought each other out.[46] Poor weather was not assisting matters, and it was not until the morning of May 7 that a series of skirmishes got under way approximately seven hundred miles to the south of the Solomon Islands. First blood was drawn by the Japanese when, on the basis of an incorrect sighting report, Takagi's big carriers launched a large-scale airstrike that found the oiler *Neosho* and the destroyer *Sims* instead of a reported American aircraft carrier; *Sims* was quickly sunk and *Neosho* crippled (and subsequently scuttled).[47] Following suit, Fletcher dispatched his own strike in response to an errantly coded sighting that indicated the presence of two enemy carriers. By the time the error had been identified, more than ninety fighters, dive-bombers, and torpedo-planes were already well on their way to intercept the reported Japanese concentration. Through good fortune, the leading elements of the strike located *Shōhō* and her consorts at 1100 hours in the vicinity of the Louisiades.[48] From 1110 to 1130 the luckless light carrier was pounded by bombs and torpedoes before she sank at 1135. To the south of the Louisiades at 1358 hours, Rear Admiral Crace's cruisers were subjected to unsuccessful attacks by approximately forty land-based bombers from Rabaul, and a subsequent mistaken effort by three USAAC aircraft flying from Townsville.[49]

The spate of misinformation and mistaken identity reached its peak with a further strike launched from Takagi's carriers just prior to dusk. Having failed to sight any enemy ships, the Japanese dive-bombers and torpedo-planes jettisoned their loads and began their return flights in foul weather. By chance they flew straight over Task Force 17, and in the melee that followed with the American combat air patrol, nine of them were shot down. Several of the surviving Japanese aircraft then compounded their difficulties by attempting to land on the American carriers by mistake.⁵⁰ In order to support the Port Moresby Group, Takagi altered course to the north. Separated by approximately 180 miles at dawn on May 8, the rival carrier forces launched their search aircraft amid low clouds and frequent rain squalls. Both forces were quickly sighted, with the Japanese launching an airstrike at 0815 hours and the American response coming an hour later. The American strike was the first to find its mark at 1015, when two coordinated assaults by eighty-four dive-bombers and torpedo-planes from *Yorktown* and *Lexington* left *Shōkaku* ablaze after she was struck by four bombs; a dozen of the attacking aircraft were shot down or otherwise lost.⁵¹ Takagi's aircrews returned serve just after 1100 hours with seventy aircraft (including fighter escort), attacking Fletcher's ships in bright sunny conditions. In a similarly coordinated fashion, the attackers caught *Lexington* with at least two torpedoes and a number of bombs that brought her to a standstill, while *Yorktown* received a single bomb that inflicted heavy internal damage and numerous casualties. Twenty-six Japanese aircraft were lost in the course of the strike, bringing total Japanese aircraft losses for the day to forty-three as opposed to thirty-three American aircraft lost through combat and other causes.⁵²

At 1247 hours a series of violent internal explosions caused by leaking fuel vapor commenced the final demise of the crippled *Lexington*. In spite of every endeavor to save the ship, she was abandoned at 1700 and scuttled two hours later. The scuttling of *Lexington* marked the final stage of the battle, with Fletch and Fitch retiring to the south while Inouye officially postponed the Port Moresby mission, and after a subsequent order from Yamamoto for Takagi to resume contact with Task Force 17 was countermanded, the *Zuikaku* and her screen withdrew the following day.⁵³ From a tactical perspective the Japanese had gained a narrow victory with the sinking of *Lexington*, but the damage to *Shōkaku* and the depletion of the Mobile Force's air groups meant that neither of the big carriers would be available for the following Midway operation. For the present, the rebuff of the Port Moresby Invasion Group along with the recall of the small forces designated to capture Nauru and Ocean Island represented a notable but temporary check to Japan's strategic momentum. Yet within the next seven months the failure to capture Port Moresby and the successful seizure of Tulagi would separately combine to halt this impetus once and for all. In the meantime, further events were brewing to the northeast of the Marshall Islands, events that were to fundamentally alter the course of the conflict within the Pacific theater as a whole.

Midway and the Mandates: May 10–December 31, 1942

The news of the repulse of the Japanese expedition and the purported destruction of at least two of Vice Admiral Inouye's carriers was received with enthusiasm and relief in Australia. Yet, as an opinion piece in the *Melbourne Age* on May 15 reflected, victory in the Coral Sea merely represented the beginning of a new campaign for which more American assistance was required as a matter of urgency:

> The enemy was massed in substantial force; his objective may have been the invasion of Australia's coast or the cutting of an important supply route. . . . It was the opening move in a new war zone. . . . Initial success in the Coral Sea must not for an instant be allowed to obscure that certainty. It is probably temperamental for the Australian people to cultivate an optimistic outlook and to plead that as there has just been a naval victory and threatening trouble has, for the meantime at least, been staved off, we may therefore somewhat relax. At this present stage, such an attitude is disloyal and could be fatal. The entire south-west Pacific campaign has shown that Japan's greatest strength and tenacity have been reserved for any second attempt that has proved necessary. Her second attempt to attack Australia is due. It may be made at any moment, and we must be ready to meet it with our maximum in men and equipment. . . . The appointment of America's distinguished soldier General MacArthur as Supreme Commander of the Allied Forces was received by Australians with enthusiasm. Everything that has happened since has served to increase their faith in his leadership. In the stern tasks that now confront him, it is to be expected that America will more lavishly than ever support him. . . . For the cause at stake is not Australia's only, it is the cause of America, and of humanity.[54]

A similar message was forthcoming from Canberra. In a cable to Evatt on May 13, Curtin sent a blunt assessment of the situation as both he and

MacArthur saw it. "MacArthur states that as the further attempt of the Japanese to move southwards has been frustrated in the recent engagement in the Coral Sea, it is of vital importance to build up and maintain adequate strength to repulse any further attacks of this nature. . . . I hope there is a full realisation in London and Washington of the grave threat with we were confronted last week."[55] For Whitehall's consumption in particular, Curtin made his feelings abundantly clear. "If Japan should move in force against Australia and obtain a foothold, as threatened to occur last week with the Coral Sea action, it may be too late to send assistance. . . . History will gravely indict such a happening to a nation which sacrificed 60,000 of its men on overseas battlefields in the last war, and, at its peril, has sent its naval, military and air forces to fight overseas in this one."[56] On May 28 Evatt advised Curtin that Churchill wished to supply Australia with an emergency reinforcement of three squadrons of Spitfires to be dispatched on a convoy in the middle of June.[57] Three days later the Japanese pulled another surprise. Since Pearl Harbor their submarines had attacked fourteen merchant vessels along the eastern Australian seaboard, sinking six of them.[58] As outlined previously, this campaign escalated to a new level on the night of May 31–June 1, 1942, when three Japanese midget submarines penetrated Sydney Harbour. A follow-up nuisance bombardment of Sydney and Newcastle by submarines on the night of June 8 did provoke some genuine panic amongst Sydneysiders from coastal suburbs who convinced themselves that an enemy invasion was imminent.[59]

Since early January the respective Japanese armed services had been grappling with future strategic proposals that included how Australia should be dealt with. These discussions took the form of study groups, and they reflected the deep levels of factionalism within the Japanese armed forces. Led by Captain Tomioka Sadatoshi from the planning division of the Naval General Staff, a number of junior grade officers recommended the capture of Darwin and several other targets in Queensland in order to cut Australia's communications with the United States and thereby force Australia to capitulate. This approach was rejected outright by the Imperial Japanese Army, whose planners did not wish to provoke another war of attrition given the ongoing struggle in China and the possibility of conflict with the Soviet Union.[60] Meanwhile Yamamoto had rejected a suggestion from the Imperial General Headquarters senior Air

Staff officer (Commander Mitsushiro) that carrier strikes be conducted against Australian ports as an alternative to the Midway operation. Yet both the Naval Staff and the Combined Fleet recognized Australia's role as a base for an American counteroffensive, and there were strong arguments advanced in favor of isolation rather than invasion. Advancing through the Solomons and seizing Fiji and Samoa would, in the view of the senior Japanese naval leadership, largely accomplish this latter task.[61] And while the principal motivation for the recent MO operation in the Coral Sea had been to strengthen Japan's imperial perimeter beyond the Caroline and Admiralty Islands, the capture of Port Moresby in particular was a critical strategic gain in any contemplated isolation strategy. Other alternative strategies, including a thrust into the Indian Ocean and war against the Soviet Union, were likewise dissected and discarded. On May 5, 1942, a final decision regarding the next offensive expedition was reached, with the following order being sent from the IGHQ to the Combined Fleet:

> By command of His Imperial Majesty to Commander in Chief Yamamoto of the Combined Fleet:
> 1. The Commander in Chief of the Combined Fleet is to cooperate with the army in the occupation of Midway and strategic points in the west of the Aleutians.
> 2. Detailed directions will be given by the chief of the Naval General Staff.[62]

Even before the first of the numerous Japanese flotillas assigned to the Midway operation began leaving their bases in mid-May, the potential flaws in Yamamoto's strategy were already apparent. As Samuel E. Morison related in his summary of Japanese planning for the MO operation, overcomplexity was a central defect. "Whenever the Japanese planners disposed of sufficient strength, they divided forces and drafted an elaborate plan, the successful execution of which required a tactical competence rare at any time in any Navy, as well as the enemy's passive acceptance of the role he was expected to play. That sort of thing worked all right in the Netherlands East Indies, where the Allied forces were heavily outnumbered, and it might have worked here [Coral Sea] too if the Allies had been surprised. But the Japanese were not sufficiently careful of security."⁶³ Nor were they any more discerning when it came to keeping the identity of an objective known as "AF" under wraps. Increasing reference to AF in Japanese naval transmissions during early May had attracted the interest of Rochefort and his codebreakers, who were already convinced that Yamamoto was intending to launch some form of major operation in the Central Pacific. Believing Midway to be the probable target, Rochefort and his staff devised a clever ruse to confirm AF's identity. A series of messages in plain English and cipher were sent from Midway to Pearl Harbor indicating difficulties with the island's fresh water supply. Intercepted by Japanese listening posts, the information was passed on to the IGHQ and Combined Fleet headquarters with reference to AF.⁶⁴ Convinced that Midway was indeed the main objective, Nimitz proceeded to set a trap for his careless opponents.

With Halsey unavailable through illness, Nimitz placed Rear Adm. Raymond Spruance in command of Task Force 16. Consisting of the carriers *Enterprise* and *Hornet* with a screen of six cruisers and eleven destroyers, Spruance's command would proceed to the northeast of Midway and be in position to intercept the Japanese carriers on June 4. To follow him from Pearl Harbor two days later was Fletcher's Task Force 17, the rapidly patched-up *Yorktown* accompanied by two heavy cruisers and six destroyers. Further to the north under the command of Rear Adm. Robert A. Theobold, Task Force 8's five cruisers and three destroyers were to intercept any Japanese attempt to attack the Aleutians, identified as the secondary target "AO" by Rochefort's command.⁶⁵ The three USN task forces were facing the single largest concentration of warships yet seen in World War II. Assembled into no less than twelve commands fielding more than 110 ships between them, the Combined Fleet's advantage in virtually every aspect of naval operations was overwhelming.⁶⁶ But the spearhead of the Japanese fleet, Vice Admiral Nagumo's First Air Fleet, did not enjoy the advantage of operating independently as it had done from Pearl Harbor to Colombo. Instead it was tucked away within the wider mission organization, a role that was to compromise its notoriously effective anonymity. And to Yamamoto's disadvantage, Nimitz had taken care to assign a seaplane tender and several smaller craft to guard French Frigate Shoal, a rocky outcrop situated between Oahu and Midway that had been previously used by Japanese submarines for refueling long-range flying boats traveling from Kwajalein. When two boats arrived there on May 26 to supply fuel for a vital reconnaissance over Pearl Harbor that would confirm the expected presence of the American carriers there, they found the enemy vessels at anchor, and the upcoming reconnaissance mission was aborted.[67]

Bereft of definitive information as to the whereabouts of the American carriers from both air and submarine reconnaissance, Yamamoto steamed on, electing not to inform Nagumo of the canceled flight and thereby break radio silence. At 0250 hours on June 3, the first blow was struck at the eastern end of the Aleutian Islands when aircraft from the carriers *Junyo* and *Ryūjō* bombed Dutch Harbor. At 0900 an American flying boat on patrol seven hundred miles to the west of Midway spotted elements of the Midway Occupation Force (Vice Admiral Kondō Nobutake), which was subsequently attacked at 1625 by a squadron of bombers from Midway, and at 0140 hours the following morning by flying boats armed with torpedoes, an oiler being slightly damaged.[68] Just before sun-up at 0534 on June 4, a reconnaissance aircraft spotted both Nagumo's carriers and a Midway-bound airstrike. Its warning message to Midway was intercepted by Fletcher's command, and the two USN carrier groups began to close the range in preparation for an attack. From 0630 to 0650 hours, Midway was subjected to bombing and strafing from more than a hundred Japanese aircraft, which failed to put the airfield out of action.[69] At the same moment the First Air Fleet came under attack from the first of several waves of Midway-based aircraft, each of these being beaten off with heavy loss to the attackers. Informed that a further strike against Midway was required, at 0715 Nagumo ordered that his standby force, armed with torpedoes as a precaution against any American naval interference, be rearmed with bombs. Ten minutes later he received a sighting report indicating the presence of enemy ships to the northeast. Though the message did not specify whether a carrier was among the sightings, Nagumo countermanded his rearmament order at 0745.[70]

At 0820 hours Nagumo received confirmation that the American formation sighted earlier did contain an aircraft carrier. Fifteen minutes later the returning aircraft from the Midway strike began to alight upon his four carriers, while preparations for an attack against the enemy carrier force were underway in the hangars below. With these approaching completion, from 0930 to 1000 the First Air Fleet was assailed by successive waves of torpedo-bombers launched from *Hornet*, *Enterprise*,

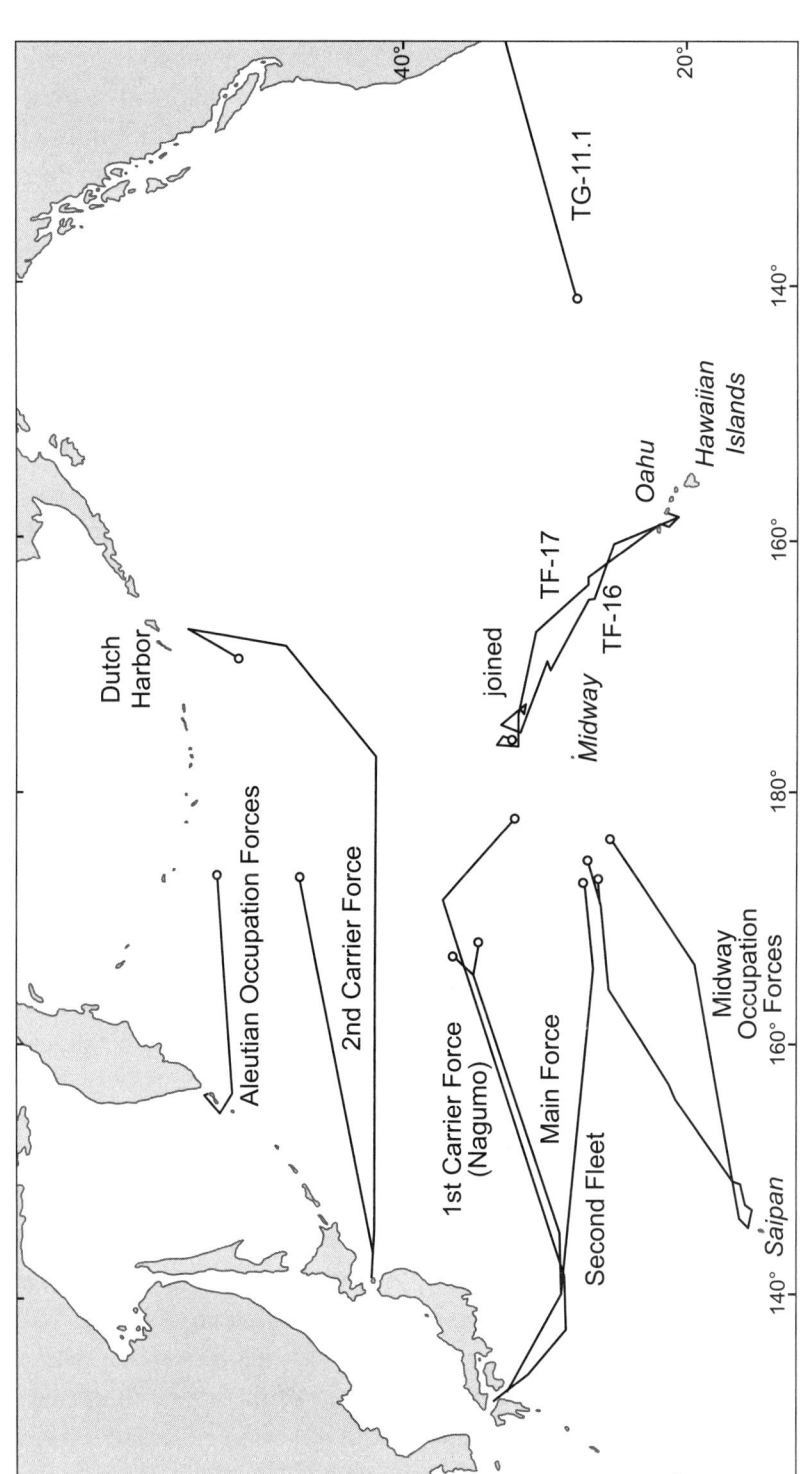

Battle of Midway, June 3–7, 1942

and *Yorktown*. In the course of these attacks no hits were scored, at the cost of thirty-five of the forty-one attackers being mown down by fighters and flak.[71] Shortly thereafter the tables were emphatically turned. Largely unhindered by enemy fighter cover, separate formations of dive-bombers from the *Yorktown* and *Enterprise* spotted three of Nagumo's carriers through broken clouds. Led by Lieutenant Commander Clarence McClusky from *Enterprise*, the dive-bombers commenced their strikes at 1026. In quick succession the carriers *Akagi*, *Kaga*, and *Sōryū* were each struck by two or more bombs, with at least one of these in each instance plunging through the carriers' unarmored flight decks. All three of the Japanese ships were subjected to a chain of internal explosions and fires fed by ordnance and avgas. *Sōryū* eventually succumbed at 1920 hours, followed five minutes later by *Kaga*, while *Akagi* was scuttled shortly before dawn the next day. Two counterstrikes from *Hiryū* at 1215 and 1440 hours scored bomb and torpedo hits on *Yorktown* before *Hiryū* herself was attacked by dive-bombers at 1700 and fatally crippled, finally sinking at 0900 hours on June 5.[72]

On board his super battleship flagship *Yamato* to the west of the First Air Fleet, Yamamoto at first considered closing upon the American task forces to pursue a night action. But the extent of the losses sustained by Nagumo dissuaded him, and he gave the order for the Midway operation to be abandoned at 2355 hours on June 4, 1942.[73] During the afternoon of June 6 the final acts were played out. At 1330 hours a Japanese submarine put two torpedoes into the stricken *Yorktown*, sinking the destroyer *Hammann* in the process, which resulted in the American carrier foundering at 0600 the following day. And in a series of attacks mounted by dive-bombers from 1300 to 1445 hours, the large light cruiser *Mikuma* was sunk and her sister ship *Mogami* heavily damaged, the latter eventually limping home to Truk.[74] To the north meanwhile, the Japanese landed troops at Attu and Kiska in the Aleutians on June 7, the sole accomplishment of the entire operation. Defeat at Midway did not spell the imminent demise of the Combined Fleet, nor, as subsequent events were to bear out, was Japan's offensive momentum fully checked, most particularly in the southwest Pacific. What Fletcher and Spruance had achieved was the permanent destruction of the Imperial Japanese Navy's most fearsome offensive instrument, the independent spearhead made up of four to six large carriers. Without it, the extra strategic flexibility that came with the deployment of a first-strike weapon that had demonstrated its capacity to annihilate targets with little or no warning was removed, leaving Yamamoto dependent upon alternative means to reacquire Japan's decisive edge.

The reaction in Australia to Yamamoto's defeat at Midway was a mixture of relief and confidence tinged with caution. This was reflected by an editorial in the *Melbourne Age* on June 15, which noted that "the further severe losses inflicted on Japan's air and sea power off Midway Island, do not give us warrant to conclude that the danger to Australia has passed. Even if the menace is to some degree lessened, our task and that of our Allies is to bring Japan to condign defeat."[75] At an Advisory War Council meeting the following day, Curtin stated his belief that while the Japanese could no longer invade Australia, what he described as marauding raids by small amphibious forces were still a possibility.[76] The principal threat Midway had removed, however, was the prospect of another Darwin: a major carrier spearhead offensive against Australia's vulnerable east coast ports and industrial centers. As forthcoming events were to prove, the remaining material menace to the continent was to be posed by long-range bombing by land-based aircraft. Prior to their cessation in November 1943, Darwin was to endure sixty-four raids by Japanese bombers flying from captured bases in the Netherlands East Indies. And from Port Gregory on the central west Australian coast to Townsville in north Queensland, forty-eight separate attacks against other targets would be undertaken, the majority of these falling into the category of nuisance raids.[77] Yet while the Japanese occupied Tulagi and could likewise threaten Port Moresby, Australia's critical sea communications with the United States lay exposed to interdiction from the still formidable fighting resources of Japan's navy.

As early as June 10, correspondence between Evatt and Curtin revealed MacArthur's desire to pursue a more active policy against the enemy in the Southwest Pacific.[78] MacArthur's ambition was shared by Admiral King in Washington, and out of this arose a short but bitter turf war. An offensive to clear New Guinea and the Solomons prior to recapturing Rabaul fell under the geographic jurisdiction of MacArthur's command, but King proved successful in persuading his fellow chiefs of staff that the initial Solomons portion of the operation be assigned to Nimitz.[79] On July 2, 1942, a compromise plan was agreed to. The overall objective remained "the seizure and occupation of the New Britain-New Ireland-New Guinea area," with MacArthur commanding all but the operation to secure the first nominated objective, Tulagi.[80] MacArthur's preparations to clear New Guinea were not assisted by his ongoing distrust of his Australian army counterparts and the friction that existed between himself and General Sir Thomas Blamey, the Australian commander of Allied Land Forces. Since his arrival in Australia in March, MacArthur had been made aware of local preparations for a Japanese invasion, the planning for which involved the feasibility of the so-called "Brisbane Line." This involved the concentration of Australia's domestic defense efforts in the southeastern portion of the country, with scorched earth methods to be carried through elsewhere.[81] Regarding the Australian attitude as defeatist, MacArthur attempted to isolate Curtin by insinuating himself as the prime minister's chief military adviser. The chief of the Australian General Staff, Lieutenant General Sir Vernon Sturdee, regarded his and Blamey's roles in MacArthur's command structure as entirely those of "housekeepers."[82] But before MacArthur could put his plans into practice, the Japanese acted otherwise.

As the New Guinea campaign was primarily determined by the ground forces involved, its conduct and outcomes are the subject of the following general summation. From July 21–22, 1942, troops of the South Seas Force (Major General Horii Tomitarō) were landed at Gona with the original intention of conducting a reconnaissance-in-force.[83] This developed into a six-thousand-strong general advance along the single track over the Owen Stanleys toward Port Moresby, and by July 29 the Japanese had pushed the Australians back from Kokoda, a small village situated roughly halfway along the track that would subsequently bear its name. While MacArthur and Blamey tussled over strategy and tactics, the fighting played out in appalling conditions. In the dense mountain jungle and fetid swamps, disease, lack of supply, and sheer exhaustion seriously hampered attacker and defender alike. On August 25 the Japanese landed a two-thousand-strong marine detachment at Milne Bay on the eastern tip of Papua with the objective of seizing three local airfields to support the advance inland from Gona.[84] Aided by a pair of RAAF fighter-bomber squadrons, two Australian brigades successfully repulsed the enemy thrust, and the surviving Japanese troops were withdrawn on September 6. By September 17 Horii's force had reached

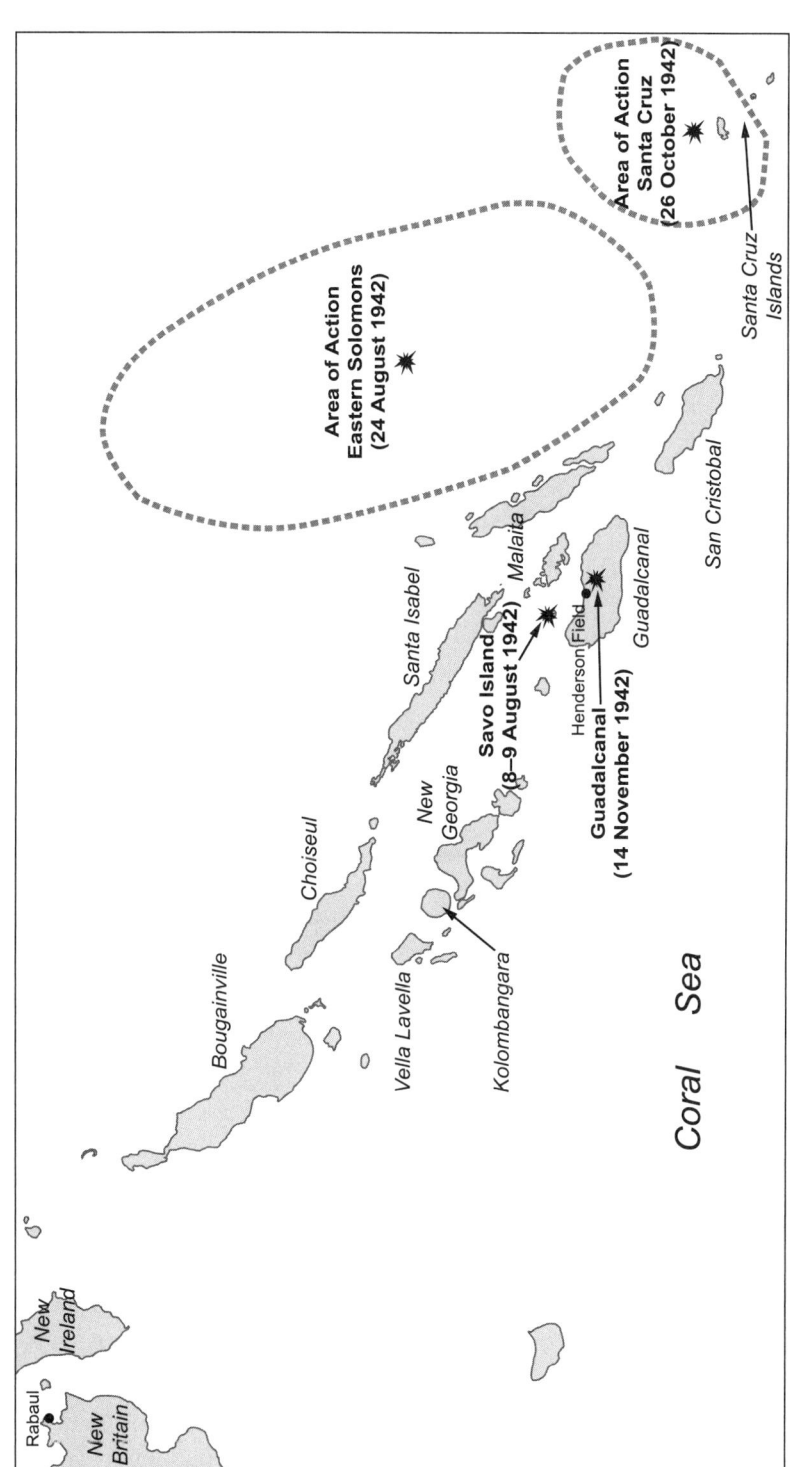

The Solomons Campaign, August–November 1942

Imita Ridge, some thirty-five miles from Port Moresby, which proved to be the furthest extent of their advance. Largely unsupplied, and with orders instructing a withdrawal to Gona due to losses sustained in the Solomons, the Japanese began their retirement on September 24, the Australians recapturing Kokoda on November 2.[85]

Once the Horii expedition had collapsed, Australian and American ground forces commenced an offensive to drive the enemy garrisons out of Gona, Buna, and Sanananda on the northeastern New Guinea coastline. Following several Allied reverses, Gona fell on December 9, 1942, while Buna and Sanananda were taken on January 2 and January 18, 1943, respectively.[86] Though the Japanese retained their principal base at Lae and remained ensconced elsewhere, a final crushing blow to their presence was dealt out in the Bismarck Sea on March 2–3, 1943. Carrying some six thousand reinforcements to Lae, a convoy containing eight transports and eight escorting destroyers was repeatedly attacked by American and Australian land-based aircraft, resulting in the sinking of all the transports together with four destroyers.[87] While the fighting continued in New Guinea until the fall of Wewak in May 1945, at the conclusion of December 1942 the prospects for a Japanese seizure of Port Moresby had been nearly extinguished. Whether undertaken by land or sea, such an assault was doomed to fail in the absence of localized air superiority, which by this time had passed to Japan's opponents and was to be employed by them with great effect in the forthcoming neutralization of Japan's remaining New Guinea garrisons.

It would not have been difficult for the Allies to appreciate why Yamamoto's planners had selected Tulagi as a target for occupation in the course of the MO operation. Aside from the deployment of flying boats, seaplanes, and submarines, the anchorage space in what was to become known as "Ironbottom Sound" was capable of accommodating the majority of the Combined Fleet. And five miles across the sound lay the island of Guadalcanal. Made up largely of fetid malarial swamps backed by jungle-clad mountains, the one area of significant flat plain within the southern Solomon Islands lay on this island's northern shoreline. The establishment of a Japanese-held airfield on Guadalcanal would directly threaten Allied naval movement in the Coral Sea and serve as a base to interdict the nearby supply routes between the United States and Australia. Late in June 1942 a Japanese convoy with the required labor and equipment arrived at Guadalcanal to commence construction. This activity was observed by Allied aerial reconnaissance in early July, and American preparations for Operation "Watchtower," which had been authorized in Washington two days beforehand, were immediately accelerated.[88] Thus the stage was set for what would become a five-month aero-amphibious war of attrition, a grim, grinding, relentless struggle ashore, afloat, and in the skies above to determine control of Guadalcanal and its vital airfield site. A. J. P. Taylor later described the coming clash as a ding-dong battle, a fitting description of the intensity and ferocity with which it would be fought.[89]

Under the overall command of Vice Adm. Robert L. Ghormley based in Noumea, the hastily assembled U.S. Navy task forces exercised for three days in the Fiji Islands before departing for the Solomons in early August. Commanded by Vice Admiral Fletcher, Task Force 61 contained the carriers *Saratoga*, *Enterprise*, and *Wasp*, the new battleship *North Carolina*, six cruisers, and sixteen destroyers. Fletcher's mission was to protect Task Force 62 (Rear Adm. Richmond Turner), which conveyed 19,000 Marines under the command of Major General Alexander Vandegrift, escorted by five American and three Australian cruisers and fifteen American destroyers.[90] On the morning of August 7, 1942, the Marines landed at Tulagi and Guadalcanal, seizing the former after a stiff fight and the latter with little resistance. Warned of the landings by a radio message from Tulagi at 0715 hours, Vice Admiral Mikawa Gunichi, based in Rabaul, ordered an immediate airstrike against the enemy transports. Escorted by eighteen fighters, the forty-three bombers were spotted in transit by a pair of Australian coast watchers, Australian, British, and New Zealand military and civilian personnel who had been inserted onto enemy-occupied islands to carry out clandestine reconnaissance and provide information by wireless.[91] Intercepted by fighters from the supporting carriers, fourteen bombers and two Zekes were downed at the cost of eleven defending fighters, the transports escaping undamaged. A repeat attack the following day by twenty-six aircraft resulted in the sinking of one transport and damage to a destroyer, with a total of seventeen Japanese planes shot down.

Believing that the invading force at Guadalcanal amounted to no more than two thousand troops, Mikawa also authorized an amphibious expedition comprising five hundred marines embarked in six transports.

This mission, however, was aborted at midnight on August 8 when one of the troopers was sunk by an American submarine.[92] Determined to wipe out the American transports before they finished unloading, Mikawa set out from Rabaul in the late afternoon of August 7. Flying his flag in the heavy cruiser *Chōkai*, his squadron included five heavy cruisers, two light cruisers, and a single destroyer. Judging that he could catch the American transports at anchor in the early morning hours of August 9, Mikawa accepted the risk of early detection and proceeded southeast down "the Slot," the American name for the long channel that ran the length of the Solomon Islands from northwest to southeast.[93] Twice on the morning of August 8 his ships were sighted by separate RAAF reconnaissance aircraft to the south of Bougainville, but an errant report detailing the presence of three cruisers, two destroyers, and two seaplane carriers did not reach Turner until 1845 hours that evening. Adjudging that these ships were being employed for other purposes, Turner ordered a conference with Vandegrift and Rear Admiral Victor Crutchley, RN, the commander of Turner's Covering Group, to discuss Fletcher's imminent withdrawal of Task Force 61.[94] Before proceeding on board the heavy cruiser *Australia* to confer with his commander at 2230, Crutchley had deployed his forces to the east of Savo Island at the entrance to Ironbottom Sound. With two destroyers performing radar picket to the north and west of Savo, the northern passage was guarded by the heavy cruisers *Vincennes*, *Quincy*, and *Astoria* with two destroyers, while the heavy cruisers *Canberra* and *Chicago*, with two destroyers, patrolled the southern entrance.[95]

As Crutchley was returning to *Australia* following his meeting with Turner on board the latter's flagship *McCawley*, Mikawa's cruisers were preparing to enter Ironbottom Sound. After sighting the enemy destroyer pickets to port and encountering no challenge, the Japanese ships proceeded to enter the sound from the south at twenty-six knots. Steaming eastward, they sighted two cruisers heading toward them on a northwesterly course. At 0138 hours Mikawa gave the order to open fire on the enemy ships, with *Chōkai* the first to launch torpedoes. Five minutes later, the Allied vessels were illuminated by parachute flares from three Japanese seaplanes circling overhead.[96] Caught almost completely by surprise, *Canberra* was raked from stem to stern with shellfire and left crippled and burning. Accompanying the Australian cruiser, *Chicago* was struck by a torpedo and thereafter steamed westward in a vain search for the Japanese ships. Next Mikawa's column came across Crutchley's northern patrollers, who were apparently none the wiser as to what had just occurred to their south. Illuminated in quick succession by enemy searchlights at 0150 hours, *Astoria*, *Quincy*, and *Vincennes* were riddled with hits. A Long Lance torpedo sent *Quincy* to the bottom at 0235, and she was followed by *Vincennes* at 0300.[97] Aside from minor damage to *Chōkai* and two of the other heavy cruisers, the Japanese ships emerged unharmed. Following a further skirmish that left an American destroyer heavily damaged, Mikawa abandoned his brief effort to fall upon Turner's transports, and at 0230 withdrew to the north of Savo. The following morning *Canberra* was scuttled, and *Astoria* sank just after midday. Returning to Kavieng, the squadron suffered its sole loss on August 10, when the heavy cruiser *Kako* was torpedoed and sunk by an American submarine.[98]

Though failing to destroy the American transports, Mikawa had nevertheless inflicted a crushing defeat upon the combined Allied cruiser force. In a subsequent inquiry it was found that defects in signaling, particularly through the use of the voice radio TBS (talk between ships) system employed on board the American vessels, together with a general lack of night fighting capability, were primarily responsible for the disaster. American analysis also attributed much of the blame to Crutchley's performance as well as the failure of the RAAF to ensure that the initial sighting report of Mikawa's ships reached Turner promptly; these claims have been subsequently disputed by some Australian scholars.[99] In the meantime, Fletcher's withdrawal, which had not been confirmed by Ghormley, and the subsequent decision by Turner to retire his transports, which now lacked air cover, left the Marines on Guadalcanal to their own devices. Despite shortages of heavy equipment, by August 20, 1942, they had made the captured airfield operational, renamed Henderson Field in honor of Major Lofton Henderson, USMC, who had been killed at Midway.[100] During the same period, the Japanese had commenced their buildup of a beachhead at Tassafaronga, a village several miles to the west of Henderson Field. The first landings were made on the night of August 17 and were followed the following evening by the use of what came to be known as the "Tokyo Express," small flotillas of destroyers and destroyer-transports ferrying troops and supplies in high-speed runs down the Slot. On this occasion their efforts were largely negated when the Marines were able to annihilate the majority of the Japanese reinforcements in battle at the entrance to the Tenaru River on August 21.[101]

With the competing demands of the New Guinea campaign upon available Japanese ground forces, only 1,500 troops could be spared for Yamamoto's next attempt to secure the Tassafaronga beachhead. Escorted by Mikawa's heavy cruisers and Rear Admiral Tanaka Raizō's Tokyo Express destroyers, the five converted transports were further protected by the Combined Fleet steaming to the north of the Solomons. Dividing his ships into four groups containing between them the carriers *Shōkaku*, *Zuikaku*, and *Ryūjō*, two battleships, and ten cruisers, Yamamoto's planning catered for both carrier and surface engagements.[102] Alerted to these deployments by aerial reconnaissance, Ghormley dispatched Task Force 61 to intercept to the north of the easternmost islands of the Solomons chain. They joined the battle on August 24, 1942. After receiving a reported sighting of an enemy carrier group some three hundred miles to his north, Fletcher directed two waves of dive-bombers and torpedo-planes to seek out the Japanese but retained all of the available Wildcat fighters to protect his own three carriers, *Enterprise*, *Saratoga*, and *Wasp*, against a retaliatory strike.[103] Owing to poor weather and confusion in target coordination due to excess radio chatter, most of the bombers missed the big Japanese carriers. Instead they concentrated their efforts against *Ryūjō*, Yamamoto's sacrificial decoy. Struck by a torpedo and numerous bombs she eventually sank at 2000 hours. In response, Nagumo's carriers launched an eighty-strong strike that reached Fletcher's ships at 1640 hours. Met by stiff fighter opposition and a wall of antiaircraft fire, three bombs inflicted serious damage upon *Enterprise* but at a frightful cost to the Japanese, with well over two-thirds of the attacking aircraft being shot down. Left totally exposed to air and surface attack, the Tanaka force soldiered on. Shortly after daylight on the August 25, his ships came under air attack, two being sunk and the remainder thereafter retiring to Truk.[104]

Having sunk a light aircraft carrier, inflicted significant losses upon Nagumo's air groups, and turned back Tanaka's convoy, the Americans emerged from the battle of the Eastern Solomons with a solid tactical victory. But true to Taylor's description, it was the Japanese who landed the next scoring punches. On August 31, 1942, *Saratoga* again fell victim to a torpedo from an enemy submarine, necessitating another lengthy stint in a home dockyard. And on September 15 a single Japanese submarine, the I-19, badly winged both *North Carolina* and a destroyer and hit the new carrier *Wasp* with two torpedoes. The explosions detonated her avgas stores, and she sank at 1452 hours with the loss of 193 lives.[105] For much of the next three weeks the combatants continued to reinforce their respective positions on Guadalcanal, though a Japanese assault against the American defensive perimeter surrounding Henderson Field was beaten back with heavy losses on September 13. The arrival of the commander of the Japanese 17th Army, Lieutenant General Hyakutake Harukichi, with fresh troops at Tassafaronga on the night of October 9–10 signaled the start of a major infusion of reinforcements, and the following night a large Tokyo Express screened by three cruisers and two destroyers attempted to repeat the exercise. Off Cape Esperance, the northernmost point of Guadalcanal, the Japanese blundered into the path of an American striking force, two heavy cruisers, two light cruisers, and five destroyers, under the command of Rear Adm. Norman Scott.[106] With the benefit of radar the American cruisers surprised the Japanese, sinking the heavy cruiser *Furutaka* and a destroyer, but further confusion led to the sinking of an American destroyer and serious damage to the light cruiser *Boise*, and the Tokyo Express arrived unhindered at Tassafaronga.[107]

Over the following nights, Yamamoto's battleships and cruisers reduced American fortunes to a new low. Though additional U.S. ground and air reinforcements arrived at Guadalcanal on October 13, two successive nights of surface bombardment destroyed or disabled at least half of the new aircraft and much of the aviation gasoline and other precious supplies between them. While there were still enough intact aircraft to attack and force ashore three enemy transports on the morning of October 15, the Japanese had seemingly seized the initiative. Conceding the gravity of the circumstances, Nimitz observed, "It now appears that we are unable to control the sea in the Guadalcanal area. Thus our supply of the positions will only be done at great expense to us. The situation is not hopeless, but it is certainly critical."[108]

Far away to the southwest in Canberra, Prime Minister Curtin and his colleagues had been observing the events in the Solomons with increasing alarm. Although the original capture of Guadalcanal had been welcomed as a turning point, they feared that a Japanese counterattack would target the Australian mainland.[109] As the situation in the Solomons ebbed and flowed during the course of September 1942, Canberra appealed to Whitehall for assistance but received little encouragement. With his gaze still fixed upon the Middle East and the Mediterranean, Winston Churchill refused Curtin's requests to send portions of the Eastern Fleet to assist in the Solomons. All the Australians could extract from Whitehall was the well-worn pledge that Britain would send assistance if Australia itself was on the point of a large-scale Japanese invasion.[110] Nor was further assistance forthcoming from Washington. In a cable to Curtin on September 16, Roosevelt informed his Australian counterpart that it was impossible to send more troops to Australia itself, "now or in the immediate future."[111] On September 30 the Australian chiefs of staff provided their latest appreciation as to the likely course of events. "The aim of the Japanese in the Southwest Pacific as we see it is to encircle Australia, thus cutting off Australian communications with America and possibly with the Middle East. . . . So long as the Solomon Islands, New Caledonia and Port Moresby are held we think an invasion of the east coast of Australia is unlikely."[112] Though conceding that a diversionary attack against northwest Australia could not be discounted, the appreciation effectively did so by pointing to Japan's fundamental strategic weakness, namely the stretching of her supply and logistics capabilities through Yamamoto's ongoing determination to recapture Guadalcanal.

The latest iteration of Yamamoto's ambition was not long in coming, but Nimitz pre-empted him with what was to emerge as a decisive change in Allied leadership. On October 18, 1942, Ghormley was relieved by Vice Admiral Halsey, a deliberate shift on Nimitz' part to a more aggressive operational policy in the Solomons.[113] As events were to unfold, the change came none too soon. With his ground forces having reached an equivalent level of numeric strength to that of the Americans, Lieutenant General Hyakutake planned to attack and overwhelm the American positions and capture Henderson Field on October 22. Supporting his operation would be the Combined Fleet (Vice Admiral Kondō), fielding four carriers, four battleships, fourteen cruisers, and several dozen destroyers; the plan was that aircraft from Kondō's carriers would land at Henderson Field as soon as it had been captured.[114] Halsey responded in typically belligerent fashion by deploying Task Force 17 (Rear Adm. George D. Murray) with *Hornet*, the battleship *South Dakota*, four cruisers, and six destroyers, and Task Force 16 (Rear Adm. Thomas C.

Kinkaid) equipped with the patched-up *Enterprise*, two cruisers, and eight destroyers, to intercept Kondō. Under the command of Rear Adm. Willis A. Lee, Task Force 64 (battleship *Washington*, three cruisers, and six destroyers) was ordered by Halsey to derail the Tokyo Express if it attempted to run the Slot in aid of Hyakutake's operation. The USN carrier task forces rendezvoused in the vicinity of the Santa Cruz Islands on October 24, with Kinkaid assuming overall command. Ashore on Guadalcanal meanwhile, Hyakutake had launched his advance on October 22 as planned. For four days the Japanese pounded the American perimeter surrounding Henderson Field with incessant attacks, culminating in a final assault on October 26, which was repelled by the Marines and GIs after vicious fighting, thereby halting Hyakutake's much-vaunted offensive in its tracks.[115]

To the north of the Santa Cruz Islands on October 26, the Japanese and American fleets clashed in a second carrier-versus-carrier duel. Once again the engagement was confused, with neither side able to land a knockout blow. After a pair of American dive-bombers had located and damaged the light carrier *Zuihō*, both combatants traded airstrikes that inflicted heavy damage. The Americans succeeded in crippling *Shōkaku* while the Japanese strikes crippled *Hornet* and rendered *Enterprise*'s forward elevator inoperable.[116] Attempts to save *Hornet* were unavailing, and she was scuttled prior to Kinkaid's retirement to the south. Kondō's carriers were likewise withdrawn, and though the Japanese had gained a similar tactical victory to that achieved at the Coral Sea, the awful casualties suffered by their aviators offset any superiority gained by reducing Halsey's available carrier contingent to the wounded *Enterprise* alone. Following a fortnight in which both sides rushed additional reinforcements into their positions on Guadalcanal, another night action off the island on November 12–13 provided more misery for the U.S. Navy. Rear Adm. Daniel Callaghan's seven cruisers and five destroyers were severely mauled while attempting to intercept a strong enemy force, including two battleships under Vice Admiral Abe Hiroaki, which was steaming to shell Henderson Field.[117] Four of the American destroyers were sunk and four cruisers crippled or otherwise badly damaged, one of these (*Juneau*) being subsequently sunk by a Japanese submarine. Both Callaghan and his deputy, Rear Admiral Scott, were killed in the fighting. One Japanese destroyer was lost, but the following day a considerable measure of revenge was extracted by the aviators from Henderson Field when they forced the eventual scuttling of the battleship *Hiei* to the north of Savo Island.[118]

Aware that the Japanese were massing their ships for another round of bombardments, Halsey ordered Rear Admiral Lee's Task Force 64 to detach from Kinkaid to the south of Guadalcanal and proceed to Ironbottom Sound. Lee's ships, however, were too far south to prevent a bombardment of Henderson Field by Vice Admiral Mikawa's cruisers and destroyers in the early hours of November 14. In the midst of his retirement up the Slot, Mikawa's ships were attacked by two waves of aircraft, which sank the heavy cruiser *Kinugasa* and damaged two others.[119] But a far greater disaster was close at hand. At 0830 hours a patrolling aircraft spotted ten Japanese merchant transports with a screen of eleven destroyers proceeding down the Slot toward Guadalcanal. Not realizing that Henderson Field remained operational following its recent bombardments, the convoy's commander, Rear Admiral Tanaka, believed he could get the slow troopers to their destination with air cover provided by the nearby light carriers *Junyō* and *Hiyō*. He was gravely mistaken. Throughout the afternoon of November 14, bombers from Henderson Field and *Enterprise* hammered the slow-moving transports, sinking six of them before nightfall.[120]

With the coming of dusk, a Japanese bombardment squadron under Vice Admiral Kondō—*Kirishima*, four cruisers, and nine destroyers—prepared to make its run into Ironbottom Sound to the west of Savo Island. Racing in from the south to meet Kondo were Lee's flagship *Washington* accompanied by *South Dakota* and four escorting destroyers. At 2304 hours *Washington*'s radar detected Kondō's outriders and twelve minutes later Lee's ships opened fire. The Japanese gained the early advantage by crippling all four of Lee's destroyers, with two of them eventually sent to the bottom. Suffering from an electrical failure that briefly knocked out her radar, *South Dakota* suffered numerous hits from both *Kirishima* and Kondō's two heavy cruisers. But just after midnight the vital blow was struck. At close range *Washington* surprised the Japanese battleship with a series of devastating salvos, reducing her to a pockmarked wreck fit only for eventual scuttling.[121] Frustrated in his attempts to reach Henderson Field, Kondō ordered retirement at 0030 hours on November 15. By daylight the American aviators returned to massacre the remnants of Tanaka's ill-fated force, which lost all ten of its merchant ships while delivering only limited supplies to a land garrison, which had been placed on the defensive. Yet it was to be Tanaka who would again remind the USN that advantages in technology alone could not better superior fighting skills. In a botched attempt to intercept the Tokyo Express off Tassafaronga on the night of November 30, the heavy cruiser *Northampton* was sunk and three other cruisers torpedoed by Tanaka's destroyers at the cost of a single Japanese destroyer being lost.[122]

It was not to be enough. Though Tanaka and his colleagues had largely outfought their radar-equipped opponents in night surface combat over the past four months, maintaining a large land presence on Guadalcanal was no longer a viable strategic option for Yamamoto and the Japanese Imperial General Headquarters. Similar to Hermann Goering's doomed attempt to supply Stalingrad by air, the Tokyo Express could not deliver enough supplies and reinforcements to reverse the situation; nor did the Japanese have enough in the first place due to the competing demands of the fighting in New Guinea. In December 1942 the Japanese leadership concluded that Guadalcanal must be evacuated, and an order to this effect was issued by the IGHQ on January 4, 1943. From February 2 through 7 the Tokyo Express pulled off one last magic trick by safely evacuating more than 11,700 troops in what Morison described as one of the cleverest evacuations in naval history (alongside the Japanese exit from Kiska).[123] By February 1943 each side had lost a total of twenty-four ships, six of those on the Japanese ledger being submarines, with dozens of others crippled or otherwise damaged, and thousands of sailors on both sides dead or wounded. In the air it was Japan that suffered most, particularly through the casualties to Nagumo's carrier air groups sustained in the battles of the Eastern Solomons and Santa Cruz. Much hard fighting remained before the Japanese were to be finally driven from this island chain, but as of December 1942 their offensive momentum in the Southwest Pacific had at last been halted, and along with it the prospect of any substantial threat to mainland Australia.

Over the course of eight months from May 1942 onwards, it was the outcomes of the stand-alone battles of Coral Sea and Midway as well as those flowing from the New Guinea and Solomons campaigns prior to January 1943 that neutralized the various means through which the Japanese could have engineered Australia's capitulation. Japan was denied the conquest of the two most vital springboards, Port Moresby and Tulagi-Guadalcanal, from which to pursue either the isolation of the continent or the eventual invasion of its eastern coastline. She had been similarly deprived of her crack carrier spearhead that posed such a destructive menace to Australia's coastal centers and shipping. The lengthy fighting in New Guinea and the Solomon Islands wore down the naval and military resources that were necessary for any future campaign against the Australian mainland. And perhaps most compelling of all, the capacity of the Japanese to support arduous operations with adequate supply and logistical arrangements was exposed as wholly deficient by the dual campaigns in the Southwest Pacific. These latter factors, attrition and support, robbed Yamamoto and his colleagues of the offensive impetus required for further southward conquest, and from then on placed Japan on the defensive. After seeing their outer defenses in the Mandates overrun with little resistance in early January 1942, the Australians stared oblivion in the face unless the United States realized the value of the continent to its own operational and strategic aims in the Pacific theater. And it was through this alignment of mutual interests that Australia's lines of communication and the physical security of the nation itself were ultimately maintained.

10

Threats and Interests

January 1919–January 1943

Throughout the year 1942 Australia confronted the gravest external military threat in that nation's history when the shores of the continent itself fell prey to the menace of the Imperial Japanese Navy. On February 19, 1942, Darwin was heavily bombed by elements of Japan's First and Eleventh Air Fleets in order to sever a critical Allied supply line to Java and facilitate the Japanese conquest of the Netherlands East Indies. With the successful accomplishment of Japan's strategic objectives in the Far East, the bulk of the Combined Fleet would be redeployed to the Pacific so that Admiral Yamamoto Isoroku's planned destruction of the weakened U.S. Pacific Fleet could be undertaken without further delay. In the course of doing so, the isolation of Australia as a threat to Yamamoto's left flank was factored into his planning for the decisive battle to be staged in the vicinity of Midway Island. Operation MO became the means through which this prerequisite was to be met via the capture of Port Moresby in Papua and Tulagi in the Solomon Islands. If both this aero-amphibious expedition and the subsequent Midway showdown had produced the outcomes Yamamoto anticipated, the subjugation of Australia by direct blockade or invasion could have been undertaken at a time of Japan's choosing. Through the decisive intervention of the U.S. Navy, events were to take a different turn. The five months of attrition at sea that took place in the struggle for Guadalcanal succeeded in blunting Japan's offensive naval momentum and placed the Japanese fleet on the defensive for the remainder of the Pacific War. Australia's security had been preserved, but not in the way the evolution of the nation's defense policies over the previous two decades had principally envisaged.

Following the end of the Great War in November 1918, Australia's political leaders and military planners undertook the formulation of defense policies in circumstances where no hostile threat was to make its presence felt for another twenty years. The previous chapters have chronicled the means, methods, and motivations through which this process was undertaken. For much of the period in question the nation's third-party naval protection remained in the hands of the Royal Navy, with the centerpiece of Anglo-Australian defense relations and the cornerstone of Australian defense strategy being the British naval base at Singapore. Yet the narrative of Australian efforts to achieve a reliable outcome for the protection of the continent and its external communications was not to be primarily shaped by the actions of any potential aggressor power. The Imperial Japanese Navy may have emerged as the single greatest peril to the country's security, but it did so in the guise of an end product. At the center of the process dwelt instead a near constant state of underlying friction between and within Australian and British strategic interests that persistently threatened to neuter the credibility of the former's naval defense when eventually confronted with the reality of war.

The genesis of this problem lay in the circumstances of Australia's colonial past and the downside of belonging to the British Empire. For the self-governing white settler colonies, the panacea of imperial protection came with strings attached. The conduct of foreign affairs and defense policy fell under the direct authority of Whitehall, which administered both upon the basis of advancing Britain's great-power interests. When the six colonies were federated in 1901, the new Australian nation remained largely beholden to these colonial-era principles. As they had done in separate negotiations with France and Germany regarding the stewardship of the islands to the continent's north and northeast in the 1880s and 1890s, the British were apparently impervious to Australian security concerns when London and Tokyo established the Anglo-Japanese Alliance in 1902. And though Australia now possessed the right to organize and maintain its own armed forces, the establishment of a naval capability beyond the needs of local defense was still subject to oversight from the British Admiralty. When the nation obtained an independent blue-water fleet in October 1913, it did so pursuant to an agreement with Whitehall that in the event of war the nascent Royal Australian Navy would be placed under overall Admiralty command. Accompanying these factors was the inherent risk, as highlighted by the likes of John Dunmore Lang, Frederic Eggleston, and Hugh Thring, that Britain's entanglement in a global conflict could lead to a situation where Whitehall was unable to dispatch naval assistance to Australia when it was most required.

Nationhood for the Australian colonies did not diminish the influence imperial patriotism exerted among the majority of the continent's Anglo-Celtic population and its leading citizens. With the British Empire approaching the zenith of its global power in the late nineteenth century, the white settler colonies became infused with the belief that they were the standard-bearers for the civilizing influence of the British race around the world. The loyalties of the colonists were not governed by the machinations of Whitehall, to which they frequently objected, but rather their adherence to the imperial ideal, and therein lay the seeds of their greatest dread. As it became known, British race patriotism was founded upon the notion of racial superiority, and the new Dominion nation-states regarded themselves as outposts of white civilization. In the case of Australia and New Zealand, the isolated presence of both to the south of Asia engendered the belief among the settler population that they dwelt under the sword of Damocles in the form of Asia's teeming faceless masses. The resulting fear of China and subsequently Japan was driven not only by the thought of military conquest but also by the prospect that the coherence of their white societies would be compromised by Asian immigration. In response to the latter dilemma, the introduction in 1901 of what became known as the White Australia policy would color the attitudes of successive Australian governments toward defense and foreign affairs policy making in the Asia-Pacific region until the late 1960s. And in the wake of the Second World War there was to be no removal of apprehension over Asia within the Australian public mindset, with the economic and military rise of China giving rise today to a similar range of concerns to those that were once reserved for Japan.

Aside from the existing strength of the Imperial Japanese Navy at her disposal, Japan in the 1920s posed no threat to Australia in spite of separate measures undertaken by Australia, the United States, and Britain that stood to provoke one. At the Paris Conference in January 1919, Prime

Minister Hughes set out to wreck Japan's proposal for a racial discrimination clause within the covenant of the League of Nations, and with the tacit approval of Britain and the United States the Japanese initiative was rejected. The resulting bitterness expressed in the moderate and nationalist elements alike of the Japanese press reflected the consequences of Australia's abject determination to preserve the integrity of the White Australia policy at all costs. Japan's sense of estrangement from the Western democracies was compounded in November 1921 with the cessation of the Anglo-Japanese Alliance at the Washington Naval Conference. With the United States unwilling to tolerate a further renewal of a treaty Washington regarded as harmful to American interests in the Pacific, a heavy war debt burden ensured that the British government was in no position to argue otherwise. For all its perceived imperfections, the Anglo-Japanese Alliance served to include the Japanese in the counsels of one of the great powers, and its removal made no small contribution to Japan's growing political isolation from the West. Nevertheless the British themselves did not assist matters by embarking upon the construction of a naval base at Singapore, a process that was justified by the Admiralty on the grounds that Japan was indeed a potential threat to imperial security in the Far East.

Or so the Admiralty said it was. Deprived of a serious European opponent by the scuttling of Germany's High Seas Fleet and with heavy budget cuts looming at home, Admiral Lord Beatty and his colleagues resorted to Japan as the new menace that would sustain the Royal Navy's funding levels and regenerate the British fleet in peacetime. Beatty, however, was to be left disappointed on both counts. Though the outcome of the Washington talks reduced British capital ship strength to a one-power standard, the first sea lord switched his focus to cruiser construction and came off second best. Pursuing an agenda of fiscal stringency, the chancellor of the exchequer, Winston Churchill, was not prepared to endorse what he regarded as an unjustifiable Admiralty extravagance, yet he saw the value in proceeding with the construction of the Singapore base as an insurance policy for more uncertain times. Its construction proceeded at no great pace, and by the onset of the 1930s there were growing questions within the Australian defense establishment as to whether their nation's military requirements would be fulfilled by its completion. What had yet to be made clear was how the presence of a British fleet in the Far

East would act to preserve Australia's security in the Pacific beyond the effects of deterrence alone. Of even greater anxiety for the Australians by the early 1930s was the increasing speculation over the length of time it would take for a fleet to reach Singapore if Japan became hostile, or whether Whitehall could dispatch a fleet to the Far East at all.

In support of the Admiralty's campaign Beatty had highlighted the vulnerability of Australia and New Zealand to attack, but this apparent display of solidarity with Dominion fears was misleading. Ever since the original concept of an Imperial Pacific Fleet had been approved by the Imperial Conference in 1909, both Australia and New Zealand harbored the desire for its eventual readoption, but the Admiralty was of a different mind. Its rebuke of Admiral Lord Jellicoe's 1919 recommendations regarding the establishment of a Pacific Fleet confirmed the sea lords' ongoing distaste for the permanent deployment of a significant element of the Royal Navy's strength abroad. Likewise the Admiralty retained its determination to shape both the composition and employment of the Dominion navies in a manner consistent with its own operational requirements. And while Beatty was prepared to emphasize Australia's situation to suit his own ends, the Admiralty was loath to seriously entertain the prospect that the naval threat posed by Japan toward Australia extended beyond the execution of light raids against military targets. By supporting the case for imperial defense to be afforded the greatest priority in Australian strategic thinking, the Royal Australian Navy placed itself at loggerheads with the other armed services in a similar debate over Japanese intentions, a debate that would blossom as the international situation began to slowly deteriorate in the early 1930s.

By September 1939 Japan had still to emerge as an overt military threat in either the Far East or the Pacific, although Japanese naval expansion was already well under way. Following its government's withdrawal from the 1936 London Treaty process, the Imperial Japanese Navy sought to achieve parity with the United States in battleships and aircraft carriers, including the construction of two enormous super battleships, in order to exert a qualitative superiority over the American battleship force. But Japan remained preoccupied with the lingering political instability that followed the February 26 Incident (1936) and the progress of the Second Sino-Japanese War, which had been under way since July 1937. Following the Manchurian crisis in 1931, both Britain and Australia had separately attempted to negotiate with Tokyo, but to little avail. With the leadership of the Imperial Japanese Army being implacably opposed to the existence of British commercial interests in China, there was little chance of making meaningful headway with the Japanese government itself. Adopting a policy of appeasement toward Japan in the latter half of the 1930s, Whitehall tolerated the increasing belligerence of the Japanese toward the British presence in China, which culminated in the Tientsin Incident in June 1939. Australia, however, was constrained in its efforts to negotiate by virtue of its adherence to British imperial foreign policy. Since 1926 the Australians had been offered the opportunity to exercise an independent foreign policy courtesy of the Balfour Declaration, but had declined to sign the Statute of Westminster, which gave legal effect to such a decision. Accordingly the Australian government could not put proposals to the Japanese that were contrary to Whitehall's wishes, and the Lyons government's ill-fated proposal for a new Pacific pact fell into this category.

Though the Australian proposal attracted Britain's qualified interest at the 1937 Imperial Conference, its value was downgraded on the grounds that it duplicated existing treaty arrangements, and the subsequent Japanese invasion of China sealed its demise. By the time the conference commenced in May 1937, British strategic priorities had turned full circle in the preceding three years. Once again Europe lay at the center of Whitehall's concerns, and the discussions concerning the Singapore strategy confirmed this. While the base itself was nearing completion, the availability of a fleet was now contingent on the prior neutralization of the new German Kriegsmarine in the event of war. The estimate of the "period before relief" stood at a minimum of fifty to seventy days, and the Admiralty representatives made it clear to Australia and the other Dominions that the need for refits would stagger the availability of the Royal Navy's capital ship force. In response to the strategic appreciations prepared by the Australians, the first lord was dismissive of any reallocation of Australian resources to homeland defense. Nevertheless, Prime Minister Lyons returned to Australia proclaiming the conference a success as his government prepared for the scheduled federal election in October. Shortly thereafter the regime of assurances in support of the Singapore strategy began to discard any remaining credibility. The estimated period before relief eventually ballooned to six months, and the need to counter the Italian fleet further complicated the issue. When Stanley Bruce confronted the Admiralty in July 1939, the only assurance he received was that events in the Mediterranean would not be allowed to interfere with the deployment of ships to Singapore. And in the course of the July 11 meeting, Australia's high commissioner learned just how far Whitehall's priorities had shifted when he was informed that there was no existent Admiralty planning for operations in the Far East.

When the Lyons government went to the polls in October 1937, the state of the nation's defenses had become a key electoral battleground between the UAP coalition and the Labor Party. During the early 1930s the debate between the Australian army and navy over the competing interests of national and imperial defense was largely motivated by the allocation of scarce defense expenditure in the midst of the Depression years. The arguments mounted on the army side by Colonel John Lavarack included the resurrection of Frederic Eggleston's warning as to the perils of a two-ocean dilemma. In 1935 Eggleston was joined by fellow skeptics Edmund Piesse and William Morris Hughes in writing a series of essays and opinion pieces that rejected the Singapore strategy as unworkable. On the naval side, the Royal Australian Navy was backed by the government in repeating the necessity for retaining the imperial system as the continent's main defense, and it gained the support of Sir Maurice Hankey when Hankey visited Australia to undertake his defense survey in 1934. The new Labor leader John Curtin came to support the army's view and fought the election campaign with a pro-domestic-defense policy. While Lyons battered Labor's alleged disloyalty toward Britain with a liberal dose of British race patriotism, he too wished to upgrade Australia's land and air defenses. This he proceeded to do upon re-election, but a portion of the RAAF's limited fighting strength was earmarked for future use at Singapore, further shifting the balance of Australian armed service deployments in favor of imperial defense.

In proceeding with the rearmament of the RAAF in 1936, the government had sought assistance from the United States in setting up the Commonwealth Aircraft Corporation and the purchase of American training aircraft along with a manufacturing license from North American Aviation. These transactions, and the further ordering of American aircraft two years later, were the practical high point of American-Australian defense relations before the outbreak of war in Europe. In the years prior to 1940, Australia was not represented at an ambassadorial level in Washington, with diplomatic contact being conducted through the British Embassy. As part of the British Empire, Australia participated in the Imperial Preference trade scheme, which sought to protect imperial markets from the influence of American trade. The other downside for the Australians was that they participated in the Singapore strategy, and by the late 1930s the Americans had made it abundantly clear to Whitehall and the Admiralty that no American battleships would be steaming to Singapore to make up for the absence of their British counterparts. Yet the possibility of a future military understanding between Australia and the United States certainly antagonized the Japanese when the USN's Combined Fleet visited Melbourne and Sydney in July 1925, a visit that was calculated to gain the attention of Japan just as the 1908 voyage of the Great White Fleet had done. But given the strength of the isolationist sentiment that existed in America during the interwar decades, there was little or no chance of an arrangement being reached even if the Australians had renounced their imperial ties, which was even more impossible to contemplate.

Bearing in mind the circumstances of the interwar period, the biggest threat to Australia's security that emerged prior to September 1939 had become the character of the chosen defense strategy upon which the nation's preparations for war were wholly based. Australia's wholesale reliance on third-party naval protection under the jurisdiction of distant foreign statesmen resulted in the chronic unpreparedness of the country's planned defense via the army and the air force. This represented an exceptionally risky gamble. If the British were unable to meet their commitments and send a fleet to the Far East, there was nothing to stand in the path of the Japanese fleet and whatever form of action it may choose to take against the Australian mainland. The alternatives to British protection, however, were practically nonexistent. Declared neutrality under the security umbrella of the League of Nations, attempting to secure a defense accommodation with a still fiercely isolationist United States, and effective negotiations with Japan while the White Australia policy lurked in the background were not the most encouraging possibilities. While Australia lacked the population and economic bases to become militarily self-sufficient, it would remain beholden to its great and powerful friends and their chosen strategic priorities. Ultimately whether or not its elected leaders had made the right choice of friends was a question that could be answered only in war.

At the beginning of December 1941 the Royal Navy had met the prerequisites for a substantial body of its available strength to be transferred to the Far East. In the fighting thus far the British had gotten the better of both the German and Italian surface fleets, though their total destruction was not yet accomplished. Despite having lost the support of the majority of the French fleet in July 1940 and having suffered heavy casualties itself, the RN's employment of aircraft carriers against its carrier-less European opponents proved decisive. Victories at Taranto in November 1940 and at Cape Matapan in March 1940 succeeded in neutralizing much of the Italian fleet, and the sinking of *Bismarck* in May 1941 effectively curtailed further raiding sorties into the Atlantic by Germany's big ships. Along the way the British had learned some bitter lessons when attempting to conduct operations in waters where the enemy enjoyed land-based air superiority, while the campaign against Germany's U-boats was still far from being resolved. In the Indian and Pacific Oceans, Australia's external sea communications remained intact in spite of their often unopposed interdiction by the disguised German auxiliary cruisers, although the loss of the cruiser *Sydney* in November 1941 was a high price to pay in the gradual elimination of the shadowy raiders and their attendant supply vessels. Missions undertaken in the Far East by long-range U-boats were not to take place until 1944 and inflicted only negligible damage. With the war in Europe under way the bulk of Australia's cruisers and destroyers eventually saw service in the Mediterranean, leaving the Australia Station badly undermanned and permitting German raiders to operate with consistent impunity when laying mines in Australian coastal waters.

By the outbreak of war with Japan the Australians had committed virtually the entirety of their first-line military strength to overseas service. The majority of the 8th Division AIF, the last of the nation's fully equipped and trained infantry divisions, was stationed in Singapore and Malaya along with four RAAF squadrons. From the ranks of the Royal Australian Navy, only the light cruiser *Perth* and a single destroyer were available for immediate service in the Far East. Most of the decisions to send the troops, ships, and squadrons to the European theater and Singapore had been made by the Menzies UAP coalition government following assurances from Whitehall that Australia's security would be protected. But the language from London now spoke of intervention if Australia itself were directly threatened, not the dispatch of a fleet to Singapore. With the fall of France in June 1940 the Singapore strategy had been revised to substitute the RAF for the Royal Navy as the base's principal means of defense. This enforced revision raised concerns in Canberra when it came to the number of aircraft that would be required for the task and when they would be deployed, and as was the case with enquiries regarding the fleet, the British prevaricated. Yet in August 1941 there was another twist to the tale as Churchill and the Admiralty began to consider afresh the composition of a future Eastern Fleet. Singapore returned to the agenda, but this time as part of the proposed Aden-Singapore-Simonstown triangle strategy for protecting Allied communications in the Indian Ocean. Should the Japanese fleet attempt to approach Darwin or other points farther to the west on the Australian coastline, a British fleet would be in position to intercept, providing it was there in the first place.

Australia's initial naval shield was nullified over the first five months of hostilities in the Far East by Japanese air superiority. From December 1941 to April 1942 the Admiralty deployed a total of seven capital ships, three aircraft carriers, nine cruisers, and twenty destroyers to the theater, a not inconsiderable portion of its available fighting strength in battleships and aircraft carriers in particular. The sinking of *Prince of Wales* and *Repulse* and the enforced withdrawal of the Eastern Fleet from Ceylon was the price paid for tangling with what was then the most powerful naval air force in the world. Bereft of the striking power wielded by Japan's First Air Fleet, no British fleet assembly at that time possessed the wherewithal to oppose it, especially given the paucity of modern fighter aircraft on board the Admiralty's carrier force as a whole. On this basis it can be reasonably deduced that neither Force Z, the Eastern Fleet, nor any other Royal Navy deployment of substance would have been able to repel a Japanese naval sortie into Australian waters. Singapore itself eventually fell in the wake of the Japanese gaining air superiority over Malaya on the first day of the war. Here the supposed impregnability of the island fortress was proven to be a myth, as was the supposed impenetrability of the Malayan landscape. Fighting seasoned combat veterans who enjoyed armored superiority as well as close air support, the British, Australian, and Indian defenders and their local allies were overwhelmed by a smaller invading force in just over two months. With the capture of Singapore and the inability of the Royal Navy to meet its Japanese opponent on equal terms, Australia's existing defense strategy had reached the point of near-total disintegration.

Given the ongoing collapse of resistance to the Japanese in Malaya and the impending loss of Singapore, the Australian government naturally enough placed the interests of its own country above those of collective grand Allied strategy. The criticism leveled by Prime Minister Curtin at the proposed evacuation of Singapore and the subsequent refusal of his government to sanction the diversion of the returning Australian divisions to Burma were a reaction to the immediate failure of the imperial scheme that left the continent defenseless. Yet when Curtin resorted to a direct appeal to the United States via his famous New Year's Day broadcast, it was not the severing of the apron strings with Britain that motivated his actions. Rather it was the repetition of what the Australians regarded as empty assurances from Whitehall, together with the shambles in Malaya and the belief that both the British and the Americans were indifferent to Australia's plight, that motivated the prime minister to take a stand. A former journalist himself, Curtin knew the value of using the press in this fashion, and he followed the path that Hughes had taken with Lloyd George back in 1918 over the implementation of President Wilson's Fourteen Points without prior consultation. He was signaling to Washington and London that with the threat Japan now posed to Australia and the rest of the Pacific, Australia must be treated as an equal in the planning of strategy to halt the Japanese offensive. The acquiescence of the Australian government to the stationing of a portion of the returning 6th Division AIF at Ceylon hardly showed a break in Anglo-Australian defense relations. Instead it demonstrated Curtin's skills as a savvy negotiator who realized that a certain degree of give-and-take was necessary in discussions with the powers in spite of the apparent desperation of Australia's defensive circumstances.

To Australia's immense good fortune, Curtin's success in forging a defense relationship with the United States benefited not only from an alignment of both nations' strategic interests but also from a degree of internal American support that the Australians had not enjoyed with the British beyond the sentimental links of kith and kin. The collapse of American resistance in the Philippines placed Australia as the last substantial piece of Allied-occupied territory in the Pacific west of Hawaii, and its isolation or capture was recognized by the Americans as directly injurious to their own defensive position. Through the presence of Admiral King as one of President Roosevelt's senior military advisers, together with the public popularity enjoyed by General MacArthur in the United States, Australia benefited from the empathy of friends in high places that had never existed within Whitehall. King's and MacArthur's desire to take the fight to the Japanese at the earliest opportunity likewise embraced Australia as the ideal springboard for future Allied counteroffensives. As a result, the eventual dispatch of American naval, ground, and air resources to the country by January 1943 had transformed eastern Australia into an armed camp, a far cry from its impoverished defenses just seven months beforehand. While the actions of the Americans were undoubtedly motivated by the desire to secure their own interests, they had nevertheless engineered the community of interest Governor Denison had urged upon Britain in 1854, and in the process preserved Australia's external security via the active presence of the U.S. Pacific Fleet.

Victory over the Japanese in the Southwest Pacific was bought at a murderous price in lives and material. The fighting in the Solomons campaign temporarily reduced the USN's carrier strength in the Pacific to the damaged *Enterprise* alone, and the American cruiser and destroyer arms were badly mauled in the frequent night combats against formidable opponents. Through the excellence of its codebreakers, astute leadership, dogged resistance, and a reasonable share of good fortune, the USN prevailed because of its ability to inflict what may be described as disproportionate attrition upon the Imperial Japanese Navy. Japan's loss of four large carriers at Midway and the heavy casualties inflicted upon its surface fleet in the Solomons could not be made up by the output of the nation's shipbuilding facilities. Even more damaging was the decimation of pilots and aircrew in the Japanese naval air arm, which had begun the war with only a shallow pool of trained reserves; this critical failing in Japan's preparations for war would be brutally exposed by the massacre of the IJN's carrier air groups at the battle of the Philippine Sea in June 1944. The shortcomings present in the Japanese supply and logistics network were likewise revealed by its inability to effectively supply ground operations on Guadalcanal and in Papua New Guinea, thereby casting doubts upon the support available for any invasion activity that may have been contemplated against Australia. In short, the Japanese war machine was well-equipped for quick decisive victories against ill-prepared opponents, but once the advantages of initial momentum were lost, a crushing defeat against the vast industrial resources of the United States became the inevitable outcome.

There remains but one question to be addressed in the analysis of the threats and interests that surrounded and molded Australia's defense policies and strategies from the end of the Great War until January 1943. Throughout the postwar era there has been an ongoing debate among Australian historians and others in the public forum regarding the issue of a potential Japanese invasion. Peter Stanley, a well-respected historian and former Principal Historian at the Australian War Memorial, recounted a particular difficulty for himself and those of his colleagues who have published assessments that have cast doubt over the capacity of the Japanese to mount an invasion. In his work *Invading Australia: Japan and the Battle for Australia, 1942*, Stanley recalled the publication of several opinion pieces by Stephen Barton, an associate lecturer in politics at Edith Cowan University, just prior to the commemoration of Anzac Day in April 2006. In these pieces, Barton contended that the threat to Australia had become greatly exaggerated in Australian national mythology. The public response to Barton's comments was scathing, as he was accused of denigrating the memory of the Australian troops who had fought at Kokoda and elsewhere in Papua New Guinea.[1] Others, including Stanley himself, have been subjected to similar responses when attempting to put forward their arguments. Australia's military past has become a centerpiece in the ongoing discourse concerning Australia's national identity as a whole, and the expressions of outrage have been extended to those who seek to understand from a nonpopulist perspective the nation's role in the ill-fated ANZAC expedition to Gallipoli in April 1915. These public disagreements testify to the role of entrenched social, political, and commercial interests in the wider so-called culture wars and history wars that have frequently colored the discussion over Australian national identity since the late 1970s.

Given a successful assault against Port Moresby in the course of the battle of Coral Sea, some form of invasion activity may well have come into Japanese calculations, and victory at Midway would have fulfilled at least one prerequisite. It was highly unlikely that Yamamoto and the Naval Staff would have planned for an amphibious attack if the U.S. Pacific Fleet was still capable of offering powerful resistance. If this hurdle were cleared and the opposition of the Imperial Japanese Army to such a campaign were removed, the prospects for an invasion would have been considerably enhanced. The Japanese certainly considered Darwin as a target for assault, and landings in North Queensland may have been readily contemplated if Port Moresby was already in Japanese hands. But to contemplate an attack against southeastern Australia was a far greater order of magnitude requiring a large infusion of manpower and merchant shipping tonnage with which to undertake the task. Without final victory in China, it is doubtful whether the required merchant shipping in particular could have been assembled due to the requirement for sufficient available tonnage to convey the economic spoils of the Far East back to Japan itself. And by committing themselves to the wholesale conquest of Australia, the Japanese would have required secure supply lines and adequate resupply for much larger forces than the ones they had failed to adequately support in both Papua New Guinea and the Solomon Islands. On balance it is unlikely that an invasion, beyond the need to capture isolated outposts for related strategic purposes, would have been ordered in the absence of all these preconditions being met, yet the invasion argument cannot be fairly discounted had Tokyo achieved more favorable military outcomes in the latter half of 1942.

For these reasons, the counterfactual that makes up the opening chapter of this work draws no conclusion as to the likelihood of a Japanese invasion of the Australian mainland. Instead it is intended to depict what I regarded to be the most probable initial threat posed to the populated southeast had Admiral Yamamoto and the naval staff determined to carry out major attacks in the area. Regardless of whether the Japanese sought to isolate Australia or invade it with conquest in mind, the southeastern region of the continent would have been a priority objective as it contained the majority of the nation's population, large urban centers, industry, and agriculture. In either event, strikes against key military targets on the seaboard would have been a task most likely assigned to the carriers from the First Air Fleet. The possibility of air attacks against eastern and southeastern Australian ports was raised during the planning conferences organized by the Japanese Naval

Staff, which preceded the decision to undertake Operation MO in the Coral Sea in May 1942. If Admiral Yamamoto had been persuaded to undertake a Pearl Harbor–style attack against Sydney Harbour and its surrounding airfields instead of the MO operation, his decision would have been entirely consistent with previous operational practice. And in the event of an airstrike against Sydney within the period of time postulated in the opening chapter, a precision attack stood to inflict far greater destruction than what had been occasioned in the first raid on Darwin, especially given that Sydney's existing defenses were wholly inadequate during the first five months of 1942.

Australia had gone to war in September 1939 with a defense strategy almost totally committed to the interests of the British Empire. With Germany's rapid conquest of western Europe in 1940, the practical intent of imperial defense became the preservation of Britain itself, and consequently the maintenance of the wider Allied cause. Such was Australia's devotion to this objective that the air and land defenses of the Australian mainland were thoroughly denuded as a result, and the prospects of the Royal Navy fulfilling its protective role were entirely predicated upon the fortunes of war on the other side of the world. In essence Australia came to totally rely on the ebb and flow of events and decisions over which the nation had little or no influence or control. The fall of Singapore and the eclipse of the Royal Navy's fighting strength at the hands of Japanese naval airpower exploded two decades of policy making in which the traditional might of British sea power had been the cornerstone of Anglo-Australian strategic thinking. Only through the fortunate coalescence of Australian and American interests were the former's irons to be plucked from the fire. In concert with the desire of the rampant Japanese to be finally rid of the specter of the U.S. Pacific Fleet, the shifting of the focal point of the Asia-Pacific conflict from the Far East to the Southwest Pacific was to be Australia's salvation. In seven months from May 1942 onwards the Japanese were fought to a standstill at the Coral Sea and Midway, and subsequently in the Solomon Islands and Papua New Guinea. Third-party naval power had indeed proven its worth in the defense of Australia's vital interests, yet its intervention had arisen from the circumstances of the moment, thereby confirming that at the instant of her greatest external peril, Australia was indeed the lucky country.

Notes

Introduction
Epigraph: *Sydney Morning Herald* (hereafter *SMH*), May 25, 1905, doc. 66, in N. Meaney, *Australia and the World: A Documentary History from the 1870s to the 1970s* (Melbourne: Longman Cheshire, 1985), 149–51.

Chapter 1. The Day That Never Dawned
1. D. Macintyre, *The Battle for the Pacific* (London: William Clowes & Sons, 1966), 15.
2. A. J. Marder, M. Jacobsen, and J. Horsfield, *Old Friends, New Enemies: The Royal Navy and the Imperial Japanese Navy*, vol. 2, *The Pacific War, 1942–1945* (Oxford: Clarendon Press, 1990), 34.
3. P. R. Stephensen and B. Kennedy, *The History and Description of Sydney Harbour* (Sydney: A. H. & A. W. Reed, 1980), 185.

Chapter 2. Foundations: 1788–1918
1. T. Frame, *No Pleasure Cruise: The Story of the Royal Australian Navy* (Sydney: Allen & Unwin, 2004), 181; G. Odgers, *The Royal Australian Navy: An Illustrated History* (Hornsby, Australia: Child & Henry, 1982), 121.
2. Port Jackson remains the official name for the various waterways that include Sydney Harbour (see Stephensen and Kennedy, *The History and Description of Sydney Harbour*, 11).
3. P. Oppenheim, *The Fragile Forts: The Fixed Defences of Sydney Harbour, 1788–1963* (Canberra: Army History Unit, 2004), 6.
4. C. Ingleton, *Matthew Flinders: Navigator and Chartmaker* (Surrey, UK: Genesis Publications, 1986), 67.
5. P. Dennis et al., *The Oxford Companion to Australian Military History* (Melbourne: Oxford University Press, 1995), 167; Frame, *No Pleasure Cruise*, 33.
6. Oppenheim, *The Fragile Forts*, 9.
7. Odgers, *The Royal Australian Navy*, 13–15.
8. Frame, *No Pleasure Cruise*; Oppenheim, *The Fragile Forts*, 21–22.
9. Stephensen and Kennedy, *The History and Description of Sydney Harbour*, 35.
10. T. Frame, *Pacific Partners: A History of Australian-American Naval Relations* (Sydney: Hodder & Stoughton, 1992), 10.
11. Frame, *No Pleasure Cruise*, 36.
12. *The Times* (London), June 25, 1846, in F. Crawley, *A Documentary History of Australia*, vol. 2, *1841–1874* (Melbourne: Thomas Nelson, 1980), 82.
13. G. Bolton, "Money: Trade, Investment, and Economic Nationalism," in *Australia's Empire*, ed. D. M. Schreuder and S. Ward (New York: Oxford University Press, 2008), 213.
14. J. Hirst, "Empire, State, Nation," in Schreuder and Ward, *Australia's Empire*, 144–45.

15. The final convict transport to Western Australia arrived in 1868.
16. J. Lahmeyer, "Population Statistics: Australia," http://www.populstat.info/Oceania/australc.htm, viewed October 25, 2017.
17. S. Ward, "Security: Defending Australia's Empire," in *Australia's Empire*, ed. D. M. Schreuder and S. Ward (New York: Oxford University Press, 2008), 232–33.
18. Ward, "Security: Defending Australia's Empire," 234; A. Lambert, "Australia, the *Trent* Crisis of 1861 and the Strategy of Imperial Defence," in *Southern Trident: Strategy, History and the Rise of Australian Naval Power*, ed. D. Stevens and J. Reeve (Sydney: Allen & Unwin, 2001), 103.
19. P. Overlack, "'A Vigorous Offensive': Core Aspects of Australian Maritime Defence Concerns before 1914," in *Southern Trident: Strategy, History and the Rise of Australian Naval Power*, ed. D. Stevens and J. Reeve (Sydney: Allen & Unwin, 2001), 147.
20. Lambert, "Australia, the *Trent* Crisis of 1861 and the Strategy of Imperial Defence," 102.
21. P. Firkins, *Of Nautilus and Eagles: History of the Royal Australian Navy* (Sydney: Hutchinson Group, 1983), 4.
22. Odgers, *The Royal Australian Navy*, 20.
23. Oppenheim, *The Fragile Forts*, 74–75.
24. B. Thomsen, *Blue and Grey at Sea: Naval Memoirs of the Civil War* (New York: Tom Doherty Associates, 2003), 282–83; Frame, *Pacific Partners*, 13–14; L. Edwards, "The Day 45 Australians Rowed Off to Fight Those Yankees," *Sydney Morning Herald* (hereinafter *SMH*) January 24, 2010, http://www.smh.com.au/national/the-day-45-australians-rowed-off-to-fight-those-yankees-20100124-msm8.html, accessed October 26, 2017.
25. Lambert, "Australia, the *Trent* Crisis of 1861 and the Strategy of Imperial Defence," 108–9.
26. Ibid., 116–17.
27. Ibid., 117–18.
28. Frame, *No Pleasure Cruise*, 54–56.
29. Editorial, *SMH*, August 25, 1870, doc. 10, in Meaney, *Australia and the World*, 51–52.
30. C. Clark, *The Encyclopaedia of Australia's Battles* (Crows Nest, Australia: Allen & Unwin, 2010), 47–49.
31. R. Parkinson, *The Late Victorian Navy—The Pre-Dreadnought Era and the Origins of the First World War* (Woolbridge, UK: Boydell Press, 2008); Firkins, *of Nautilus and Eagles*, 7–8.
32. Frame, *No Pleasure Cruise*, 61–62; Firkins, *Of Nautilus and Eagles*, 10.
33. Great Britain, *Parliamentary Papers*, 1887 session, vol. 56, C. 5091, Pf. I, pp. 507–9, doc. 30, in Meaney, *Australia and the World*, 85–86.
34. New South Wales, *Parliamentary Debates, Legislative Council*, 1884–1885 session, vol. 16, 5–9, March 17, 1885, doc. 21, in Meaney, *Australia and the World*, 73–75.
35. Thomas McIlwraith, Queensland colonial secretary, to Sir A. E. Kennedy, governor of Queensland, February 26, 1883; Queensland, *Votes and Proceedings of the Legislative Assembly*, 1883 session, vol. 2, "The Annexation of New Guinea (Correspondence Respecting)," doc. 12, in Meaney, *Australia and the World*, 58; Dispatch, Lord Derby, British colonial secretary, to officer administering the government of Queensland, July 11, 1883; Queensland, *Journals of the Legislative Council*, 1883–1884 session, vol. 23, 3–4, doc. 13, in Meaney, *Australia and the World*, 60–62.

36. B. Nicholls, *Statesmen & Sailors: Australian Maritime Defence 1870–1920* (Sydney: B. Nicholls, 1995), 33.
37. R. Hillsborough, *Samurai Revolution: The Dawn of Modern Japan Seen through the Eyes of the Shogun's Last Samurai* (Tokyo: Tuttle Publishing, 2014), 218, 400.
38. New South Wales, *Votes and Proceedings of the Legislative Assembly*, 1895–1896 session, vol. 6, 1320–25, doc. 42, in Meaney, *Australia and the World*, 103–5.
39. Ward, "Security: Defending Australia's Empire," 239; Odgers, *The Royal Australian Navy*, 35.
40. P. M. Kennedy, *The Rise and Fall of British Naval Mastery* (London: Macmillan Press, 1983), 185; Parkinson, *The Late Victorian Navy*, 92.
41. J. Beeler, "Steam, Strategy and Schurman: Imperial Defence in the Post-Crimean Era, 1856–1905," in *Far Flung Lines: Studies in Imperial Defence in Honour of Donald Mackenzie Schurman*, ed. K. Neilson and G. Kennedy (London: Frank Cass, 1996), 32–33.
42. *SMH*, February 14, 1902, doc. 50, in Meaney, *Australia and the World*, 125–28.
43. Nicholls, *Statesmen & Sailors*, 55.
44. Copy of letter, H. Eitaki, consul for Japan, to E. Barton, prime minister of Australia, May 3, 1901, TAA: PRO C.O. 418/10/287, doc. 47, in Meaney, *Australia and the World*, 121–22.
45. Commonwealth Parliamentary Debates (CPD), 1901–1902 session, vol. 4, 4812, September 12, 1901, doc. 48, in Meaney, *Australia and the World*, 122–23.
46. N. Meaney, *A History of Australian Defence and Foreign Policy, 1901–23*, vol. 1, *The Search for Security in the Pacific 1910–14* (Sydney: Sydney University Press, 1976), 76–77.
47. Nicholls, *Statesmen & Sailors*, 53.
48. Nicholls, *Statesmen & Sailors*, 83; Firkins, *Of Nautilus and Eagles*, 14–15.
49. *SMH*, November 3, 1906, doc. 62, in Meaney, *Australia and the World*, 143–44.
50. A. J. Marder, *From the Dreadnought to Scapa Flow*, vol. 1, *The Road to War 1904–1914* (London: Oxford University Press, 1961), 40.
51. "Memorandum for the Prime Minister: Conditions affecting the Naval defence of the Commonwealth," February 6, 1907: NAA CP 103/12, bundle 6, doc. 72, in Meaney, *Australia and the World*, 164–67; Nicholls, *Statesmen & Sailors*, 45–47.
52. G. Freudenberg, *Churchill and Australia* (Sydney: Pan Macmillan, 2008), 32–34; Great Britain, *Parliamentary Papers*, 1907 session, vol. 55, Cd. 3523, "Colonial Conference 1907. Minutes of the Proceedings of the Colonial Conference, 1907," 71–72, doc. 74, in Meaney, *Australia and the World*, 169–70.
53. R. Parkin and D. Lee, *Great White Fleet to Coral Sea: Naval Strategy and the Development of Australia-United States Relations 1900–1945* (Canberra: Department of Foreign Affairs and Trade, 2008), 13.
54. Frame, *Pacific Partners*, 17.
55. J. A. Reckner, "'A Sea of Troubles': The Great White Fleet's 1908 War Plans for Australia and New Zealand," in *Southern Trident: Strategy, History and the Rise of Australian Naval Power*, ed. D. Stevens and J. Reeve (Sydney: Allen & Unwin, 2001), 175.
56. Ibid., 188–93.
57. Ibid., 195.
58. Marder, *The Road to War 1904–1914*, 44–45; Nicholls, *Statesmen & Sailors*, 152; N. Lambert, "Sir John Fisher, the Fleet Unit Concept, and the Creation of the Royal Australian Navy," in *Southern Trident: Strategy, History and the Rise of Australian Naval Power*, ed. D. Stevens and J. Reeve (Sydney: Allen & Unwin, 2001), 219–20.

59. Meaney, *The Search for Security*, 177.
60. Frame, *No Pleasure Cruise*, 90; Nicholls, *Statesmen & Sailors*, 152–53.
61. Firkins, *Of Nautilus and Eagles*, 19; Nicholls, *Statesmen & Sailors*, 156.
62. Meaney, *The Search for Security*, 184; Nicholls, *Statesmen & Sailors*, 161–63.
63. *Commonwealth Parliamentary Papers* (hereafter *CPP*), 1909 session, vol. 2, no. 64, "Imperial Conference—Conference with Representatives of the Self-Governing Dominions on the Naval and Military Defence of the Empire, 1909," 19–20, 22, 28–29, doc. 84, in Meaney, *Australia and the World*, 182–83.
64. Lord Crewe, British colonial secretary, to Alfred Deakin, prime minister, December 15, 1909, Deakin Papers, NLA, Ms. 1540, doc. 89, in Meaney, *Australia and the World*, 189–90; Nicholls, *Statesmen & Sailors*, 161–62.
65. Frame, *No Pleasure Cruise*, 92–93; Nicholls, *Statesmen & Sailors*, 181–85.
66. Minutes of 111th Meeting of the Committee of Imperial Defence, June 26, 1911, the National Archives: UK (TNA): PRO Cab. 2/2, doc. 94, in Meaney, *Australia and the World*, 196–97; Marder, *The Road to War 1904–1914*, 238–39.
67. Great Britain, *Parliamentary Papers*, 1911 session, vol. 54, Cd. 5745, "Imperial Conference, 1911, Dominion No. 17. Minutes of the Proceedings of the Imperial Conference, 1911," 97–98, doc. 96, in Meaney, *Australia and the World*, 199.
68. Meaney, *The Search for Security*, 217.
69. Marder, *The Road to War 1904–1914*, 240.
70. Nicholls, *Sailors & Statesmen*, 196–97.
71. Marder, *The Road to War 1904–1914*, 295–98.
72. Meaney, *The Search for Security*, 234–235; Nicholls, *Statesmen & Sailors*, 197–98.
73. Pearce to Muirhead-Collins 3/12/, Australian War Memorial (AWM), Pearce Papers, 7/106.
74. Nicholls, *Statesmen & Sailors*, 197.
75. Odgers, *The Royal Australian Navy*, 41–42; Freudenberg, *Churchill and Australia*, 44.
76. Joseph Cook, prime minister, to Lord Denman, governor-general, November 28, 1914, AA, CP290/15/2 enclosed in dispatch, Lord Denman to Lewis Harcourt, British colonial secretary, March 3, 1914 (received in the Colonial Office, April 11, 1914), TNA: PRO C.O.532/66 doc. 101, in Meaney, *Australia and the World,* 203–4.
77. Great Britain, *Parliamentary Debates*, House of Commons, 1914 session, vol. 59, cols. 1931–1933, March 17, 1914, doc. 102, in Meaney, *Australia and the World*, 205–6.
78. Meaney, *The Search for Security*, 256.
79. Frame, *Pacific Partners*, 20.
80. Ward, "Security: Defending Australia's Empire," 243.
81. Frame, *No Pleasure Cruise*, 106–7.
82. A. Marder, *From the Dreadnought to Scapa Flow, Volume II: The War Years: To the Eve of Jutland 1914–1916* (London: Oxford University Press, 1965), 104.
83. Nicholls, *Statesmen & Sailors*, 240.
84. M. Carlton, *First Victory: 1914—HMAS Sydney's Hunt for the German Raider Emden* (North Sydney: William Heinemann, 2013), 226.
85. Frame, *No Pleasure Cruise*, 107.
86. Firkins, *Of Nautilus and Eagles*, 33.
87. Carlton, *First Victory*, 236–39.
88. Firkins, *Of Nautilus and Eagles*, 29–30.
89. Frame, *No Pleasure Cruise*, 123–24.
90. Cablegram, secretary of state for the colonies to governor-general of Australia, August 6, 1914, Office of the Governor General, General Correspondence

1912–1927; "War 1914–15. Expeditions to the Pacific and Pacific Generally," 1914–1915, Australian Archives (AA) CP 78/23, item 14/89/10.
91. N. Meaney, *A History of Australian Defence and Foreign Policy, 1901–23, vol, 2, Australia and World Crisis 1914–1923* (Sydney: Sydney University Press, 2009), 65.
92. Cablegram, secretary of state for the colonies, to governor-general of Australia, August 11, 1914, Australian Archives Act (AAA), CRS 19981; Memorandum, official secretary to the governor-general of Australia, September 11, 1914, AAA CRS 19981.
93. Cablegram, secretary of state for the colonies to governor-general of Australia, October 13, 1914, AA CP 78/23, item 14/89/10; Office of the Prime Minister to official secretary to the governor-general of Australia, November 16, 1914, AAA CRS 19981.
94. "Occupation of Islands North of the Equator," Minute Paper, Department of Defence, November 14, 1914, AAA CRS 19981; Cablegram, secretary of state for the colonies to governor-general of Australia, November 24, 1914, AA CP 78/23, item 14/89/10; Cable, Sir Conyngham Greene, British ambassador in Tokyo, to Sir Edward Grey, British foreign secretary, December 1, 1914, TNA: PRO F.O. 371/2018, doc. 119, in Meaney, *Australia and the World*, 228–29; Memorandum, secretary of state for the colonies to governor-general of Australia, December 3, 1914, AAA CRS 19981.
95. Lewis Harcourt, British colonial secretary, to Sir Ronald Munro-Ferguson, governor-general, December 6, 1914, NLA, Munro-Ferguson Papers, 696/1306-09, doc. 113, in Meaney, *Australia and the World*, 223–24.
96. Memorandum, Department of Defence, December 30, 1914, "Captured German Possessions in the Pacific 1915–1920," External Affairs H & T 1916 Correspondence Files, AA CRS A1, item 20/7685; F. Wallin, Burns Philp & Company Limited, to resident commissioner of Gilbert & Ellice Island Protectorate, December 24, 1914, "Captured German Possessions in the Pacific 1915–1920," External Affairs H & T 1916 Correspondence Files, AA CRS A1, item 20/7685.
97. Cable, Sir Conyngham Greene, British ambassador in Tokyo, to Sir Edward Grey, British foreign secretary, December 1, 1914, TNA: PRO F.O. 371/2018, doc. 119, in Meaney, *Australia and the World*, 228–29.
98. M. MacCallum, *Political Anecdotes* (Sydney: Duffy & Snellgrove, 2003), 100–101. Author's note: The distance by road between Inverell and Broken Hill is 714 miles.
99. "Post-Belligerent Naval Policy for the Pacific," Minute Paper (& attached Annexures) "Australian Naval Defence," 06/11/15, AA MP1049/1, 1915/054.
100. Memorandum, Sir Edward Grey, March 23, 1916, FO 371 2693 XC 16464: Memoranda regarding Japanese attitudes in Pacific 1916; Memorandum, Special Commissioner in the East (government of New South Wales) November 1, 1916, NAA A981, 9 JAP 38 PT.1.; "Australia's Peril and Australia's Need: Compulsory training for Home Defence; Voluntary enlistment for Empire Service," Memorandum, J. H. Catts May 29, 1916, AA CRS A1, Item 16/15272.
101. William Morris Hughes, prime minister, to Senator George Pearce, acting prime minister, April 21, 1916, AWM, Pearce Papers, bundle 3, folder 3, doc. 125, in Meaney, *Australia and the World*, 234–35; Meaney, *Australia and World Crisis 1914–1923*, 153; C. M. H. Clark, *A History of Australia*, vol. 6, "*The Old Dead Tree and the Young Tree Green 1916–1935*" (Melbourne: Melbourne University Press, 1987), 18.

102. CPD, 1914–1917 session, vol. 80, 8952–60, September 22, 1916, doc. 128, in Meaney, *Australia and the World*, 238; CPD, 1914–1917 session, vol. 80, 8807, September 22, 1916, doc. 127, in Meaney, *Australia and the World*, 237.
103. Meaney, *Australia and World Crisis 1914–1923*, 186–87.
104. A. J. P. Taylor, *The First World War—An Illustrated History* (London: Penguin, 1968), 177–80.
105. Great Britain, *Parliamentary Debates*, vol. 93, cols., 1790–1792, May 17, 1917, doc. 137, in Meaney, *Australia and the World*, 252–53; Meaney, *Australia and World Crisis 1914–1923*, 267.
106. Cable (Secret), Walter H. Long, British colonial secretary, to Sir Ronald Munro Ferguson, governor-general, February 2, 1917, NAA CP 447/2, item SC472; National Library of Australia (NLA), Hughes Papers, 950/3/40, doc. 130, in Meaney, *Australia and the World*, 241–42; Cable, Sir Ronald Munro Ferguson, governor-general, to Walter H. Long, British colonial secretary, January 10, 1917, Public Records Office: UK (PRO) C.O. 532/91/232, doc. 133, in Meaney, *Australia and the World*, 243.
107. Meaney, *Australia and World Crisis 1914–1923*, 256.
108. Clark, *A History of Australia*, 92; Parkin and Lee, *Great White Fleet to Coral Sea*, 47.
109. Meaney, *Australia and World Crisis 1914–1923*, 258; Frame, *Pacific Partners*, 20.
110. Cable, W. M. Hughes, prime minister, to W. A. Watt, acting prime minister, November 11, 1918, NLA W. M. Hughes Papers, Ms.950/3/37, doc. 142, in Meaney, *Australia and the World*, 259–60.
111. Clark, *A History of Australia*, 100; *Times* (London), November 8, 1918, doc. 141, in Meaney, *Australia and the World*, 256–57.
112. Freudenberg, *Churchill and Australia*, 140.

Chapter 3. Paris, Washington, and Singapore: 1919–1923

1. Meaney, *Australia and World Crisis 1914–1923*, 95.
2. J. Winton, *War in the Pacific: Pearl Harbour to Tokyo Bay* (London: Sidgwick & Jackson, 1978), 113.
3. C. Hosoya, "Britain and the United States in Japan's View of the International System," in *Anglo-Japanese Alienation 1919–1952: Papers of the Anglo-Japanese Conference on the History of the Second World War*, ed. I. Nish (Cambridge: Cambridge University Press, 1982), 5.
4. Meaney, *Australia and World Crisis 1914–1923*, 304.
5. D. Judd, *Balfour & the British Empire* (London: Macmillan, 1968), 323.
6. W. M. Hughes, prime minister, to David Lloyd George, British prime minister, November 4, 1918, House of Lords Library, Lloyd George Papers, box 38, folder 5, doc. 143, in Meaney, *Australia and the World*, 260–62.
7. Cable, "Very Urgent and Most Secret," W. A. Watt, acting prime minister, to W. M. Hughes, prime minister, January 31, 1919; CPD, 1920 session, vol. 94, 5797–98, December 20, 1920, doc. 149, in Meaney, *Australia and the World*, 273–74.
8. Meaney, *Australia and World Crisis 1914–1923*, 326.
9. M. Lake and H. Reynolds, *Drawing the Global Colour Line: White Men's Countries and the Question of Racial Equality* (Melbourne: Melbourne University Press, 2008), 286.
10. Ibid., 288.
11. "Australia and Japan," translated article from *Nishi Nishi*, December 16, 1919, AA 1877/5/144: Department of Defence Association CRS B197 Secret and Confidential Correspondence Files, multiple number series, 1906–1935.

12. M. Fraser (with C. Roberts), *Dangerous Allies* (Melbourne: Melbourne University Press, 2014), 46; Clark, *A History of Australia*, 111.
13. MacCallum, *Political Anecdotes*, 79.
14. Clark, *A History of Australia*, 112.
15. P. Stanley, *Invading Australia: Japan and the Battle for Australia, 1942* (Camberwell, Vic.: Australian Penguin Group, 2008), 36.
16. FRUS (United States Foreign Relations Document Series), "The Paris Peace Conference, 1919," vol. 3, 720–22, doc. 146, in Meaney, *Australia and the World*, 265–66.
17. Meaney, *Australia and World Crisis 1914–1923*, 349.
18. Ibid., 351.
19. Ibid., 354.
20. P. H. Kerr, British prime minister David Lloyd George's private secretary, to Lord Milner, British colonial secretary, January 31, 1919, Bodleian Library, Add. Milner Papers C700/193–200, doc. 151, in Meaney, *Australia and the World*, 276–81.
21. FRUS, "The Paris Peace Conference, 1919," vol. 3, 785–800, doc. 147, in Meaney, *Australia and the World*, 266–72.
22. David Hunter Miller, *My Diary at the Conference of Paris*, 21 vols. (New York, Appeal Printing Co., 1924), vol. 1, 99–100, doc. 148, in Meaney, *Australia and the World*, 272–73.
23. Hosoya, "Britain and the United States in Japan's View of the International System," 5.
24. *Melbourne Herald*, February 14, 1919.
25. Lake and Reynolds, *Drawing the Global Colour Line*, 289.
26. Meaney, *Australia and World Crisis 1914–1923*, 366.
27. Clark, *A History of Australia*, 115.
28. Lake and Reynolds, *Drawing the Global Colour Line*, 297.
29. Cable, W. M. Hughes, prime minister, to W. A. Watt, acting prime minister, March 27, 1919, NLA, Hughes Papers, Ms.950/3/37, doc. 154, in Meaney, *Australia and the World*, 262–63.
30. Meaney, *Australia and World Crisis 1914–1923*, 372.
31. Lake and Reynolds, *Drawing the Global Colour Line*, 303; Meaney, *Australia and World Crisis 1914–1923*, 371.
32. Hosoya, "Britain and the United States in Japan's View of the International System," 7.
33. Lake and Reynolds, *Drawing the Global Colour Line*, 304.
34. Copy of letter, Major E. L. Piesse, (Melbourne) director of the Pacific Branch of the Prime Minister's Department, to Lieutenant Commander J. G. Latham, member of Australian delegation to the Paris Peace Conference, May 7, 1919, NLA Piesse Papers Ms882/5/25, doc. 155, in Meaney, *Australia and the World*, 263.
35. Clark, *A History of Australia*, 111.
36. *Melbourne Herald*, February 21, 1919.
37. Telegram, W. M. Hughes, prime minister, to David Lloyd George, British prime minister, October 8, 1920, TNA PRO CO 418/204/310-11, doc. 167, in Meaney, *Australia and the World*, 309.
38. Meaney, *Australia and World Crisis 1914–1923*, 467.
39. Parkin and Lee, *Great White Fleet to Coral Sea*, 67.
40. R. L. Buell, *The Washington Conference* (New York: D. Appleton and Company, 1922), 140.

41. Ibid., 148.
42. H. and M. Sprout, *Toward a New Era of Sea Power: American Naval Policy and the World Scene, 1918–1922* (Princeton NJ: Princeton University Press, 1940), 83.
43. Meaney, *Australia and World Crisis 1914–1923*, 479; Frame, *No Pleasure Cruise*, 139.
44. Meaney, *Australia and World Crisis 1914–1923*, 482.
45. "Notes of a Meeting of Prime Ministers of the Empire," July 20, 1921, TNA (UK): CAB 32/4 169473.
46. Letter (unpublished), Hughes to Sir Maurice Hankey, secretary to the Imperial Conference, undated, Lloyd George Papers, House of Lords Record Office, F/25/2/5.
47. Meaney, *Australia and World Crisis 1914–1923*, 492.
48. CPD, 1921 session, vol. 94, 7262–70, April 7, 1921, doc. 168, in Meaney, *Australia and the World*, 310–15; "Notes of a Meeting of Prime Ministers of the Empire," July 27, 1921, TNA (UK): CAB 32/4 169473.
49. "Notes of a Meeting of Prime Ministers of the Empire," July 19, 1921, TNA (UK): CAB 32/4 169473.
50. S. Asada, "Japanese Admirals and the Politics of Naval Limitation: Kato Tomasaburo versus Kato Kanji," in *Naval Warfare in the Twentieth Century: Essays in Honour of Arthur Marder*, ed. G. Jordan (London: Croome Helm Ltd, 1977), 141.
51. Buell, *The Washington Conference*, 139.
52. H. Agawa, *The Reluctant Admiral: Yamamoto and the Imperial Navy* (Tokyo: Kodansha International Ltd, 1979), 28.
53. Sprout and Sprout, *Toward a New Era of Sea Power*, 151.
54. Ibid.
55. Buell, *The Washington Conference*, 401.
56. J. McCarthy, *Australia and Imperial Defence 1918–39: A Study in Air and Sea Power* (St. Lucia, Australia: University of Queensland Press, 1976), 10.
57. Meaney, *Australia and World Crisis 1914–1923*, 495–96.
58. Buell, *The Washington Conference*, 181.
59. Judd, *Balfour and the British Empire*, 87.
60. E. L. Piesse, "The Quadruple Pacific Treaty," paper, NLA, Piesse Papers, doc. 171, in Meaney, *Australia and the World*, 321–23.
61. Hosoya, "Britain and the United States in Japan's View of the International System," 8.
62. Ibid.
63. Ibid.
64. McCarthy, *Australia and Imperial Defence 1918–39*, 11.
65. Sprout and Sprout, *Toward a New Era of Sea Power*, 298–306; Buell, *The Washington Conference*, 374–84.
66. G. Bennett, *Naval Battles of World War Two* (Barnsley, UK: Pen and Sword Military Classics, 2003), 23.
67. Buell, *The Washington Conference*, 163.
68. Sprout and Sprout, *Toward a New Era of Sea Power*, 307–8.
69. J. Terraine, *White Heat: The New Warfare 1914–18* (London: Book Club Associates, 1982), 247.
70. Sprout and Sprout, *Toward a New Era of Sea Power*, 259, 267.
71. Ibid., 260.
72. B. Nicholls, *War to War: Australia's Navy 1919–1939* (Sydney: Bob Nicholls, 2012), 58; Sprout and Sprout, *Toward a New Era of Sea Power*, 263.

73. Agawa, *The Reluctant Admiral*, 29.
74. Hosoya, "Britain and the United States in Japan's View of the International System," 8.
75. CPD, 1922 session, vol. 99, 786–93, July 26, 1922, doc. 172, in Meaney, *Australia and the World*, 323–26.
76. CPD, 1922 session, vol. 99, 821–23, July 27, 1922, doc. 173, in Meaney, *Australia and the World*, 326–29.
77. Buell, *The Washington Conference*, 386; Firkins, *Of Nautilus and Eagles*, 63.
78. Nicholls, *Statesmen & Sailors*, 270; G. Hermon Gill, *Royal Australian Navy 1939-1942* (Adelaide: Griffin Press, 1957), 2.
79. D. Stevens, "'Defend the North': Commander Thring, Captain Hughes-Onslow and the Beginnings of Australian Naval Strategic Thought," in *Southern Trident: Strategy, History and the Rise of Australian Naval Power*, ed. D. Stevens and J. Reeve (Sydney: Allen & Unwin, 2001), 240.
80. "Report on the Naval Defences of Australia," Commander W. H. Thring, RAN, July 5, 1913, AA (VICRO) MP1587/1 184J.
81. Meaney, *Australia and World Crisis 1914–1923*, 425–26; Nicholls, *Statesmen & Sailors*, 263.
82. "Naval Defence of the British Empire," Admiralty memorandum for the War Cabinet, May 17, 1918, British Admiralty (ADM) 116/1815 XC169040; Nicholls, *Statesmen & Sailors*, 263–66.
83. Sir Joseph Cook to Sir Eric Geddes, November 16, 1918, ADM 116/1815 XC169040.
84. Admiral Sir R. H. Bacon, *The Life of John Rushworth, Earl Jellicoe GCB, OM, GCVO, LLD, DCL* (London: Cassell, 1936), 369.
85. Ibid., 390.
86. "Proposed Visit of Lord Jellicoe to the Dominions and India to advise on Naval Matters," Admiralty memorandum for War Cabinet, December 17, 1918, ADM 116/1815 XC169040.
87. "Statement of Objects and Duties for Pacific Branch," June 20, 1919, NAA CP447/3, item No. SC12 "Eastern Question," doc. 157, in Meaney, *Australia and the World*, 285–87.
88. Meaney, *Australia and World Crisis 1914–1923*, 416.
89. D. Gillison, *Royal Australian Air Force 1939–42* (Adelaide: Griffin Press, 1962), 6.
90. Bacon, *The Life of John Rushworth, Earl Jellicoe*, 402–3; Frame, *No Pleasure Cruise*, 133.
91. "Instructions for Lord Jellicoe," December 23, 1918, ADM 116/1815 XC169040.
92. External Affairs (2), Correspondence Files, Alphabetical Series: "Imperial Defence-Naval, 1918–1920," AA CRS A981, Item Defence 350, pt. I.
93. Bacon, *The Life of John Rushworth, Earl Jellicoe*, 427.
94. Jellicoe Report on Naval Defence, vol. 4 (secret), 221–23, NAA CRS A65/2, doc. 160, in Meaney, *Australia and the World*, 290–91; Bacon, *The Life of John Rushworth, Earl Jellicoe*, 427–28; Frame, *No Pleasure Cruise* 133; Nicholls, *War to War*, 37–38.
95. Newcastle is located 101 miles (60 nautical miles) to the north of Sydney.
96. Nicholls, *War to War*, 37–38.
97. "Lord Jellicoe's Report to the Commonwealth Government of Australia," Report to first lord, October 31, 1919, ADM 116/1815 XC 169040.
98. "Imperial Naval Defence," Admiralty Memorandum, July 9, 1919, ADM 116/3104 169081.
99. Ibid.

100. Cable, Australian prime minister W. M. Hughes to British prime minister, David Lloyd George, October 7, 1919, *Lloyd George Papers*, House of Lords Record Office, F133/2/75(a); Meaney, *Australia and World Crisis 1914–1923*, 433.
101. Admiralty Minute December 5, 1919, ADM 116/1815 XC 169040.
102. "Naval Mission to India and the Dominions," general remarks, Lord Jellicoe to secretary of the Admiralty, February 3, 1920, ADM 116/1815 XC 169040.
103. "Naval Defence," statement by the minister for the navy explanatory of the Navy Estimates, 1920–1921, September 23, 1920, External Affairs (2), Correspondence Files, Alphabetical Series: "Imperial Defence-Naval," 1918–1920. AA CRS A981, Item Defence 350, part I.
104. Report of the conference held on board HMS *Hawkins* at Penang between the commanders in chief of the China, East Indies, and Australian Stations, from March 7, 1921, onward, March 13, 1921, ADM 116/3100 169081; Nicholls, *War to War*, 53–54.
105. Report of the conference held on board HMS *Hawkins* at Penang between the commanders in chief of the China, East Indies, and Australian Stations, from March 7, 1921, onward, March 13, 1921, ADM 116/3100 169081.
106. "Development of Singapore as a Naval Base," conclusion, Standing Defence Subcommittee of the Committee of Imperial Defence, June 13, 1921, CAB/24/125–0040; Minutes, Cabinet Meeting, June 16, 1921, CAB/23/26-0005.
107. W. S. Churchill, "Report of Committee to Examine Part 1 (Defence Departments) of the Report of the Geddes Committee on National Expenditure," memorandum, February 4, 1922, CAB/24/132–0091; "Report of the Committee on National Expenditure," cabinet conclusions, February 17, 1922, CAB/23/29-0011.
108. "Singapore—Proposed Naval Base," cabinet memorandum, February 15, 1923, CAB/24/159–0018.
109. Nicholls, *War to War*, 59–60.
110. "Naval Estimates 1922/23," minute paper and attachments, Department of the Navy, April 7, 1922, AA MP 1049/1 27/0307.
111. Gillison, *Royal Australian Air Force 1939–42*, 12–13.
112. "Policy—Royal Australian Air Force," Air Council memorandum, April 6, 1922, Department of Defence MS1538, series 19, folder 5.
113. "General Minute Covering the Defence Policy of the Various Branches of the Service," letter, minister for defense to prime minister, April 7, 1922, Department of Defence MS1538, series 19, folder 5.
114. McCarthy, *Australia and Imperial Defence 1918–39*, 45.
115. Ibid., 4.
116. Nicholls, *War to War*, 61.
117. McCarthy, *Australia and Imperial Defence 1918–39*, 24.
118. "Singapore—Proposed Naval Base," cabinet memorandum, February 15, 1923, CAB/24/159–0018; "Singapore—Development as a Naval Base," memorandum (No. 501M) by the Oversea Sub-Committee of the Committee of Imperial Defence, June 7, 1921, Prime Minister's Department, Correspondence and other papers relating to the Imperial and Economic Conferences—"Imperial Conference 1921," AA CD 103/3, vol. 2.
119. Gill, *Royal Australian Navy 1939–1942*, 15; Firkins, *Of Nautilus and Eagles*, 63.
120. Gill, *Royal Australian Navy 1939–1942*, 16.
121. McCarthy, *Australia and Imperial Defence 1918–39*, 46.
122. Ibid., 47; Nicholls, *War to War*, 60–61.

123. *Imperial Conference 1923: Summary of Proceedings* (Melbourne: Victorian Government Printer, 1924).
124. CPD, 1924 session, vol. 104, 43–45, March 27, 1924.

Chapter 4. Not a Cloud in the Sky: 1924–1929

1. McCarthy, *Australia and Imperial Defence 1918–39*, 49.
2. *Imperial Conference 1923: Summary of Proceedings*.
3. "Dimensions and Particulars of British and Foreign Warships," in *Brassey's Naval Annual 1936* (hereafter *BSY 1936*), ed. C. N. Robinson (London: William Clowes, 1936), 194–98.
4. *The Battleships* (DVD), Australian Broadcasting Corporation, 2002, accessed February 2, 2018.
5. "Cruise Itinerary: Special Service Squadron," H.M.S. Hood Association, http://hmshood.com/history/empirecruise/index.htm, accessed February 2, 2018.
6. L. Kennedy, *Pursuit: The Sinking of the Bismarck* (London: Cassell Military Paperbacks, 1974), 60.
7. *Perth Call*, March 7, 1924, https://trove.nla.gov.au/newspaper/article/210904811, accessed February 2, 2018.
8. "Australian Naval Defence," *Hobart World*, March 24, 1924, https://trove.nla.gov.au/newspaper/article/190366781, accessed February 2, 2018.
9. "Australia's Problems: Admiral Field's Advice," *Brisbane Daily Mail*, March 21, 1924, https://trove.nla.gov.au/newspaper/article/217619948, accessed February 2, 2018.
10. "Parliamentary Dinner: Admiral Field's Speech," *Hobart World*, March 22, 1924, https://trove.nla.gov.au/newspaper/article/190366636, accessed February 2, 2018.
11. "Erroneous Assertions: Admiral Field's Response," *West Australian*, March 22, 1924, https://trove.nla.gov.au/newspaper/article/31221729, accessed February 2, 2018.
12. Ibid., 182–83.
13. H. C. Bywater, *Sea Power in the Pacific: A Study of the American-Japanese Naval Problem* (London: Constable, 1921), 254.
14. Sprout and Sprout, *Toward a New Era of Sea Power*, 300–301.
15. W. R. Braisted, "On the American Red and Red-Orange Plans, 1919–1939," in Jordan, *Naval Warfare in the Twentieth Century*, 168–71.
16. Parkin and Lee, *Great White Fleet to Coral Sea*, 83–84.
17. Ibid., 84.
18. "Visit of American Fleet" Report, E. M. Lawton, American consul-general, to the secretary of state, Washington, July 14, 1925, Department of State, Division of Western European Affairs, Index Bureau 811.3347/91.
19. "Visit of American Fleet" Report, E. M. Lawton, American consul-general, to the secretary of state, Washington, June 22, 1925, Department of State, Division of Western European Affairs, Index Bureau 811.3347/87.
20. "Visit of American Fleet" Report, E. M. Lawton, American consul-general, to the secretary of state, Washington, August 4, 1925, Department of State, Division of Western European Affairs, Index Bureau 811.3347/92; "Visit of American Fleet" Report, Norman L. Anderson, American consul (Melbourne), to the secretary of state, Washington, August 12, 1925, Department of State, Division of Western European Affairs, Index Bureau 811.3347/95; "Visit of American Fleet" Report, E. M. Lawton, American consul-general, to the

secretary of state, Washington, August 14, 1925, Department of State, Division of Western European Affairs, Index Bureau 811.3347/94; Frame, *Pacific Partners*, 29.

21. "Cruise to Australia—New Zealand: 1 July to 26 September, 1925, by a Detachment of the U.S. Fleet," memorandum, commander in chief to chief of naval operations, United States Fleet, USS *Seattle* Flagship September 26, 1925, CINC File No. C-34-21.
22. Parkin and Lee, *Great White Fleet to Coral Sea*, 92.
23. "Cruise to Australia—New Zealand: 1 July to 26 September, 1925, by a Detachment of the U.S. Fleet."
24. C. Cantrill, "UK Expenditure 1880–1914," http://www.ukpublicspending.co.uk, accessed February 2, 2018.
25. H. Montgomery-Hyde, *British Air Policy Between the Wars 1918–1939* (London: William Heinemann Ltd, 1976), 118.
26. "The Relations of the Navy and the Air Force," Cabinet Conclusions July 31, 1923, TNA (UK): CAB/23/46-0015; "Report of a Sub-Committee on National and Imperial Defence," November 15, 1923, TNA (UK): CAB/24/162-0061.
27. G. Till, *Airpower and the Royal Navy 1914–1945—A Historical Survey* (London: Jane's, 1979), 40.
28. "The Relations of the Navy and the Air Force," Cabinet Conclusions, July 31, 1923, CAB/23/46-0015.
29. A. Boyle, *Trenchard* (London: Collins, 1962), 524–25; E. C. Shepherd, *The Air Force of Today* (Glasgow: Blackie & Son, 1939), 29; Till, *Airpower and the Royal Navy 1914–1945*, 31.
30. "The Navy and its Fleet Air Arm," in *Brassey's Naval and Shipping Annual 1925*, ed. A. Richardson & A. Hurd (hereinafter BSY 1925). (London: W. M. Clowes & Sons Ltd, 1925), 90.
31. "The Question of the Capital Ship in the Royal Navy," Report of the Sub-Committee of the Committee of Imperial Defence, March 2, 1921, Long Papers 947/716/3.
32. J. Ferris, "The Last Decade of British Maritime Supremacy 1919–1929," in Neilson and Kennedy, *Far Flung Lines*, 137.
33. O. Babij, "The Royal Navy and the Defence of the British Empire 1928–1934," in Neilson and Kennedy, *Far Flung Lines*, 173.
34. Beatty, "To his Wife," January 22, 1925, doc. 150 [BTY/17/69/76–79], in *The Beatty Papers: Selections from the Private and Official Correspondence of Admiral of the Fleet Earl Beatty*, vol. 2: *1916–1927*, ed. B Ranft (Aldershot: Scolar Press for the Navy Records Society, 1995), 277.
35. W. S. Churchill, "Navy Estimates 1925–1926," cabinet memorandum, January 29, 1925, TNA (UK): CAB/24/171-0039.
36. W. Bridgeman, "Navy Estimates," memorandum by the first lord of the admiralty, February 5, 1925, TNA (UK): CAB/24/171-0068.
37. Ibid.
38. Babij, "The Royal Navy and the Defence of the British Empire 1928–1934," 174.
39. Ferris, "The Last Decade of British Maritime Supremacy 1919–1929," 143.
40. Babij, "The Royal Navy and the Defence of the British Empire 1928–1934," 172.
41. Lord Birkenhead, "Report on Cruisers," Naval Programme Committee, December 14, 1927, TNA (UK): CAB/24/190-0005.
42. W. W. Fisher and G. C. Upcott, "Navy Estimates 1930," Joint Reply by Admiralty-Treasury on Navy Estimates, December 13, 1929, TNA (UK):

CAB/24/209-0014; P. Snowden, "Memorandum by Treasury on Financial Aspects of the Naval Conference," December 16, 1929, TNA (UK): CAB/24/209-0012.
43. Babij, "The Royal Navy and the Defence of the British Empire 1928–1934," 171.
44. Beatty, "To His Wife."
45. Gillison, *Royal Australian Air Force 1939–42*, 22.
46. CPD, 1924 session, vol. 106, 43–45, March 27, 1924, doc. 181, in Meaney, *Australia and the World*, 343–46.
47. CPD, 1924 Session, vol. 107, 2115-7, July 16, 1924, doc. 183, in Meaney, *Australia and the World*, 348–51.
48. Cable, S. M. Bruce, prime minister, to Sir. L. E. Groom, minister for trade and customs and for health, Geneva, July 17, 1924, NAA CRS A3934, item SC 11 [8], doc. 184, in Meaney, *Australia and the World*, 352–53.
49. Judd, *Balfour & the British Empire*, 326.
50. CPD, 1924 Session, vol. 114, 4772, August 3, 1926.
51. J. Curran, *Curtin's Empire* (Melbourne: Cambridge University Press, 2011), 51.
52. CPD, 1924 Session, vol. 114, 4772, August 3, 1926.
53. Curran, *Curtin's Empire*, 51.
54. Gillison, *Royal Australian Air Force 1939–42*, 17.
55. McCarthy, *Australia and Imperial Defence 1918–39*, 33–34.
56. A. Stephens, *The Royal Australian Air Force* (Melbourne: Oxford University Press, 2001), 43–44.
57. R. Williams, "Memorandum regarding the Air Force of Australia," April 21, 1925, AA MP826/1/10; McCarthy, *Australia and Imperial Defence 1918–39*, 37; Nicholls, *War to War*, 89.
58. Gillison, *Royal Australian Air Force 1939–42*, 33.
59. "Summary of Proceedings: General Meeting of the Council of Defence," July 8, 1929, AAA MP 1049/9, file 1851/4/17.
60. Ibid.
61. "Summary of Proceedings: General Meeting of the Council of Defence," November 12, 1929, AAA MP 1049/9, file 1851/4/17.
62. "Summary of Proceedings: General Meeting of the Council of Defence," November 12, 1929, AAA MP 1049/9, file 1851/4/17; Nicholls, *War to War*, 96–98.
63. "Singapore Naval Base: Copy of Telegrams from the Dominion Governments," March 12, 1924, TNA (UK): CAB/24/165-0082.
64. CPD, 1924 session, vol. 107, 1702–1703, June 27, 1924, doc. 182, in Meaney, *Australia and the World*, 346–48.
65. "Singapore Naval Base: Copy of Telegrams from the Governments of Australia, New Zealand, and the Straits Settlements regarding the Singapore Naval Base," December 9, 1924, TNA (UK): CAB/24/169-0035.
66. "The Singapore Base: Memorandum by the Chairman of the Committee of Imperial Defence," February 27, 1925, TNA (UK): CAB/24/172-0024.
67. Churchill, "Navy Estimates 1925–1926," January 29, 1925, CAB/24/171-0039.
68. *Melbourne Age*, March 21, 1925; "Secret and Confidential Correspondence 1923–1950," Department of Defence/Navy: AA MP1185/8, file 1846/4/25.
69. *Melbourne Age*, March 23, 1923; *Argus*, March 25, 1923; AA MP1185/8, file 1846/4/25.
70. *Melbourne Herald*, March 25, 1925; AA MP1185/8, file 1846/4/25.
71. *Melbourne Age*, July 6, 1925; AA MP1185/8, file 1846/4/25.
72. McCarthy, *Australia and Imperial Defence 1918–39*, 48.

73. "The Singapore Base: The Defences and Development of the Naval Base," draft minutes, 23rd meeting of the Committee of Imperial Defence, December 13, 1928, TNA (UK): CAB/24/199-0050.
74. *Melbourne Herald*, June 18, 1925, AA MP1185/8, File 1846/4/25.
75. "Singapore: Scale of Attack and Scale of Defence," interim report by the Chiefs-of-Staff subcommittee, March 28, 1928, TNA (UK): CAB/24/194-0013.
76. Ibid.
77. Ibid.
78. "The Fuller Employment of Air Power in Imperial Defence 1919–1929," memorandum by the chief of the air staff, November 1, 1929, TNA (UK) CAB/24/207-0033.
79. "Fighting Services Committee: Policy as Regards the Singapore Base," memoranda, October 22, 1929, TNA (UK): CAB/24/206-0039.
80. Ibid.
81. C. N. Robinson and H. M. Ross, eds., *Brassey's Naval Annual 1930* (BSY 1930) (London: William Clowes, 1930), 15.
82. McCarthy, *Australia and Imperial Defence 1918–39*, 47.
83. *Melbourne Herald* 23/03/1925; AA MP1185/8, file 1846/4/25; *Perth Call*, March 7, 1924.
84. Gillison, *Royal Australian Air Force 1939–42*, 21–22.
85. Collier, *Japanese Aircraft of World War II*, 102.

Chapter 5. The Onset of the Two-Ocean Dilemma: 1930–1935

1. Ward, "Security: Defending Australia's Empire," 243.
2. "International Treaty for the Limitation and Reduction of Naval Armament." http://www.navweaps.com/index_tech/tech-089_London_Treaty_1930.php, first viewed March 8, 2018.
3. Bennett, *Naval Battles of World War Two*, 27.
4. Ferris, "The Last Decade of British Maritime Supremacy 1919–1929," 157.
5. Babij, "The Royal Navy and the Defence of the British Empire 1928–1934," 172.
6. P. Williamson, *National Crisis and National Government: British Politics, the Economy and Empire, 1926–1932* (Cambridge: Cambridge University Press, 1992), 15–16.
7. Ibid., 505.
8. "Limitation of Naval Armaments," memorandum by the first lord of the admiralty, September 30, 1931, TNA (UK): CAB/24/223-0053.
9. D. Van der Vat, *The Pacific Campaign: The U.S.-Japanese Naval War 1941–1945* (New York: Simon & Schuster, 1991), 52.
10. Ibid.
11. S. Ienaga, *Japan's Last War: World War II and the Japanese, 1931–1945* (Canberra: Australian National University Press, 1979), 14–18.
12. Ibid.
13. Van der Vat, *The Pacific Campaign*, 49.
14. Ienaga, *Japan's Last War*, 36.
15. Van der Vat, *The Pacific Campaign*, 54; D. Reynolds, *Britannia Overruled—British Policy and World Power in the 20th Century* (London: Longman, 2000), 120.
16. "Situation in the Far East," cabinet memorandum March 15, 1934, TNA (UK): CAB/24/248-0012; Hosoya, "Britain and the United States in Japan's View of the International System," 15.
17. "The Far East–Chino-Japanese Dispute," cabinet conclusions, February 27, 1933, TNA (UK): CAB/23/75-0012.

18. Hosoya, "Britain and the United States in Japan's View of the International System," 20; "The Importance of Anglo-Japanese Friendship," memorandum, secretary of state for war, January 11, 1936, TNA (UK): CAB/24/259-0012.
19. "Imperial Defence Policy: Annual Review 1933," memorandum, Chiefs of Staff Sub-Committee, November 10, 1933, TNA (UK): CAB/24/244-0014.
20. "The Far East–Chino-Japanese Dispute," CAB/23/75-0012; "Situation in the Far East," CAB/24/248-0012.
21. "Imperial Defence Policy: The Annual Review by the Chiefs-of-Staff Sub-Committee," memorandum, March 17, 1932, TNA (UK): CAB/24/229-0005.
22. "The Situation in the Far East," memorandum, Committee of Imperial Defence May 17, 1933, TNA (UK): CAB/24/239-0045; "Imperial Defence Policy," Interim Report Ministerial Committee on Disarmament Dealing with Air Defence, July 16, 1934, TNA (UK): CAB/24/250-0018.
23. "Imperial Defence Policy," CAB/24/250-0018.
24. Reynolds, *Britannia Overruled*, 112.
25. "Imperial Defence Policy," CAB/24/250-0018.
26. A. J. P. Taylor, *The Second World War: An Illustrated History* (New York: Penguin Books, 1976), 26.
27. Eric Raeder, *My Life* (Annapolis, MD: Naval Institute Press, 1960), 267–69.
28. L. Sansonetti, "The Royal Italian Navy," in *Brassey's Naval Annual 1938*, ed. H. G. Thursfield (London: W. M. Clowes, 1938), 78–83.
29. A. Tusa and J. Tusa, *The Nuremberg Trial* (London: Papermac, 1984), 303.
30. G. Corrigan, *The Second World War: A Military History* (London: Atlantic Books Ltd, 2010), 72.
31. I. Kershaw, *Making Friends with Hitler: Lord Londonderry and Britain's Road to War* (London: Allen Lane, 2004), 122.
32. "The Singapore Base," report, Committee of the Fighting Services, October 14, 1930, TNA (UK): CAB/24/215-0044.
33. "Coast Defence," report of Sub-Committee, Committee of Imperial Defence, July 11, 1932, TNA (UK): CAB/24/231-0039.
34. "The Far East–Chino-Japanese Dispute," CAB/23/75-0012.
35. "The Situation in the Far East," CAB/24/239-0045.
36. Ibid.
37. "Imperial Defence Policy: Annual Review 1933," CAB/24/244-0014.
38. Ibid.
39. Ibid.
40. Ibid.
41. "Situation in the Far East," CAB/24/248-0012.
42. "Imperial Defence Policy: Annual Review 1933," CAB/24/244-0014; "Situation in the Far East," CAB/24/248-0012.
43. "Situation in the Far East," CAB/24/248-0012.
44. "Singapore Defences," Sub-Committee on Defence Policy and Requirements, Committee of Imperial Defence, July 19, 1935, TNA (UK): CAB/24/256.
45. Ibid.
46. "'*Status Quo*' in the Pacific: Article 19 of the Washington Treaty," memorandum by the minister for League of Nations affairs, December 7, 1935, TNA (UK): CAB/24/257-0058.
47. "The Singapore Base," BSY 1930, 15.
48. G. Bolton, "Money: Trade, Investment and Economic Nationalism," in Schreuder and Ward, *Australia's Empire*, 223.
49. Parkin and Lee, *Great White Fleet to Coral Sea*, 98–99.

50. D. Horner, *Defence Supremo: Sir Frederick Shedden and the Making of Australian Defence Policy* (St. Leonards, Australia: Allen & Unwin, 2000), 32–33.
51. Stanley, *Invading Australia*, 62.
52. Horner, *Defence Supremo*, 32.
53. "Submarines 'Oxley' and 'Otway,'" memorandum by the chief of naval staff, November 22, 1930. Department of Defence Association CRS B197 Secret and Confidential Correspondence Files, multiple number series, 1906–1935, AA 1855/1/181.
54. Horner, *Defence Supremo*, 37.
55. Curran, *Curtin's Empire*, 61.
56. *League of Nations Journal* (11th Ordinary Session), Assembly, Ninth Plenary Meeting, September 15, 1930, 74–75, doc. 194, in Meaney, *Australia and the World*, 376–79.
57. Horner, *Defence Supremo*, 33.
58. Parkin and Lee, *Great White Fleet to Coral Sea*, 100.
59. Horner, *Defence Supremo*, 34.
60. "Estimates of Expenditure, 1930/31," Minutes of Defence Committee Meeting, April 11, 1930, Department of External Affairs II, Correspondence file; "Imperial Conference 1930—Memoranda for delegates—Foreign policy and defence," 1930, AA CRS A981, item Imperial 126.
61. Ibid.
62. Ibid.
63. Ibid.
64. P. Hasluck, *Australia in the War of 1939–45: The Government and the People 1939–41* (Canberra: Australian War Memorial, 1952), 38.
65. "Draft Disarmament Convention," memorandum by chief of the general staff, October 26, 1931, AA MP729/2, File 1846/1/26.
66. Clark, *A History of Australia*, 381–89.
67. Ibid., 392.
68. McCarthy, *Australia and Imperial Defence 1918–39*, 54; Horner, *Defence Supremo*, 40.
69. McCarthy, *Australia and Imperial Defence 1918–39*, 39–41.
70. Gillison, *Royal Australian Air Force 1939–42*, 28.
71. McCarthy, *Australia and Imperial Defence*, 27.
72. Extract of Minutes, Committee of Imperial Defence June 9, 1932, contained within "Coast Defence," report of Sub-Committee, Committee of Imperial Defence, July 11, 1932, CAB/24/231-0039.
73. "The Defence of Australia," extracts of CID Paper 372C and CID 249C provided to an ordinary meeting of the Military Board, March 29, 1933, Department of Defence Association CRS B197 Secret and Confidential Correspondence Files, multiple number series, 1906–1935, AA 1855/1/165.
74. Ibid.
75. Hasluck, *Australia in the War of 1939–45*, 40.
76. "The Defence of Australia," AA 1855/1/165.
77. "The Situation in the Far East," CAB/24/239-0045.
78. Hasluck, *Australia in the War of 1939–45*, 41.
79. Cable, S. M. Bruce, high commissioner to London, to J. G. Latham, minister for external affairs, March 3, 1933, NAA CRS A981, item China 114 ("Old") pt. 5, doc. 197, in Meaney, *Australia and the World*, 386.
80. "The Australian Eastern Mission, 1934: Report of the Right Honourable J. G. Latham, Leader of the Mission," prime minister's department, papers

collected in the offices of the secretary and the prime minister: "[Reports of the Australian Eastern Mission]," 1934, AA CP209/1 item 10.
81. Ibid.
82. "Report upon the International Position in the Far East," in letter (secret), J. G. Latham, minister for external affairs, to J. A. Lyons, prime minister, July 3, 1934, NLA, Papers of Sir Earle Page, Ms. 1633/288, doc. 199, in Meaney, *Australia and the World*, 388–90.
83. Notes of the third meeting of British Commonwealth prime ministers, held in the Prime Minister's Room at the House of Commons on May 9, 1935, NAA, CRS A981, item Imperial Relations 135, doc. 202, in Meaney, *Australia and the World*, 393–94.
84. Notes of the fourth meeting of British Commonwealth prime ministers, held in the Prime Minister's Room at the House of Commons on May 23, 1935, NAA CRS A981, item Imperial Relations 135, doc. 203, in Meaney, *Australia and the World*, 394–95.
85. Senator G. F. Pearce, minister for external affairs, to secretary, External Affairs Department, May 23, 1935, NLA, Latham Papers, Ms. 1633/648, doc. 204, in Meaney, *Australia and the World*, 396.
86. Nancy Harvison Hooker, ed., *The Moffat Papers* (Cambridge, MA: Harvard University Press, 1956), 126–30, doc. 205, in Meaney, *Australia and the World*, 396–97.
87. Horner, *Defence Supremo*, 45.
88. McCarthy, *Australia and Imperial Defence 1918–39*, 57.
89. Horner, *Defence Supremo*, 45.
90. "Report by Sir Maurice Hankey, Secretary to the Committee of Imperial Defence, on Certain Aspects of Australian Defence," November 15, 1934. PRO PREM1/174 XC 17793, TNA (UK): CAB/21/386.
91. Ibid.
92. Ibid.
93. Ibid.
94. McCarthy, *Australia and Imperial Defence 1918–39*, 60.
95. Horner, *Defence Supremo*, 46.
96. N. Meaney, *Fears and Phobias: E. L. Piesse and the Problem of Japan* (Canberra: National Library of Australia, 1996), 42; McCarthy, *Australia and Imperial Defence 1918–39*, 59.
97. W. M. Hughes, *Australia and War Today: The Price of Peace* (Sydney: Angus & Robertson, 1935), 118–19, doc. 206, in Meaney, *Australia and the World*, 397–99.
98. "Albatross," *Japan and the Defence of Australia* (Melbourne: Robertson & Mullens, 1935), 28.
99. Ibid., 50.
100. Stanley, *Invading Australia*, 52; "Albatross," *Japan and the Defence of Australia*, 21; Hasluck, *Australia in the War of 1939–45*, 46.
101. "Albatross," *Japan and the Defence of Australia*, 36.
102. *Melbourne Herald*, December 31, 1935.
103. Ibid.
104. Ibid.

Chapter 6. Something Less Than Fools: January 1936–August 1939

1. Horner, *Defence Supremo*, 35.
2. McCarthy, *Australia and Imperial Defence 1918–39*, 132.

3. "Notes on the Naval Disarmament Conference, 1935–36," chief of naval staff to minister of defense, January 23, 1936, AA MP1049/9, File 1846/4/48.
4. Gill, *Royal Australian Navy 1939–1942*, 34–35.
5. "London Conference 1936: International Treaty for the Limitation and Reduction of Naval Armament," http://www.navweaps.com/index_tech/tech-089_London_Treaty_1930.php, first viewed March 8, 2018.
6. "Notes on the Naval Disarmament Conference, 1935–36," AA MP1049/9, File 1846/4/48.
7. "Statement Relating to Defence," P.M. statement to the House of Commons, March 3, 1936, TNA (UK): CAB/24/260-0029.
8. "Progress in Defence Requirements," memorandum by the minister for the co-ordination of defense, February 1, 1937, TNA (UK): CAB/24/267-0041.
9. McCarthy, *Australia and Imperial Defence 1918–39*, 135.
10. "Progress in Defence Requirements," CAB/24/267-0041.
11. "Plan for Further Expansion of the First-Line Strength of the Royal Air Force," memorandum by the secretary of state for air, January 14, 1937, TNA (UK): CAB/24/267-0019.
12. Hosoya, "Britain and the United States in Japan's View of the International System," 21–23.
13. I. Nish, "Japan in Britain's View of the International System, 1919–37," in Nish, *Anglo-Japanese Alienation 1919–1952*, 45; "Review of Relations between the United Kingdom and Japan 06/03/1937," doc. 11 in R. G. Neale, ed., *Documents on Australian Foreign Policy 1937–49*, vol. 1, 1937–38 (hereafter known as *DOAFP, VI: 1937–38*) (Canberra: Australian Government Publishing Service, 1975), 35.
14. Van der Vat, *The Pacific Campaign*, 55.
15. C. Waters, *Australia and Appeasement: Imperial Foreign Policy and the Origins of World War II* (London: I. B. Tauris, 2012), 50–52.
16. Corrigan, *The Second World War*, 77.
17. Kershaw, *Making Friends with Hitler*, 150–53.
18. Waters, *Australia and Appeasement*, 246; Taylor, *The Second World War*, 30.
19. Corrigan, *The Second World War*, 78–80.
20. Taylor, *The Second World War*, 26.
21. McCarthy, *Australia and Imperial Defence 1918–39*, 136.
22. Ibid., 131.
23. "Council of Defence Meeting 24/08/1936: Summary of Proceedings," National Archives of Australia A5954 910/14, https://recordsearch.naa.gov.au/SearchNRetrieve/Interface/ViewImage.aspx?B=652410, first viewed April 24, 2018.
24. Horner, *Defence Supremo*, 49.
25. Hasluck, *The Government and the People 1939–41*, 80–81.
26. Curran, *Curtin's Empire*, 65.
27. Hasluck, *Australia in the War of 1939–45*, 84.
28. Gill, *Royal Australian Navy 1939–1942*, 36; Nicholls, *War to War*, 160–61.
29. "Secret Admiralty Note on Australian Naval Requirements: Appendix 'B', Estimates 1935/36 and New Programme Proposals," May 22, 1936, general correspondence 1923–50, AA MP1049/9, File 1855/2/41.
30. Firkins, *Of Nautilus and Eagles*, 65.
31. Gillison, *Royal Australian Air Force 1939–1942*, 43; McCarthy, *Australia and Imperial Defence 1918–39*, 113.
32. Cable, No. 12, J. A. Lyons, prime minister, to S. M. Bruce, high commissioner in London, March 16, 1936, NAA CRS A981, item Europe 4 ("Old"), Part I, doc. 208, in Meaney, *Australia and the World*, 402–3.

33. CPD, 1936 session, vol. 150, 2211–17, May 22, 1936, doc. 209, in Meaney, *Australia and the World*, 403–6.
34. CPD, vol. 151, 622–23, September 29, 1936, doc. 211, in Meaney, *Australia and the World*, 408.
35. "Reform of the Covenant of the League of Nations," external affairs memorandum for Imperial Conference, September 11, 1936, doc. 5, *DOAFP, VI: 1937–38*, 22.
36. "Relations between United Kingdom and Germany," external affairs memorandum for Imperial Conference, n.d. [after February 9, 1937], doc. 6, *DOAFP, VI: 1937–38*, 29–30.
37. "Paper No. 4—Problems Relating to the Basis of Australian Defence Policy—No. 3—Defence against Invasion," summary of papers and questions on defense submitted by delegation to Imperial Conference, April 28, 1937, doc. 20, *DOAFP, VI: 1937–38*, 58–59.
38. "Paper No. 3—Problems Relating to the Basis of Australian Defence Policy—No. 1—Priority for Provision of Defence and the Time Factor," summary of papers and questions on defense submitted by Delegation to Imperial Conference, April 28, 1937, doc. 20, *DOAFP, VI: 1937–38*, 58.
39. Hasluck, *Australia in the War of 1939–45*, 55.
40. Ibid., 56.
41. "Reform of the Covenant of the League of Nations," doc. 5, *DOAFP, VI: 1937–38*, 22; Waters, *Australia and Appeasement*, 15.
42. Waters, *Australia and Appeasement*, 19.
43. Hasluck, *Australia in the War of 1939–45*, 71.
44. Ibid., 56.
45. Waters, *Australia and Appeasement*, 22.
46. "Minutes of Third Meeting of Principal Delegates to Imperial Conference 21/05/1937," doc. 27, *DOAFP, VI: 1937–38*, 75.
47. "Minutes of Twelfth Meeting of Principal Delegates to Imperial Conference 03/06/1937," doc. 39, *DOAFP, VI: 1937–38*, 128–29.
48. "Minutes of Tenth Meeting of Principal Delegates to Imperial Conference 01/06/1937," doc. 34, *DOAFP, VI: 1937–38*, 96–97.
49. "Minutes of Fourth Meeting of Principal Delegates to Imperial Conference 22/05/1937," doc. 28, *DOAFP, VI: 1937–38*, 79.
50. Ibid., 79–80.
51. "Most Secret" memorandum E. (37) 29, May 28, 1937, NAA CRS A981, Item Pacific 23, doc. 214, in Meaney, *Australia and the World*, 411–15.
52. "Mr J. A. Lyons, Prime Minister, to Sir George Pearce, Minister for External Affairs 10/06/1937," doc. 44, *DOAFP, VI: 1937–38*, 158–59.
53. "Minutes of Seventh Meeting of Principal Delegates to Imperial Conference 26/05/1937," doc. 32, *DOAFP, VI: 1937–38*, 86.
54. Ibid., 86–87.
55. "Minutes of Seventh Meeting of Principal Delegates to Imperial Conference 26/05/1937," doc. 32, *DOAFP, VI: 1937–38*, 89–90; Nicholls, *War to War*, 167.
56. "Minutes of Meeting to Discuss Defence Questions 01/06/1937," doc. 35, *DOAFP, VI: 1937–38*, 101–3.
57. Ibid., 108.
58. Ibid., 106.
59. "Minutes of Meeting to Discuss Defence Questions 01/06/1937," doc. 35, *DOAFP, VI: 1937–38*, 107; Nicholls, *War to War*, 166–67.

60. "Minutes of Meeting to Discuss Defence Questions 01/06/1937," doc. 35, *DOAFP, VI: 1937–38*, 109.
61. "Questions Raised by the Australian Delegation," report by Chiefs-of-Staff Sub-Committee, June 9, 1937, TNA (UK): CAB/21/2525 XC17491, 11–12.
62. Ibid., 8.
63. Ibid., 6.
64. Ibid., 10.
65. Ibid.
66. CPD, 1937 session, vol. 154, 22–31, August 24, 1937, doc. 221, in Meaney, *Australia and the World*, 428–33.
67. Ibid.
68. Ibid.
69. Waters, *Australia and Appeasement*, 27.
70. "Mr S. M. Bruce, High Commissioner in London, to Prime Minister's Department 22/11/1937," doc. 109, *DOAFP, VI: 1937–38*, 231–32.
71. "Mr S. M. Bruce, High Commissioner in London, to Mr J. A. Lyons, Prime Minister 22/02/1938," doc. 127, *DOAFP, VI: 1937–38*, 266–67; Waters, *Australia and Appeasement*, 30–31.
72. K. Usui, "A Consideration of Anglo-Japanese Relations: Japanese Views of Britain, 1937–41," in Nish, *Anglo-Japanese Alienation 1919–1952*, 85.
73. Ibid.
74. Ibid., 88.
75. Van der Vat, *The Pacific War*, 57–59.
76. "Mr R. G. Menzies, Prime Minister, to Mr S. Bruce, High Commissioner in London 19/05/1939," doc. 90 in *Documents on Australian Foreign Policy 1937–49*, vol. 2: 1939, ed. R. G. Neale (hereafter referred to as *DOAFP, VII: 1939*) (Canberra: Australian Government Publishing Service, 1976), 120.
77. McCarthy, *Australia and Imperial Defence 1918–35*, 140.
78. "Questions Raised by the Australian Delegation," report by Chiefs-of-Staff Sub-Committee, June 9, 1937, CAB/21/2525 XC17491, 4.
79. G. Kennedy, *Anglo-American Strategic Relations and the Far East, 1933–39* (London: Routledge, 2013), 39–40; McCarthy, *Australia and Imperial Defence 1918–39*, 141.
80. Kennedy, *Anglo-American Strategic Relations and the Far East, 1933–39*, 40.
81. A. E. Percival, "Operation of Malaya Command from 8 December 1941 to 15 February 1942," *London Gazette* (Supplement) (hereafter referred to as *LDNGZT*), no. 38215, February 20, 1948, 1250, https://www.thegazette.co.uk/London/issue/38215/supplement/1250, first viewed May 8, 2018.
82. R. Grenfell, *Main Fleet to Singapore: An Account of Naval Actions of the Last War* (Oxford: Oxford University Press, 1987), 71.
83. Percival, "Operation of Malaya Command from 8 December 1941 to 15 February 1942," 1250.
84. M. Murfett, "Reflections on an Enduring Theme: The 'Singapore Strategy' at Sixty," in *Sixty Years On: The Fall of Singapore Revisited*, ed. B. Farrell and S. Hunter (Singapore: Eastern Universities Press, 2003), 16–18.
85. Ibid.
86. Percival, "Operation of Malaya Command from 8 December 1941 to 15 February 1942," 1250.
87. *SMH*, September 29, 1937, doc. 223, in Meaney, *Australia and the World*, 435–37.
88. *SMH*, September 21, 1937, doc. 222, in Meaney, *Australia and the World*, 433–35.
89. Ibid.

90. Hasluck, *Australia in the War of 1939–45*, 85.
91. Curran, *Curtin's Empire*, 73.
92. Horner, *Defence Supremo*, 54.
93. Waters, *Australia and Appeasement*, 115–17.
94. Ibid., 231.
95. "Mr J. K. Waller, Department of External Affairs, to Mr H. A. Peterson, Department of External Affairs 03/05/1937," doc. 22, *DOAFP, VI: 1937–38*, 60.
96. "Mr Longford Lloyd, Trade Commissioner in Japan, to Mr J. F. Murphy, Secretary of Department of Commerce 06/10/1937," doc. 111, *DOAFP, VI: 1937–38*, 234–35.
97. "Mr J. A. Lyons, Prime Minister, to Sir Earle Page, Minister for Commerce 02/06/1938," doc. 213, *DOAFP, VI: 1937–38*, 166–67; "Mr Torao Wakamatsu, Japanese Consul-General in Sydney, to Mr J. A. Lyons, Prime Minister 14/06/1938," doc. 216, *DOAFP, VI: 1937–38*, 371–73.
98. Waters, *Australia and Appeasement*, 140.
99. Stanley, *Invading Australia*, 63.
100. "Mr R. G. Menzies, Attorney-General and Minister for Industry, to Mr J. A. Lyons, Prime Minister 05/01/1939," doc. 2, *DOAFP, VII: 1939*, 5.
101. "Mr F. K. Officer, Australian Counsellor at U.K. Embassy, Washington, to Mr R. G. Casey, Treasurer 22/03/1939," doc. 52, *DOAFP, VII: 1939*, 79.
102. "Broadcast Speech by Mr R. G. Menzies, Prime Minister 26/04/1939," doc. 73, *DOAFP, VII: 1939*, 97–98.
103. "Mr S. M. Bruce, High Commissioner in London (in America), to Mr R. G. Menzies, Prime Minister 08/05/1939," doc. 82, *DOAFP, VII: 1939*, 108.
104. Horner, *Defence Supremo*, 55.
105. Hasluck, *Australia in the War of 1939–45*, 85; Nicholls, *War to War*, 182–83.
106. Hasluck, *Australia in the War of 1939–45*, 105; Nicholls, *War to War*, 185–86.
107. Horner, *Defence Supremo*, 71; Nicholls, *War to War*, 183–84.
108. McCarthy, *Australia and Imperial Defence 1918–39*, 86–87.
109. Gillison, *Royal Australian Air Force 1939–42*, 74–76.
110. McCarthy, *Australia and Imperial Defence 1918–39*, 103–4; Nicholls, *War to War*, 186.
111. McCarthy, *Australia and Imperial Defence 1918–39*, 110.
112. "Mr N. Chamberlain, U.K. Prime Minister, to Mr J. A. Lyons, Prime Minister 11/03/1938," doc. 134, *DOAFP, VI: 1937–38*, 273–75; "Report of Discussion by Committee of Imperial Defence 04/03/1938," doc. 189, *DOAFP, VI: 1937–38*, 335.
113. "Mr S. Bruce, High Commissioner in London, to Mr J. A. Lyons, Prime Minister 01/11/1938," doc. 315, *DOAFP, VI: 1937–38*, 511–12; "Mr S. Bruce, High Commissioner in London, to Mr J. A. Lyons, Prime Minister 31/10/1938," doc. 314, *DOAFP, VI: 1937–38*, 510–11.
114. "Mr M. MacDonald, U.K. Secretary of State for Dominion Affairs, to Commonwealth Government 07/12/1938," doc. 331, *DOAFP, VI: 1937–38*, 527.
115. "Admiral Sir Ragnar Colvin, First Naval Member, Naval Board, to Admiral Sir Roger Backhouse, U.K. First Sea Lord 14/03/1939," doc. 37, *DOAFP, VII: 1939*, 60.
116. "Sir Harry Batterbee, U.K. High Commissioner to New Zealand, to Sir Thomas Inskip, U.K. Secretary of State for Dominion Affairs 26/04/1939," doc. 74, *DOAFP, VII: 1939*, 99.
117. McCarthy, *Australia and Imperial Defence 1918–39*, 145; Nicholls, *War to War*, 203–4.

118. "Admiral Sir Roger Backhouse, U.K. First Sea Lord, to Admiral Sir Ragnar Colvin, First Naval Member, Naval Board 17/03/1939," doc. 41, *DOAFP, VII: 1939*, 68.
119. "Note by Mr J. S. Duncan, Acting High Commissioner in London, of Conversation with Major-General H. L. Ismay, Secretary of U.K. Committee of Imperial Defence 17/03/1939," doc. 42, *DOAFP, VII: 1939*, 69; Nicholls, *War to War*, 205.
120. "Mr N. Chamberlain, U.K. Prime Minister, to Mr J. A. Lyons, Prime Minister 20/03/1939," doc. 46, *DOAFP, VII: 1939*, 75; "Mr N. Chamberlain, U.K. Prime Minister, to Mr R. G. Menzies, Prime Minister 29/06/1939," doc. 113, *DOAFP, VII: 1939*, 144.
121. "Record of Meeting Held at Dominions Office 11/07/1939," doc. 118, *DOAFP, VII: 1939*, 152.
122. Ibid.
123. "Commonwealth Government to Sir Thomas Inskip, U.K. Secretary of State for Dominion Affairs 30/08/1939," doc. 169, *DOAFP, VII: 1939*, 205. HMAS *Perth* was then located in the West Indies on her delivery voyage to Australia.
124. "Broadcast Message by Mr R. G. Menzies, Prime Minister 03/09/1939," doc. 189, *DOAFP, VII: 1939*, 221.
125. R. Adkins and L. Adkins, *The War for All the Oceans: From Nelson at the Nile to Napoleon at Waterloo* (London: Abacus, 2006), 101.

Chapter 7. Conduits: September 1939–December 1941

1. S. Roskill, *The War at Sea 1939–1945*, vol. 1, *The Defensive* (London: Her Majesty's Stationery Office, 1954), 584–85.
2. Frame, *No Pleasure Cruise*, 153.
3. Gill, *Royal Australian Navy 1939–1942*, 126.
4. Firkins, *Of Nautilus and Eagles*, 70.
5. J. Goldrick, "Australian Naval Policy 1939–45," in *Royal Australian Navy in World War II*, ed. D. Stevens (Sydney: Allen & Unwin, 1996), 5.
6. Gill, *Royal Australian Navy 1939–1942*, 87.
7. Gill, *Royal Australian Navy 1939–1942*, 117; Goldrick, "Australian Naval Policy 1939–45," 4–5.
8. S. W. Roskill, *The Navy at War 1939–1945* (London: Collins, 1960), 51.
9. Raeder, *My Life*, 311; Roskill, *The Navy at War 1939–1945*, 68–71, 73–78.
10. Gill, *Royal Australian Navy 1939–1942*, 162.
11. Taylor, *The Second World War*, 62.
12. Roskill, *The War at Sea 1939–1945*, vol. 1, 615–16.
13. C. Forbes, dispatch, July 17, 1940: *The Norway Campaign*, LDNGZT issue 38011, July 8, 1947: 3170, http://www.london.gazette.co.uk/Issues/3801/supplements.
14. B. Ramsey, dispatch, June 18, 1940: *The Evacuation of the Allied Armies from Dunkirk and Neighbouring Beaches*, LDNGZT issue 38017, June 17, 1947, 5141, http://www.london.gazette.co.uk/Issues/38017/supplements.
15. Roskill, *The War at Sea 1939–1945*, vol. 1, 615–16.
16. S. E. Morison, *History of United States Naval Operations in World War II*, vol. 3: *The Rising Sun in the Pacific 1931–April 1942* (Boston: Little, Brown and Company, 1965), 41.
17. K. Usui, "A Consideration of Anglo-Japanese Relations: Japanese Views of Britain, 1937–41," in Nish, *Anglo-Japanese Alienation 1919–1952*, 90–91;

Hosoya, "Britain and the United States in Japan's View of the International System 1937–41," 64–65.
18. Hosoya, "Britain and the United States in Japan's View of the International System 1937–41," 65.
19. Usui, "A Consideration of Anglo-Japanese Relations: Japanese Views of Britain, 1937–41," 91.
20. "Far Eastern Policy," report by the British chiefs of staff to the War Cabinet, July 27, 1940, TNA (UK): CAB/66/10/20-0001.
21. Morison, *History of United States Naval Operations in World War II*, vol. 3, 41.
22. Ibid., 43.
23. Parkin and Lee, *Great White Fleet to Coral Sea*, 137.
24. Morison, *History of United States Naval Operations in World War II*, vol. 3, 43; Parkin and Lee, *Great White Fleet to Coral Sea*, 136.
25. "Mr R. G. Menzies, Prime Minister, to Mr S. M. Bruce, High Commissioner in London 05/09/1939," doc. 195, *DOAFP, VII: 1939*, 232.
26. D. Day, *Menzies and Churchill at War: A Revealing Account of the 1941 Struggle for Power* (Sydney: Simon & Schuster, 2001), 25.
27. Parkin and Lee, *Great White Fleet to Coral Sea*, 136.
28. Parkin and Lee, *Great White Fleet to Coral Sea*, 136; Frame, *Pacific Partners*, 36–37.
29. "Lord Caldecote, Secretary of State for Dominion Affairs, to Commonwealth Government 28/06/1940," doc. 459 in H. Kenway, H. J. W. Stokes, and P. G. Edwards, eds., *Documents on Australian Foreign Policy 1937–49*, vol. 3, *January–June 1940* (hereafter known as *DOAFP, VIII*: January–June 1940) (Canberra: Australian Government Publishing Service, 1979), 517–18.
30. "Mr S. M. Bruce, High Commissioner in London, to Mr R. G. Menzies, Prime Minister 03/07/1940," doc. 7 in *Documents on Australian Foreign Policy 1937–49*, vol. 4: *July 1940–June 1941* (hereafter known as *DOAFP, VIV*: July 1940–June 1941), ed. W. J. Hudson and H. J. W. Stokes (Canberra: Australian Government Publishing Service, 1980), 10.
31. W. S. Churchill, "Australian and New Zealand Naval Defence," memorandum by the first sea lord, November 21, 1939, PRO: CAB99/1, doc. 112, in J. Robertson and J. McCarthy, eds., *Australian War Strategy 1939–1945: A Documentary History* (St. Lucia, QL: University of Queensland Press, 1985), 144–45.
32. "Maj Gen H. L. Ismay, Chief of Staff to U.K. Minister of Defence, to Mr S. Bruce, High Commissioner in London 04/07/1940," doc. 9, *DOAFP, VIV*: July 1940–June 1941, 13.
33. Freudenberg, *Churchill and Australia*, 211.
34. Odgers, *The Royal Australian Navy*, 75.
35. Hasluck, *Australia in the War of 1939–45*, 168.
36. Day, *Churchill and Menzies at War*, 24.
37. "Commonwealth Government to Lord Caldecote, Secretary of State for Dominion Affairs 26/06/1940," doc. 442, *DOAFP, VIII*: January–June 1940, 498–99; "Mr A. Eden, U.K. Secretary of State for Dominion Affairs, to Mr R. G. Menzies, Prime Minister 21/03/1940," doc. 110, *DOAFP, VIII*: January–June 1940, 154–55; "Mr R.G. Menzies, Prime Minister, to Lord Caldecote, U.K. Secretary of State for Dominion Affairs 13/03/1940," doc. 372, *DOAFP, VIII*: January–June 1940, 420–21.
38. "The Far East," appreciation by the chiefs of staff, July 31, 1940, TNA (UK): CAB/66/10/33-0001.

39. Ibid.
40. Frame, *No Pleasure* Cruise, 155; Odgers, *The Royal Australian Navy*, 88.
41. Gill, *Royal Australian Navy 1939–1942*, 279–81.
42. Frame, *No Pleasure Cruise*, 158–59.
43. Roskill, *The War at Sea 1939–1945*, vol. 1, 282.
44. Roskill, *The Navy at War 1939–1945*, 122.
45. Frame, *No Pleasure* Cruise, 166; Roskill, *The War at Sea 1939–1945*, vol. 1, 618.
46. Raeder, *My Life*, 351–52.
47. Bennett, *Naval Battles of World War Two*, 138–40, 145–46.
48. Raeder, *My Life*, 358.
49. R. Hough, *The Longest Battle: The War at Sea 1939–45* (London: Cassell, 2003), 38.
50. Roskill, *The Navy at War 1939–1945*, 136–38.
51. E. Grove, "The Royal Australian Navy in the Mediterranean in World War II," in Stevens, *Royal Australian Navy in World War II*, 74.
52. W. S. Churchill, *The Second World War*, vol. 3: *The Grand Alliance* (London: Penguin, 1985), 286.
53. Morison, *History of United States Naval Operations in World War II*, vol. 3, 139.
54. Roskill, *The War at Sea 1939–1945*, vol. 1, 618.
55. Morison, *History of United States Naval Operations in World War II*, vol. 3, 45.
56. Hosoya, "Britain and the United States in Japan's View of the International System 1937–41," 67.
57. "Minutes of the 29th Liaison Conference, 11/06/1941," in *Japan's Decision for War: Records of the 1941 Policy Conferences*, ed. N. Ike (Stanford, CA: Stanford University Press, 1967), 50.
58. "Minutes of the 36th Liaison Conference, 30/06/1941," in Ike, *Japan's Decision for War*, 70–74.
59. Hosoya, "Britain and the United States in Japan's View of the International System 1937–41," 66.
60. P. Lowe, "Britain and the Opening of the War in Asia, 1937–41," in Nish, *Anglo-Japanese Alienation 1919–1952*, 112–13.
61. Morison, *History of United States Naval Operations in World War II*, vol. 3, 59–60.
62. Ibid., 62.
63. Frame, *Pacific Partners*, 36.
64. Morison, *History of United States Naval Operations in World War II*, vol. 3, 51.
65. R. Brooke-Popham, dispatch, May 28, 1942: *Operations in the Far East from 17 October 1940 to 27 December 1941*, LDNGZT issue 38183, February 20, 1948, 543–44, http://www.gazettes-online.co.uk/home.aspx?Geotype+London.
66. Ibid.
67. Morison, *History of United States Naval Operations in World War II*, vol. 3, 55.
68. "Lord Caldecote, U.K. Secretary of State for Dominion Affairs, to Sir Geoffrey Whiskard, U.K. High Commissioner in Australia 11/08/1940," doc. 65, *DOAFP, VIV*: July 1940–June 1941, 87–89; "Lord Caldecote, U.K. Secretary of State for Dominion Affairs, to Sir Geoffrey Whiskard, U.K. High Commissioner in Australia 11/08/1940," doc. 66, *DOAFP, VIV*: July 1940–June 1941, 89–99.
69. "Lord Caldecote, U.K. Secretary of State for Dominion Affairs, to Sir Geoffrey Whiskard, U.K. High Commissioner in Australia 11/08/1940," doc. 64, *DOAFP, VIV*: July 1940–June 1941, 84–86.
70. Horner, *Defence Supremo*, 86.

71. "Far Eastern Position Appreciation," report by the Australian chiefs of staff, August 23, 1940, doc. 115 in Robertson and McCarthy, *Australian War Strategy 1939–1945: A Documentary History*, 148–49.
72. Hasluck, *Australia in the War of 1939–45*, 272.
73. "Report of Singapore Defence Conference 1940: Review by Chiefs-of-Staff 16/11/1940," War Cabinet minute, November 26, 1940, doc. 118, in Robertson and McCarthy, *Australian War Strategy 1939–1945: A Documentary History*, 151.
74. Day, *Menzies and Churchill at War*, 34.
75. Ibid., 45.
76. Frame, *No Pleasure Cruise*, 158–59; Freudenberg, *Churchill and Australia*, 236–38.
77. Horner, *Defence Supremo*, 105.
78. Day, *Menzies and Churchill at War*, 152.
79. "Lord Cranborne, U.K. Secretary of State for Dominion Affairs, to Sir Geoffrey Whiskard, U.K. High Commissioner in Australia 16/02/1941," doc. 304, *DOAFP, VIV*: July 1940–June 1941, 416–18.
80. D. Day, *The Politics of War* (Sydney: Harper Collins, 2003), 108.
81. "Combined Far Eastern Appreciation of the Australian Chiefs-of-Staff: February 1941," War Cabinet minute, February 14, 1941, doc. 122, in Robertson and McCarthy, *Australian War Strategy 1939–1945: A Documentary History*, 154–56.
82. D. Horner, *High Command: Australia's Struggle for an Independent War Strategy 1939–1945* (Sydney: Allen & Unwin, 1982), 56.
83. "Mr R. G. Menzies, Prime Minister, to Mr S. M. Bruce, High Commissioner in London 03/12/1940," doc. 214, *DOAFP, VIV*: July 1940–June 1941, 289; "Lord Cranborne, U.K. Secretary of State for Dominion Affairs, to Commonwealth Government 23/12/1940," doc. 236, *DOAFP, VIV*: July 1940–June 1941, 314–15.
84. "Mr A. W. Fadden, Acting Prime Minister, to Lord Cranborne, U.K. Secretary of State for Dominion Affairs 12/02/1941," doc. 285, *DOAFP, VIV*: July 1940–June 1941, 382–84; "Lord Cranborne, U.K. Secretary of State for Dominion Affairs, to Commonwealth Government 23/02/1941," doc. 317, *DOAFP, VIV*: July 1940–June 1941, 438–39.
85. "Note of Conversation at U.K. Admiralty 08/03/1941," doc. 343, *DOAFP, VIV*: July 1940–June 1941, 482–84.
86. Parkin and Lee, *Great White Fleet to Coral Sea*, 141.
87. Morison, *History of United States Naval Operations in World War II*, vol. 3, 56.
88. "Mr A. S. Watt, First Secretary of the Legation in Washington, to Mr R. G. Casey, Minister to the United States 12/02/1941," doc. 288, *DOAFP, VIV*: July 1940–June 1941, 387.
89. "Mr R. G. Casey, Minister to the United States, to Department of External Affairs 02/05/1941," doc. 445, *DOAFP, VIV*: July 1940–June 1941, 635.
90. "Mr R. G. Casey, Minister to the United States, to Department of External Affairs 26/07/1940," doc. 18 in W. J. Hudson & H. J. W. Stokes, *Documents on Australian Foreign Policy 1937–49*, vol. 5, *July 1941–June 1942* (hereafter known as *DOAFP, VV*: July 1941–June 1942) (Canberra: Australian Government Printing Service, 1982), 26–27.
91. Roskill, *The Navy at War 1939–1945*, 141.
92. Gill, *Royal Australian Navy 1939–1942*, 453–54; Frame, *No Pleasure Cruise*, 168–69.
93. Gill, *Royal Australian Navy 1939–1942*, 455–57.
94. Goldrick, "Australian Naval Policy 1939–45," 8.

95. Roskill, *The Navy at War 1939–1945*, 171–73.
96. Churchill, *The Grand Alliance*, 768–69.
97. Ibid., 771–72.
98. Ibid., 773–74.
99. Morison, *History of United States Naval Operations in World War II*, vol. 3, 70–71; "Minutes of the Imperial Conference, 06/09/1941," in Ike, *Japan's Decision for War*, 133–39.
100. Morison, *History of United States Naval Operations in World War II*, vol. 3, 72.
101. "Minutes of the 59th Liaison Conference 23/10/1941," in Ike, *Japan's Decision for War*, 184–86.
102. "Minutes of the Imperial Conference 05/11/1941," in Ike, *Japan's Decision for War*, 233.
103. "Minutes of the Imperial Conference 01/12/1941," in Ike, *Japan's Decision for War*, 280.
104. M. Tsuji, *Singapore—The Japanese Version* (Sydney: Ure Smith, 1960), 45–51.
105. Ibid.
106. Day, *Menzies and Churchill at War*, 228.
107. Hasluck, *Australia in the War of 1939–45*, 516–17.
108. "Advisory War Council Minute 533, 16/10/1941," doc. 84, *DOAFP, VV*: July 1941–June 1942, 141–44.
109. "Mr A. W. Fadden, Prime Minister, to Mr Winston Churchill, U.K. Prime Minister 15/09/1941," doc. 68, *DOAFP, VV*: July 1941–June 1942, 111–13; "Mr Winston Churchill, U.K. Prime Minister, to Mr A. W. Fadden, Prime Minister 30/09/1941," doc. 73, *DOAFP, VV*: July 1941–June 1942, 120–21.
110. "Mr Winston Churchill, U.K. Prime Minister, to Mr John Curtin, Prime Minister 26/10/1941," doc. 91, *DOAFP, VV*: July 1941–June 1942, 153–54.
111. Roskill, *The War at Sea 1939–1945*, vol. 1, 556–57.
112. Grenfell, *Main Fleet to Singapore*, 96–97; Churchill, *The Grand Alliance*, 524–25.
113. "Advisory War Council Minute 560, 07/11/1941," doc. 104, *DOAFP, VV*: July 1941–June 1942, 176.
114. Ibid., 180–81.
115. "Commonwealth Government to Lord Cranborne, U.K. Secretary of State for Dominion Affairs 22/11/1941," doc. 121, *DOAFP, VV*: July 1941–June 1942, 214–15.
116. Brooke-Popham, dispatch, May 28, 1942, LDNGZT 38183, 545–46.
117. "Lord Cranborne, U.K. Secretary of State for Dominion Affairs, to Mr John Curtin, Prime Minister 05/12/1941," doc. 162, *DOAFP, VV*: July 1941–June 1942, 275.
118. Gillison, *Royal Australian Air Force 1939–42*, 200–202.
119. Roskill, *The War at Sea 1939–1945*, vol. 1, 559.
120. Gillison, *Royal Australian Air Force 1939–42*, 202.
121. Ibid.
122. Ibid., 208.
123. W. S. Churchill, *The Second World War*, vol. 1, *The Gathering Storm* (London: Cassell, 1948), 475.

Chapter 8. The Far East: December 1941–April 1942

1. Report of the conference held on board H.M.S. "Hawkins" at Penang between the commanders-in-chief of the China, East Indies, and Australia Stations, from March 7, 1921, onwards, March 13, 1921, ADM 116/3100 169081.
2. Churchill, *The Grand Alliance*, 771–72.
3. Gillison, *Royal Australian Air Force 1939–1942*, 214–15.

4. Ibid.
5. J. Burton, *Fortnight of Infamy: The Collapse of Allied Airpower West of Pearl Harbor* (Annapolis MD: Naval Institute Press, 2013), 109.
6. Ibid., 113.
7. P. Maltby, *Report on the Air Operations during the Campaigns in Malaya and the Netherlands East Indies from 5 December 1941 to 12 March 1942*, LDNGZT issue 38216, February 26, 1948, http://www.london.gazette.co.uk/issues/38216/supplements.
8. Ibid.
9. Burton, *Fortnight of Infamy*, 129–31, 150–51.
10. Grenfell, *Main Fleet to Singapore*, 110.
11. Churchill, *The Grand Alliance*, 548.
12. G. Layton, dispatch December 17, 1941, *Loss of H.M. Ships Prince of Wales and Repulse*, LDNGZT issue 38214, February 26, 1948, http://www.london.gazette.co.uk/issues/38214/supplements; Grenfell, *Main Fleet to Singapore*, 115.
13. Gillison, *Royal Australian Air Force 1939–1942*, 251.
14. Burton, *Fortnight of Infamy*, 164–65.
15. Layton, dispatch, December 17, 1941, LDNGZT; Roskill, *The War at Sea 1939–1945*, vol. 1, 564.
16. Roskill, *The War at Sea 1939–1945*, vol. 1, 564; Macintyre, *The Battle for the Pacific*, 36.
17. Layton, dispatch, December 17, 1941, LDNGZT.
18. Ibid.
19. Ibid.
20. Churchill, *The Grand Alliance*, 551.
21. Ibid., 547.
22. Roskill, *The War at Sea 1939–1945*, vol. 1, 568.
23. Grenfell, *Main Fleet to Singapore*, 136.
24. W. H. Bartsch, *Doomed at the Start: American Pursuit Pilots in the Philippines, 1941–1942* (College Station: Texas A&M University Press, 1995), 5, 42.
25. Grenfell, *Main Fleet to Singapore*, 129.
26. Burton, *Fortnight of Infamy*, 11.
27. *Daily Telegraph*, December 12, 1941, https://trove.nla.gov.au/newspaper/article/248711119.
28. *Argus*, December 11, 1941, https://trove.nla.gov.au/newspaper/article/8221886.
29. *Newcastle Morning Herald and Miner's Advocate*, December 11, 1941, https://trove.nla.gov.au/newspaper/article/134076325.
30. *Wellington Times*, December 11, 1941, https://trove.nla.gov.au/newspaper/article/141623436.
31. "Sir Earle Page, Special representative in the United Kingdom, to Mr John Curtin, Prime Minister 08/12/1941," doc. 175, *DOAFP, VV*: July 1941–June 1942, 289–93.
32. "Commonwealth Government to Lord Cranborne, U.K. Secretary of State for Dominion Affairs, 11/12/1941," doc. 182, *DOAFP, VV*: July 1941–June 1942, 299; "Mr S. M. Bruce, High Commissioner in the United Kingdom, to Mr John Curtin, Prime Minister, 13/12/1941," doc. 189, *DOAFP, VV*: July 1941–June 1942, 307–8.
33. "Dr H. V. Evatt, Minister for External Affairs, to Mr R. G. Casey, Minister to the United States, 16/12/1941," doc. 196, *DOAFP, VV*: July 1941–June 1942, 316.
34. "Mr Winston Churchill, U.K. Prime Minister (in the United States), to Mr John Curtin, Prime Minister, 29/12/1941," doc. 240, *DOAFP, VV*: July 1941–June 1942, 387–88.

35. "Mr R. G. Casey, Minister to the United States, to Department of External Affairs, 29/12/1941," doc. 241, *DOAFP, VV*: July 1941–June 1942, 389–90.
36. "Mr John Curtin, Prime Minister, to Mr Winston Churchill, U.K. Prime Minister (in the United States), 01/01/1942," doc. 247, *DOAFP, VV*: July 1941–June 1942, 396–97; Goldrick, "Australian Naval Policy 1939–45," 9.
37. "Mr R. G. Casey, Minister to the United States, to Department of External Affairs, 03/01/1942," doc. 253, *DOAFP, VV*: July 1941–June 1942, 408–9.
38. "Lord Cranborne, U.K. Secretary of State for Dominion Affairs, to Mr John Curtin, Prime Minister, 11/12/1941," doc. 185, *DOAFP, VV*: July 1941–June 1942, 303.
39. "Lord Cranborne, U.K. Secretary of State for Dominion Affairs, to Commonwealth Government, 21/12/1941," doc. 211, *DOAFP, VV*: July 1941–June 1942, 335.
40. "Lord Cranborne, U.K. Secretary of State for Dominion Affairs, to Mr John Curtin, Prime Minister, 23/12/1941," doc. 215, *DOAFP, VV*: July 1941–June 1942, 342–43.
41. "Mr John Curtin, Prime Minister, to Mr R. G. Casey, Minister to the United States, 29/12/1941," doc. 237, *DOAFP, VV*: July 1941–June 1942, 382–86; Goldrick, "Australian Naval Policy 1939–45," 9.
42. "Mr Winston Churchill, U.K. Prime Minister (in the United States), to Mr John Curtin, Prime Minister, 03/01/1942," doc. 255, *DOAFP, VV*: July 1941–June 1942, 411–12.
43. "Mr Winston Churchill, U.K. Prime Minister (in the United States), to Mr John Curtin, Prime Minister, 12/02/1942," doc. 273, *DOAFP, VV*: July 1941–June 1942, 435–36.
44. "Lord Cranborne, U.K. Secretary of State for Dominion Affairs, to Mr John Curtin, Prime Minister, 23/12/1941," doc. 215, *DOAFP, VV*: July 1941–June 1942, 346–47; "Mr R. G. Casey, Minister to the United States, to Department of External Affairs, 24/12/1941," doc. 223, *DOAFP, VV*: July 1941–June 1942, 357–58.
45. Gillison, *Royal Australian Air Force 1939–1942*, 340.
46. "Mr S. M. Bruce, High Commissioner in the United Kingdom, to Mr John Curtin, Prime Minister, 24/12/1941," doc. 221, *DOAFP, VV*: July 1941–June 1942, 354–56.
47. "Mr R. G. Casey, Minister to the United States, to Department of External Affairs, 24/12/1941," doc. 223, *DOAFP, VV*: July 1941–June 1942, 357–58.
48. Curtin's "America" speech and its implications are addressed in chapter 10.
49. "Mr Winston Churchill, U.K. Prime Minister (in the United States), to Mr John Curtin, Prime Minister, 12/01/1942," doc. 271, *DOAFP, VV*: July 1941–June 1942, 432–35; "Mr John Curtin, Prime Minister, to Mr Winston Churchill, U.K. Prime Minister, 17/01/1942," doc. 278, *DOAFP, VV*: July 1941–June 1942, 441–43; "Mr Winston Churchill, U.K. Prime Minister, to Mr John Curtin, Prime Minister, 19/01/1942," doc. 278, *DOAFP, VV*: July 1941–June 1942, 445–46.
50. "Sir Earle Page, Special Representative in the United Kingdom, to Mr John Curtin, Prime Minister, 22/01/1941," doc. 292, *DOAFP, VV*: July 1941–June 1942, 459–61.
51. "Mr John Curtin, Prime Minister, to Mr Winston Churchill, U.K. Prime Minister, 23/01/1942," doc. 294, *DOAFP, VV*: July 1941–June 1942, 463–67.
52. "Mr V. G. Bowden, Official Representative in Singapore, to Dr H. V. Evatt, Minister for Foreign Affairs, 14/12/1941," doc. 193, *DOAFP, VV*: July 1941–June 1942, 312–13.

53. "Mr V. G. Bowden, Official representative in Singapore, to Dr H. V. Evatt, Minister for External Affairs, 23/12/1941," doc. 217, *DOAFP, VV*: July 1941–June 1942, 349–50.
54. "Mr V. G. Bowden, Official representative in Singapore, to Department of External Affairs, 23/01/1942," doc. 297, *DOAFP, VV*: July 1941–June 1942, 468.
55. W. S. Churchill, *The Second World War*, vol. 4, *The Hinge of Fate* (London: Cassell & Co, 1951), 43.
56. N. Barber, *Sinister Twilight: The Fall of Singapore* (London: Fontana Books, 1970), 67.
57. "Mr V. G. Bowden, Official Representative in Singapore, to Dr H. V. Evatt, Minister for Foreign Affairs, 26/10/1941," doc. 306, *DOAFP, VV*: July 1941–June 1942, 482–83.
58. F. Owen, *The Fall of Singapore* (London: Penguin, 1960), 170–72.
59. *Sydney Morning Herald*, February 17, 1942, https://trove.nla.gov.au/newspaper/article/17788305?searchTerm=Singapore.
60. Morison, *History of United States Naval Operations in World War II*, vol. 3, 294–95.
61. Morison, *History of United States Naval Operations in World War II*, vol. 3, 288–91; Gillison, *Royal Australian Air Force 1939–42*, 391–95.
62. Gillison, *Royal Australian Air Force 1939–42*, 426.
63. Clark, *The Encyclopaedia of Australia's Battles*, 204–5.
64. Ibid, 205.
65. Gillison, *Royal Australian Air Force 1939–42*, 466–67.
66. *Sydney Morning Herald*, February 20, 1942, https://trove.nla.gov.au/newspaper/article/17788820?searchTerm=Darwin.
67. Morison, *History of United States Naval Operations in World War II*, vol. 3, 335.
68. Gill, *Royal Australian Navy 1939–1942*, 606.
69. Ibid., 609.
70. J. A. Collins, dispatch, March 17, 1942, *Battle of the Java Sea 27 February 1942*, LDNGZT issue 38346, July 6, 1948, http://www.london.gazette.co.uk/issues/38346/supplements.
71. Ibid.
72. S. K. Roskill, *The War at Sea 1939–1945*, vol. 2, *The Period of Balance* (London: Her Majesty's Stationery Office, 1956), 13–14.
73. Collins, dispatch, March 17, 1942, LDNGZT.
74. Morison, *History of United States Naval Operations in World War II*, vol. 3, 340–41.
75. Gill, *Royal Australian Navy 1939–1942*, 620–22.
76. Roskill, *The War at Sea 1939–1945*, vol. 2, 17.
77. Gill, *Royal Australian Navy 1939–1942*, 629–30.
78. "Commonwealth Government to U.K. Dominions Office, 06/01/1942," doc. 255, *DOAFP, VV*: July 1941–June 1942, 415.
79. "Mr John Curtin, Prime Minister, to Mr Winston Churchill, U.K. Prime Minister, 23/01/1942," doc. 294, *DOAFP, VV*: July 1941–June 1942, 463–66; "Mr R. G. Casey, Minister to the United States, to Department of External Affairs, 24/01/1942," doc. 299, *DOAFP, VV*: July 1941–June 1942, 471–72.
80. "Mr John Curtin, Prime Minister, to General Sir Archibald Wavell, Allied Supreme Commander of the A.B.D.A. Area, 12/02/1942," doc. 329, *DOAFP, VV*: July 1941–June 1942, 516–17; "Mr John Curtin, Prime Minister, to Sir Earle Page, Special Representative to the United Kingdom, 13/02/1942," doc. 332, *DOAFP, VV*: July 1941–June 1942, 519–20.

81. "Mr John Curtin, Prime Minister, to Lord Cranborne, U.K. Secretary of State for Dominion Affairs, 17/02/1942," doc. 336, *DOAFP, VV*: July 1941–June 1942, 527–28.
82. Gill, *Royal Australian Navy 1939–1942*, 626–27.
83. "Sir Earle Page, Special Representative to the United Kingdom, to Mr John Curtin, Prime Minister, 19/02/1942," doc. 347, *DOAFP, VV*: July 1941–June 1942, 542.
84. "Mr Clement Attlee, U.K. Secretary of State for Dominion Affairs, to Mr John Curtin, Prime Minister, 22/02/1942," doc. 362, *DOAFP, VV*: July 1941–June 1942, 561.
85. "Mr John Curtin, Prime Minister, to Mr Clement Attlee, U.K. Secretary of State for Dominion Affairs, 23/02/1942," doc. 366, *DOAFP, VV*: July 1941–June 1942, 564.
86. "Mr Clement Attlee, U.K. Secretary of State for Dominion Affairs, to Mr John Curtin, Prime Minister, 23/02/1942," doc. 367, *DOAFP, VV*: July 1941–June 1942, 565.
87. "Mr John Curtin, Prime Minister, to Mr Clement Attlee, U.K. Secretary of State for Dominion Affairs, 02/03/1942," doc. 385, *DOAFP, VV*: July 1941–June 1942, 593.
88. Gill, *Royal Australian Navy 1939–1942*, 632.
89. "Mr Winston Churchill, Prime Minister, to Mr John Curtin, Prime Minister, 19/01/1942," doc. 385, *DOAFP, VV*: July 1941–June 1942, 445–47.
90. J. Somerville, "Report of Proceedings of Eastern Fleet from 29th March to 13th April 1942," office of the British naval commander in chief, Eastern Fleet, April 18, 1942, number 4, S/4682, http://www.naval-history.net/xDKWD-EF1942.
91. Churchill, *The Hinge of Fate*, 156.
92. Somerville, "Report of Proceedings of Eastern Fleet from 29th March to 13th April 1942," S/4682.
93. Ibid.
94. Ibid.
95. "Chiefs-of-Staff Weekly Review (hereafter COSWR) (No. 136) of the Naval, Military and Air Situation from 0700 April 2nd to 0700 April 9th, 1942," TNA (UK): CAB/66/27/6-0001.
96. M. Okumiya, J. Horikoshi, and M. Caidin, *Zero! The Story of Japan's Air War in the Pacific: 1947–45*. New York: Ballatine Books, 1973, 90–92; van der Vat, *The Pacific Campaign*, 135.
97. Roskill, *The War at Sea 1939–1945*, vol. 2, 27.
98. Somerville, "Report of Proceedings of Eastern Fleet from 29th March to 13th April 1942," S/4682.
99. The sixth, *Kaga*, was undergoing maintenance in Japan.
100. COSWR No. 136, April 2, 1942–April 9, 1942, CAB/66/27/6-0001.
101. Gillison, *Royal Australian Air Force 1939–1942*, 499–500.
102. Roskill, *The War at Sea 1939–1945*, vol. 2, 28.
103. Ibid.
104. "Mr Clement Attlee, U.K. Secretary of State for Dominion Affairs, to Mr John Curtin, Prime Minister, 15/04/1942," doc. 466, *DOAFP, VV*: July 1941–June 1942, 719.
105. "Mr John Curtin, Prime Minister, to Mr Clement Attlee, U.K. Secretary of State for Dominion Affairs, 17/04/1942," doc. 467, *DOAFP, VV*: July 1941–June 1942, 719–20.
106. "Dr H. V. Evatt, Minister for External Affairs, to Mr John Curtin, Prime Minister, 28/05/1942," doc. 501, *DOAFP, VV*: July 1941–June 1942, 795–97.
107. Macintyre, *The Battle for the Pacific*, 165.

Chapter 9. The Pacific: December 1941–December 1942

Epigraph: *Melbourne Herald*, December 27, 1941, doc. 253, in Meaney, *Australia and the World*, 472–73.

1. Morison, *History of United States Naval Operations in World War II*, vol. 3, 230–31.
2. Ibid., 171–72.
3. van der Vat, *The Pacific Campaign*, 28–29.
4. Morison, *History of United States Naval Operations in World War II*, vol. 3, 251–52.
5. Ibid, 175–176.
6. *Sydney Morning Herald*, December 9, 1941, https://trove.nla.gov.au/newspaper/article/17777931.
7. *Courier Mail*, December 9, 1941, https://trove.nla.gov.au/newspaper/article/41922931.
8. *Sydney Morning Herald*, December 9, 1941.
9. Parkin and Lee, *Great White Fleet to Coral Sea*, 132–33; Frame, *Pacific Partners*, 40–41.
10. "Dr H. V. Evatt, Minister for External Affairs, to Mr R. G. Casey, Minister to the United States, 13/12/1941," doc. 188, *DOAFP, VV*: July 1941–June 1942, 305–6; "Mr John Curtin, Prime Minister, to Mr R. G. Casey, Minister to the United States, 23/12/1941," doc. 214, *DOAFP, VV*: July 1941–June 1942, 341–42.
11. "Mr R. G. Casey, Minister to the United States, to Mr John Curtin, Prime Minister, and to Dr H. V. Evatt, Minister for External Affairs, 14/12/1941," doc. 192, *DOAFP, VV*: July 1941–June 1942, 310–12; "Mr R. G. Casey, Minister to the United States, to Mr John Curtin, Prime Minister, and to Dr H. V. Evatt, Minister for External Affairs, 22/12/1941," doc. 213, *DOAFP, VV*: July 1941–June 1942, 339–40; "Dr H. V. Evatt, Minister for External Affairs, to Mr R. G. Casey, Minister to the United States, 25/12/1941," doc. 224, *DOAFP, VV*: July 1941–June 1942, 359–60.
12. "Mr R. G. Casey, Minister to the United States, to Department of External Affairs, 20/12/1941," doc. 210, *DOAFP, VV*: July 1941–June 1942, 334; "Mr R. G. Casey, Minister to the United States, to Department of External Affairs, 27/12/1941," doc. 230, *DOAFP, VV*: July 1941–June 1942, 369–70; "Mr R. G. Casey, Minister to the United States, to Mr John Curtin, Prime Minister, and to Dr H. V. Evatt, Minister for External Affairs, 17/12/1942," doc. 204, *DOAFP, VV*: July 1941–June 1942, 325–26.
13. "Mr R. G. Casey, Minister to the United States, to Department of External Affairs, 27/12/1941."
14. Horner, *Defence Supremo*, 130.
15. "Mr R. G. Casey, Minister to the United States, to Mr John Curtin, Prime Minister, and to Dr H. V. Evatt, Minister for External Affairs, 22/12/1942," doc. 213, *DOAFP, VV*: July 1941–June 1942, 339–40.
16. "Mr R. G. Casey, Minister to the United States, to Department of External Affairs, 17/12/1941," doc. 203, *DOAFP, VV*: July 1941–June 1942, 323–25.
17. Morison, *History of United States Naval Operations in World War II*, vol. 3, 255–57; I. Cowman, "Forging an Alliance? The American Naval Commitment to the South Pacific, 1940–42," in Stevens, *Royal Australian Navy in World War II*, 32–33.
18. Morison, *History of United States Naval Operations in World War II*, vol. 3, 259–68; Firkins, *Of Nautilus and Eagles*, 152.

19. Agawa, *The Reluctant Admiral*, 300.
20. Clark, *The Encyclopaedia of Australia's Battles*, 199–200.
21. Morison, *History of United States Naval Operations in World War II*, vol. 3, 387.
22. *Sydney Morning Herald*, January 26, 1942, https://trove.nla.gov.au/newspaper/article/17785014.
23. "Department of External Affairs to Mr R. G. Casey, Minister to the United States, 02/02/1942," doc. 314, *DOAFP, VV*: July 1941–June 1942, 490.
24. "Mr R. G. Casey, Minister to the United States, to Department of External Affairs, 02/02/1942," doc. 315, *DOAFP, VV*: July 1941–June 1942, 491–93; "War Cabinet Submission by Dr H. V. Evatt, Minister for External Affairs, and Mr J. B. Chifley, Treasurer, 10/02/1942," doc. 324, *DOAFP, VV*: July 1941–June 1942, 504–9.
25. "Department of External Affairs to Mr R. G. Casey, Minister to the United States, 10/02/1942," doc. 325, *DOAFP, VV*: July 1941–June 1942, 510–13; "Mr John Curtin, Prime Minister, to Dr H. V. Evatt, Minister for External Affairs (in Washington), 07/04/1942," doc. 457, *DOAFP, VV*: July 1941–June 1942, 704–7; "Mr J. B. Brigden, Financial Counsellor at the Legation in Washington, to Department of External Affairs, 03/05/1942," doc. 480, *DOAFP, VV*: July 1941–June 1942, 743–45.
26. "Mr R. G. Casey, Minister to the United States, to Department of External Affairs, 17/02/1942," doc. 340, *DOAFP, VV*: July 1941–June 1942, 533–34.
27. Cowman, "Forging an Alliance?" 35.
28. "Mr R. G. Casey, Minister to the United States, to Mr John Curtin, Prime Minister, 21/02/1942," doc. 355, *DOAFP, VV*: July 1941–June 1942, 549–50; M. Fraser, with C. Roberts, *Dangerous Allies*, 76.
29. "Mr R. G. Casey, Minister to the United States, to Mr John Curtin, Prime Minister, 22/02/1942," doc. 361, *DOAFP, VV*: July 1941–June 1942, 559–60.
30. "Dr H. V. Evatt, Minister for External Affairs, to Mr John Curtin, Prime Minister, 21/03/1942," doc. 433, *DOAFP, VV*: July 1941–June 1942, 668–69.
31. "Dr H. V. Evatt, Minister for External Affairs, to Mr John Curtin, Prime Minister, 01/04/1942," doc. 451, *DOAFP, VV*: July 1941–June 1942, 696–97.
32. "Dr H. V. Evatt, Minister for External Affairs, to Mr John Curtin, Prime Minister, 01/04/1942," doc. 469, *DOAFP, VV*: July 1941–June 1942, 722–25.
33. Van der Vat, *The Pacific Campaign*, 168.
34. Horner, *Defence Supremo*, 142.
35. "Dr H. V. Evatt, Minister for External Affairs, to Mr John Curtin, Prime Minister, 07/04/1942," doc. 458, *DOAFP, VV*: July 1941–June 1942, 707–8.
36. Horner, *Defence Supremo*, 146.
37. "Mr R. G. Casey, Minister to the United States, to the Department of External Affairs, 12/03/1942," doc. 407, *DOAFP, VV*: July 1941–June 1942, 632–33.
38. P. Burns, *The Brisbane Line Controversy: Political Opportunism versus National Security, 1942–45* (Sydney: Allen & Unwin, 1998), 102.
39. Ibid., 103.
40. "Mr John Curtin, Prime Minister, to Dr H. V. Evatt, Minister for External Affairs (in Washington), 28/04/1942," doc. 475, *DOAFP, VV*: July 1941–June 1942, 733–34.
41. Van der Vat, *The Pacific Campaign*, 172; Cowman, "Forging an Alliance?" 41.
42. S. E. Morison, *History of United States Naval Operations in World War II*, vol. 4, *Coral Sea, Midway and Submarine Actions May 1942–August 1942* (Boston: Little, Brown and Company, 1949), 19–20.

43. Ibid., 17–18.
44. Frame, *Pacific Partners*, 51–52.
45. Macintyre, *The Battle for the Pacific*, 55.
46. Morison, *History of United States Naval Operations in World War II*, vol. 4, 32.
47. Frame, *Pacific Partners*, 55.
48. Macintyre, *The Battle for the Pacific*, 57–58.
49. Firkins, *Of Nautilus and Eagles*, 154–55.
50. Macintyre, *The Battle for the Pacific*, 59.
51. Morison, *History of United States Naval Operations in World War II*, vol. 4, 50–52.
52. Ibid., 56.
53. Macintyre, *The Battle for the Pacific*, 64; Morison, *History of United States Naval Operations in World War II*, vol. 4, 61.
54. *Melbourne Age*, May 15, 1942, https://trove.nla.gov.au/newspaper/article/206818488.
55. "Mr John Curtin, Prime Minister, to Dr H. V. Evatt, Minister for External Affairs (in London), 13/05/1942," doc. 487, *DOAFP, VV*: July 1941–June 1942, 757.
56. Ibid., 760.
57. "Dr H. V. Evatt, Minister for External Affairs, to Mr John Curtin, Prime Minister, 28/05/1942," doc. 469, *DOAFP, VV*: July 1941–June 1942, 793.
58. D. Jenkins, *Battle Surface! Japan's Submarine War Against Australia* (Sydney: Random House, 1992), 254–55.
59. Ibid., 250.
60. Stanley, *Invading Australia: Japan and the Battle for Australia, 1942*, 155.
61. Gillison, *Royal Australian Air Force 1939–42*, 532; Agawa, *The Reluctant Admiral*, 294.
62. Agawa, *The Reluctant Admiral*, 304.
63. Morison, *History of United States Naval Operations in World War II*, vol. 4, 13.
64. Van der Vat, *The Pacific Campaign*, 180.
65. Morison, *History of United States Naval Operations in World War II*, vol. 4, 90–92; Van der Vat, *The Pacific Campaign*, 180–81.
66. Morison, *History of United States Naval Operations in World War II*, vol. 4, 87–89.
67. Agawa, *The Reluctant Admiral*, 313.
68. Morison, *History of United States Naval Operations in World War II*, vol. 4, 99–100.
69. Van der Vat, *The Pacific Campaign*, 184.
70. Morison, *History of United States Naval Operations in World War II*, vol. IV, 107.
71. Van der Vat, *The Pacific Campaign*, 188.
72. Macintyre, *The Battle for the Pacific*, 67–68.
73. Agawa, *The Reluctant Admiral*, 320.
74. Macintyre, *The Battle for the Pacific*, 68.
75. *Melbourne Age*, June 15, 1942, https://trove.nla.gov.au/newspaper/article/206822776.
76. Stanley, *Invading Australia: Japan and the Battle for Australia, 1942*, 181.
77. Ibid., 166.
78. "Dr H. V. Evatt, Minister for External Affairs, to Mr John Curtin, Prime Minister, 10/06/1942," doc. 523, *DOAFP, VV*: July 1941–June 1942, 841.
79. Van der Vat, *The Pacific Campaign*, 200; Cowman, "Forging an Alliance?" 40–41.
80. S. E. Morison, *History of United States Naval Operations in World War II*, vol. 5: *The Struggle for Guadalcanal August 1942–February 1943* (Boston: Little, Brown and Company, 1966), 12.

81. Burns, *The Brisbane Line Controversy*, 99–100.
82. Horner, *Defence Supremo*, 150.
83. P. Brune, *A Bastard of a Place: The Australians in Papua* (Sydney: Allen & Unwin, 2004), 99.
84. Ibid., 263.
85. Stanley, *Invading Australia*, 187.
86. M. McKernan, *The Strength of a Nation: Six Years of Australians Fighting for the Nation and Defending the Homefront in WWII* (Sydney: Allen & Unwin, 2008), 425–27.
87. Gillison, *Royal Australian Air Force 1939–42*, 695.
88. Morison, *History of United States Naval Operations in World War II*, vol. 5, 12.
89. Taylor, *The Second World War*, 168.
90. Macintyre, *The Battle for the Pacific*, 72.
91. Ibid., 73.
92. Morison, *History of United States Naval Operations in World War II*, vol. 5, 18.
93. B. Loxton, "Savo in Retrospect," in Stevens, *Royal Australian Navy in World War II*, 80.
94. Morison, *History of United States Naval Operations in World War II*, vol. 5, 31; Loxton, "Savo in Retrospect," 81.
95. Van der Vat, *The Pacific Campaign*, 212.
96. Macintyre, *The Battle for the Pacific*, 79–80.
97. Ibid., 83.
98. Van der Vat, *The Pacific Campaign*, 214.
99. Macintyre, *The Battle for the Pacific*, 88; Loxton, "Savo in Retrospect," 84–86.
100. Morison, *History of United States Naval Operations in World War II*, vol. 4, 110.
101. Morison, *History of United States Naval Operations in World War II*, vol. 5, 71–73.
102. Macintyre, *The Battle for the Pacific*, 90.
103. Van der Vat, *The Pacific Campaign*, 220.
104. Morison, *History of United States Naval Operations in World War II*, vol. 5, 97–99; Macintyre, *The Battle for the Pacific*, 95.
105. Morison, *History of United States Naval Operations in World War II*, vol. 5, 134–36.
106. Macintyre, *The Battle for the Pacific*, 96.
107. Van der Vat, *The Pacific Campaign*, 227–28.
108. Macintyre, *The Battle for the Pacific*, 105.
109. "Evatt to [Admiral] King, 14/08/1942," doc. 24 in *Documents on Australian Foreign Policy 1937–49*, vol. 6, July 1942–December 1943 (hereafter *DOAFP, VVI: July 1942–December 1943*), ed. W. J. Hudson and H. J. W. Stokes (Canberra: Australian Government Publishing Service, 1980), 46–47.
110. "Curtin to Churchill, 25/08/1942," doc. 27, *DOAFP, VVI*: July 1942–December 1943, 57–58; "Churchill to Curtin, 08/09/1942," doc. 41, *DOAFP, VVI*: July 1942–December 1943, 84.
111. "Dixon to Curtin, 17/09/1942," doc. 48, *DOAFP, VVI*: July 1942–December 1943, 103.
112. "Appreciation by the Chiefs of Staff on the Defence of Australia, 30/09/1942," doc. 53, *DOAFP, VVI*: July 1942–December 1943, 119–22.
113. Morison, *History of United States Naval Operations in World War II*, vol. 5, 183.
114. Macintyre, *The Battle for the Pacific*, 106.
115. Morison, *History of United States Naval Operations in World War II*, vol. 5, 190–93, 203.

116. Macintyre, *The Battle for the Pacific*, 107–110.
117. Morison, *History of United States Naval Operations in World War II*, vol. 5, 237.
118. Ibid., 252; Macintyre, *The Battle for the Pacific*, 123.
119. Van der Vat, *The Pacific Campaign*, 236.
120. Ibid.
121. Morison, *History of United States Naval Operations in World War II*, vol. 5, 277–79.
122. Macintyre, *The Battle for the Pacific*, 137–39.
123. Morison, *History of United States Naval Operations in World War II*, vol. 5, 370–71.

Chapter 10. Threats and Interests: January 1919–January 1943
1. Stanley, *Invading Australia*, 8–9.

Bibliography

Note: Archival sources, reports, memoranda, and correspondence are listed in chronological order.

Primary Sources: Public Papers

AUSTRALIAN DEPARTMENT OF DEFENCE
"Policy—Royal Australian Air Force." Air Council Memorandum April 6, 1922. Department of Defence MS1538, series 19, folder 5.
"General Minute Covering the Defence Policy of the Various Branches of the Service." Letter, Minister for Defence to Prime Minister, April 7, 1922. Department of Defence MS1538, series 19, folder 5.

NATIONAL ARCHIVES OF AUSTRALIA
Department of Defence Association 1906–1935: Secret and Confidential Correspondence Files. Multiple number series, 1906–1935: AA 1855/1/165; multiple number series, 1906–1935: AA 1855/1/181; multiple number series, 1906–1935: AA 1877/5/144.
Department of Defence/Navy Secret and Confidential Correspondence, 1923–1950: AA MP1185/8, file 1846/4/25.

REPORTS AND CORRESPONDENCE PERTAINING TO THE DEFENSE OF AUSTRALIA, 1913–1918
"Report on the Naval Defences of Australia." Commander W. H. Thring, R.A.N. July 5, 1913: AA (VICRO) MP1587/1 184J.
Office of the Governor General, General Correspondence 1912–1927. "War 1914–15. Expeditions to the Pacific and Pacific Generally." 1914–1915: AA CP 78/23 (14/89/10).
"Captured German Possessions in the Pacific 1915–1920." External Affairs H & T 1916 Correspondence Files: AA CRS A1, item 20/7685.
Marshall and Caroline Islands (2): AA CRS 19981.
"Australian Naval Defence." 1915/054: AA MP1049/1.
"Australia's Peril and Australia's Need: Compulsory Training for Home Defence; Voluntary Enlistment for Empire Service." Memorandum, J. H. Catts, May 29, 1916: AA CRS A1, item 16/15272.
External Affairs (2), Correspondence Files, Alphabetical Series: "Imperial Defence-Naval," 1918–1920: AA CRS A981, item defense 350, part 1.
Memorandum, Special Commissioner in the East (Government of New South Wales). November 1, 1916: NAA A981 9 JAP 38 PT.1.

REPORTS AND CORRESPONDENCE PERTAINING TO THE DEFENSE OF AUSTRALIA, 1919–1936
External Affairs (2), Correspondence Files, Alphabetical Series: "Imperial Defence-Naval," 1918–1920: AA CRS A981, item defense 350, part 1.
Memorandum, Special Commissioner in the East (Government of New South Wales), November 1, 1916: NAA A981 9 JAP 38 PT.1.
"Naval Defence." Statement by the Minister for the Navy Explanatory of the Navy Estimates, 1920–1921, September 23, 1920. External Affairs (2),

Correspondence Files, Alphabetical Series: "Imperial Defence-Naval," 1918–1920: AA CRS A981, item defense 350, part 2.
"Empire Naval Policy and Co-Operation." Admiralty Outline, February 1921. External Affairs (2), Correspondence Files, Alphabetical Series: "Imperial Defence-Naval," 1918–1920: AA CRS A981, item defense 350, part 2.
"Singapore—Development as a Naval Base." Memorandum (No. 501M) by the Oversea Sub-Committee of the Committee of Imperial Defence, June 7, 1921. Prime Minister's Department. Correspondence and other papers relating to the Imperial and Economic Conferences—"Imperial Conference 1921": AA CD 103/3, vol. 2.
"Empire Naval Policy." Summary of Admiralty Recommendations, July 11, 1921. Prime Minister's Department. Correspondence and other papers relating to the Imperial and Economic Conferences—"Imperial Conference 1921": AA CD 103/3, vol. 2.
Cablegram, Senator G. Pearce to Prime Minister W. M. Hughes, December 5, 1921. External Affairs Department, Correspondence Files, Alphabetical Series: "Washington Disarmament Conference" 1921–1922: AA CRS A981, item disarmament 1, part 2.
"Naval Estimates 1922/23." Minute Paper and Attachments, Department of the Navy, April 7, 1922: AA MP 1049/1 27/0307.
Cablegram, Prime Minister of Australia to Prime Minister of Great Britain, September 20, 1922. Governor General's Office; Copies of Telegrams Exchanged by the Governor-General and the Secretary of State in Connection with the "Chanak Incident" Sept 1922—Feb 1923 "Near East Crisis 1922. Turkish Aggression Terminating in Treaty of Lausarne" 1922–1923: AA CP78/32 item 1922–1923.
R. Williams. "Memorandum regarding the Air Force of Australia." April 21, 1924: AA MP 826/1/10.
"Summary of Proceedings: General Meeting of the Council of Defence," July 8, 1929: AA MP 1049/9, file 1851/4/17.
"Summary of Proceedings: General Meeting of the Council of Defence," November 12, 1929: AA MP 1049/9, file 1851/4/17.
"Estimates of Expenditure, 1930/31." Minutes of Defence Committee Meeting, April 11, 1930. Department of External Affairs II, Correspondence file. "Imperial Conference 1930—Memoranda for delegates—Foreign policy and defence," 1930: AA CRS A981, item imperial 126.
"Draft Disarmament Convention." Memorandum by Chief of the General Staff, October 26, 1931: AA MP 729/2, File 1846/1/26.
"The Australian Eastern Mission, 1934: Report of the Right Honourable J. G. Latham, Leader of the Mission." Prime Minister's Department; Papers Collected in the Offices of the Secretary and the Prime Minister: "[Reports of the Australian Eastern Mission]" 1934: AA CP209/1 item 10.
"Notes on the Naval Disarmament Conference, 1935–36." Chief of Naval Staff to Minister of Defence, January 23, 1936: AA MP1049/9, file 1846/4/48.
"Secret Admiralty Note on Australian Naval Requirements: Appendix 'B', Estimates 1935/36 and New Programme Proposals," May 22, 1936. General Correspondence 1923–50: AA MP1049/9, file 1855/2/41.

COMMONWEALTH PARLIAMENTARY DEBATES
CPD, 1924 session, vol. 14, August 3, 1926.

BIBLIOGRAPHY

BRITISH ADMIRALTY (ADM)
"Naval Defence of the British Empire." Admiralty Memorandum for the War Cabinet, May 17, 1918: ADM 116/1815 XC169040.
Letter, Joseph Cook to Sir Eric Geddes, November 16, 1918: ADM 116/1815 XC169040.
"Proposed Visit of Lord Jellicoe to the Dominions and India to Advise on Naval Matters." Admiralty Memorandum for War Cabinet, December 17, 1918: ADM 116/1815 XC169040.
"Instructions for Lord Jellicoe," December 23, 1918: ADM 116/1815 XC169040.
"Imperial Naval Defence." Admiralty Memorandum, July 9, 1919. ADM 116/3104 169081.
"Lord Jellicoe's Report to the Commonwealth Government of Australia." Report to First Lord October 31, 1919: ADM 116/1815 XC 169040.
Admiralty Minute, December 5, 1919: ADM 116/1815 XC 169040.
"Naval Mission to India and the Dominions." General Remarks, Lord Jellicoe to Secretary of the Admiralty, February 3, 1920: ADM 116/1815 XC 169040.
Report of the Conference held on board H.M.S. "Hawkins" at Penang between the Commanders-in-Chief of the China, East Indies and Australia Stations, from March 7, 1921 onwards, March 13, 1921: ADM 116/3100 169081.

BRITISH FOREIGN OFFICE
Memoranda regarding Japanese attitudes in Pacific 1916: FO 371 2693 XC 16464.

THE NATIONAL ARCHIVES/PUBLIC RECORDS OFFICE (UNITED KINGDOM) (CAB)
"Notes of a Meeting of Prime Ministers of the Empire," July 19, 1921: CAB 32/4 169473.
"Notes of a Meeting of Prime Ministers of the Empire," July 20, 1921: CAB 32/4 169473.
"Notes of a Meeting of Prime Ministers of the Empire," July 27, 1921: CAB 32/4 169473.
"Development of Singapore as a Naval Base." Conclusion, Standing Defence Sub-Committee of the Committee of Imperial Defence, June 13, 1921: CAB/24/125-0040.
Minutes, Cabinet Meeting, June 16, 1921: CAB/23/26-0005.
W. S. Churchill. "Report of Committee to Examine Part 1 (Defence Departments) of the Report of the Geddes Committee on National Expenditure." Memorandum, February 4, 1922: CAB/24/132-0091.
"Report of the Committee on National Expenditure." Cabinet Conclusions, February 17, 1922: CAB/23/29-0011.
"Singapore–Proposed Naval Base." Cabinet Memorandum, February 15, 1923: CAB/24/159-0018.
"The Relations of the Navy and the Air Force." Cabinet Conclusions, July 31, 1923: CAB/23/46-0015.
"Report of a Sub-Committee on National and Imperial Defence," November 15, 1923: CAB/24/162-0061.
"Singapore Naval Base: Copy of Telegrams from the Dominion Governments," March 12, 1924: CAB/24/165-0082.
"Singapore Naval Base: Copy of Telegrams from the Governments of Australia, New Zealand, and the Straits Settlements Regarding the Singapore Naval Base," December 9, 1924: CAB/24/169-0035.

W. S. Churchill. "Navy Estimates 1925–1926." Cabinet Memorandum, January 29, 1925: CAB/24/171-0039.
W. Bridgeman. "Navy Estimates." Memorandum by the First Lord of the Admiralty, February 5, 1925: CAB/24/171-0068.
"The Singapore Base: Memorandum by the Chairman of the Committee of Imperial Defence," February 27, 1925: CAB/24/172-0024.
Lord Birkenhead. "Report on Cruisers." Naval Programme Committee, December 14, 1927: CAB/24/190-0005.
"Singapore: Scale of Attack and Scale of Defence." Interim Report by the Chiefs-of-Staff Sub-Committee, March 28, 1928: CAB/24/194-0013.
"The Singapore Base: The Defences and Development of the Naval Base." Draft Minutes, 23rd meeting of the Committee of Imperial Defence, December 13, 1928: CAB/24/199-0050.
"The Fuller Employment of Air Power in Imperial Defence 1919–1929." Memorandum by the Chief of the Air Staff, November 1, 1929: CAB/24/207-0033.
"Fighting Services Committee: Policy as Regards the Singapore Base." Memoranda, October 22, 1929: CAB/24/206-0039.
W. W. Fisher and G. C. Upcott. "Navy Estimates 1930." Joint Reply by Admiralty-Treasury on Navy Estimates, December 13, 1929: CAB/24/209-0014.
P. Snowden. "Memorandum by Treasury on Financial Aspects of the Naval Conference," December 16, 1929: CAB/24/209-0012.
"The Singapore Base." Report, Committee of the Fighting Services, October 14, 1930: CAB/24/215-0044.
"Limitation of Naval Armaments." Memorandum by the First Lord of the Admiralty, September 30, 1931: CAB/24/223-0053.
"Imperial Defence Policy: The Annual Review by the Chiefs-of-Staff Sub-Committee." Memorandum, March 17, 1932: CAB/24/229-0005.
"Coast Defence." Report of Sub-Committee, Committee of Imperial Defence, July 11, 1932: CAB/24/231-0039.
"The Far East–Chino-Japanese Dispute." Cabinet Conclusions, February 27, 1933: CAB/23/75-0012.
"The Situation in the Far East." Memorandum, Committee of Imperial Defence, May 17, 1933: CAB/24/239-0045.
"Imperial Defence Policy: Annual Review 1933." Memorandum Chiefs-of-Staff Sub-Committee, November 10, 1933: CAB/24/244-0014.
"Situation in the Far East." Cabinet Memorandum, March 15, 1934: CAB/24/248-0012.
"Imperial Defence Policy." Interim Report Ministerial Committee on Disarmament Dealing with Air Defence, July 16, 1934: CAB/24/250-0018.
"Report by Sir Maurice Hankey, Secretary to the Committee of Imperial Defence, on Certain Aspects of Australian Defence," November 15, 1934. PRO PREM1/174 XC 17793. TNA (UK): CAB/21/386.
"Singapore Defences." Sub-Committee on Defence Policy and Requirements, Committee of Imperial Defence, July 19, 1935: CAB/24/256.
"'Status Quo' in the Pacific: Article 19 of the Washington Treaty." Memorandum by the Minister for League of Nations Affairs, December 7, 1935: CAB/24/257-0058.
"The Importance of Anglo-Japanese Friendship." Memorandum Secretary of State for War, January 11, 1936: CAB/24/259-0012.
S. Baldwin. "Statement Relating to Defence." P.M. Statement to the House of Commons, March 3, 1936: CAB/24/260-0029.

Viscount Swindon. "Plan for Further Expansion of the First-Line Strength of the
    Royal Air Force." Memorandum by the Secretary of State for Air, January 14,
    1937: CAB/24/267-0019.
T. Inskip. "Progress in Defence Requirements." Memorandum by the Minister for
    the Co-ordination of Defence, February 1, 1937: CAB/24/267-0041.
"Questions Raised by the Australian Delegation [1937 Imperial Conference]." Report
    by Chiefs-of-Staff Sub-Committee, June 9, 1937: CAB/21/2525 XC17491.
"Far Eastern Policy." Report by the British Chiefs-of-Staff to the War Cabinet, July
    27, 1940. CAB/66/10/20-0001.
"The Situation in the Far East in the Event of Japanese Intervention against Us."
    Cabinet Memorandum, July 31, 1940: CAB/66/10/33-0001.
"Chiefs-of-Staff Weekly Review (No. 136) of the Naval, Military and Air Situation
    from 0700 April 2nd to 0700 April 9th, 1942." CAB/66/27/6-0001.

UNITED STATES GOVERNMENT: DEPARTMENT OF STATE
"Visit of American Fleet." Report, E. M. Lawton, American Consul-General, to the
    Secretary of State, Washington, June 22, 1925. Department of State, Division
    of Western European Affairs, Index Bureau 811.3347/87.
"Visit of American Fleet." Report, E. M. Lawton, American Consul-General, to the
    Secretary of State, Washington July 14, 1925. Department of State, Division
    of Western European Affairs, Index Bureau 811.3347/91.
"Visit of American Fleet." Report, E. M. Lawton, American Consul-General, to
    the Secretary of State, Washington, August 2, 1925. Department of State,
    Division of Western European Affairs, Index Bureau 811.3347/92.
"Visit of American Fleet." Report, Norman L. Anderson, U.S. Consul (Melbourne),
    to the Secretary of State, Washington, August 12, 1925. Department of State,
    Division of Western European Affairs, Index Bureau 811.3347/95.

UNITED STATES NAVY
"Cruise to Australia—New Zealand: 1 July to 26 September, 1925, by a Detachment
    of the U.S. Fleet." Memorandum, Commander in Chief to Chief of Naval
    Operations. United States Fleet, USS Seattle Flagship, September 26, 1925.
    CinC File No C-34-21.

Primary Sources: Private Papers
Lloyd George Papers, House of Lords Record Office, F/25/2/5.
Long Papers 947/716/3.
Pearce Papers (unpublished). Australian War Memorial 7/106.

Published Primary Sources (Books)
"Albatross." *Japan and the Defence of Australia*. Melbourne: Robertson & Mullens,
    1935.
Beatty, David. "To His Wife." In *The Beatty Papers: Selections from the Private
    and Official Correspondence of Admiral of the Fleet Earl Beatty*, volume 2,
    1916–1927, edited by B. Ranft. Aldershot: Scolar Press for the Navy Records
    Society, 1995.
Churchill, W. S. *The Second World War*. Vol. 1, *The Gathering Storm*. London:
    Cassell, 1948.
———. *The Second World War*. Vol. 3, *The Grand Alliance*. London: Penguin, 1985.
———. *The Second World War*. Vol. 4, *The Hinge of Fate*. London: Cassell & Co.,
    1951.

Crawley, F. *A Documentary History of Australia. Vol. 2, 1841–1874*. Melbourne: Thomas Nelson, 1980.

"Dimensions and Particulars of British and Foreign Warships." In *Brassey's Naval Annual 1936*, edited by C. N. Robinson. London: William Clowes, 1936.

Goldstein, D. M., and K. V. Dillon, eds. *The Pacific War Papers: Japanese Documents of World War II*. Dulles, VA: Potomac Books, 2004.

Hudson, W. J., and H. J. W. Stokes, eds. *Documents on Australian Foreign Policy 1937–49*. Vol. 4, July 1940–June 1941. Canberra: Australian Government Publishing Service, 1980.

———. *Documents on Australian Foreign Policy 1937–49*. Vol. 5, July 1941–June 1942. Canberra: Australian Government Publishing Service, 1982.

———. *Documents on Australian Foreign Policy 1937–49*. Vol. 6, July 1942–December 1943. Canberra: Australian Government Publishing Service, 1983.

Ike, N., ed. *Japan's Decision for War: Records of the 1941 Policy Conferences*. Stanford, CA: Stanford University Press, 1967.

Imperial Conference 1923: Summary of Proceedings. Melbourne: Victorian Government Printer, 1924.

Kenway, H., H. J. W. Stokes, and P. G. Edwards, eds. *Documents on Australian Foreign Policy 1937–49*. Vol. 3, January–June 1940. Canberra: Australian Government Publishing Service, 1979.

Meaney, N. *Australia and the World: A Documentary History from the 1870s to the 1970s*. Melbourne: Longman Cheshire, 1985.

"The Navy and its Fleet Air Arm." In *Brassey's Naval and Shipping Annual 1925*, edited by A. Richardson and A. Hurd. London: W. M. Clowes & Sons, 1925.

Neale, R. G., ed. *Documents on Australian Foreign Policy 1937–49*, Vol. 1, 1937–38. Canberra: Australian Government Publishing Service, 1975.

———. *Documents on Australian Foreign Policy 1937–49*, Vol. 2, 1939. Canberra: Australian Government Publishing Service, 1976.

Raeder, E. *My Life*. Annapolis MD: Naval Institute Press, 1960.

Ranft, B., ed. *The Beatty Papers: Selections from the Private and Official Correspondence of Admiral of the Fleet Earl Beatty*, Vol. 2, *1916–1927*. Aldershot: Scolar Press for the Navy Records Society, 1995.

"Review of Relations between the United Kingdom and Japan 06/03/1937." In *Documents on Australian Foreign Policy 1937–49*. Vol. 1, 1937–38, edited by R. G. Neale, doc. 11. Canberra: Australian Government Publishing Service, 1975.

Richardson, A., and A. Hurd, eds. *Brassey's Naval and Shipping Annual 1925*. London: W. M. Clowes & Sons, 1925.

Robertson, J., and J. McCarthy, eds. *Australian War Strategy 1939–1945: A Documentary History*. St. Lucia: University of Queensland Press, 1985.

Robinson, C. N., ed. *Brassey's Naval Annual 1936*. London: William Clowes, 1936.

Robinson, C. N., and H. M. Ross, eds. *Brassey's Naval Annual 1930*. London: William Clowes, 1930.

———. *Brassey's Naval Annual 1932*. London: William Clowes, 1932.

Sansonetti, L. "The Royal Italian Navy." In *Brassey's Naval Annual 1938*, edited by H. G. Thursfield. London: W. M. Clowes, 1938.

Thursfield, H. G., ed. *Brassey's Naval Annual 1938*. London: W. M. Clowes, 1938.

Tsuji, M. *Singapore—The Japanese Version*. Sydney: Ure Smith, 1960.

BIBLIOGRAPHY

Primary Sources: Internet

TROVE (NATIONAL LIBRARY OF AUSTRALIA)
Brisbane Courier Mail, December 9, 1941. https://trove.nla.gov.au/newspaper/article/41922931.
Brisbane Daily Mail, March 21, 1924. https://trove.nla.gov.au/newspaper/article/217619948.
Hobart World, March 22, 1924. https://trove.nla.gov.au/newspaper/article/190366636.
Hobart World, March 24, 1924. https://trove.nla.gov.au/newspaper/article/190366781.
Melbourne Age, May 15, 1942. https://trove.nla.gov.au/newspaper/article/206818488.
Melbourne Age, June 15, 1942. https://trove.nla.gov.au/newspaper/article/206822776.
Melbourne Argus, December 11, 1941. https://trove.nla.gov.au/newspaper/article/8221886.
Newcastle Morning Herald and Miner's Advocate, December 11, 1941. https://trove.nla.gov.au/newspaper/article/134076325.
Perth Call, March 7, 1924. https://trove.nla.gov.au/newspaper/article/210904811.
Sydney Daily Telegraph, December 12, 1941. https://trove.nla.gov.au/newspaper/article/248711119.
Sydney Morning Herald, December 9, 1941. https://trove.nla.gov.au/newspaper/article/17777931.
Sydney Morning Herald, January 26, 1942. https://trove.nla.gov.au/newspaper/article/17785014.
Sydney Morning Herald, February 17, 1942. https://trove.nla.gov.au/newspaper/article/17788305?searchTerm=Singapore.
Sydney Morning Herald, February 20, 1942. https://trove.nla.gov.au/newspaper/article/17788820?searchTerm=Darwin.
Wellington Times, December 11, 1941. https://trove.nla.gov.au/newspaper/article/141623436.
The West Australian, March 22, 1924. https://trove.nla.gov.au/newspaper/article/31221729.

HMS HOOD ASSOCIATION
"Cruise Itinerary: Special Service Squadron." H.M.S. Hood Association. http://hmshood.com/history/empirecruise/index.htm.

NATIONAL ARCHIVES OF AUSTRALIA
"Council of Defence Meeting 24/08/1936: Summary of Proceedings." National Archives of Australia, A5954 910/14. https://recordsearch.naa.gov.au/SearchNRetrieve/Interface/ViewImage.aspx?B=652410.

"NAVWEAPS": NAVAL WEAPONS, NAVAL TECHNOLOGY, AND NAVAL REUNIONS
"International Treaty for the Limitation and Reduction of Naval Armament." http://www.navweaps.com/index_tech/tech-089_London_Treaty_1930.php.
"London Conference 1936: International Treaty for the Limitation and Reduction of Naval Armament." http://www.navweaps.com/index_tech/tech-089_London_Treaty_1936.php.
Somerville, J. "Report of Proceedings of Eastern Fleet from 29th March to 13th April 1942." Office of the British Naval Commander-in-Chief, Eastern Fleet, April 18, 1942, Number 4. S/4682. http://www.naval-history.net/xDKWD-EF1942.

The London Gazette (LNDGZT)

Brooke-Popham, R. Dispatch, May 28, 1942. *Operations in the Far East from 17 October 1940 to 27 December 1941.* LDNGZT issue 38183, February 20, 1948. http://www.gazettes-online.co.uk/home.aspx?Geotype+London.

Collins, J. A. Dispatch, March 17, 1942. *Battle of the Java Sea 27 February 1942.* LDNGZT issue 38346, July 6, 1948. http://www.london.gazette.co.uk/issues/38346/supplements.

Forbes, C. Dispatch, July 17, 1940. *The Norway Campaign.* LDNGZT issue 38011, July 8, 1947. http://www.london.gazette.co.uk/Issues/3801/supplements.

Layton, D. Dispatch, December 17, 1941. *Loss of H.M. Ships Prince of Wales and Repulse.* LDNGZT issue 38214, February 26, 1948. http://www.london.gazette.co.uk/issues/38214/supplements.

Maltby, P. *Report on the Air Operations during the Campaigns in Malaya and the Netherlands East Indies from 5 December 1941 to 12 March 1942.* LDNGZT issue 38216, February 26, 1948. http://www.london.gazette.co.uk/issues/38216/supplements.

Percival, A. E. Report, April 25, 1946. *Operation of Malaya Command from 8 December 1941 to 15 February 1942.* LDNGZT issue 38215, February 20, 1948. https://www.thegazette.co.uk/London/issue/38215/supplement/1250.

Ramsey, B. Dispatch, June 18, 1940. *The Evacuation of the Allied Armies from Dunkirk and Neighbouring Beaches.* LDNGZT issue 38017, June 17, 1947. http://www.london.gazette.co.uk/Issues/38017/supplements.

Published Secondary Sources (Books)

Adkins, R., and L. Adkins. *The War for All the Oceans: From Nelson at the Nile to Napoleon at Waterloo.* London: Abacus, 2006.

Agawa, H. *The Reluctant Admiral: Yamamoto and the Imperial Navy.* Tokyo: Kodansha, 1979.

Asada, S. "Japanese Admirals and the Politics of Naval Limitation: Kato Tomasaburo versus Kato Kanji." In *Naval Warfare in the Twentieth Century: Essays in Honour of Arthur Marder,* edited by G. Jordan. London: Croome Helm, 1977.

Babij, O. "The Royal Navy and the Defence of the British Empire 1928–1934." In *Far Flung Lines: Studies in Imperial Defence in Honour of Donald McKenzie Schurman,* edited by K. Neilson and G. Kennedy. London: Frank Cass, 1996.

Bacon, Admiral Sir R. H. *The Life of John Rushworth, Earl Jellicoe GCB, OM, GCVO, LLD, DCL.* London: Cassell and Company, 1936.

Barber, N. *Sinister Twilight: The Fall of Singapore.* London: Fontana Books, 1970.

Bartsch, W. H. *Doomed at the Start: American Pursuit Pilots in the Philippines, 1941–1942.* College Station: Texas A&M University Press, 1995.

Beeler, J. "Steam, Strategy and Schurman: Imperial Defence in the Post-Crimean Era, 1856–1905." In *Far Flung Lines: Studies in Imperial Defence in Honour of Donald Mackenzie Schurman,* edited by K. Neilson and G. Kennedy. London: Frank Cass, 1996.

Bennett, G. *Naval Battles of World War Two.* Barnsley, UK: Pen and Sword Military Classics, 2003.

Bolton, G. "Money: Trade, Investment, and Economic Nationalism." In *Australia's Empire,* edited by D. M. Schreuder and S. Ward. New York: Oxford University Press, 2008.

Boyle, A. *Trenchard.* London: Collins, 1962.

Braisted, W. R. "On the American Red and Red-Orange Plans, 1919–1939." In *Naval Warfare in the Twentieth Century: Essays in Honour of Arthur Marder*, edited by G. Jordan. London: Croome Helm, 1977.
Brune, P. *A Bastard of a Place: The Australians in Papua*. Sydney: Allen & Unwin, 2004.
Buell, R. L. *The Washington Conference*. New York: D. Appleton and Company, 1922.
Burns, P. *The Brisbane Line Controversy: Political Opportunism versus National Security, 1942–45*. Sydney: Allen & Unwin, 1998.
Burton, J. *Fortnight of Infamy: The Collapse of Allied Airpower West of Pearl Harbor*. Annapolis, MD: Naval Institute Press, 2016.
Bywater, H. C. *Sea Power in the Pacific: A Study of the American-Japanese Naval Problem*. London: Constable, 1921.
Carlton, M. *First Victory: 1914–HMAS Sydney's Hunt for the German Raider Emden*. North Sydney: William Heinemann, 2013.
Clark, C. *The Encyclopaedia of Australia's Battles*. Crows Nest, Australia: Allen & Unwin, 2010.
Clark, C. M. H. *A History of Australia*. Vol. 6, "*The Old Dead Tree and the Young Tree Green 1916–1935.*" Melbourne: Melbourne University Press, 1987.
Collier, B. *Japanese Aircraft of World War II*. New York: Mayflower Books, 1979.
Corrigan, G. *The Second World War: A Military History*. London: Atlantic Books, 2010.
Cowman, I. "Forging an Alliance? The American Naval Commitment to the South Pacific, 1940–42." In *Royal Australian Navy in World War II*, edited by D. Stevens. Sydney: Allen & Unwin, 1996.
Curran, J. *Curtin's Empire*. Melbourne: Cambridge University Press, 2011.
Day, D. *Menzies and Churchill at War: A Revealing Account of the 1941 Struggle for Power*. Sydney: Simon & Schuster, 2001.
———. *The Politics of War*. Sydney: Harper Collins, 2003.
Dennis, P., J. Grey, E. Morris, and J. Prior. *The Oxford Companion to Australian Military History*. Melbourne: Oxford University Press, 1995.
Farrell, B., and S. Hunter, eds. *Sixty Years On: The Fall of Singapore Revisited*. Singapore: Eastern Universities Press, 2003.
Ferris, J. "The Last Decade of British Maritime Supremacy 1919–1929." In *Far Flung Lines: Studies in Imperial Defence in Honour of Donald McKenzie Schurman*, edited by K. Neilson and G. Kennedy London: Frank Cass, 1996.
Firkins, P. *Of Nautilus and Eagles: History of the Royal Australian Navy*. Sydney: Hutchinson Group, 1983.
Frame, T. *No Pleasure Cruise: The Story of the Royal Australian Navy*. Sydney: Allen & Unwin, 2004.
———. *Pacific Partners: A History of Australian-American Naval Relations*. Sydney: Hodder & Stoughton, 1992.
Fraser, M., with C. Roberts. *Dangerous Allies*. Melbourne: Melbourne University Press, 2014.
Freudenberg, G. *Churchill and Australia*. Sydney: Pan Macmillan, 2008.
Gill, G. Hermon. *Royal Australian Navy 1939–1942*. Adelaide: Griffin Press, 1957.
Gillison, D. *Royal Australian Air Force 1939–1942*. Adelaide: Griffin Press, 1962.
Goldrick, J. "Australian Naval Policy 1939–45." In *Royal Australian Navy in World War II*, edited by D. Stevens. Sydney: Allen & Unwin, 1996.
Greene, J. *War at Sea: Pearl Harbor to Midway*. New York: Gallery Books, 1988.
Grenfell, R. *Main Fleet to Singapore: An Account of Naval Actions of the Last War*. Oxford: Oxford University Press, 1987.

Grove, E. "The Royal Australian Navy in the Mediterranean in World War II." In *Royal Australian Navy in World War II*, edited by D. Stevens. Sydney: Allen & Unwin, 1996.
Hasluck, P. *Australia in the War of 1939–45: The Government and the People 1939–41*. Canberra: Australian War Memorial, 1952.
Hezlet, A. *Aircraft and Sea Power*. London: Wyman & Co., 1970.
Hillsborough, R. *Samurai Revolution: The Dawn of Modern Japan Seen through the Eyes of the Shogun's Last Samurai*. Tokyo: Tuttle Publishing, 2014.
Hirst, J. "Empire, State, Nation." In *Australia's Empire*, edited by D. M. Schreuder and S. Ward. New York: Oxford University Press, 2008.
Horner, D. *Defence Supremo: Sir Frederick Shedden and the Making of Australian Defence Policy*. St Leonards, Australia: Allen & Unwin, 2000.
———. *High Command: Australia's Struggle for an Independent War Strategy 1939–1945*. Sydney: Allen & Unwin, 1982.
Hosoya, C. "Britain and the United States in Japan's View of the International System." In *Anglo-Japanese Alienation 1919–1952: Papers of the Anglo-Japanese Conference on the History of the Second World War*, edited by I. Nish. Cambridge: Cambridge University Press, 1982.
Hough, R. *The Longest Battle: The War at Sea 1939–45*. London: Cassell, 2003.
Ienaga, S. *Japan's Last War: World War II and the Japanese, 1931–1945*. Canberra: Australian National University Press, 1979.
Ingleton, G. C. *Matthew Flinders: Navigator and Chartmaker*. Surrey, UK: Genesis Publications, 1986.
Jenkins, D. *Battle Surface! Japan's Submarine War Against Australia*. Sydney: Random House, 1992.
Jordan, G., ed. *Naval Warfare in the Twentieth Century: Essays in Honour of Arthur Marder*. London: Croome Helm Ltd, 1977.
Judd, D. *Balfour & the British Empire*. London: Macmillan, 1968.
Kennedy, G. *Anglo-American Strategic Relations and the Far East, 1933–39*. London: Routledge, 2013.
Kennedy, L. *Pursuit: The Sinking of the Bismarck*. London: Cassell Military Paperbacks, 1974.
Kennedy, P. M. *The Rise and Fall of British Naval Mastery*. London: Macmillan Press, 1983.
Kershaw, I. *Making Friends with Hitler: Lord Londonderry and Britain's Road to War*. London: Allen Lane, 2004.
Lake, M., and H. Reynolds. *Drawing the Global Colour Line: White Men's Countries and the Question of Racial Equality*. Melbourne: Melbourne University Press, 2008.
Lambert, A. "Australia, the *Trent* Crisis of 1861 and the Strategy of Imperial Defence." In *Southern Trident: Strategy, History and the Rise of Australian Naval Power*, edited by D. Stevens and J. Reeve. Sydney: Allen & Unwin, 2001.
Lambert, N. "Sir John Fisher, the Fleet Unit Concept, and the Creation of the Royal Australian Navy." In *Southern Trident: Strategy, History and the Rise of Australian Naval Power*, edited by D. Stevens and J. Reeve. Sydney: Allen & Unwin, 2001.
Lowe, P. "Britain and the Opening of the War in Asia, 1937–41." In *Anglo-Japanese Alienation 1919–1952: Papers of the Anglo-Japanese Conference on the History of the Second World War*, edited by I. Nish. Cambridge: Cambridge University Press, 1982.
Loxton, B. "Savo in Retrospect." In *Royal Australian Navy in World War II*, edited by D. Stevens. Sydney: Allen & Unwin, 1996.

MacCallum, M. *Political Anecdotes*. Sydney: Duffy & Snellgrove, 2003.
McCarthy, J. *Australia and Imperial Defence 1918–39: A Study in Air and Sea Power*. St. Lucia, Australia: University of Queensland Press, 1976.
McKernan, M. *The Strength of a Nation: Six Years of Australians Fighting for the Nation and Defending the Homefront in WWII*. Sydney: Allen & Unwin, 2008.
Macintyre, D. *The Battle for the Pacific*. London: William Clowes & Sons Ltd, 1966.
Marder, A. J. *From the Dreadnought to Scapa Flow*. Vol. 1, *The Road to War 1904–1914*. London: Oxford University Press, 1961.
———. *From the Dreadnought to Scapa Flow*. Vol. 2, *The War Years: To the Eve of Jutland 1914–1916*. London: Oxford University Press, 1965.
Marder, A. J., Jacobsen M., and Horsfield J. *Old Friends, New Enemies: The Royal Navy and the Imperial Japanese Navy*. Vol. 2, *The Pacific War, 1942–1945* Oxford: Clarendon Press, 1990.
Meaney, N. *Fears and Phobias: E. L. Piesse and the Problem of Japan*. Canberra: National Library of Australia, 1996.
———. *A History of Australian Defence and Foreign Policy, 1901–23*. Vol. 1, *The Search for Security in the Pacific 1910–14*. Sydney: Sydney University Press, 1976.
———. *A History of Australian Defence and Foreign Policy, 1901–23*. Vol. 2, *Australia and World Crisis 1914–1923*. Sydney: Sydney University Press, 2009.
Montgomery-Hyde, H. *British Air Policy Between the Wars 1918–1939*. London: William Heinemann Ltd, 1976.
Morison, S. E. *History of United States Naval Operations in World War II*. Vol. 3, *The Rising Sun in the Pacific 1931–April 1942*. Boston: Little, Brown and Company, 1965.
———. *History of United States Naval Operations in World War II*. Vol. 4, *Coral Sea, Midway and Submarine Actions May 1942–August 1942*. Boston: Little, Brown and Company, 1949.
———. *History of United States Naval Operations in World War II*. Vol. 5, *The Struggle for Guadalcanal August 1942–February 1943*. Boston: Little, Brown and Company, 1966.
Murfett, M. "Reflections on an Enduring Theme: The 'Singapore Strategy' at Sixty." In *Sixty Years On: The Fall of Singapore Revisited*, edited by B. Farrell and S. Hunter. Singapore: Eastern Universities Press, 2003.
Neilson, K., and G. Kennedy, eds. *Far Flung Lines: Studies in Imperial Defence in Honour of Donald McKenzie Schurman*. London: Frank Cass, 1996.
Nicholls, B. *Statesmen & Sailors: Australian Maritime Defence 1870–1920*. Sydney: Bob Nicholls, 1995.
———. *War to War: Australia's Navy 1919–1939*. Sydney: Bob Nicholls, 2012.
Nish, I. "Japan in Britain's View of the International System, 1919–37." In *Anglo-Japanese Alienation 1919–1952: Papers of the Anglo-Japanese Conference on the History of the Second World War*, edited by I. Nish. Cambridge: Cambridge University Press, 1982.
———, ed. *Anglo-Japanese Alienation 1919–1952: Papers of the Anglo-Japanese Conference on the History of the Second World War*. Cambridge: Cambridge University Press, 1982.
Odgers, G. *The Royal Australian Navy: An Illustrated History*. Hornsby, Australia: Child & Henry, 1982.
Okumiya, M., J. Horikoshi, and M. Caidin. *Zero! The Story of Japan's Air War in the Pacific: 1941–45*. New York: Ballantine Books, 1973.

Oppenheim, P. *The Fragile Forts—The Fixed Defences of Sydney Harbour 1788-1963.* Canberra: Army History Unit, 2004.
Overlack, P. "'A Vigorous Offensive': Core Aspects of Australian Maritime Defence Concerns before 1914." In *Southern Trident: Strategy, History and the Rise of Australian Naval Power,* edited by D. Stevens and J. Reeve. Sydney: Allen & Unwin, 2001.
Owen, F. *The Fall of Singapore.* London: Penguin, 1960.
Parkin, R., and D. Lee. *Great White Fleet to Coral Sea: Naval Strategy and the Development of Australia-United States Relations 1900-1945.* Canberra: Department of Foreign Affairs and Trade, 2008.
Parkinson, R. *The Late Victorian Navy—The Pre-Dreadnought Era and the Origins of the First World War.* Woolbridge, UK: The Boydell Press, 2008.
Reckner, J. A. "'A Sea of Troubles': The Great White Fleet's 1908 War Plans for Australia and New Zealand." In *Southern Trident: Strategy, History and the Rise of Australian Naval Power,* edited by D. Stevens and J. Reeve. Sydney: Allen & Unwin, 2001.
Reynolds, D. *Britannia Overruled—British Policy and World Power in the 20th Century.* London: Longman, 2000.
Roskill, S. W. *The Navy at War 1939-1945.* London: Collins, 1960.
———. *The War at Sea 1939-1945.* Vol. 1, *The Defensive.* London: Her Majesty's Stationery Office, 1954.
———. *The War at Sea 1939-1945.* Vol. 2, *The Period of Balance.* London: Her Majesty's Stationery Office, 1956.
Ross, L. *John Curtin for Labor and Australia.* Canberra: National University Press, 1971.
Schreuder, D. M., and S. Ward. *Australia's Empire.* New York: Oxford University Press, 2008.
Shepherd, E. C. *The Air Force of Today.* Glasgow: Blackie & Son, 1939.
Sprout, H. and M. *Toward a New Era of Sea Power: American Naval Policy and the World Scene, 1918-1922.* Princeton NJ: Princeton University Press, 1940.
Stanley, P. *Invading Australia: Japan and the Battle for Australia, 1942.* Camberwell, VIC: Australian Penguin Group, 2008.
Stephens, A. *The Royal Australian Air Force.* Melbourne: Oxford University Press, 2001.
Stephensen, P. R., and B. Kennedy. *The History and Description of Sydney Harbour.* Sydney: A. H. & A. W. Reed, 1980.
Stevens, D. "'Defend the North': Commander Thring, Captain Hughes-Onslow and the Beginnings of Australian Naval Strategic Thought." In *Southern Trident: Strategy, History and the Rise of Australian Naval Power,* edited by D. Stevens and J. Reeve. Sydney: Allen & Unwin, 2001.
Stevens, D. *The Royal Australian Navy in World War II.* Sydney: Allen & Unwin, 1996.
Stevens, D., and J. Reeve, eds. *Southern Trident: Strategy, History and the Rise of Australian Naval Power.* Sydney: Allen & Unwin, 2001.
Taylor, A. J. P. *The First World War—An Illustrated History.* London: Penguin, 1968.
———. *The Second World War: An Illustrated History.* New York: Penguin Books, 1976.
Terraine, J. *White Heat: The New Warfare 1914-18.* London: Book Club Associates, 1982.
Thomsen, B. *Blue & Gray at Sea: Naval Memoirs of the Civil War.* New York: Tom Doherty Associates, 2003.

Till, G. *Airpower and the Royal Navy 1914–1945—A Historical Survey.* London: Jane's Publishing Co., 1979.
Tusa, A., and J. Tusa. *The Nuremberg Trial.* London: Papermac, 1984.
Usui, K. "A Consideration of Anglo-Japanese Relations: Japanese Views of Britain, 1937–41." In *Anglo-Japanese Alienation 1919–1952: Papers of the Anglo-Japanese Conference on the History of the Second World War,* edited by I. Nish. Cambridge: Cambridge University Press, 1982.
Van der Vat, D. *The Pacific Campaign: The U.S.-Japanese Naval War 1941–1945.* New York: Simon & Schuster, 1991.
Ward, S. "Security: Defending Australia's Empire." In *Australia's Empire,* edited by D. M. Schreuder and S. Ward. New York: Oxford University Press, 2008.
Waters, C. *Australia and Appeasement: Imperial Foreign Policy and the Origins of World War II.* London: I. B. Tauris, 2012.
Williamson, P. *National Crisis and National Government: British Politics, the Economy and Empire, 1926–1932.* Cambridge: Cambridge University Press, 1992.
Winton, J. *War in the Pacific: Pearl Harbour to Tokyo Bay.* London: Sidgwick & Jackson, 1978.

Secondary Sources: Internet
Cantrill, C. "UK Expenditure 1880–1914." http://www.ukpublicspending.co.uk. Viewed February 9, 2018.
Edwards, L. "The Day 45 Australians Rowed Off to Fight Those Yankees." *Sydney Morning Herald,* January 24, 2010. http://www.smh.com.au/national/the-day-45-australians-rowed-off-to-fight-those-yankees-20100124-msm8.html. Viewed October 27, 2017.
Lahmeyer, J. "Population Statistics: Australia." http://www.populstat.info/Oceania/australc.htm. Viewed October 25, 2017.
"Locations of Warships of the United States Navy 07.12.1941." *NavSource Naval History.* http://www.navsource.org/Naval/usf.htm. Viewed June 15, 2018.

Index

Abyssinia, 113, 121, 136, 141, 145, 147, 149, 154
ADB Plan, 191
Adelaide (Australia), 9, 14, 177, 185
Admiralty Islands, 248, 252, 258
Advisory War Council (AWC), 9–10, 193, 203
aircraft and naval aviation: aeronautical development and naval combat, 108–10; dismissive attitudes toward Japanese aviation, 195, 205, 206, 216–17; Fleet Air Arm and naval aviation, 95–96, 103, 146; Imperial Japanese Navy naval air power development, 110–11; Washington Conference failure to address policies on, 69
aircraft carriers: ASW tactics from, 178–79; Coral Sea battle, 242, 253–55; Easter Fleet clash with First Air Fleet, 236–38, 242, 322n99; Japanese carrier strength, 140; London Conference (1930) and design of, 114–15; London Conference (1936) and design of, 144; Washington Naval Treaty limits on, 68
Aleutians, 4, 5
Amery, Leo, 80, 81, 110
Anglo-Australian relationship: Anglo-Japanese agreement and, 28; British garrison troops withdrawal from Australia, 25–26; British overruling of Australian ambitions, 27–28; defense policies and naval security of Australia, 49–50, 151–53, 278–87; lack of consultation before decisions, 134, 219–25; neglect of Australian security by British, 21, 23; New South Wales units in defense of England, 27; priority of Australia in British strategic thinking, 151–53; shaping of during interwar years, 1

Anglo-German Naval Agreement, 120–21, 141–42, 157
Anglo-Japanese Alliance, 29–30, 32, 36, 46, 62–63, 65–67, 278, 280
Anglo-Japanese Commercial Treaty, 28, 43, 46, 119
Anti-Comintern Pact, 122, 151, 163
antisubmarine warfare (ASW), 178–79
Atlantic Conference (1941), 198
Atlantic Ocean: *Bismarck* sinking in, 186–87, 188; British naval success in South Atlantic, 197; convoy escort operations in, 189, 197; German warship and U-boat raiding operations in, 177, 186–87, 285; lines of supply and communication protection in, 221; merchant ship sinkings in, 189; two-ocean dilemma and British naval interests in, 113, 121, 124, 158
Australia: British overruling ambitions of colonies, 27–28; casualties of Japanese attacks, 239–40; citizen military training in, 45, 104, 129; colonies in, 21–22; colonization and imperial expansion of Britain, 17–18, 278; commerce protection from Japanese navy, 29–30; communication vacuum and submarine cable completion, 19, 26; compulsory military service proposal for, 183; conscription in, 46–47; constitution and federation of, 28–29, 278–79; convict transport to, 21, 22, 294n15; Crimean War and concerns about, 22–23, 113; debate and controversy over defense during WWII, 2, 17, 289–91; economic prosperity in, 21, 22; foreign policy and diplomatic representation to foreign powers, 168–69; foreign policy and pursuit of Pacific pact, 151–53, 155–56, 161; foreign policy of and Balfour

343

Declaration, 101–3, 282; foreign policy trip and diplomacy in Far East, 134–37; free settler immigration to, 21, 22; German-controlled Pacific islands, possession of after WWI, 47–48, 53; governance of colonies, 22; immigration restrictions and racial identity of, 28, 30–31, 46, 55, 57–58, 101, 125, 140, 279–80, 284–85; invasion by China, concerns about, 28; invasion by Japan, Churchill opinion about, 192–93; invasion by Japan, Japanese capabilities for, 288–91; iron ore deposit and embargo of iron ore exports, 167–68; Japanese attack on, 1–2, 228–29; Mandated Territories, Japanese seizure of, 242–43, 276; national identity related to military past, 289–91; prison colony establishment in, 18; radio announcement about accepting the authority of Japan, 16; self-sufficiency of, 21; trade policy of, 150–51; Washington Conference and naval treaty, 62–71. *See also* Anglo-Australian relationship; defense and security of Australia; Sydney and Sydney Harbour

Australia (Australia), 14, 15, 36, 39, 86, 91, 177, 194, 252, 268

Australia and War Today (Hughes), 139–40

Australian Army, 79–80, 103–4, 138, 161

Australian Army Reserve, 45

Australian Auxiliary Squadron: cost sharing among colonies, 27; establishment of, 26–27

Australian Imperial Force (AIF): convoy of Second AIF to the Middle East, 176; overseas deployment of, 181, 183, 193, 194, 203, 285; siege of in Tobruk, 203–4; withdrawal of troops request to Churchill, 204

Australian Squadron, Royal Navy: auxiliary squadron as supplement to, 26–27; cost of hosting, 26, 31; establishment of, 23–24; second Maori War engagement of, 24

Backhouse, Roger, 165, 171, 172
Baldwin, Stanley, 106, 121–22, 137, 145–46, 153–54, 162
Balfour Declaration, 101–3, 282
Barton, Stephen, 289

Baudin, Thomas, 18–19
Beatty, David, 97, 100, 280–81
Bismarck (Germany), 186–87, 188, 285
Brooke-Popham, Robert, 191, 194, 195, 203, 206–8, 211, 216, 219
Bruce, Stanley Melbourne: appeasement policy support by, 167; Australian defense and concern about overseas deployment of troops, 181; British defense commitment, questions about reliability of, 170–73; funding and defense priorities of, 80–82; Imperial Conference attendance by, 153; imperial defense policy of, 132, 134, 170–73; prime minister role of, 80; RAAF overseas deployment opinion of, 100; racial identity of Australia support from, 101; reversal of British imperial defense policy, 182–83; RN deployment of ships request from, 196; Singapore base opinion of, 105, 107
Burma: aircraft for defense of, 203, 287; Australian troops deployment to, 232–33; closure of Burma Road, 179–81, 190; Japanese invasion of, 236; strategic importance of, 232–34

Canberra (Australia), 7–8, 14, 177, 186, 268–69
Caroline Islands, 41, 43, 51, 60, 258
Casey, Richard: assistance from U.S., proposal for, 181; Australia Area proposal for defense responsibilities, 220; Australian representation in strategy development, 219; Imperial Conference attendance by, 153; Pacific Fleet transfer, opinion about, 197; Singapore defense by U.S., 246
Ceylon: battle cruiser basing at, 196; Eastern Fleet assembly at, 234–35; Eastern Fleet limit and check operations from, 235–36; Eastern Fleet withdrawal from, 237–39, 286; Japanese attack on Colombo's port facilities and airfields, 236–37; Japanese attack on Trincomalee, 238; lines of supply and communication protection near, 175; naval disposition decisions for, 199–200; Special Service Squadron visit to Trincomalee, 86; strategic importance of, 234; Trincomalee basing for flying

INDEX

squadron, 166; withdrawal of forces from Singapore to, 210–11
Chamberlain, Neville, 162–63, 167, 170–71, 172
Chanak Crisis, 79
Chatfield, Ernle, 123–24, 157–59, 165, 172–73
Chicago, 7–8, 14, 196, 252, 268–69
China: arms embargo against, 118–19, 123, 134; demand for closure of supply route to, 179–80; immigrants from, fear of, 28, 279; Marco Polo Bridge incident and Second Sino-Japanese War, 161–62, 167, 281; Nanking, Rape of, 162; Shanghai incursion by Japan, 117, 118, 122, 134
Churchill, Winston Spencer: attitude toward Australian defense and strategic interests, 37–40, 185; Australian naval defense policy questions to, 238–39; British naval strategy for Pacific and Far East, 219–25; Curtin relationship with, 224; defense funding opinion of, 97–98; diplomacy efforts with Japan, 190; Force Z attack, reaction to, 214, 217–18; Force Z operational rationale of, 216; forfeiture of Mediterranean in event of Japanese threat to Australia, 182–83; French fleet destruction order from, 177–78; Menzies trip to meet with, 194, 195; message to Menzies about imperial defense to, 192–93; naval disposition decisions of, 198–201, 204–7, 210–11; naval superiority strategy of, 208; RN deployment of ships request to, 196; Singapore base opinion of, 106–7; WWI Pacific theater naval activity, 42
codebreaking and intelligence intercepts, 235–36, 253, 259
Colonial Naval Defense Act, 25
Colvin, Ragnar, 171–72, 176
Commonwealth of Australia Constitution Act, 28
Cook, Joseph, 38–39, 43, 52, 72
Coral Sea: air strike exchanges between carrier formations at, 242; battle of the, 241, 253–57, 275–76, 289–90; intelligence about Japanese operations in, 253; MO operation and battle in, 17, 258, 277, 290–91
Courageous (Great Britain), 68, 177, 178

Creswell, R. W., 31, 32
Crete, 188–89
Crimean War, 22–23, 113
Curtin, John: address to nation after attack, 16; Advisory War Council support from, 193; America speech by, 224, 246–47, 287, 320n48; American-Australian unified command agreement of, 251–52; appeal for U.S. assistance from, 2; Burma defense, forces for, 232–33; Churchill relationship with, 224; disarmament and possibility of peace, speech about, 129; Easter Fleet request to assist in Solomons campaign, 272; foreign policy independence of Australia, 150; intentions of Japanese, cautions to about drawing premature, 13; lack of consultation with before defense strategy development, 219–25; MacArthur promise of defense support batteries, 12–13; military readiness as election issue for, 142; national defense policy of, 149, 166–67; national defense resources of, 203–4; national defense strategy and call for total war by, 218–19; naval defense policy questions from, 238–39; prime minister role of, 203; reaction to Sydney attack, 9–10; reversal of British imperial defense policy, reaction to, 221–25; Singapore strategy opinion of, 203; Sydney air raid notification to, 6; vulnerability of Australia to Japanese invasion, 256–57, 263, 271–72

Dalley, William Bebe, 27
Darwin, 13, 15, 228–29, 239–40, 263, 277, 290, 291
De Ruyter (Netherlands), 230–31
Deakin, Alfred, 30, 32–33, 34, 35–36
defense and security of Australia: American-Australian unified command for, 251–52, 287; Anglo-Australian relationship and naval security of Australia, 49–50, 278–87; Australia Area/Anzac Area proposal for defense responsibilities, 220, 222–23; British honoring naval commitments for, 166, 170–74, 205–6; Churchill's attitude toward Australian defense and strategic interests, 37–40, 185;

commerce raiding as major security concern, 31; Commonwealth control of colonial land and naval units, 31; defense against raids or invasion, 159–61; defense funding and budgets, 79, 94, 95–101, 111, 127–41, 149–50, 169–70; defense initiatives of Hughes, 45–46; deficiencies in armed services for, 144; federation and British role in naval security, 28–29, 278–79; foreign visits and defense concerns of new colonies in, 17–22; funding and defense priorities, 79–83; great-power intervention for security, 2, 284–85, 291; Imperial Conference and discussion of, 153–61, 166; inadequacies of imperial naval defenses, 143–44; integrity of naval security, 161; Japanese advances in South Pacific and threat to, 247–49, 275–76, 277, 290–91; lack of consultation before strategy development for, 219–25; local naval forces development by colonies, 25, 31, 278–79; localized naval defense of Australia as a whole, 26; military partnership with U.S. for, 224, 242, 245–47, 249–52, 283–85, 287–90; national defense strategy of Curtin and call for total war by, 218–19; national or imperial defense plan, division over, 89, 283; naval attacks as primary threat to, 128, 139; naval defense and Japanese capabilities, 208–9, 288–89; naval defense policy after Eastern Fleet withdrawal, 238–39, 286; Pacific Fleet defense responsibilities for, 1–2, 40, 222–23, 239–40, 277–78, 288–91; raids-versus-invasion debate, 127–41; reversal of British imperial defense policy, 182–85, 191–93, 221–27; troop and force strength under for, 252; two-ocean dilemma, operational readiness, and imperial defense, 113–14, 118–27, 130–34, 139–42, 166–67, 280–81, 282–84, 291; U.S. assistance for, 142, 164, 169, 170; vulnerability of Australia to Japanese invasion, 256–58, 263, 271–72, 275–76, 277, 290–91. *See also* Singapore
Denison, William, 23, 27, 288
Dobbie, William, 164–65
Doolittle, James H., 248

Doorman, Karel, 230–31
Dreadnought and *Dreadnought*-class battleships (Great Britain), 32, 34, 68, 144
Duff Cooper, Alfred, 205–6

Eden, Anthony, 126, 155, 162
Eggleston, Frederic, 40, 54, 113, 141, 279, 283
Egusa Takashiga, 6, 7, 10
Ellington, Edward, 169–70
Empire Air Training Scheme (EATS), 183
Empire Day address, 1
Empire Men, 55
Enterprise, 259, 260, 262, 267, 270, 273, 274, 288
Exeter (Great Britain), 230–31

Fadden, Arthur, 195, 196, 203–4
Far East: abandonment of Mediterranean in event attacks, 173, 193, 205–6, 283; Australian foreign policy trip and diplomacy in, 134–37; British naval strategy for Pacific and Far East, 219–25; Japanese areo-amphibious operations in, 227–28; RAF and RAAF success in, 228; RN deployment of ships to, 204–7; submarine naval war in, 239
Far Eastern Air Force, U.S., 212, 217, 251
Field, Frederick, 86, 87, 88–89, 100, 115, 123
Fisher, Andrew, 35, 36–37, 38–39, 40, 43–44, 45, 51, 144
Fisher, John "Jacky," 32, 34, 35
Fitch, Aubrey W., 253–54, 255
Five-Power Pact (Washington Naval Treaty), 67–71, 78, 84, 86, 114, 141
Fleet Air Arm (FAA), 95–96, 103, 146
Fletcher, Frank J.: Coral Sea battle, 253–54, 255; Marshall and Gilbert operations under, 247; Solomons campaign, 267, 268, 269, 270; Wake Island relief operation under, 244
Flinders, Matthew, 19
Four-Power Pact, 65–67, 78
France: Agadir incident, 37; arms limitation treaties and force strength of, 114, 115; Asia-Pacific colonies of, 164; British assistance to France, 147–48; collapse of French resistance, 177–78, 286; exploration of Australia by,

18–19, 20; force strength of navy, 121; Franco-Prussian War, 26; threat to from remilitarization of Germany, 147–48; war with Britain, 19; Washington Conference and naval treaty, 65–70; WWI Pacific theater naval activity, 41

Garden Island naval depot, 10–11, 14
Geneva arms limitations negotiations, 119
German navy/Kriegsmarine: Anglo-German Naval Agreement and force strength of, 120–21, 141–42, 157; British ship losses to, 177–78; force strength of, 159, 160, 174
Germany: Agadir incident, 37; annexation campaign of National Socialists, 141, 151–52, 155; Anti-Comintern Pact signing by, 122, 151, 163; appeasement policy toward, 147, 155, 162–63, 167; bombing of Britain by, 193; British declaration of war against Germany, 174; British diplomacy efforts with, 146, 147, 167; conscription in, 121; fleet expansion by, 30; Franco-Prussian War, 26; Greece invasion by, 194–95; High Seas Fleet internment at Scapa Flow, 61; League of Nations withdrawal of, 120, 141; military alliance with Italy, 147; National Socialist rise in, 60, 120, 121–22; nationalist-militarist rise in, 118; naval arms race with British, 34–35; New Guinea negotiation with Britain, 27, 53; Pacific island possessions of, 40, 43–45, 47–48, 51, 52–53, 57; Poland invasion by, 163, 167, 173–74; rearmament of military, 124; rehabilitation as European power, 120; remilitarization of the Rhineland, 147–48, 150; reparations from after WWI, 48, 60–61; Russia invasion by, 189; threat to France from remilitarization of, 147–48; Tripartite Pact signing by, 3, 189–90; WWI Pacific theater naval activity, 40–46
Glorious (Great Britain), 68, 177
gold, discovery of, 22
Graf Spee (Germany), 176, 177
Great Britain/Britain: aircraft production and export policies, 170; American Civil War participation by, 24–25; conscription in, 46–47; Crimean War, 22–23, 113; declaration of war against Germany, 174; defense funding and budgets, 77, 78–79, 94, 95–101, 115–16; diplomacy efforts with Germany, 146, 147, 167; diplomacy efforts with Italy, 146, 147; diplomacy efforts with Japan, 146, 163, 179–81, 190, 281–82; diplomacy efforts with Soviets, 163; Europe first policy of, 190–91; foreign policy discussions at Imperial Conference, 154–56; French assistance from, 147–48; German bombing of, 193; New Guinea negotiation with Germany, 27, 53; potential hostilities with Russia, 26; Ten-Year Rule and defense funding, 77, 97, 98, 118; Tientsin incident and anti-British demonstrations, 163, 169, 282; two-ocean dilemma, operational readiness, and imperial defense, 113–14, 166–67, 280–81, 282–84; two-ocean dilemma, operational readiness, and imperial defense policy, 118–27, 130–34, 139–42, 291; U.S. war plan against, 90; war debt owed by, 64, 66, 77; war with France, 19; Washington Conference and naval treaty, 62–71; WWII focus of, 1. *See also* Anglo-Australian relationship
Great Depression, 127, 141
Greece, 194–95, 224
Grenfell, Russell, 216, 217
Guadalcanal campaign, 241, 266–68, 269–76, 277

Halsey, William F., 247, 259, 272–74
Hankey, Maurice, 137–39, 283
Harding, Warren, 62, 65
Henderson, Lofton, 269
Henderson Field, 265, 269–70, 271, 272–74
Hitler, Adolf, 60, 113, 120, 124, 147, 155
Hobart (Australia), 14, 15, 230, 252
Hong Kong: air defense reinforcements at, 124, 126–27; defenselessness of base at, 115, 123; demand for closure of, 179–80; fall of, 244; Japanese attack plan for, 201; naval base at, 69, 76, 78, 81
Honjo Sueo, 111
Hood (Great Britain), 85–88, 89, 160, 187
Hornet, 248, 259, 260, 272–73
Houston, 230–31
Hughes, William Morris "Billy": armistice terms opposition by, 48–49; *Australia*

and War Today, 139–40; British defense commitment, questions about reliability of, 170; conscription policy of, 46–47; defense initiatives of, 45–46; external affairs role of, 170; funding and defense priorities of, 80; German reparations negotiation role of, 60–61; intelligence, temperament, and oratorial skills of, 45; Paris Peace Conference negotiation role of, 52–61, 279–80; peace settlement role of Australia under, 47–48, 49; prime minister role of, 45; racial identity of Australia support from, 46, 55, 279–80; two-ocean dilemma and impossibility of British naval assistance, 139–40; Washington Naval Treaty, opinion about, 70

Hull, Cordell, 180–82

immigration and White Australia policy, 28, 30–31, 46, 55, 57–58, 67, 101, 106–7, 125, 140, 279–80, 284–85

Immigration Restriction Act, 30

Imperial Japanese Army: Army Plan and pre-emptive strikes against Malaya and Singapore, 179; Central Agreement for war objectives of, 201–3; nationalist-militarist sentiment in, 117, 118; rearmament of and British negotiations and diplomacy, 146

Imperial Japanese Navy (IJN): aircraft lost in Sydney raid, 12; attack plan for Pearl Harbor, 188; Australian commerce protection by, 29–30; British fleet strength against invasion by, 159–61; British training of and assistance to, 28; Central Agreement for war objectives of, 201–3; dismissive attitudes toward Japanese aviation, 195, 205, 206, 216–17; Eight-Eight program, 64–65; Far East invasion operations of, 227–28; First Air Fleet attack on Ceylon, 236–38, 322n99; First Air Fleet force strength, 3; First Air Fleet QP operation, 3, 4–6; fleet exercises of, 76; force strength of, 110–11, 145, 281; invasion of Australia, capabilities for, 288–91; MO operation, 4, 258, 277, 290–91; nationalist-militarist sentiment in, 117; naval bases on Pacific islands, 51, 60, 68–69; range of aircraft in, 111; Royal Navy failure against air power of, 1; southern advance of, 4–5; supply and logistic network of, 288–89, 290

Imperial Pacific Fleet: composition of, 35, 75; firepower and strength of, 50, 77; funding for, 63; opposition to, 37; resistance to formation of, 77–78; support for formation of, 35, 45–46, 47, 281

Indian Ocean: commerce raiding in, 41, 42–43, 197–98; lines of supply and communication protection in, 166, 172, 175–76, 185–86, 208, 221, 285; merchant ship sinkings in, 185–86; naval disposition decisions of Churchill in, 198–201, 204–5, 210–11; Singapore base to protect interests in, 75; Stepsister transfer of Middle East through, 233–34

Indo-China, 180, 189–90

intelligence intercepts and codebreaking, 235–36, 253, 259

Italy: Abyssinia invasion by, 113, 121, 136, 141, 145, 147, 149, 154; appeasement policy toward, 155, 162; arms limitation treaties and force strength of, 114; arms limitation treaty rejection by, 144–45; British diplomacy efforts with, 146, 147; British ship losses in, 177–78; economic sanctions against, 145, 147, 149; Fascism rise in, 121; force strength of navy, 121, 142, 174; Japanese aircraft downing by, 179; League of Nations withdrawal of, 141; Mediterranean force of, 157, 161, 172–73; military alliance with Germany, 147; Tripartite Pact signing by, 3, 189–90; Washington Conference and naval treaty, 65–70, 141

Japan: ambitions for dominance and the war in Europe, 175; Anti-Comintern Pact signing by, 122, 151, 163; anxieties in Australia about, 28; appeasement policy toward, 162, 190, 282; arms embargo against, 118–19, 123, 134; arms limitation treaties and force strength of, 114, 117; arms limitation treaty rejection by, 144–45; arms limitation treaty withdrawal of, 122; Australian diplomatic relations with, 169; Australian foreign policy trip to, 135; Australian Mandated Territories, seizure of, 242–43, 276;

British diplomacy efforts with, 146, 163, 179–81, 190, 281–82; Central Agreement for war objectives of, 201–3; economic issues and poverty in, 118; economic sanctions and embargoes against, 181, 190, 201; factionalism over Australian operations, 257–58; foothold policy and commercial infiltration by, 167–68; German-controlled Pacific islands, interest in and occupation of, 40, 43–45, 48, 51, 52–53, 57; immigration restrictions for people from, 30–31, 46, 67, 125, 140, 279–80, 284–85; Indo-China annexation by, 189–90; League of Nations withdrawal of, 118, 141; Manchuria (Manchukuo) annexation by, 113, 116–17, 122, 134, 281–82; Marco Polo Bridge incident and Second Sino-Japanese War, 161–62, 167, 281; military intentions toward Australia, 2, 43; moral embargo of, 162; Nanking, Rape of, 162; nationalist-militarist rise in, 60, 82, 91, 116–18; Nomonhan hostilities, 163; Paris Peace Conference negotiation role of, 52, 53–54; political roller coaster in and pro-Axis attitude in, 179–81; racial discrimination issues related to, 57–60, 279–80; radio announcement in about attack and accepting authority of, 16; scrap metal and pig-iron exports to, 168; Shanghai incursion to end economic boycott by China, 117, 118, 122, 134; Singapore overland attack by, possibility for, 164–65; Soviet skirmishes with along Manchukuo border, 163; Thailand annexation by, 189–90; Tientsin incident and anti-British demonstrations, 163, 169, 282; Tokyo bombing by Doolittle, 248; trade policy toward, 150–51; Tripartite Pact signing by, 3, 189–90; U.S. war plan against, 90; Washington Conference and naval treaty, 62–70, 141; WWI Pacific theater naval activity, 40–46
Java, 228, 229–33, 234, 277
Java (Netherlands), 230–31
Jellicoe, Lord, 71, 72–77, 84, 137, 281

Kellogg-Briand Pact, 101, 155
King, Ernest J., 247, 250, 263–64, 288

King George V (Great Britain), 187, 188, 200
Knox, Frank, 197

Latham, John, 54, 60, 132, 133, 134–37
Lavarack, John, 130, 139, 148–49, 283
League of Nations: British Empire relationship with, 154; disarmament initiative of, 129, 132, 134; dispute resolution role of, 82–83, 129; formation of, 48, 52; Germany withdrawal from, 120, 141; Italy withdrawal from, 141; Japan rejection of, 53; Japan withdrawal from, 118, 141; Manchuria annexation response by, 118; mandate system for islands under, 53, 54–60, 66; Permanent Court of International Justice under, 101; racial discrimination clause in covenant of, 55, 57–58, 280
Leander (New Zealand), 8, 11, 14
Lend-Lease arrangement, 245–46
Lexington, 241, 247, 255
Lloyd George, David: armistice terms discussion by, 48; Dardanelles campaign support from, 79; Paris Peace Conference negotiation role of, 52, 56; war policy participation under, 47
London Conference and London Naval Treaty (1930), 69, 109, 112, 114–16, 117, 122
London Naval Treaty (1936), 137, 144–45, 281
Lyons, Joseph: acquisition of U.S. aircraft by, 170; British fleet for imperial defense, 148, 172; death of, 167; foreign policy of and loyalty toward Britain of, 150–53; foreign policy trip and diplomacy in Far East under, 134–37; Imperial Conference and foreign policy and defense discussions, 153, 155–56, 161, 166; imperial defense policy of, 132–36, 166–67, 283; Pacific Pact pursuit by, 151–53, 155–56, 161; prime minister role of, 132; trade policy of, 150–51

MacArthur, Douglas: antiaircraft and searchlight batteries for Sydney from, 12–13; defeatist attitude of Australian, opinion about, 264; dismissive attitudes toward Japanese aviation, 216–17; New Guinea campaign, 263–64, 266;

popularity of with Australians, 256, 288; Southwest Pacific Area command of, 251–52; troop and force strength under for defense of Australia, 252; vulnerability of Australia to Japanese invasion, 256–57

MacDonald, Ramsay, 87, 99, 105–6, 109, 115–16, 118, 121, 123

Madden, Charles, 99–100, 115

Maginot Line, naval, 124, 227

Malaya: AIF division deployment to, 193, 194; air support for defense of, 223–24; Army Plan of Japan and pre-emptive strikes against, 179; Australian division deployment to, 182–83; construction of defensive lines in, 165; evacuation recommendation for, 224–25; fall of, 226–27, 286–87; inclusion in defense plan for Singapore and focus of Singapore strategy, 165; Japanese attack on, 208, 211–12, 213; Japanese attack on, possibility for, 165; Japanese attack plan for, 201–3; Japanese control of, 249, 286–87; Japanese invasion of, 211, 214, 216, 217; Matador operation, 206–7; RAAF role in defense of, 184–85, 202–3, 211, 285–86; RAF role in defense of, 211–12; reversal of British imperial defense policy, 191–93; weakness of land and air defenses in, 202

Manchuria: annexation of, 113, 116–17, 122, 134, 281–82; British response to annexation of, 118

Manoora (Australia), 8, 11, 14, 176

Marks, Walter M., 110–11

Marshall Islands, 43, 60, 90, 243, 247, 256

McCarthy, John, 66, 67, 80, 110, 145

Mediterranean Sea: abandonment of in event of Far East attacks, 173, 193, 205–6, 283; Anglo-French naval force against Italian navy in, 174; British fleet maintenance in, 192–93, 221; British fleet operations against Italy in, 178, 187–88; British naval force in, 37–38, 124, 148, 157; British naval success in, 187–88, 208, 285; British ship losses in, 177–78, 198, 208; French fleet destruction order after collapse of French resistance, 177–78; French naval force in, 121, 148; German U-boat attacks in, 198; Gibraltar base to safeguard interests in, 37; Italian fleet in, 157, 161, 172–73

Menzies, Robert: appeasement policy support by, 167; Australia at war because of British declaration of war, informing nation of, 174; Australian defense and concern about overseas deployment of troops, 181, 183; Australian division deployment under, 183; Churchill message about imperial defense to, 192–93; compulsory military service proposal of, 183; foreign policy and establishment of diplomatic representation under, 168–69; London trip to meet with Churchill, 194, 195; national defense policy of, 170, 285–86; national government formation by, 193, 203; Pig-Iron Bob moniker for, 168; regional nonaggression pact opinion of, 151; resignation of, 203; scrap metal and pig-iron exports to Japan, negotiation of, 168

Middle East: AIF division deployment to, 193, 194; convoy of Second AIF to, 176; Stepsister transfer of Australian divisions to, 233–34

Midway Island: aircraft carriers available for battle, 255; battle of, 258–63, 275–76, 288, 289–90; diversionary operations against, 4, 5; sinking of Japanese carrier in battle near, 17; strategic importance of, 5; U.S. defense of, 17

MO operation, 4, 17, 258, 266, 277, 290–91

Molotov-Ribbentrop Pact, 163, 179

Mussolini, Benito, 113, 121, 145, 147, 174

Nagumo Chūichi: First Air Fleet attack on Ceylon under, 237–38, 242; Midway battle, 17, 259–62; Pearl Harbor attack role of, 243; relief of by Ozawa, 5; Solomons campaign, 270, 275

Naval Defense Act, 27

Navy, U.S.: Combined Fleet visit to Australia, 89–94, 111; confrontation of Japanese fleet by, 247; convoy escort duties in Atlantic, 197; Europe first policy of, 190–91; Great White Fleet visit to Australia, 33–34, 283–85; Naval Appropriations Act and strengthening of, 62; Plan RED for defense of eastern coastline of U.S., 34; success of in South

INDEX 351

Pacific, 288–89; visits to Australia by, 20, 196–97; war plan development by, 90; war plan in event of war with British and Japanese, 34; war planning and visit to Australia, 91, 92–94. *See also* Pacific Fleet, U.S.
Nelson, Horatio, 174
Nelson-class battleships, 68, 160, 188, 199–200, 204
Netherlands East Indies: co-existence and co-prosperity policy for, 180; collapse of Holland and status of, 179; fall of, 4, 227; Japanese attack plan for, 202; Japanese control of, 249; Japanese foothold policy and commercial infiltration by, 167; Java battles and surrender of, 229–33; Matador operation, 206–7
New Guinea and Port Moresby: attack on Japanese on, 247; Australia Area inclusion of, 220; Australian bases in, 71; Coral Sea battle, 241, 253–56, 289–90; German control of, 27, 53; Japanese base on, 248, 252, 266; MO operation, 4, 258, 277, 290–91; offensive to clear Japanese from, 263–64, 266, 270, 275–76; Queensland annexation of, 27
New Hebrides, 32
New South Wales, 1, 19–22, 27, 28
Nimitz, Chester, 4, 5, 247, 253, 259–60, 263, 271, 272

Ozawa Jisaburō: First Air Fleet attack on Ceylon, 237, 238; nuisance attacks on coastline by, 9, 15–16; QP operation, 3, 4–6; success of mission of, 12

Pacific Fleet, U.S.: attack on in Pearl Harbor, 4, 208, 243, 244; defense of Australia by, 1–2, 40, 222–23, 239–40, 277–78, 288–91; destruction of as Yamamoto's objective, 3–4, 12, 277; Japanese attack plan for Pearl Harbor, 188, 201; Pearl Harbor, transfer to fleet to, 181; strategy for operations of, 190–91; success of, 288–89; transfer to portion to Atlantic, 197
Pacific Ocean/South Pacific: British naval strategy for Pacific and Far East, 219–25; British-German agreement on islands in, 27; Combined Fleet visit to, 89–94; commerce raiding in, 197–98; coordination of naval forces and strategy in, 190–91; exploration and coastline charting by France in, 18–19, 20; Japanese areo-amphibious operations in, 227–28; Japanese attack plan for, 201–2; lines of supply and communication protection in, 175–77, 185, 208, 285; merchant ship sinkings in, 185, 186; mines and mine laying in, 185; Monroe Doctrine in, 27; naval disposition decisions of Churchill in, 204–7; naval strategy of U.S. and Japan in, 244–45; Navy task group visit to, 196–97; price in lives and material for victory in, 288–89; RAF and RAAF success in, 228; strategic importance of Australia to U.S., 249–52
Page, Earle, 80, 100, 105, 132, 218–19, 224
Paris Peace Conference, 52–61, 279–80
Parkhill, Archdale, 137, 148–50, 153, 157, 167
Pearce, George: defense funding and budget under, 134; defense minister role of, 38, 132; diplomacy support for external security of Australia, 136–37; loss of seat by, 167; Pacific island handover role of, 44; positive comments about Japanese delegation at Washington Conference, 70; RAAF defense role, 133; Washington Conference role of, 63, 66
Percival, Arthur, 164–65, 206, 226
Perth (Australia), 173, 177, 230–31, 285, 314n123
Philippines: Cavite naval base attack, 244; Clark Field attack, 212, 216–17, 244; dispatch of U.S. fleet to, 164; fall of Manila, 244, 287; Japanese attack plan for, 201–2; plans to relieve U.S. forces based in, 182; U.S. defense role of, 90
Phillips, Tom, 196, 212–14, 216–17
Piesse, Edmund, 60, 66–67, 73, 140–41, 283
Poland: attitude toward German invasion of, 167; German invasion of, 163, 173–74
Port Jackson, 18, 19, 20, 293n2 (chap 2)
Portland, 196
Prince of Wales (Great Britain), 187, 188, 204–5, 213–18, 286

Queensland: establishment of, 22; New Guinea annexation by, 27

Rabaul: Coral Sea battle, 241; defense of, 246, 248; German surrender and Australian control of, 43, 53; Japanese capture of, 248–49

Reid, George, 1

Repulse (Great Britain), 85–87, 160, 199, 204, 207, 213–18, 286

Richmond, 6, 7, 9, 10, 13, 15

Richmond, Herbert, 143

Rochefort, Joseph J., 253, 259

Rodney (Great Britain), 187, 199–200, 204

Roskill, Stephen, 216, 217

Royal Air Force (RAF): aircraft for, 195; arms limitation treaties and operational readiness of, 119–20; ASW coordination with RN, 178–79; Australian bomber diversion to, 183; Australian pilots training with, 183; Dual Control system over, 95–96; Far East successes of, 228; formation of, 95; funding for, 78, 95–101; Malaya defense role of, 211–12; Matador operation, 207; Singapore deployment of squadrons, 195

Royal Australian Air Force (RAAF): acquisition of U.S. aircraft for, 142, 170; air raid alert from, 6; aircraft for, 142, 150, 170, 195, 203, 223–24, 282–84; budget and funding for, 79–80, 169–70; casualties from Japanese air raid, 13; creation of, 79; debate about future of, 103–5, 132–33; expansion of, 161; Far East successes of, 228; force strength of, 134, 161; imperial defense role of, 132–33, 139, 149–50, 161; Japanese aircraft downing by, 9, 10; Malaya defense role of, 184–85, 202–3, 211, 285–86; Matador operation, 207; overseas deployment of, 100; retention of, decision about, 129; Singapore basing of squadron, 170; Singapore defense role of, 133, 184–85, 203, 285–86; Singapore deployment of squadrons, 183–84; *Sydney* loss as worst single disaster suffered by, 197–98; training and flying standards of, 169

Royal Australian Navy (RAN): absorption into an imperial fleet, 89; bases for, 75, 301n95; boat and submarine purchases for, 33, 35, 36, 169; budget and funding for, 86, 103, 169–70; convoys of AIF to the Middle East, 176; cooperation with RN by, 137–38; creation of, 31–39; deployment of destroyers for overseas service, 176–77; dreadnought for, 35; eight-eight ship plan for, 75, 84; force strength of, 75, 105, 129, 134, 161, 169; imperial defense role of, 149–50, 161; naval development plan for, 36; WWI Pacific theater naval activity, 40–46

Royal Navy (RN): Anglo-German Naval Agreement and force strength of, 120–21, 141–42, 157; arms limitation treaties and operational readiness of, 113–16, 119–20; ASW and commerce protection doctrine of, 178–79; ASW coordination with RAF, 178–79; budget and funding for, 95–101, 115–16, 280; cost of hosting overseas deployments, 26, 31; dominance of and defense of Australia, 21; East Indies and China Station squadrons, 35, 175–76; Eastern Fleet, 199–200, 234–39, 242, 272, 286; Europe first policy of, 190–91; failure against Japanese naval air power by, 1; Far East deployment of ships, 204–7; flying squadron deployment to Singapore, 165–66; flying squadrons to safeguard trade and commerce, 24–25, 26, 38; force strength of, 138, 140, 144, 156–57, 159–61; honoring naval commitments for Australian defense, 166, 170–74, 205–6; imperial and continental schools on naval defense, 29–30; Japanese navy training and assistance from, 28; Mediterranean force of, 37–38, 148, 157; naval arms race with Germany, 34–35; Naval Defense Act and power and size of, 27; naval superiority strategy of, 208; overseas squadrons of, 25, 26, 29; rearmament program for, 145–46; ship losses to Germany and Italy, 177–78; Singapore deployment of ships, 196, 282; Special Service Squadron visit to Australia, 85–89, 92, 93, 110, 111; two-ocean dilemma, operational readiness, and imperial defense, 113–14, 118–27, 130–34, 139–42, 166–67, 280–81, 282–84, 291; two-ocean fleet construction by, 145–46; war readiness of, 99–100, 111–12, 141, 174; WWI Pacific theater naval activity, 40–46. *See also* Australian Squadron, Royal Navy

Russia/Soviet Union: American Civil War sympathies of, 24; Australian commerce protection from, 29–30; British diplomacy efforts with, 163; Crimean War, 22–23, 113; German invasion of, 189; influences of in China, 118; Japanese skirmishes with along Manchukuo border, 163; Kellogg-Briand Pact agreement by, 101; Nomonhan hostilities, 163; potential hostilities with Britain, 26; tyranny under Stalin, 147; visits to Australia by, 10, 24; WWI Pacific theater naval activity, 41
Russo-Japanese War, 31–32

Santa Cruz Islands, 12, 265, 273, 275
Saratoga, 68, 244, 267, 270
Savo Island, 265, 268, 269, 274
Shedden, Frederick, 128–30, 132, 137, 143, 153, 169, 246
Simson, Ivan, 225–26
Singapore: abandonment of base development in, 86–87, 115, 116; air defense reinforcements at, 124, 126–27, 137, 158–59; air power versus coastal artillery for base defense, 108–10; air support for defense of, 223–24; Army Plan of Japan and pre-emptive strikes against, 179; base development in, 78–79, 84, 93, 100–101, 122–23, 126, 278; base site selection in, 110; capture of British base in, 4; completion of base at, 156; debate about base in, 105–11; defensive structures on, 226; dispatch of a British fleet to for imperial defense, 130–31, 137, 148, 153, 156–58, 170–74, 182–83, 185, 205–6, 282; evacuation recommendation for, 224–25, 287; fall of, 226–27, 286–87; flying squadron deployment to, 165–66; Force Z departure and Japanese attack on Force Z, 212–18; funding for base in, 94, 126; importance of base in, 106, 158, 197, 206, 280–81; inclusion of Malaya in defense plan for Singapore and focus of defense strategy, 165; Japanese attack on, 208, 224, 226; Japanese attack plan for, 202–3; Japanese overland attack on, possibility for, 164–65; naval disposition decisions for, 199–200; as naval Maginot Line, 124, 227; opening of base at, 165; RAAF role in defense of, 133, 184–85, 203, 285–86; RAAF squadron basing in, 170; RAAF squadron deployment to, 183–84; RAF squadron deployment to, 195; reliability of naval defense strategy, 170–74; reversal of British imperial defense policy in, 182–85, 191–93, 221–27; RN deployment of ships to, 196, 205, 282; strategy for naval defense, 71–82, 133–34, 139, 152–53, 156–59, 161, 280–81, 282–83, 284, 286; U.S. fleet deployment to, proposal for, 181–82; U.S. role in defense of, 246; U.S. role in naval defense at, 164; viability of a base in, 81, 123, 130, 139, 148; weakness of land and air defenses in, 202, 210–11
Sino-Japanese War, 28
Sino-Japanese War, Second, 161–62, 167, 281
Solomon Islands: campaign in, 263–76, 277, 288; Curtin's request for Eastern Fleet to assist in, 272; Japanese offensive operations in, 248, 252; MO operation, 4, 258, 277; Tokyo Express run down the Slot in, 269–70, 271, 273, 274, 275
Somerville, James, 178, 235–37
South Australia colony, 21
South Pacific. *See* Pacific Ocean/South Pacific
Soviet Union. *See* Russia/Soviet Union
Spain, visits to Australia by, 19–20
Spectacle Island bunkers, 11–12, 15
Spruance, Raymond, 259, 262
Stanley, Peter, 289
submarines: British ASW and commerce protection doctrine, 178–79; Far East naval war carried out by, 239; midget submarine attack on Sydney, 17; Washington Conference limits on, 69
Sudan, 27
Sydney (Australia), 39, 42–43, 197–98, 285
Sydney and Sydney Harbour: air raid on, 5–12; aircraft and ship damage from air raid, 7–10, 11, 13–15; casualties from attacks on, 13, 14, 15, 17; defenses against air attacks on, 9–10; destruction of facilities to support naval operations from, 7–12, 13–15; early defense concerns of, 21; importance of base in, 110; MacArthur promise of defense support batteries for, 12–13; midget

submarine attack on, 17; nuisance attacks on coastline north of, 9, 15–16; Pearl Harbor–style attack on, 290–91; radar site damage and shutdown of detection equipment in, 6; radio announcement in Japan about attack on, 16

Tasmania colony, 21
Thailand: annexation by Japan, 189–90; Japanese attack plan for, 203; Japanese invasion of, 191; Japanese occupation of, 180; Matador operation, 206–7, 212
Tirpitz (Germany), 188, 199, 200–201, 204
Toowoomba (Australia), 9, 14
Tripartite Pact, 3, 189–90
Truk, 51
Tryon, George, 26
Tulagi, 4, 253–54, 255–56, 263–64, 266–67, 276, 277

United States (U.S.): arms limitation treaties and force strength of, 114; assistance to Australia in event of hostilities, 142, 164, 169; assistance to Australia, proposals for, 181–82; Australian diplomatic relations with, 169; Civil War in, 24–25; Europe first policy of, 190–91; exports from and National Defense Act passage in, 190; Far East strategic problem of, 89–91; military partnership for Australian defense, 224, 242, 245–47, 249–52, 283–85, 287–90; Neutrality Act and WWII, 180, 284; trade policy toward, 150–51; visits to Australia by, 10; war debt owed to, 64, 66, 77; Washington Conference and naval treaty, 62–70

Valiant (Great Britain), 160, 187–88, 198, 234–35
Victoria colony, 21
Vincennes, 8, 11, 14, 20, 268–69

Wake Island, 243–44, 247
Warspite (Great Britain), 160, 187–88, 234–35

Washington Naval Treaty (Five-Power Pact), 67–71, 78, 84, 86, 114, 141
Webb, Richard, 143–44
Wellington Conference, 171–72
Western Australia (Swan River Colony), 20, 21, 22, 294n15
White Australia policy and immigration, 28, 30–31, 46, 55, 57–58, 67, 101, 106–7, 125, 140, 279–80, 284–85
Wilson, Woodrow, 48, 52, 53, 54–57, 58, 59, 61–62
World War I (WWI): casualties of, 47, 49; conscription for, 46–47; defeat of Central Powers and end of, 47–49; Pacific theater naval activity, 40–46; Paris Peace Conference and agreement, 52–61, 279–80; peace settlement at end of, 47–48, 49; start of, 40
World War II (WWII): Allied grand strategy during, 1; British declaration of war against Germany, 174; British ship losses to Germany and Italy, 177–78; debate and controversy over Australian defense during, 2, 289–91; Dunkirk operation, 177, 178, 188; foundations for Axis tripartite alliance for, 113–14, 121–22; international tensions leading to, 143–44; island-hopping campaign, 94; Japanese ambitions for dominance and the war in Europe, 175; Japanese pro-Axis attitude and threat of war with Western powers, 179–81; lines of supply and communication protection during, 175–77, 185, 189, 208, 285; Matador operation, 206–7, 212; Neutrality Act of U.S. during, 180, 284; Norwegian campaign, 177, 178, 188; Pearl Harbor attack, 4, 208; Tripartite Pact, 3, 189–90

Yamamoto Isoroku: factionalism over Australian operations, 257–58; Midway Island battle, 258–63, 277, 290; Pacific Fleet destruction objective of, 3–4, 12, 277; Pearl Harbor attack role of, 3; Solomons campaign, 12, 270, 271, 272, 275, 276, 277
Yorktown, 241, 247, 253–54, 255, 259, 262